Psychology
for you

Tracy Cullis

Larry Dolan

David Groves

Stanley Thornes (Publishers) Ltd

First published in 1999 by:

Stanley Thornes (Publishers) Ltd
Ellenborough House
Wellington Street
CHELTENHAM
GL50 1YW
United Kingdom

99 00 01 02 03 / 10 9 8 7 6 5 4 3 2 1

A catalogue record for this book is available from the British Library

ISBN 0-7487-3627-1

Illustrations by John Crawford Fraser, Oxford Designers & Illustrators and Shaun Williams

Typeset by Paul Manning

Printed and bound in Great Britain by Redwood Books, Trowbridge, Wiltshire

Contents

Acknowledgements

The authors and publishers are grateful to the following for permission to reproduce previously published material:

United Press Syndicate: p.99
Jared Scheiman Design: p.143
Prentice Hall Inc.: p.157
Wadsworth Publishing: p.158
British Psychological Society: p.213
Society for Research in Child Development Inc: pp.244, 247
Harvard University Press: p.271
Academic Press: p.375
NTL Institute for Applied Behavioural Science, 300 N Lee Suite 300, Alexandria, VA 22314: p.380
Ikliyo Tagawa Garber: p.386

The following examination boards gave permission for the use of their exam questions:

OCR (MEG)
Northern Examinations & Assessment Board
Southern Examining Group

Every attempt has been made to contact copyright holders, and we apologise if any have been overlooked. Should copyright have been unwittingly infringed in this book, the owners should contact the publishers who will make corrections at reprint.

Photo credits

Getty Images: pp.45, 112 (*left & right*), 114, 148 (*bottom*), 190, 265, 289, 313, 331, 385 (*bottom*), 394, 425, 444, 452

Corbis: pp.3 (*top & bottom*), 4, 27, 29, 42, 80 (*bottom*), 84, 93, 184, 383 (*left*)

Mike Wyndham: p.191

University of Wisconsin Primate Library: p.82

The Hutchinson Library: p. 176 (*right*)

Central Washington Chimpanzee and Human Communication Institute (April Ottley): p.282

Philip G. Zimbardo Inc: p.391

Angela Hampton – Family Life Picture Library: pp.74 (*all photos*), 80 (*top*), 149 (*bottom*), 233, 318

The Ronald Grant Archive: pp.175, 186, 338, 350

Janine Weidel: pp. 254, 382 (*top*), 449

Cordon Art B.V. – Baarn – Holland: p.198

Royal Liverpool Children's Trust: p.90

Stuart Boreham © Stanley Thornes (Publishers) Ltd: p.252

Martin Sookias © Stanley Thornes (Publishers) Ltd: p.382 (*middle*)

Dedications

To Sue and Michael, for all their support. *T.C.*

To my Arlene, for loving me. *L.D.*

To Amanda, without whom… *D.G.*

An Introduction to Psychology

Different perspectives in psychology propose fundamentally different views of people, what we are and how we develop. This section outlines the six main approaches within psychology.

1 Defining Psychology

If you've decided to study psychology you may be wondering what you have let yourself in for. In this first section, it might be useful to consider what studying psychology will actually involve. If you are new to psychology, you will want to know:

Questions	Issues raised
What subject areas does psychology cover?	Psychology covers a number of areas such as personality, memory, social influence and stress.
How do psychologists go about collecting their data?	Psychologists use a variety of research methods including experiments, surveys and case studies.
Is psychology concerned with focusing on the individual or is it concerned with people in general?	Some psychological theory focuses on the individual (i.e. has an *idiographic* focus) while other areas focus on groups of people (called a *nomothetic* focus).
Do all psychologists think alike or are there different ways of approaching the subject?	There are a number of different approaches in psychology as well as areas of controversy – for example, the 'nature–nurture' debate.

It is fair to say that not all psychologists think alike because they approach issues and topics from different perspectives. There are several main approaches in psychology. Each approach is based on certain assumptions about human nature and focuses on explaining a particular part of human experience. Different approaches also vary in terms of methodology. You will discover that behaviourists are very fond of the experimental method, while psychoanalytic psychologists prefer case studies.

Six main approaches are:

- psychoanalytic
- behavioural
- humanistic
- cognitive
- biological
- socio-cultural

Although the theories which make up these approaches are explained in detail in different chapters, it is worth having a brief overview of them now so that you can get a 'feel' for what psychology is about.

Approaches in psychology

1. The psychoanalytic approach

This approach began with the work of **Sigmund Freud** (1856–1939). Freud was trained as a physician and worked with patients suffering from emotional problems. Freud came to the view that we are driven by certain basic **instincts** – such as aggression and sex. These provide the motivation for much of our behaviour, but these motivations are largely hidden from us in our **unconscious** mind. Freud believed that in many cases, the problems his patients suffered were the result of unconscious conflicts. He developed a theory of personality development, and argued that early childhood experiences play a major role in determining our adult personality. Strangely, perhaps, for such a theory, his research was almost entirely conducted on adults who were suffering from emotional disorders. Based on case studies and his observations of his patients, he developed not only a theory of child development, but also a model of personality and a therapeutic technique called **psychoanalysis**.

Freud's theory inspired other researchers such as **Carl Jung** (1875–1961) and **Erik Erikson** to provide alternative theories of personality and development.

Sigmund Freud (1856–1939) ▲

2. The behavioural approach

This approach was initiated by an American psychologist, **John Watson** (1878–1958). Watson believed that psychology should be the study of overt (observable) behaviour. He was interested in what people *do*, rather than what they think or feel. He argued that psychology should be a *science* and therefore psychologists needed to use objective methods such as controlled observation and experimentation. Since thoughts and feelings cannot be directly observed, studying them should not be a part of the science of psychology.

Behaviourism focuses on how factors in the external environment affect human behaviour. Watson's work was expanded by other researchers such as **Pavlov** (1849–1936), who developed **classical conditioning**, and **B.F. Skinner** (1904–1990) who developed **operant conditioning**. These theories explain how humans and animals learn and acquire new behaviours. The extent to which learning in animals is comparable to learning in humans is one area of controversy within this approach. The emphasis here, then, is not on internal forces such as instincts, but the way in which our learning history, and external rewards and punishments, shape our behaviour and make us into the sort of people we are. The behaviourist approach is sometimes referred to as **Stimulus–Response (S–R)** psychology. This is because of its focus

B.F. Skinner (1904–1990) ▲

on observable events. A **stimulus** is some event in the environment, and a **response** is how the organism reacts. Behaviourism has provided us with ways of treating mental disorders.

*Abraham Maslow
(1916–1972)* ▲

3. The humanistic approach

This approach focuses on the positive side of human nature. It developed as a reaction against both the behavioural and psychoanalytic approaches described above. **Humanism** aimed to offer a 'third force' in psychology, by providing an alternative perspective on human nature. Humanism assumes that humans are inherently good and worthy of respect. Theorists focus less on unconscious forces or childhood conflicts, and more on how people *consciously* interpret and think about the world around them now. Unlike behaviourists who see us as the product of our environment and learning history, humanistic psychologists believe we have **free will**, and that we actively shape our environment, as well as being shaped by it. They also believe we all wish to grow and develop to fulfill our potential, i.e. we have a drive towards **self-actualisation**. Of course, terms like free will and self-actualisation are abstract and difficult to measure, and this in part is why behaviourists want nothing to do with them.

The main exponents of the humanistic approach include **Abraham Maslow** (1916–1972), who developed a theory of motivation, and **Carl Rogers** (1902–1987), who made significant contributions to the development of therapy.

4. The cognitive approach

The cognitive approach also developed as a reaction against behaviourism and psychoanalytic theory. **Cognitive** psychologists emphasise the importance of internal mental processes such as perceiving and thinking. They reject the notion that the environment has a direct influence on behaviour. Instead they argue that cognitive processes mediate between the stimulus and the response. In other words, it is not the stimulus itself which influences our behaviour but how we perceive and make sense of the stimulus. **Jean Piaget** (1896–1980) was a cognitive psychologist interested to discover how children's thinking develops (see Chapter 9, page 92). The chapters in this book on memory, perception and problem-solving also examine the work of cognitive psychologists.

5. The biological approach

Psychologists who adopt the **biological approach** try to explain human behaviour in terms of our internal physiological processes. This assumes that our thoughts, feelings and behaviour are intricately linked to our physiological make-up. As a result, the biological approach focuses on two main areas of research:

● how the nervous and hormonal systems affect behaviour

● the influence of genes on behaviour.

For example, it is generally accepted that there are sex differences in our levels of aggression, and that on average, males tend to be more aggressive than females. The biological approach seeks to explain differences in aggression by pointing to the influence of hormones (such as testosterone), or to genetic differences. Darwin's *The Origin of Species* (1859) detailing his views on evolution has also led researchers to study animals, on the basis that humans are not fundamentally different from animals and that animal study can shed light on human behaviour.

6. *The socio-cultural approach*

The socio-cultural approach emphasises how our behaviour is influenced by the society and culture in which we live. Psychologists from this approach are interested in studying how a person's behaviour is affected by **social norms** (widely shared, accepted ways of behaving) and **cultural values**. For example, research has shown that a person's sense of self is influenced by their culture. People from Western cultures tend to view themselves as individuals. When asked to describe themselves, they tend to focus on their personality characteristics ('I am outgoing', 'I am hardworking'). By contrast, people from other cultures often see themselves more in terms of their roles ('I am a daughter', 'I am Hindu'). Later in the book we shall be looking at the influence of cultural factors and how they affect areas such as aggression and the development of gender roles.

TIME CHART						
Psychological approach	1880	1900	1920	1940	1960	1980
Psychoanalytical		▬▬	▬▬▬▬	▬▬▬▬	▬▬▬▬	▬▬▬
Behaviourist			▬▬▬	▬▬▬▬	▬▬▬▬	▬▬▬
Cognitive			▬▬	▬▬▬▬	▬▬▬▬	▬▬▬
Humanistic					▬▬▬	▬▬▬
Biological	▬▬▬	▬▬▬▬	▬▬▬▬	▬▬▬▬	▬▬▬▬	▬▬▬
Socio-cultural	▬▬▬	▬▬▬▬	▬▬▬▬	▬▬▬▬	▬▬▬▬	▬▬▬

Chronological chart showing key developments in psychology

Some conclusions

What are we to make of the fact that psychology embraces so many different perspectives? Take the example of a student – Susan – who has just started at college to study GCSE psychology. As psychologists, we are interested in people. We want to know what they are like and why they do the things that they do. So we may ask, 'Why has Susan gone to college to study psychology?' It is a question that is simply put. It is not, however, a simple question. People are complicated. They can do different things for the same reason, and the same thing for different reasons. Discovering human motives is no easy task.

Why has Susan gone to college to study psychology? ▲

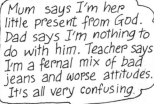

Most of us have a natural curiosity about ourselves and other people ▲

Susan may not be sure why she is at college. Perhaps she fancies another student at the college, even if she won't admit this to herself. Freud would have something to say about that. Perhaps she does well at school. She gains praise from her teachers and respect from her peers. Studying is therefore associated with rewards for Susan – and behaviourists would have something to say about this.

Perhaps Susan is unsatisfied with her life. Perhaps she feels unfulfilled and is searching for something more that will make her life a bit less boring or hollow. Humanistic psychologists would have something to say here. Perhaps Susan realises that, although an education doesn't guarantee a good job, the *lack* of an education makes good jobs more difficult to find in this culture. Education has cultural value, and this is something on which the socio-cultural approach would focus. Cognitive psychologists would be interested to know how Susan thinks about education and the strategies she uses to solve problems.

We can see that Susan may attend college for a number of different reasons – perhaps a mixture of the above, perhaps for other reasons altogether. Whatever her motives are, we must confront the fact that people are the most complex creatures we know. To hope to understand them we must be willing to consider a wide variety of issues and undertake a variety of different forms of research.

Most of us have a natural curiosity about ourselves, wanting to know what we are like and how we came to be that way. The different perspectives in psychology have each tended to focus on different sorts of explanations. None of these approaches on their own can explain the diversity of human behaviour. Understanding people requires a willingness to consider alternative perspectives. The different perspectives provide us with some tools for the job and help us to gain some important insights, but ultimately it is a hard task and our understanding is still limited. There is nothing so fascinating, important or difficult as the study of other people. If you are willing to embark on such a task, then we invite you to read on.

Research Methods

Everyone is a psychologist in the sense that they have ideas about what people are like and why they do what they do. But professional psychologists cannot rely on everyday beliefs if they wish to get an accurate picture of human behaviour. They use a variety of methods to investigate people – and sometimes get surprising results. This section introduces some of these methods, the ethical issues they raise, and ways of presenting the findings of research.

2 Carrying out Research: Experimental Methods

This book invites you to explore the world around you in new ways: to look at the world through the eyes of a psychologist and to examine human behaviour, including your own, in a systematic way. In later chapters you will be looking at the work done by a wide variety of different researchers. But to understand their work, and know what to make of it, you first need to understand:

- how their research was conducted
- why it was conducted in that way
- what the research can and cannot tell us.

The aim of this chapter is for you to familiarise yourself with the different methods that psychologists use, and to help you gain some understanding of their strengths and weaknesses.

The psychologist's 'toolkit'

Every psychologist has a kind of 'toolkit' of investigative methods. Each tool can be used in a special way to do a specific job, and the researcher must choose the appropriate tool for the job. Before we look at the tools or methods that psychologists use, however, we must first consider the people who are the subjects of psychological research.

Populations and samples

Psychologists often want to know about large numbers of people. They want to be able to say things like 'most people are like this.' This means that psychologists often do research on groups of people. The term **population** refers to the big group of people the researcher wants to find out about. For example, if you want to know about college students, then the population is 'all college students'. If you want to know about students at school x, then the population is 'all the students at school x'. Usually it is either too difficult or expensive to test all the members of a group. Instead, just some members of the group are tested. The portion of the group that is actually used in the research is called the **sample**.

When we carry out research on a sample of people from the population, we need to be able to say that whatever we find out about the sample

The 'population' of students ▲

A 'sample' from the student population ▲

tested can also be applied to the population from which the sample is drawn. The risk here is that the sample may not be typical of the population as a whole. For example, if your population is 'all college students' but you only test students at one college, there may be a problem if students at other colleges are different in some way from the ones in your sample. Ideally, the people in the sample should have similar characteristics to the people in the population. That is, the sample should be **representative** of the population. If it is representative, the researcher can then **generalise** the findings from the sample to the population.

Random sampling aims to select a mixture of subjects similar to those in the population as a whole ▲

A technique used to obtain representative samples is **random sampling**. In a random sample, every member of the population has an equal chance of being selected. Picking names out of a hat or using a computer to select people at random are ways of achieving this. This should result in a mixture of different people in the sample, and the hope is that this mixture is similar to the mixture of people in the population as a whole.

For your own project work, you will often be using friends, family, or anybody you can persuade to take part in your research. This sort of sample is called an **opportunity sample**, and for college project work it is quite acceptable. But you should realise that this means your samples cannot be said to be representative of any group of the public at large, and so you cannot generalise your findings with any certainty.

The experimental method

The **experiment** is a unique method of research and the only way to obtain reliable information about cause and effect. This is because in an experiment conditions can be kept the same, apart from one thing that is deliberately changed. The experimenter can therefore be sure that anything new that happens is the result of the condition or factor that was changed. The thing that is changed is called the **independent variable (IV).** This is what the experimenter is interested in finding out about. In order to do this, he or she must measure the effect it has, or the difference it makes. What is measured is called the **dependent variable (DV).**

Independent variable
= Variable manipulated

Dependent variable
= Variable measured

For example, if we want to know how alcohol affects people's driving ability, we could test them once while they are sober, and again after they have had a drink. Here, the independent variable is the alcohol and dependent variable is some measure of driving ability.

The independent variable is the thing manipulated by the experimenter. To take another example, if you want to know if a drug makes people happy, you could give the drug to some people and not others, and then test their levels of happiness. Here, the drug is the independent variable, and the dependent variable is people's happiness.

Many experiments use a **control group** (in the control condition) and an **experimental group** (in the **experimental condition**). The control group is the group of people who are *not* given the IV (e.g. alcohol, drug, or whatever is being tested). The experimental group are the ones who *are* given the IV. The performance of the two groups is then compared. The control group is simply used to provide a means of comparison.

Not all experiments employ a control group. You could have two experimental groups (e.g. if you compared the effects of one drug with the effects of a different one). In this case both groups receive the IV in a different treatment. GCSE and A level research does not require students to investigate more than two conditions or treatments, though theoretically you can have any number of them.

Natural experiments
Sometimes experimenters want to compare the effects of some *naturally occurring* variable, like sex or age. The independent variable is not manipulated in the sense of being 'fiddled with'. The researcher simply exploits an opportunity to investigate variables that has presented itself in everyday life. Comparing the performance of one class of people with another in a company or school are examples. This is called a **natural experiment**.

QUESTIONS

Imagine that you want to find out if students learn more effectively if pop music is played gently in the background during class. You could choose a selection of students, and test them for recall of a lesson with music in the background and without music.

In this case:

1   What is the **independent variable**?
2   What is the **dependent variable**?
3   Which is the **experimental** condition and which the **control**?
4   What is the **population**? How would you **select** the students to use in this study?

Can you think of any difficulties in doing this research? Remember that you want to be reasonably sure that any differences in the performance between the two conditions are due to the playing of the music. But are there other factors that might have an impact on how well the students do? Think about the people you choose, the room in which you carry out the research and the type of lessons.

An advantage of this method is that, sometimes, participants may be unaware that they are part of an experiment. This means participants should behave 'naturally'. That is, they are unlikely to change their behaviour simply because they are being researched, since they do not know that they are being researched (see **demand characteristics**, page 14). This method has the disadvantage of giving the researcher less control over the situation, which makes statements about cause and effect difficult. This lack of control means that some researchers are reluctant to label this kind of research as experimental. There is debate and disagreement on this issue. This type of research is sometimes called *quasi-experimental* to reflect this uncertainty.

Hypotheses

Experiments aim to test a **hypothesis**. All experimental hypotheses have the same general form:

The aim of all experiments ▲
is to test a hypothesis

>   **something** (the **IV**) *will affect* **something** (the **DV**)

An experimental hypothesis, therefore, predicts a relationship between the IV and the DV. So we could predict that 'Drinking will affect driving', or that 'Drug *x* will affect speed of running', etc. It is important for the IV and DV to be **operationalised** so that it is clear just what you mean by them. 'Drinking affects driving' is vague, in that it is not clear exactly what the two terms mean. 'A double measure of whisky affects the number of cones knocked over in a weave-through-the-cones driving task' is operationalised. Now we are clearer about what the variables mean and what the experiment will entail.

A hypothesis may be **one-tailed** or **two-tailed**. A two-tailed hypothesis is **non-directional**. This means that it predicts that the IV will have an effect, but doesn't say precisely what *sort* of effect. 'Drinking will affect driving' is two-tailed, because the prediction is that driving could get better or worse. Either way, driving is affected, and so either of two different outcomes will satisfy a two-tailed hypothesis. A one-tailed hypothesis is **directional**. 'Drinking will impair driving' is one-tailed. 'Drinking will improve driving' is also a one-tailed hypothesis. Only *one* outcome will satisfy a one-tailed hypothesis. This distinction between one- and two-tailed hypotheses is particularly important for A-level students who may need to use statistical tests on data.

Notice that an experimenter does not aim to prove a hypothesis *true*. This implies the experimenter is biased and wants to get a particular result. Researchers should be unbiased in their research. If a hypothesis is not supported by the research findings, this information is no less valuable than if it is.

Confounding variables

The key feature about an experiment is that everything apart from the independent variable is kept the same. Only then can you say that any change that you measure is due to the influence of the IV. Keeping everything else the same, however, is often difficult. If other factors change, this will distort the results of your study. Such things are

He's *never* done that before!

Subjects may not always behave naturally in laboratory conditions

referred to as **confounding variables**, or sometimes **extraneous variables**. To conduct a good experiment, confounding variables must be minimised or eliminated.

There are three broad sources of confounding variables:

1. The **environment** in which the experiment takes place
2. The **participants** (the people used to conduct the research on)
3. The **experimenters** themselves

1. Environmental (or situational) variables

Psychologists must consider the surroundings in which an experiment takes place. Any changes in the environment can affect what people do and obscure or confuse the effect of the IV. Environmental variables can include temperature, lighting, background noise or distractions. For this reason, many experiments are carried out in a laboratory.

The advantage of a laboratory experiment is that the researcher can have close control over the environment. However, this also has its drawbacks. The way in which people behave in a laboratory setting may be different to the way in which they behave in real life. Laboratory research, then, may lack **ecological validity**. Ecological validity refers to the extent to which the findings of the research can be applied beyond the testing situation to behaviour in the real world. Since a laboratory environment is an artificial environment, whatever is discovered in a laboratory setting may not tell the experimenter much about how people behave elsewhere.

One form of experiment that has good ecological validity is the **field experiment**. In a field experiment the researcher manipulates variables in a real-life setting.

For example, Piliavin and others (1969) wanted to investigate helping behaviour. In their study, a **confederate** (i.e. a party to the experiment) 'collapsed' on a train. The researchers recorded how many people offered help and how quickly they responded. The IV in the study was the appearance of the confederate and whether they looked drunk or sober. Field experiments, though, have the disadvantage of giving the experimenter less control over the situation. For example, someone *else* could fall over, etc.

2. Participant variables

If you conduct research on two groups of people, they may give you very different results simply because the people involved are different. For example, if we wanted to test whether a drug increases speed of running by giving the drug to one group and not the other, we should bear in mind that if one group are mostly young children and the other group are mostly young adults, then the adult group is likely to run faster regardless of whether or not they are given a drug.

Repeated measures design

One way to avoid participant variables is to employ a **repeated measures** design. Here, you test the *same* group of people twice (e.g. test them

---

In summary

- *Laboratory experiments may provide good control over conditions but poor ecological validity.*

- *Field experiments may provide good ecological validity but less control over conditions.*

Repeated measures testing can be boring for the participants ▲

Sometimes improvements in performance can be the result of order effects ▲

without and then with a drug). This means that you don't have to worry about differences between the people in each group affecting the results. It has the added advantage that the experimenter needs fewer people on whom to experiment.

A disadvantage of this approach is what are known as **order effects**. Since people will be doing a task twice, it is possible they may do it better the second time simply through *practice*. Alternatively, they may do worse the second time because they have become *tired* or *bored* with the task – particularly if it is a long one.

One way to deal with this is to use **counterbalancing**. Here, half of the group do one treatment or condition (Condition A) first and then the other; and the other half of the group do the second condition (Condition B) first and then switch to the first.

For example, if you wish to know if alcohol affects people's driving ability, you could test them by asking them to weave through a series of cones and count the number of cones they knock over. But if you test them all first when they are sober and then again after alcohol, you may find that they do better the second time. It would be a mistake, though, to conclude that alcohol improves driving ability. The improvement may simply reflect the fact that the participants had more practice the second time.

In a counterbalanced design, you would test half the participants when sober, and then after alcohol, and the other half of the group would first be tested after having alcohol and tested again while sober. Notice that counterbalancing does *not* prevent order effects from occurring. Rather, it aims to balance out these effects so that differences between the performance of the group in each condition can be attributed to the IV.

However, sometimes order effects are so strong that counterbalancing is pointless and a different experimental design is needed. For example, if you want to compare the effectiveness of two different methods of teaching people to drive a car, it would be absurd to test Method A and then Method B on the same group of people. Once people have learned to drive, then they can drive – in theory, at least.

Let us turn to consider two other experimental designs which avoid the problem of order effects:

- matched participants design
- independent measures design

Matched participants design

In a matched design, the experimenter uses two different groups of people – one in **Condition A** and the other in **Condition B**. A matching process is used to ensure that the two groups are as similar as possible in important respects – for example, age and sex. Identical twins would be very useful for experiments of this kind, since one twin can be assigned to Condition A and the other to Condition B. Unfortunately, identical twins are rare.

Identical twins can provide useful data in matched participant testing

It is also important to match people on the variable that is to be measured. For example, if the aim is to measure driving ability, people should initially be matched for (lack of) driving skill. It is then possible to teach one group to drive using Method A, and a different group using Method B. Since different people are used in each condition we no longer have to worry about order effects, and if one group learns faster we can attribute this to the IV – in this case the method of teaching.

Matching people up, however, can be time-consuming and expensive, particularly if they have to be tested first. It can also be difficult sometimes to find people who are equally matched. A way to address this difficulty is to choose an **independent design**.

Independent design

An **independent** design involves using *different* people in each condition, but without matching the people. It therefore avoids the problems of the matching process and of order effects.

However, the obvious difficulty with an independent design is that the people used in each group can be very different from each other. As a result, each group may provide very different results, and this may have little or nothing to do with the IV. For example, if one group is mostly young and the other group old, or one group mostly male and the other group female, these differences will introduce a bias into the research findings. To avoid this, the researcher must use random allocation.

In **random allocation** each person has an equal chance of being assigned to either condition. This can be achieved by pulling names out of a hat or tossing a coin to decide who is in which group. In this way it is hoped that you will get an even mixture of different sorts of people in each group, and systematic bias will be eliminated.

QUESTIONS

Refer back to your study of whether music assists learning (see page 10).

1 What problems might there be here with a repeated measures design?
2 Suppose instead you decide to use a matched design. What variables do you think it would be good to match the students for?

Demand characteristics

A final difficulty that may arise from the people used in experiments is what are known as **demand characteristics**. If people know, or think they know, what the experimenter is looking for, this can affect the way they behave. Some people can be nice and try and help you get the results you want; others can deliberately try and prevent you from getting what you want, perhaps because they want to show that they know what you are up to and are not going to be taken in by it! Either way, it can distort the result of the study.

A way to combat this is to run the experiment as a **single blind**. In a single blind design, the participants are not told what the experimenter is looking for until after the experiment is finished. Sometimes the experimenter may actually lie to them about the true nature of the research to prevent them finding out the aim of the experiment. This raises ethical issues which we will examine later.

The reason for conducting research as a single blind is that, if people do not know what is being looked for, they cannot deliberately give you the results you want or prevent you from getting them. However, the simple knowledge that they are in an experiment may mean that people do not perform in ways that they otherwise would.

3. Experimenter variables
Apart from the environment and the participants, a third possible source of confounding variables is the experimenters themselves. There are two issues to consider here:

Experimenter bias
Experimenter bias occurs if the expectations of the experimenter unconsciously influence the way in which he or she behaves or interprets what is happening in the experiment. Research has revealed that people often see what they expect to see. Rosenthal and Fode (1963) gave a group of 12 students 5 rats each and told them to run their rats 10 times a day in a T-shaped maze. The rats had to learn to distinguish between one arm of the maze, which was painted dark grey, and the other arm, which was painted white. The position of the arms was swapped at random, and the rats were always rewarded for running the grey arm and never rewarded for running the white arm. The students were told that their rats were specially bred to be either 'maze-bright' or 'maze-dull'. The maze-bright rats were expected to learn the maze quickly; the dull rats were not.

The students recorded the number of correct responses each rat made over five days. The students who believed they had bright rats recorded that their rats made more correct responses and learned the maze more quickly than the students who believed they had dull rats. Afterwards, those with bright rats also reported that their rats were more clean and tame than the dull rats, and that they handled their rats more and were more gentle with them.

The key point is that *there was actually no difference in the rats*. The rats in each group had *not* been specially bred as the students believed. The rats were allocated randomly to each group of students, and the rats in each group had the same average age. None of the rats had experience of a T-maze. This study revealed that the experimenters' expectations can affect the way in which they treat their participants and how they interpret their behaviour. If this is true for research with rats, it is likely to also be true for research with human participants.

Counteracting experimenter bias
One way to counteract experimenter bias is to use a **double blind**

technique. Here, not only are the participants not told of the true nature of the study, but neither are the people who collect the results. The experimenter sets up the experiment and then lets other people run the research. Afterwards, he or she simply collects the data for analysis. In this way, it is hoped the data is collected in an unbiased way.

The use of a double blind technique is quite common in drug-testing and medical experiments. Some people are given the drug, and others a **placebo** (i.e. a substance known to have no effect). Neither the volunteers or the doctors know which they have been given. The true situation is only revealed once the results have been collected.

Experimenter effects

Experimenters can influence how people respond to them in a number of ways. The influence that researchers can have on participants in an experiment simply by virtue of their sex, age, personality and how they treat the participants is known as **experimenter effects**.

THINK ABOUT IT

Psychologists test *people*. If you were about to take your driving test and the examiner was grumpy and rude, how would this affect your chances of passing? What does this tell us about the importance of the way in which psychologists treat the participants in their experiments?

Of course, experimenters cannot help being a certain age or sex. But they can and should ensure that all their participants are treated in the same way. To this end, experimenters use **standardised instructions**. Typically, these are written down and given to the participants to read, or else are read aloud to each participant in an identical fashion. The aim is to ensure that differences in the performance of two groups cannot be blamed on the way they were treated by the experimenter.

Evaluation of the experimental method

Strengths

+ Experiments can tell us about cause and effect. They are the only form of research that can do this.
+ Experiments allow close measurement and can usually be repeated. This replicability means it is relatively easy for other researchers to test the claims made by the experimenter.
+ Laboratory experiments allow good control of environmental conditions.
+ Different designs allow researchers to control for participant variables, experimenter effects and bias too.
+ Field experiments allow variables to be investigated in a natural setting.

Weaknesses

– If people know they are being experimented upon, they may alter their behaviour – that is, experiments may introduce demand characteristics. However, if people do not know they are being experimented upon, or if they are not told what the research is about, this may raise ethical questions.

- A laboratory setting is artificial and may have low ecological validity.
- Field experiments have poorer control over variables.
- Experimental methods are not always appropriate for ethical reasons. For example, you could not deliberately remove children from their mothers to see what effect this might have on their development. In many cases, the researcher must select a different research tool.

Summary

- Experiments provide the only research method for looking at what causes what. They do this by manipulating and controlling variables.
- The independent variable is manipulated deliberately to see if it has any effect. The dependent variable is what is measured.
- The experimental condition has the IV present; the control condition does not and provides a means of comparison.
- Confounding variables are things which confuse the research. They occur if everything apart from the IV is not constant between the two conditions. Major sources of confounding variables are the environment, the participants and the experimenters themselves.
- Environmental variables can be held constant under laboratory conditions, but this may lower ecological validity. Field experiments provide better ecological validity but less control.
- Repeated, matched or independent designs may be used, depending on how you wish to allocate people to each condition. Each method has advantages and disadvantages.
- Standardised instructions can help minimise experimenter effects.
- Double blind research can help minimise the effects of participant and experimenter bias.
- An experiment tests an experimental hypothesis which predicts the relationship between the IV and the DV.

TRY THIS

Match the **terms** on the left to the **definitions** on the right.

independent variable	when different people are used in each condition
single blind	serves as a comparison with the experimental group
confounding variable	a mechanism for counteracting order effects
ecological validity	allocating people to each condition by chance
repeated measures	the variable measured by the experimenter
counterbalancing	a technique to counteract participant bias
random allocation	the same people are used in each condition
dependent variable	a variable which causes confusion in the research
independent measures	how far findings can be generalised to the real world
control condition	the variable manipulated by the experimenter

3 Carrying out Research: Non-Experimental Methods

Observing people's behaviour without their knowledge may be unethical ▲

In **observational research**, a researcher looks to see what is there and might be of interest. In general, observational studies are useful in that they may reveal information that can generate further research, or else they may be used to check the extent to which findings obtained in a laboratory apply in the real world. A difficulty for all observational research is that, if participants know that they are being watched, this may alter the way in which they behave, and this will distort the findings of the research. To counter this, researchers sometimes use **covert** observation. This means they observe people without them realising it. One-way mirrors are sometimes used for this purpose. But this raises the ethical issue of whether or not researchers have the right to spy on people without their knowledge or consent.

THINK ABOUT IT

The graph on the right is based on observation of children's behaviour in various settings. It *seems* to suggest that boys are more aggressive than girls. But does it prove that gender is a **cause** of aggression?

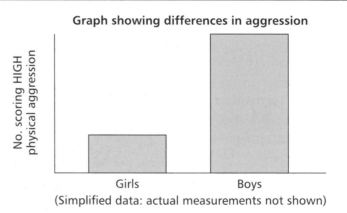

Graph showing differences in aggression

No. scoring HIGH physical aggression

Girls · Boys
(Simplified data: actual measurements not shown)

Source: Maccoby, E.E., & ▲
Jacklin, C.N., *The
Psychology of Sex
Differences* (Stanford
University Press,
Stanford, Ca., 1974)

Types of observational research
Three different kinds of observational research are:

1. Naturalistic observation
The observer watches, but does not interfere with, people in a natural setting, going about their normal activities – for example, children playing in a playground. **Ethologists** often use this method to observe the behaviour of animals in the natural environment.

Strengths

+ This research has good ecological validity.
+ It can sometimes allow a researcher to gather information which, for ethical reasons, could not be gathered by deliberate experimentation – for example, information about how people behave at funerals.

Weaknesses

– The lack of control may mean confounding variables affect the research.
– The lack of control may make research findings difficult to replicate.
– It may be difficult to generalise the findings to a different setting.

2. Participant observation

The researcher joins the group as an 'inside observer'. Ideally, the group do not know the observer's real purpose. This may raise ethical issues. An example would be the case of a researcher joining a group of football supporters in order to observe football hooliganism. The film *ID* is a fictional story about police undercover research in this area, and is a good example of such research and some of the possible pitfalls. Rosenhan (1973) used this approach when he gained admission to psychiatric hospitals as a patient in order to observe the behaviour of patients and doctors (see page 181).

It may be difficult to record data at the same time as participating in a group's activities

Strengths

+ The research has good ecological validity.
+ It may allow observation of the behaviour of groups who wish to keep their activities hidden from 'outsiders'.
+ Participation may allow the researcher to develop a deeper understanding of the attitudes and motives of the group.

Weaknesses

– It may be unethical to mislead people or spy on them without their knowledge.
– It may be difficult to record data while participating in the activities of the group.
– Group membership may lead the researcher to form personal feelings about group members. This may lead to bias in the interpretation of events and the data recorded.

3. Structured observation

The researcher deliberately arranges the environment in a particular way (usually in a laboratory setting) to observe how people behave in that environment. Ainsworth and others (1978) used this technique to observe the behaviour of young children when with their mothers, alone, or with a stranger (see page 75).

Strengths

+ This technique gives the researcher better control over the environment. This enables variables to be studied in a systematic way, and reduces the impact of confounding variables.
+ Better control means such research is easier to replicate.

Weaknesses
- The research may have lower ecological validity. The artificial environment may affect behaviour so that the results cannot be generalised to more natural settings.

Where data is gathered by more than one observer, the research must show good **inter-observer reliability**. That is, the different observers must agree on what happens, or the research is worthless. One thing researchers must do here is to clearly define what they are looking for (for example, if they are studying aggression, they must define what counts as aggressive behaviour). Another problem for observational research is that observers may miss events that are important. Increasingly, researchers are using video cameras and other techniques to improve accuracy of recording.

Survey questionnaires

Surveys involve gathering data from lots of people, and questionnaires or interviews are used to do this. A **postal questionnaire** (one that is sent out in the mail) provides a quick way to contact a large number of people. Questionnaires can be **closed** or **open-ended**. Closed questions force people to choose from a list of possible answers, perhaps by ticking a box. Possible responses may include 'Yes' or 'No', or options such as 'Agree', 'Don't Know' or 'Disagree'. Open-ended questions invite people to describe what they think or feel about a situation, e.g. *'What do you feel about making students pay fees to go to university'*?

Strengths
+ Postal questionnaires provide a quick way to contact large numbers of people.
+ Questionnaires allow researchers to find out things that cannot easily be discovered by experimentation or observation (e.g. people's attitude to sexual behaviour).
+ Closed questionnaires are easy to score objectively.
+ Open-ended questionnaires allow the researcher to gain a detailed understanding of peoples' views on particular issues.

Weaknesses
- Closed questionnaires may not offer participants the opportunity to say what they really think, and may force them to give an answer they are not happy with.
- Replies to open-ended questionnaires have to be interpreted by the researcher, which makes them harder to score objectively.
- Postal questionnaires have a low return rate. Many get thrown straight in the bin with other 'junk mail'. This means that many questionnaires must be sent out, which can make it expensive.
- Those who bother to respond may think differently to those who don't. (Perhaps the questions are about an issue the respondents feel strongly about).
- People may lie when answering the questions. To try and detect this, some questionnaires include a **lie scale**. This involves asking the same question in a different way at a later point, so that truthful

responses require a different answer. For example, the question 'Is **x** a *good* thing?' can be followed by 'Is **x** a *bad* thing?' This helps reveal whether participants are lying, and also counters **response set**, which is the tendency by participants to keep giving the same answer to all questions.

A key requirement for any questionnaire is that the questions asked should not be **ambiguous**. If a question is ambiguous it means that different people interpret the question in different ways. An example might be: *Do you agree/disagree with the following: 'Swearing in class is not a problem for me'*. Questionnaires are often tested on small numbers of people (this is called **piloting**) to help to identify and avoid such problems, as well as problems to do with lying and response set.

Interviews

An **interview** is like a verbal questionnaire, and involves asking people questions face to face. The same points about ambiguous questions, lying and response set apply to interviews in the same way as to questionnaires. **Acquiescent response set** refers to the tendency of participants to agree with whatever it is they are asked about, perhaps because they do not want to disagree with the interviewer. The researcher may use a **structured** interview, in which they work through a number of predetermined questions, or an **unstructured** interview, which is a relaxed conversation aimed at finding out what the participant thinks about certain issues. Piaget used a technique called the **clinical interview** (see page 93). This involves chatting to people, perhaps setting them problems and listening to how they go about solving these problems to get an insight into their thought processes.

Strengths

+ Unstructured interviews provide good descriptive data and are a good way to gain detail and insight into a person's views and understanding of particular issues.
+ A structured interview is less likely to deviate from the topic of interest.
+ Structured interviews are relatively easy to score and reduce the risk of interviewer bias. (This occurs if the researcher gains a distorted understanding of a person's views as a result of interpreting them in the light of the researcher's own beliefs or expectations).

Weaknesses

– Interviews can be time consuming and expensive.
– People may give answers they feel to be 'socially desirable'. They may not want to admit to an interviewer that they have unpleasant characteristics.
– Asking people about events that happened a long time ago may get answers that are inaccurate because memory can be unreliable.
– There is a risk of **interviewer effects**. That is, the characteristics of the interviewer, (e.g. their age, sex, ethnicity) may influence the way in which people respond.

Survey respondents may not like to admit to having unpleasant or antisocial habits

An IQ test should give valid results ▲

Psychometric testing

Psychometric tests are designed to measure mental abilities or psychological characteristics. Examples include **IQ tests** and **personality inventories**. They may involve face-to-face testing, but many are pen-and-paper tests which provide a quick and easy way to gather a lot of information about many different people.

Since they are a measuring tool, all such tests should be reliable and valid. If a test is **reliable** it gives consistent results. An IQ test that says someone is a genius one day and an idiot the next would hardly inspire confidence. A test is only **valid** if it measures what it says it does. Just as a psychology test should measure knowledge of psychology, a personality test should measure personality and not something else. (However, you should note that a test can be reliable but still not valid.)

Strengths

+ Pen-and-paper tests are quick and easy to administer and score.
+ They can be used to diagnose difficulties that particular people may have (specific learning difficulties, for example)
+ They can be used as a tool for selection and recruitment.

Weaknesses

– Good tests are time-consuming and expensive to design.
– Tests may help describe a person (e.g. as an extravert), but they do not explain *why* they are the way they are.
– They only give a snapshot of what a person is like at the time they sit the test. On another occasion, they might perform quite differently.
– Tests such as IQ or personality tests are often culture-biased. In other words, they are only suitable for the particular group of people who were involved in their construction.
– Labelling people (for example as 'mentally ill' or 'unintelligent') may damage their self-esteeem and reinforce other people's prejudices against them.

❓ THINK ABOUT IT

The Eysenck Personality Inventory (1964) was designed to measure personality. One question in the inventory was:

'Do you prefer early classical music to swinging jazz?' (Yes/No/Don't know).

Can you think of any problems with asking such a question?

Case studies

A **case study** is an in-depth study of an individual or small group of people. Data may be gathered using a variety of techniques, including interviews, observations, psychometrics and examination of records (archival data). The purpose is to gain as full an understanding of the participants as possible.

For example, if someone has behavioural problems (say, they are depressed), then it is useful to learn a lot about their background and recent experiences. Their behaviour may reflect something that has happened to them – perhaps the loss of a loved one. On the other hand, if they are prone to extreme mood swings for no apparent reason they may suffer from a condition known as manic depression.

Strengths
+ Case studies provide a lot of information about an individual or group.
+ This method can help to explain why people are as they are, and is often used for investigating the causes of psychological disorders.
+ It offers the chance to study people in circumstances which could not have been pre-arranged by the researcher, e.g. convalescence after an illness or an accident.

Weaknesses
– Case studies often rely on subjects' memories, which are not always reliable.
– If researchers get too involved with participants it may lead to bias.
– The small number of people studied means the researcher cannot generalise the findings to any wider group.

Longitudinal and cross-sectional research

Longitudinal research involves collecting data from the same people over a long period of time, perhaps years, to see how they change over time. **Cross-sectional** research looks at groups of people at the same moment in time, who *differ* in some way, e.g. sex, social class or age.

A famous example of longitudinal research is the television documentary, originally called *Seven Up*, which charts the development of a group of people by returning to look at them every seven years. It first looked at them at the age of seven years, and has recently returned to look at them at the age of 42.

Strengths
+ Both methods are often used by developmental psychologists to study age-related change.
+ Since longitudinal research always uses the same people, participant variables cannot affect the research.
+ Compared to longitudinal research, cross-sectional research is quicker, cheaper, and easier to replicate.

Weaknesses
– Longitudinal research can be very time-consuming and expensive.
– In a longitudinal study people may be hard to retain. They may leave for all kinds of reasons (e.g. die, become ill, emigrate or decide to drop out of the research).
– Participant variables may confound the results of cross-sectional research. For example, if younger people have different educational experiences from older people, this, rather than age, may affect their performance in certain tests of ability.

Cross-cultural research

Cross-cultural studies look at the way in which people from various ethnic and cultural backgrounds differ from one another. They provide a good way to examine the influence of environmental factors. If all people are the same in some respects, this points to the influence of **biology**. If people in one culture are different from people in another culture, this points to the impact of the **environment**.

This technique is often used in social and developmental psychology and we shall refer to it in looking at areas such as aggression, perceptual development and moral development.

Strengths

+ By identifying universal characteristics, cross-cultural studies can help clarify issues in the nature/nurture debate concerning the relative impact of biology and learning.
+ The knowledge gained by studying different cultures can challenge accepted ways of thinking about and looking at things and provide new and interesting insights.

Weaknesses

– Cross-cultural studies can be expensive and time-consuming.
– Differences in language and background may make it difficult to be sure that people from different cultures fully understand the aim of the research and what is required of them.
– Cultural differences may make it difficult for the researcher to understand the behaviour of the people being studied.
– Differences that are discovered between groups of people may be used to support prejudice.

TRY THIS

Match the **terms** on the left to the **definitions** on the right.

structured interview	in-depth research of an individual or small group
participant observation	looking at different groups of people at the same time
acquiescent response set	a flexible, conversational technique used by Piaget
clinical interview	extent to which research gives consistent, repeatable results
case study	interview with a set sequence of questions
cross-sectional research	researcher joins group to observe their behaviour
reliability	tendency of survey participants to agree with every question asked

Methods and perspectives

We have seen that the choice of research method depends very much on the type of research the psychologist wishes to carry out. All methods have their advantages and disadvantages. Different methods provide different kinds of data.

Some data is referred to as **quantitative data**. This kind of data is gained by careful measurement and can be expressed in numbers and fixed quantities. In a controlled experiment, for example, it should be possible to measure performance. Similarly, in a psychometric test the candidate will achieve a certain score.

Other types of data are more descriptive, and cannot easily be expressed in numbers. For example, if someone tells you what they felt about their father when they were young, this may be interesting, but cannot be expressed in numbers. This is called **qualitative data**.

Some psychologists take the view that qualitative data is largely uninformative and should be ignored. Behaviourists, for example, believe that psychology should be scientific. In scientific research, results can be repeated and subjected to objective testing. Behaviourists therefore prefer to use methods like the experiment to conduct their research. They distrust qualitative data because it is not obtained by direct, objective measurement.

Qualitative data usually requires subjective interpretation by the researcher. However, other psychologists such as Freud believe that qualitative data can give important insights into the ways in which people really think and feel about things, and are happy to use methods like case studies and clinical interviews. It is probably fair to say that most psychologists believe that all the different methods have their uses, and use them as they think appropriate.

QUESTIONS

Which would be the best method to use to conduct the following research:

Research topic	Research method
To find out how people feel about the amount of violence on TV	....
To see if boys play more aggressively than girls	....
To find out why a man is frequently aggressive towards his family	....
To see if 20-year-olds watch more violent videos than 50-year-olds	....

Summary

- In order to choose the 'right' research method, you need to think carefully about what you want to find out. The different methods all have their strengths and weaknesses and what is best for investigating one question may not be best for another.

- An understanding of the strengths and weaknesses of the different techniques is vital. In the same way, you need to be aware of the pitfalls and advantages of different research methods when you read about the work of other psychologists. Finding out about people is often hard, and weaknesses in research design can seriously affect the validity of the resulting data.

- All the different research techniques raise ethical questions. Sometimes a technique cannot be used at all because it would be wrong to do so. The next section will consider the different ethical questions raised in doing research.

4 Ethical Issues in Research

Animal experimentation raises serious ethical concerns ➤

Professional ethics

Professional people whose work brings them into direct contact with other people are expected to behave in certain ways. Doctors, priests and teachers, for example, must be trusted by the people they serve, and must never abuse the privileges of their position. In extreme cases, individuals who are guilty of professional misconduct may lose the right to practise their profession.

As professionals, psychologists are subject to certain rules and expectations. Over 90% of psychological research is carried out on human participants. Since psychologists work within society and with the consent of society, they have a responsibility to make sure that they do not cause distress or harm to fellow human beings.

The **British Psychological Society** is the governing body of registered psychologists in Britain and provides a code of conduct which all psychologists are expected to follow. The main rules are:

● **Be open and honest with your participants**. Whenever possible, people taking part in experiments should be made fully aware of the nature of the research. This may sometimes be difficult, as when a researcher wishes to run the study as a 'single blind', but information which might result in participants not wishing to take part in the research should never be witheld.

- **Obtain the informed consent of your participants**. The researcher should obtain the prior informed consent of participants to protect their welfare and dignity. They should be allowed to withdraw from the study at any time, and they must be told they can do this before the study begins. Afterwards, if participants are unhappy with the research for any reason, they have the right to order any data they have provided to be destroyed. With some research, telling people in advance that they can withdraw at any time is difficult. For example, it is hard to test obedience (see Milgram's research, page 319) if you have already explained to people that this is what you intend to do – and even more difficult if there is an option *not* to obey. An advantage of field research is that people behave naturally. However, they may not do so if you ask for their consent and reveal to them that you are there in order to study their behaviour.

- **Avoid deceiving participants as far as possible**. If psychologists acquire a reputation for being deceitful and lying to participants, people will stop volunteering to take part in research. Those who do take part will expect to be lied to, and will try to 'second-guess' the researcher, which will affect their behaviour and distort the findings of the study. Sometimes deception is necessary, but it should never be used unless it is the only realistic way to carry out the research.

- **Ensure the physical and psychological safety of participants**. Psychologists have a primary responsibility to protect participants from physical and mental harm in the course of their research. Where participants are exposed to risk, this risk should be no greater than the risks that they would encounter in normal daily life. Research which involves putting participants under stress may be unethical, particularly if the stress levels involved are high. Cultural differences should also be respected and allowed for. When conducting research on members of a different culture, researchers should consult members of that culture in advance to make sure that the research will not prove harmful or upsetting to them.

- **Debrief thoroughly**. At the end of a research study, participants are entitled to have the nature and objectives of the research in which they have taken part explained to them. They should be made to feel comfortable with their role, and should not go away from the study feeling worse about themselves than before they took part. If necessary, researchers should conduct follow-up research to ensure that participants have not been adversely affected in any way.

You may feel a teeny weeny tingly sensation

3000000 VOLTS

Psychologists have a duty to be honest with participants and protect them from mental and physical harm

- **Ensure confidentiality**. Psychologists have a duty to maintain the confidentiality of any information provided by participants and to conceal their identity in subsequent publications.

- **Do not exploit vulnerable people**. In the case of research involving vulnerable groups in society such as prisoners, the mentally handicapped or children, psychologists must not only seek consent from the participants themselves, but also from those charged with caring for them.

- **Observe professional guidelines**. Researchers should consult with colleagues if they believe they are at risk of breaching professional guidelines and amend procedures that are ethically dubious. They must weigh the costs and benefits of their research, and never risk breaching guidelines without reason.

Animal research

In his study of attachment, Harlow reared baby monkeys in isolation with only a cloth/wire 'surrogate mother'. The monkeys grew up to be severely disturbed and were unable to mate or play properly with other monkeys ▶

Psychological research is sometimes conducted using animals. In this book you will find several examples of research involving rats, monkeys and other creatures – for example, Harlow's research on baby rhesus monkeys on page 81. Over 80% of animal research is carried out on mice and rats. The kind of research varies, from testing animals' ability to run mazes to observing how they respond to surgery.

There are a number of advantages in using animals for research. They are cheaper and easier to look after than humans and they breed and develop more quickly, which is useful when looking at developmental changes or cross-generational influences.

However, animals cannot give their consent to research – and this worries those concerned with animal welfare. Most of us would agree that simply because animal research is convenient and cheap, that does not make it right. Animal rights campaigners believe that human beings have no right to inflict suffering on animals. To mistreat people because they belong to a different ethnic group to our own reflects a prejudice called **racism**. To mistreat women (or men) because of their gender reflects a prejudice called **sexism**. Singer (1976) argued that to mistreat animals for the benefit of humans reflects a prejudice called **speciesism**, and is morally wrong. Not everyone shares this view. Most of us are willing to eat animals, and to use them in various other ways – for example, as guide dogs for the blind or as police sniffer dogs. Many psychologists believe that, provided there is no unnecessary or undue cruelty, animal research has a part to play in their work. Gray (1987) argued that we have a moral *duty* to experiment on animals if the research will advance scientific knowledge and lead to medical advances that reduce human suffering.

This debate is a difficult one. Ultimately, researchers must decide for themselves whether they want to use animals in their research. But all psychologists need to be aware of the laws governing animal research.

Animal protection laws

Animals used in research are protected under the **Animals (Scientific Procedures) Act 1986**, and by ethical guidelines produced by the British Psychological Society governing the ways in which animal research must be conducted. Three main points are:

- **Research must be legal**. Psychologists are not above the law. They must know and conduct themselves within the limits of the 1986 Act. A Home Office licence and relevant certificate are needed before a researcher can perform surgery, administer drugs or carry out euthanasia on any animal. Researchers must also satisfy the government that their procedures are necessary and not cruel. Home Office Inspectors regularly visit institutions carrying out such research to ensure that animals do not suffer unnecessarily.
- **Pain and distress must be avoided if possible**. Researchers should always explore alternative methods (for example, tissue sampling or computer modelling), rather than cause animals to suffer. Where suffering is unavoidable it should be the least amount possible and justified by the knowledge gained.
- **The species must be understood by the researcher**. Researchers must allow for an animal's natural behaviour, habits and needs (e.g. for food, water and company). For example, some animals 'freeze' when in pain, and unless the researcher is aware of this, he or she may wrongly think the animal is not suffering.

Some researchers such as Bateson (1986) have argued that performing research on animals is justified if:

- the certainty of benefit is high
- research procedures are of a high quality
- the level of animal suffering is minimal

For others, animal research will always be the 'unacceptable face' of psychology.

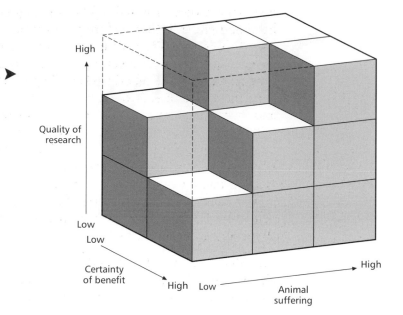

The function of the Bateson Cube is to help researchers determine whether or not research should proceed. When a research proposal falls into the shaded part of the cube, it is recommended that the experimental work should not be done

High

Quality of research

Low

Low

Certainty of benefit

High   Low

High

Animal suffering

❓ THINK ABOUT IT

A gorilla ▲

In 1999, the New Zealand parliament considered introducing a law giving great apes the right to life and protection from cruel or degrading treatment. Animal rights campaigners hoped that this might lead to the United Nations declaring the animals a protected species.

The move to protect the great apes was partly prompted by the close evolutionary links which exist between apes and humans. Great apes share over 98% of their genes with humans. They have distinct personalities, form strong emotional bonds and have some ability to understand language and to count.

Do you think that apes ought to be granted rights? If so, are there other animals that ought to be given the same protection? How would you make decisions here?

Summary

- Codes of conduct for researchers are wide-ranging, and set out good practice. They are designed to protect the good name of psychology and ensure the welfare of people and animals used in research.
- Students as well as professional psychologists are expected to be aware of these guidelines and follow them. You must show you have followed these guidelines in your own project work, and you will need to be able to demonstrate an understanding of them in your exams.

5 Presenting the Results of Research

In the last two chapters we looked at how to carry out research in a professional and ethical way using an appropriate 'tool' or method, and with the right sample of participants. We are now left with results or data to examine. We have to decide how best to analyse this data and present our findings in a written report that can be read and understood by others.

Tables and graphs

The simplest way of presenting data is to use pictures or simple graphs to put the data into a form that is easy to understand. Depending on the type of data you have collected, there are a number of options:

● frequency tables
● graphs

Frequency tables

A **table** is simply an orderly arrangement of information. The information is known as **raw data** because so far nothing has been done to change it.

One of the first things that you might do when organising your data is to count how often each value occurs. This is called the **frequency** of each value or score. This information can be presented in a **frequency table** that has two columns. The first column consists of the individual values or scores listed in order from lowest to highest. It is customary to use **x** as the column heading for the scores. The second column (which has **f** as a heading) shows how many times each score occurs in the data. For example, the following marks were obtained on a statistics test where the maximum mark was 10.

The figures below represent the scores on a statistics test:

  8, 7, 4, 9, 8, 8, 10, 9, 10, 6, 7, 9, 5

The frequency table for this data is shown on the left.

X	f
4	1
5	1
6	1
7	2
8	3
9	3
10	2

Frequency table for ▲
scores on a statistics test

Questions

1. Based on the data, how many students had perfect scores on the statistics test?
2. Based on the results, how well prepared do you think the students were for the test?

It is worth noting that if you add up the frequencies, this will give you the total number of scores in the data.

Graphs

Graphs are another way to present data in a more visual way. This involves plotting information on a horizontal (**x**) and vertical (**y**) axis. Scores are placed along the **x** axis in increasing value from left to right. In general, where the two axes meet should have a value of zero.

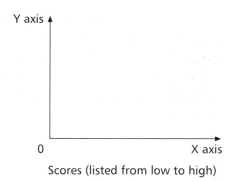

Scores (listed from low to high)

There are a number of different types of graphs that you can use, depending on your data:

● Frequency histogram
● Frequency bar chart
● Line graph
● Scattergrams

Frequency histogram

If you are going to construct either a frequency histogram or a bar chart, it helps if you have already put the data into a frequency table.

For a histogram, you need to :

● place the scores in order from lowest to highest on the x axis
● label the y axis with (f) for frequency
● draw a vertical box above each score that corresponds to the number of times the score occurs.

For example, a histogram for the marks from the statistics test would look like this:

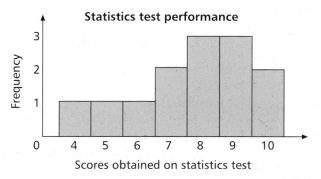

As you can see, the bars of the histogram touch each other.

Frequency bar chart

A bar chart is constructed in exactly the same way as a histogram with scores on the x axis and a vertical bar drawn above each score showing the frequency. The only difference is that the bars do not touch each other in a bar chart. The separate bars emphasise that the data consists of separate, distinct categories. For example, if you measured personality using Eysenck's Personality Inventory, you could identify which participants were extravert, neurotic or psychotic. Because these categories are all independent of each other, a bar chart would be the most appropriate way to display the results.

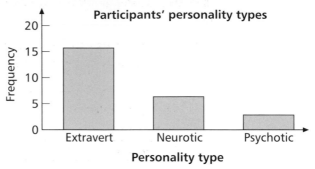

Other types of graphs

Both bar charts and histograms display the frequencies of the scores. Graphs can also be used to show **relationships between variables**. Two other graphs which you need to be familiar with are:

● line graphs
● scattergrams

Line graph

A **line graph** is most commonly used to show the changes in the relationship between two variables. If you have carried out an experiment, you might like to show graphically how the independent variable has affected the dependent variable. The values of the independent variables should be plotted on the x axis and the values of the dependent value should be plotted on the y axis.

For example, imagine you have carried out an experiment to see how caffeine affects levels of anxiety. Participants are given either no caffeine, or one, two, three or four cups of tea. Anxiety is measured by a questionnaire. The results are shown in the following line graph:

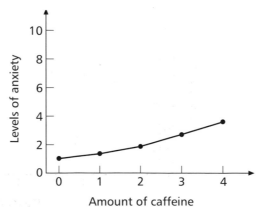

THINK ABOUT IT

According to the graph, how does caffeine affect levels of anxiety?

Scattergram

The term **correlation** refers to a statistical technique for measuring the relationship between two variables. To compute a correlation, you need to have two scores which are paired in some way (each participant can have two scores *or* you can have one score from each of the variables measured).

The pairs of scores can be listed in a table like the one shown below or they can be presented graphically in a scattergram.

Relationship between number of hours spent studying and scores on the theory part of the driving test		
Participant	Hours studied	Theory test score
1	4	22
2	0	15
3	3	22
4	7	27
5	9	29
6	1	18
7	3	21
8	2	20
9	3	20
10	5	23

On a scattergram, each pair of scores is represented by a single point on the graph. The relationship between hours studied and test scores is displayed below:

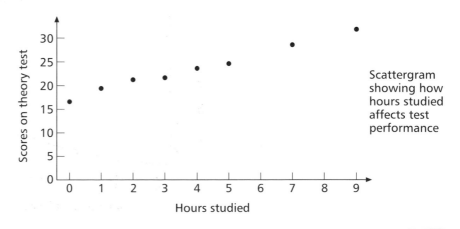

Scattergram showing how hours studied affects test performance

In correlation, if one variable increases as another variable increases, this is called a **positive correlation**. For example, it is now accepted that the more cigarettes a person smokes, the greater the risk of lung cancer. If one variable increases as the other variable *decreases*, this is called a **negative correlation**. For example, the more classes a student misses, the less likely they are to pass their exams.

There are three basic shapes of scattergrams:

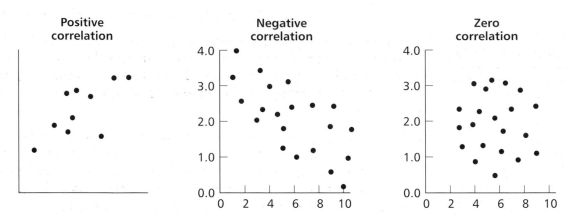

Notice that the closer the data forms to a straight line, the stronger the correlation between the variables. One important point to remember is that *a correlation does not show causation*. In other words, where a link is found between two variables, we cannot automatically conclude that one thing causes another.

For example, there is clearly a link between the size of peoples' left feet and the size of their right feet, but left feet don't cause right feet to be the length they are, or vice versa. In the same way, a correlation between smoking and cancer does not prove that smoking causes cancer. Only experiments can tell us about cause and effect.

Working with numerical data

Measures of central tendency

When you are confronted with an enormous amount of data (e.g. you have carried out a survey on 550 participants) it is helpful to try and summarise the data in a single figure. For example, in a holiday brochure it is more useful to know that the average number of daily hours of sunshine for a resort in August is 8.3 than to be given the daily temperature in August over the last ten years!

A **measure of central tendency** is a statistical measure that identifies the most typical or representative score for the data. There are three different measures of central tendency:

● mean
● median
● mode

The mean

The mean is the most familiar average – the one we are familiar with from our schooldays. To calculate the mean, simply add up all the scores and divide the total by the number of scores. The symbol $\bar{x}$ is used to refer to the mean. The formula for the mean is:

$$\bar{x} = \frac{\sum (x)}{\eta} \quad \text{where:}$$

$\sum$ means 'add up'

x refers to the scores

η refers to the total number of scores

Preferences for TV Soaps		
Participant	Neighbours	Eastenders
1	1	4
2	3	7
3	3	5
4	4	5
5	4	2
6	3	4
7	1	6
8	2	6
9	3	6
10	7	6
Totals	31	51
Means	3.1	5.1

Table showing viewers' preferences for TV soaps ▲

For example, suppose we have investigated preferences for TV soaps using ten participants who were asked to rate the programmes from 1 to 7, with 7 being the best rating. From the table on the left you can see that the mean rating for *Coronation Street* was 3.1 and the mean for *Eastenders* was 5.1

The mean is generally considered to be the best measure of central tendency. This is because the mean is based on every score and therefore is a representative value. However, one disadvantage of the mean is that it is very sensitive to extreme values. To see this for yourself, find the mean of the following sets of scores.

a) 2, 3, 5, 7, 8
b) 2, 3, 5, 7, 33

The only difference between the two sets of data is the last score. How does this affect the mean?

The median

If a set of scores has been placed in order from lowest to highest, the **median** is the score that divides the set exactly in half. This means that half of the scores will be above the median and half of the scores will be below the median. There are two ways of finding the median:

● When the sample size is an odd number
● When the sample size is an even number

When the sample size is an odd number, all you need to do is put the scores in order from lowest to highest and locate the middle score.

Example:

To calculate the median for the following set of scores:

9, 7, 5, 12, 10 (*sample size:* 5)

1 Arrange the scores in ascending order:

5, 7, 9, 10, 12

2 Locate the middle score: **9**

Where there is an even number of scores in the distribution, calculating the median requires an extra step:

Example:

To calculate the median for the following set of scores:

9, 7, 5, 12, 10, 11

1 Arrange the scores in ascending order:

5, 7, 9, 10, 11, 12 (*sample size*: 6)

2 Locate the middle pair of scores:

9, 10

3 Add them together and divide by 2:

$19 \div 2 = 9.5$

Unlike the mean, the median is a good measure of central tendency to use if there are extreme scores. Because the median is based on the position of scores, it is unaffected by extreme values.

Example:

| 2, 3, 5, 7, 8 | median = 5 |
| 2, 3, 5, 7, 33 | median = 5 |

Mode

The **mode** is the value that occurs most frequently in the data. In a sense, the mode is the most 'popular' value. For example, the mode of the following scores is 5 because this value occurs three times and no other value appears more than twice:

3, 4, 4, **5, 5, 5**, 8, 9

TRY THIS

What is the mode of the scores: 2, 3, 6, 6, 6, 8, 7, 7, 7 10

Here, both **6** and **7** are modes because they are the most frequently occurring scores. A set of scores which has more than one mode is said to be **bimodal**.

Although the mode is very easy to identify, it is not often used as a measure of central tendency because it does not take into account the values of the other scores.

In psychological research, measures of central tendency are very useful because they identify the single most representative score in the data. Unfortunately, measures of central tendency do not tell us everything that we need to know about a set of data.

TRY THIS

Consider the following sets of scores:

Participant A: 55, 51, 52, 55, 57, 55, 59, 58, 54, 53, 56, 55
Participant B: 52, 40, 55, 45, 55, 55, 55, 65, 55, 58, 55, 70

Calculate the mean, median and mode for each set of data.

The mean, median and mode for both sets of data is 55. Yet by looking at the sets of data, you can see that, despite having the same measures of central tendency, the scores for Participant B range from 40 (lowest score) to 70 (highest score). Participant A's scores are more clustered together, ranging from 51 to 59.

Measures of dispersion

Some way of recording how spread out scores are, then, is also useful. **Measures of dispersion** provide us with ways to record the spread of scores by measuring the extent to which individual scores differ from each other. There are several different measures of dispersion including:

- range
- standard deviation

Range

To calculate the **range**, subtract the lowest score from the highest score:

Range = Highest score – Lowest score

The range is very easy to calculate. However, it is not a very reliable measure of dispersion because it is based only on the highest and lowest scores.

TRY THIS

Calculate the range of the following scores:

a) 31, 33, 37, 41, 49, 52, 52, 51   b) 8, 10, 12, 13, 14, 16

Standard deviation

The **standard deviation** is the most commonly used measure of dispersion. The standard deviation uses the mean as reference point. It measures the spread of the scores by taking into account the distance between each score and the mean. Although the formula for calculating standard deviation looks complicated, it is a good way of seeing how close scores are to the mean. The formula for standard deviation is:

$$\text{Standard deviation} = \sqrt{\frac{\Sigma\,(x - \bar{x})^2}{\eta - 1}}$$

Example:
Imagine you measured reaction time and obtained the following scores:

2, 4, 6, 8

The first step in computing the standard deviation is to find the mean of the scores as shown in the table below.

Step 1	Step 2
x (scores)	*(x − x̄)*
2	2 – 5 = –3
4	4 – 5 = –1
6	6 – 5 = 1
8	8 – 5 = 3
Total = 20	
Mean = 5	

At this point it is worth noting that you have some positive differences and some negative differences. If you added up this column, the positive numbers and negative numbers would cancel each other out and you would end up with zero which isn't very helpful. Therefore you need some way of getting rid of the negative signs. One way of doing this is to square the differences since squaring a negative number makes it positive.

Step 3	Step 4
$(x − x̄)^2$	$\sum (x − x̄)^2$
$(–3)^2 = 9$	9
$(–1)^2 = 1$	1
$(1)^2 = 1$	1
$(3)^2 = 9$	9
	Total = 20

The final step involves putting the numbers into the formula. The standard deviation of these scores is 2.58.

The standard deviation tells you that on average the scores differed from the mean by 2.58. Some of the scores differ more than 2.58, other scores differ less, but on average the scores in this data differ from the mean by 2.58.

$$\text{Standard deviation} = \sqrt{\frac{\sum (x − x̄)^2}{\eta − 1}} = \sqrt{\frac{20}{4 − 1}} = \sqrt{\frac{20}{3}} = \sqrt{6.6} = 2.58$$

Summary

- There are a number of ways to present and organise data using tables and graphs.
- Frequency tables can be used to display visually how often scores have occurred in the data.
- A number of graphs can be used to display data. Frequency histograms and bar charts both display the frequencies of scores.
- Line graphs are used to show the changes in the relationship between two variables.
- Scattergrams are used to show the correlation between variables.
- Measures of central tendency include the mean, median and mode.
- Measures of dispersion indicate the extent to which individual scores differ from each other. The range and standard deviation are both measures of dispersion.

Two Major Approaches to Development

Chapter 6

Freud and
Psychoanalytic Theory

Chapter 7

The Behavioural
Approach

In **Section 1**, we outlined the six main schools of thought in psychology: the cognitive, biological, humanistic, socio-cultural, psychoanalytical and behavioural. Although each of these is important in its own right, and will be discussed in detail, two deserve special attention: the psychoanalytic and behavioural. The next two chapters explore these two approaches in detail.

6 Freud and Psychoanalytic Theory

Sigmund Freud is one of the great figures in the history of psychology. Many people who know very little about psychology have heard of 'Freudian slips' or Freud's theory of the interpretation of dreams.

Freud was born in Moravia in 1856 and spent most of his life working in Vienna as a neurologist. Following the Nazi take-over of Austria, he moved to England where he lived and worked until his death in 1939.

During his lifetime, Freud wrote over three and a half million words explaining his theories. But what was Freud really about? And how much influence did he have on psychology?

The overview diagram below shows the key elements in Freud's theory in relation to the human mind and personality.

Overview of Freud's theory

Structure of the personality

Conscious
Pre-conscious
Unconscious

A map of the mind

Id
Ego
Superego

Psychosexual development

Oral stage
Anal stage
Phallic stage
Latency stage
Genital stage

Techniques for studying the unconscious

Slips of the tongue
Dream analysis
Free association

Freud and psychoanalysis

Freud was the founder of the **psychoanalytic** movement. He developed a theory of personality development and a type of therapy known as **psychoanalysis**.

In Vienna in the late 1880s, Freud treated several patients suffering from a variety of extreme physical symptoms such as the loss of feeling in, and control over, their limbs. What really puzzled Freud was that there appeared to be nothing physically wrong with them. He concluded that the root cause of their symptoms was to be found in the unconscious level of their mind. Unpleasant memories get pushed into the unconscious and so out of awareness, to protect us from anxiety. This is a defence mechanism called **repression**. Freud believed that the physical symptoms his patients were experiencing were the result of these repressed memories or past experiences.

Based on his clinical case studies, Freud went on to develop a theory or model of the structure of the human mind, which he compared to an enormous iceberg, of which consciousness represents only the exposed tip. An illustration and explanation of this theory is shown below.

Freud's model of the human mind

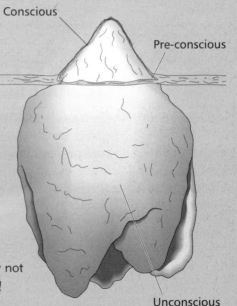

Conscious

Pre-conscious

Unconscious

The conscious level

The 'tip' of the iceberg consists of what we are aware of at any moment in time. For example, right now your conscious mind includes the words you are reading on this page. This level handles all the information which you receive from the outside world through your eyes and other senses.

The pre-conscious level

This level lies just below the surface of consciousness. It can be compared to a filing cabinet where we store everything we need to remember. The material in the preconscious level can easily be brought into conscious awareness. For example, at the moment you are probably not thinking about the taste in your mouth – but you are now!

The unconscious level

According to Freud, the largest part of the iceberg is the unconscious, which contains all our instinctual drives and repressed memories, thoughts and experiences. The unconscious consists of material which we keep from conscious awareness because it may cause us psychological distress. Although we are not aware of these repressed memories, they are able to influence our behaviour. The unconscious contains our 'secret files' which are beyond the direct reach of memory. As a result, Freud believed that the real study of the mind involved probing beneath the surface of consciousness.

THINK ABOUT IT

Mr C. is aged 40 and has spent all his working life with the same engineering company. He has recently become a supervisor and has the job of making up the overtime list for the weekend shift. Most of the people he works with are young apprentices who want weekends to themselves and regularly refuse to work extra shifts. Mr C. is finding it impossible to complete the overtime list and is being criticised by his supervisor for failing to sort the problem out.

One Friday morning he wakes up to find that he is unable to open his eyes. After a series of medical tests, it becomes clear that there is no physical cause for his temporary 'blindness'. Mr C. is referred for psychological therapy. In the process of his therapy, his anxiety about his sense of failure at work is brought to light and dealt with. Suddenly Mr C. can see again!

What helped Mr C. overcome his problem was bringing out into the open his repressed anxiety about his work. Freud called the process of confronting repressed emotions **catharsis**.

Despite the long name, catharsis can be a common experience. Can you remember a time when you overreacted to a situation at college or in your home? It is possible that you had not dealt with the unconscious emotions from a previous experience and that this new situation acted as a trigger for pent-up emotions.

Techniques of psychoanalysis

By the early 1900s, Freud had developed some basic techniques that he used with his patients in order to explore what was going on in their unconscious mind. Let us look at each of these techniques.

Free association
Mention the name 'Freud' and most people immediately think of a patient lying on a couch and a psychiatrist taking notes. Freud encouraged his patients to relax and talk freely about whatever thoughts or feelings came into their head. This process, which he called **free association**, provided clues to what was going on in their unconscious mind.

Dream analysis
Freud believed that dreams were the 'royal road into the unconscious' and that they contained hidden meanings and symbols that provided clues to a person's unconscious thoughts and desires. It was the therapist's task to listen to the patient retelling the 'story' of the dream, which he called the **manifest content**. The therapist would then try to interpret or decode the **latent content**, consisting of the hidden or disguised meaning of the dream.

Techniques of psychoanalysis pioneered by Freud are still widely used today ▶

For Freud, dreams are rather like coded messages from the unconscious. The therapist's task is to decode the dream and uncover the unconscious meaning. Then the patient can use this interpretation to confront the real problem.

You may have seen books with titles like *Understand Your Own Dreams* in bargain bookshops. These books often contain hundreds of examples of dreams, together with explanations of their 'real meaning'. Many of these books are based on simplified versions of Freud's original ideas.

Freudian slips (parapraxes)

According to Freud, the silly errors we all make are not quite as trivial as we may think. For example, what you may think of as a 'slip of the tongue' – or pen – Freud believed may reveal your unconscious attitudes and wishes. A colleague of the author's reported going for a job interview. On meeting a fellow interviewee she shook hands and said, 'Pleased to beat you'. No prizes for guessing what thought this slip revealed! Freud also believed that if you drop some household ornament and damage it, it may mean that you do not really like the object and have a secret desire to destroy it. Similarly, if you leave a hat or glove at someone's house 'by mistake' it may mean you have a secret wish to return there.

As we have seen, Freud claimed that much of our behaviour is influenced by unconscious motives. He also believed that free association, dream analysis and slips of the tongue could provide unconscious clues about our real wishes and desires.

Freud's theory about how the mind functions was based on the idea of a continuing struggle between conscious thoughts and unconscious forces. Now let's look at how that struggle takes place within the human personality.

TRY THIS

Check that you understand what you have read so far by filling in the missing words in the following passage. Choose from the following terms:

- dream analysis
- Freudian slips
- free association
- three

Freud developed .... techniques for probing the unconscious. A technique that encourages patients to talk about any thoughts or images that come to mind is called

....

A technique to interpret the hidden meanings and symbols in dreams is called

...

A therapist can also analyse the mistakes or .... that the patient makes in everyday speech.

The structure of the personality

According to Freud, our behaviour is nearly always the result of interaction between the three parts of our personality: the **id, ego and superego**.

1. The id

The **id**, Freud believed, is innate or present from birth and contains all our instincts and drives, including the two instincts known as the life and death instincts. The **life instinct** (or **eros**) includes all of our drives for survival such as finding food, warmth and sexual gratification. Freud called the energy associated with the life instinct the **libido**.

To express the relationship of the ego and id, Freud used the image of a rider struggling to control an unruly horse

The **death instinct** (or **thanatos**) is a destructive instinct which may show itself in high-risk behaviours. According to Freud, the energy associated with the death instinct was **aggression**.

According to Freud, the id is ruled by the **pleasure principle** which means that it seeks immediate gratification, rather like an impulsive child who must have its needs met *now*!

However, children have to learn that not all of their needs can be instantly satisfied. Children have to learn self-control – and that brings us to the second part of the personality, the ego.

2. The ego
The task of the **ego** is to try to find safe and socially acceptable ways of satisfying the basic needs and desires of the id. While the id is ruled by the pleasure principle, the ego is guided by the **reality principle**. When the id tells us to go ahead and satisfy our needs, the ego tells us to wait and think about it!

One image which Freud used to describe the relationship of ego to id was that of 'a man on horseback, who has to hold in check the superior strength of the horse.' The 'horse' is the id and the 'rider' is the ego.

3. The superego
At about the age of four, the third part of the personality, the **superego**, develops. The superego is like our moral guardian. It is the part of our personality which reminds us of the morals and values that we learned from our parents. Developing a superego means learning that you have to follow rules and regulations and consider the needs of others.

According to Freud, the superego consists of two parts: the **conscience** and **ego ideal**. The conscience contains all the things we should not do. If we do wrong, our conscience punishes us with guilt. The ego ideal contains all the things we should do – and it rewards us with a feeling of self-esteem or approval when we are good.

To sum up, according to Freud, personality is made up of three components: the id, ego and superego. In a healthy, well-adjusted person these three parts are in balance.

The structure of the personality

Ego
- ruled by the reality principle
- tries to satisfy needs of the id in a socially acceptable way
- is rational and logical

Superego
- strives for perfection rather than pleasure
- consists of ego ideal and conscience
- forces the ego to act on moral considerations rather than just rational ones

Id
- ruled by the pleasure principle
- seeks immediate gratification of needs
- the source of basic instincts or drives

TRY THIS

Check that you understand the previous section by filling in the missing words in the following passage. Choose from the following terms:

- **superego**
- **ego**
- **id**
- **reality**
- **gratification**
- **pleasure**

Freud believed that the human personality consisted of three major parts. The part that contains the biological drives and instincts is called the ....

This part of the personality is ruled according to the .... principle which demands ....

The part of personality that develops during infancy and has to find socially acceptable ways of meeting needs and desires is called the ....

This part of the personality is ruled by the .... principle, which involves satisfying a need only if there is a socially acceptable way of doing so.

The part of the personality which contains moral values and beliefs is called the ....

THINK ABOUT IT

Freud's theory of personality was based largely on the results of his adult patients recalling their childhood experiences. Can you think of a drawback of this approach? (You may find it helpful to refer back to page 23.)

Psychosexual development

As well as developing a model of the personality and developing psychoanalysis as a therapeutic technique, Freud is also famous for his theory of how personality develops. This theory is referred to as **psychosexual development**. It is based on the case studies of some of the patients he treated.

In 1905, Freud published *Three Essays on Sexuality*, in which he outlined the five stages that he claimed all children go through as they develop. According to Freud, most of the stages are associated with a particular part of the body which, if stimulated, gives the child pleasure. Freud called these sensitive areas **erogenous zones**. They include the mouth, the anus and the genitals. These areas are the focus of feeding and cleaning for the young infant.

At each stage of psychosexual development, Freud claimed that there is a crisis or conflict that the child must deal with. If the child is not successful in resolving it, he/she may become fixated in a stage of development. **Fixation** means that the child's later personality may include characteristics from an earlier stage of development.

The five stages which Freud identified are each associated with a certain part of the body, as follows:

- the oral stage
- the anal stage
- the phallic stage
- the latency stage
- the genital stage

1. The oral stage

The **oral stage** begins at birth and continues until the infant is about one year old. The erogenous zone during this stage is the mouth, lips and tongue, and children get pleasure from sucking and biting. Children in this stage according to Freud, are quite passive and their sense of well-being depends on the actions of those who are caring for them.

According to Freud, an oral personality seeks gratification by chewing, smoking and sucking

The conflict which occurs in this stage is weaning. If the child has feeding problems, or if the weaning process is traumatic, the child may become fixated in the oral stage and may develop an **oral** personality. Such a person may be passive and very dependent on other people. However, if fixation occurs after the child has developed teeth, Freud believed that the child may turn out to be aggressive and verbally sarcastic. A person with an oral personality may try to meet their oral needs by smoking, sucking their thumb or chewing sweets. (Interestingly, in many photographs Freud is shown smoking a large cigar.)

2. The anal stage

During the **anal stage** (ages 2–3), the erogenous zone is the anus and the child gets pleasure from defecation. Freud believed that having a full bowel caused physical tension which is relieved and gives pleasure when the child goes to the toilet. This time, the conflict is that the child has to become potty-trained – something that often develops into a battle of wills between the child and its parents. Parents want the child to learn how to control bowel movements and to 'perform' at the right place (preferably the potty) and the right time. Freud claimed that the child may rebel, either by holding onto their bowel movements or by letting go at an inappropriate time or place.

Anal-retentive personalities can be stubborn

If parents are patient and easy-going about potty training, in most cases the child will go through the anal stage without any problems. But if potty training becomes problematic, the child may become fixated in this stage. According to Freud, fixation in the anal stage can result in an anal-retentive or anal-expulsive personality. An **anal-retentive** personality is the result of a child holding onto their faeces. As an adult, this person may be very stubborn, will tend to procrastinate (put things off) and be stingy. This person may also be excessively tidy and controlled. As an adult, the **anal-expulsive** personality may be very untidy, disorganised and possibly generous. An **anal-expulsive** personality is the result of a child defecating whenever and wherever they want!

3. The phallic stage

During the **phallic stage** (ages 3–5), the erogenous zone is the genitals. Until now, development has been much the same for boys and girls. However, boys and girls go through the phallic stage very differently. Freud believed that the phallic stage was an important stage of psychosexual development because it resulted in the development of the superego (see page 47) and in the psychological differences between boys and girls.

It is easier to start with Freud's ideas about what happens to the boy. The boy gets pleasure from exploring his genitals. These pleasurable feelings may then be transferred to his mother, because she is usually the person who has the most contact with him. This means that the natural affection that the boy feels for his mother may now also include sexual feelings. The boy may begin to see his father as a rival for his mother's attention and may feel resentment. Freud believed that these feelings were unconscious so the boy is unaware of them. This conflict of feeling – desire for the mother, and resentment towards the father – was called the **Oedipus complex**. It is based on the Greek myth in which Oedipus unknowingly kills his father and marries his mother.

Freud claimed that the boy begins to worry that his father will punish him for desiring his mother. He worries that his father will take revenge by cutting off his penis. Freud called this **castration anxiety**. The boy is faced with the choice of giving up the desire for his mother or losing his penis – not much of a choice! So, according to Freud, the boy decides that he cannot have mummy for himself and instead he decides to be 'like' Daddy. He begins to **identify** with his father and accepts him as a role model. This means the boy will internalise his father's beliefs and values. At this point, the boy's superego develops.

Freud's description of the girl's development is more complicated. The girl also gets pleasure from her genitals and initially connects this pleasure with her mother. However, when she sees the genitals of her brother or a male playmate, she realises that he has a penis – and that she doesn't. According to Freud, the girl:

> 'notices the penis of a brother or playmate, strikingly visible and of large proportions, at once recognises it as the superior counterpart of her own small and inconspicuous organ, and from that time forward falls a victim to envy for the penis... She makes her judgement and decision in a flash. She has seen it and knows that she is without it and wants to have it.'[1]

As Freud describes in the passage above, the girl begins to suffer from **penis envy**. She may also blame her mother for bringing her into the world without a penis. As a result, she switches her affection away from her mother to her father and in the process comes to view her mother as a rival.

This part of the girl's psychosexual development Freud called the **Electra complex**. However, since the girl does not suffer from the same

Freud viewed castration anxiety as an expression of the son's guilt for desiring the mother

type of castration anxiety, her Electra complex is never really resolved. She realises that she can't have Daddy to herself, so she decides to identify with her mother. Freud believed that the girl's identification with her mother was not very strong and this means that her superego will not be very strong either. Freud was implying that girls are not as morally developed as boys. He claimed that women:

> 'show less sense of justice than men, (that) they are less ready to submit to the great necessities of life, that they are more often influenced in their judgements by feelings of affection or hostility'[2]

All in all, not a very positive picture for the girl!

4. The latency stage
The **latency stage** (ages 6–12) is a quiet period compared to the phallic stage of development. The child's sexual energy (libido) is resting and most children at this stage prefer to play with same-sex friends. (If you observe schoolchildren of this age, you will notice that boys tend to play with boys, and girls tend to play with girls). It is interesting that the latency stage covers a wider age-range (6–12) than the phallic stage, and clearly many changes occur during these years. However, Freud has very little to say about this period of development, believing that most of the human personality is determined by the age of five!

5. The genital stage
At this final stage of psychosexual development (ages 12+), sexual feelings re-emerge. However, now these feelings are directed towards a person of the opposite sex, but of the same age. Again, it is interesting that Freud has very little to say about development during this stage, despite the fact that young people go through enormous changes at this time of their life.

Defence mechanisms

According to Freud, most of the time, the three parts of the personality (id, ego and superego) work together in order to satisfy our needs. However, sometimes there may be conflict between them. For example, right now your id may be urging you to stop reading and watch television instead. Your ego may weigh up this option against your need to do well in your exams.

The effect of such conflict may be anxiety, which is an unpleasant feeling. Most of the time the ego is able to deal with this, but if the anxiety is overwhelming and the ego can't cope, it has other strategies called **defence mechanisms** to help deal with unpleasant emotions like guilt or anxiety.

Because defence mechanisms operate unconsciously, we are not aware that we are using them. Freud described many different types of defence mechanisms – some are listed on page 52. As you read through them, see if anyone you know uses these strategies.

Defence mechanism	Description	Example
Repression	when unacceptable thoughts, memories or emotions are pushed into the unconscious	**Victims of traumatic events may not remember what happened to them**
Regression	when we behave in a way that is typical of an earlier stage of development	**People may suck their thumbs for comfort when they are distressed**
Denial	when we refuse to admit something unpleasant or embarrassing is happening	**A person with an incurable disease may refuse to admit that anything is wrong with them**
Reaction formation	when we behave in a way that is exactly opposite to how we really feel	**Sometimes we may be especially nice to someone to disguise the fact that we really dislike them**
Sublimation	when we re-direct an anti-social or forbidden desire into an acceptable activity	**Contact sports like rugby or boxing may be a socially acceptable way of behaving aggressively**

Typical defence mechanisms ▲

According to Freud, we all use defence mechanisms some of the time as a way of protecting our ego and reducing anxiety. However, they can become a source of concern if we rely on them too much. This can lead to unhealthy patterns of thought and behaviour and, potentially, to psychological problems.

Evaluation of Freud's theory

Many psychology students argue that since Freud's theory developed in Victorian times, it may not be very relevant today. But in order to assess Freud's theory more objectively, we really need to consider both the positive and the negative aspects of his thinking.

Strengths

+ Freud's theory has helped us to appreciate how childhood experiences can influence personality development.
+ Freud developed psychoanalysis as a therapeutic technique to help people with psychological problems. Some of the techniques he used during psychoanalysis, such as free association, hypnosis and dream analysis, are still used today.
+ Freud was the founding father of the psychoanalytic movement and inspired many other theorists. Some of the best-known are **Carl Jung** (1875–1961), **Alfred Adler** (1870–1937) and **Karen Horney** (1885–1952). However, although Freud inspired these theorists, they strongly disagreed with some aspects of Freud's original theory.

  Adler focused more on the role of the ego, while Freud emphasised the role of the unconscious. Adler believed that humans are motivated by the need to overcome a feeling of inferiority.

Karen Horney agreed with Freud that childhood experiences affect how personality develops. However, she was more interested in the role of social and cultural influences. She attacked Freud's concept of penis envy and argued that it was based on an inadequate and biased interpretation of the evidence. Horney even suggested that 'womb envy', in which men are jealous of women's ability to bear children, was more likely to occur than penis envy.

+   Freud increased our awareness of the role of the unconscious in human behaviour. Carl Jung expanded Freud's theory of the unconscious. Jung believed that the 'personal unconscious' was very similar to Freud's unconscious in that it consisted of repressed memories and experiences. Jung also suggested that we have a collective unconscious which stores the memories and experiences which we inherit from our ancestors.

+   Freud formulated a stage theory of personality development. The notion of developmental stages has been used by others (e.g. Piaget). Freud also developed a model of the personality (id, ego, superego).

Weaknesses

–   Freud's theory is based on the observations he made of his patients during psychoanalytic sessions. Freud did not take notes during these sessions because he thought this might make it more difficult to form a relationship with his patients. However, this meant that he had to rely on his memory when he wrote up his notes after the session had ended. It is possible that Freud selected the details which fitted in with his theory and ignored those that did not.

–   Freud used the case study method. The patients he observed during psychoanalysis were mostly middle-class adults who were suffering from emotional problems. These patients were not a representative sample of the population as a whole, and yet Freud claimed his theory of personality was universal.

–   Although Freud developed a stage theory of child development, he only ever studied one child – a small boy he referred to as 'Little Hans' who had an irrational fear of horses. In fact, Freud did not treat Hans himself but wrote letters giving advice to Hans's father.

–   It is very difficult to test Freud's theories scientifically. Many Freudian concepts are very difficult to define and measure. Also, many of Freud's ideas are stated in such a way that they can neither be proved or disproved.

Summary

- According to Freud, there are three levels of awareness: the conscious, preconscious and unconscious.
- Freud's theory was based on his observations of emotionally disturbed patients. Some of the techniques he used during therapy were free association, dream analysis and hypnosis.
- Freud's model of personality consisted of three parts: the id, ego and superego.
- Psychosexual development consists of five stages: oral, anal, phallic, latency and genital.
- Freud believed that when the ego is under threat, we use defence mechanisms to help us cope with anxiety.

7 The Behavioural Approach

Behaviourism emphasises the role of environmental factors in human behaviour

The **behavioural approach** to psychology was developed by John Watson in America in the early 1900s. Until that time, psychologists had tended to study:

● internal mental processes
● physiological processes such as reaction time
● the nature of conscious experience.

The methods used were fairly subjective. Watson believed that psychology should be a science and that psychologists should use objective methods such as direct observation and laboratory experiments to collect data. He also argued that psychology should be the study of overt behaviour rather than the study of internal mental processes. A famous quote from Watson may help to clarify the nature of the behavioural approach:

'Give me a dozen healthy infants, well-formed and my own specified world to bring them up in and I'll guarantee to take any one at random and train him to become any type of specialist I might select – doctor, lawyer, artist, merchant-chief and yes, even beggar-man and thief, regardless of his talents, penchants, tendencies, abilities, vocations, and race of his ancestors.'[3]

The role of environment

As the quote suggests, the behavioural approach focuses on the role the **environment** plays in behaviour. Watson is suggesting that learning and experience determine the person we become – that, in other words, we are what we learn.

Behaviourism as an approach in psychology consists of a number of different theories. However, the theories all share certain basic assumptions and characteristics:

● a focus on the **external conditions** in which behaviour occurs
● a focus on the role of **learning and experience**
● a belief that changing the **environment** can result in a change in behaviour.

Comparing the behavioural approach with other approaches in psychology, Hirschorn suggests that behaviourism views humans as:

'...the proverbial inscrutable black box. Instead of attempting to open the box to see what may be inside, the behaviourists poke at it, prod it, and observe how it responds to external situations they contrive. In the process, they give no more than a brief, polite nod to psychobiologists who are wallowing in the box's contents.'[4]

Hirschorn points out that behaviourists are not interested in internal processes, whether physiological or mental. Instead, behaviourists are concerned with how organisms respond to external factors within the environment. These factors are called **stimuli**. Hirschorn's quote also provides an appropriate explanation of how behaviourists carry out their research, in that they observe how organisms respond to certain situations. When you read the section on operant conditioning later in this chapter, it will help to keep this quote in mind.

The behavioural approach has its limitations, but its achievement lies in recognising the impact of the environment on behaviour. It is also true that behavioural techniques have been successfully applied in a number of areas, including child development, education and abnormal psychology. The aim of this chapter is to explain in some detail the principles of behavioural theory.

Behavioural theories

Classical conditioning

During 1902, the Russian physiologist Ivan Pavlov carried out a series of studies on the digestive system of dogs. In particular, Pavlov was interested to find out how much saliva a dog produced when it was presented with food. Pavlov knew that if you presented food to a hungry dog it would trigger salivation, which is a **reflex** behaviour. A **reflex** is a response which happens automatically and does not involve learning. However, he also observed that if he used the same dogs over a period of time, he did not have to wait until the food was presented before they began to salivate. In fact, the dogs would already begin to salivate when the trainer appeared or when they saw the food bowl. Pavlov believed that the animals had made a mental association or link between the:

● food and the presence of the trainer

● food and the presence of the food bowl.

Pavlov decided to investigate this phenomenon in more detail.

THINK ABOUT IT

Some dogs salivate at the sound of a cupboard opening. How would you explain this in terms of conditioning?

Pavlov's methods

Pavlov knew that presenting food to hungry animals would result in salivation. He therefore suggested that food was acting as an **unconditional stimulus (UCS)**. A UCS is any stimulus which automatically elicits a response. He also suggested that the salivation to the food was an **unconditional response** or **UCR**. A UCR is a response that does not depend on learning but happens automatically.

UCS   UCR
Food ——————▶ Salivation to food

(a hungry animal will automatically salivate at the sight of food)

Pavlov found that if he repeatedly paired a neutral stimulus (any stimulus which would not normally affect the animal) with a UCS, the animal would start to respond to it. For example, if he repeatedly paired the ringing of a bell with food, eventually presenting the bell on its own would cause the animal to salivate.

CS + UCS   UCR
Bell + food ——————▶ Salivation to food

CS   CR
Bell ——————▶ Salivation to bell

Pavlov believed that the bell was a **conditional stimulus** or **CS**. A conditional stimulus is defined as any neutral stimulus which, if paired with an unconditional stimulus, will elicit a response. Salivation to the bell was considered to be a **learned response** or **conditional response (CR)**.

According to Pavlov, **classical conditioning** is a learning process which involves forming an association between two stimuli: the conditional stimulus and the unconditional stimulus. As a result of classical conditioning, a **conditional stimulus (CS)** acquires the ability to elicit a response.

Pavlov's theories were based on scientific study of animal responses to stimuli such as lights and bells ▶

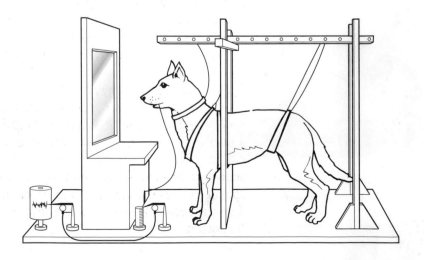

TRY THIS

Look at the terms listed in the table below and decide whether each one is a UCS or a UCR (reflex response). Then match each stimulus or response with its correct pair by ticking the appropriate column (one has already been done for you).

Terms	UCS	UCR	Links with
fear		✓	*loud noise*
blinking			
pepper			
loud noise			
puff of air on eye			
sneezing			

Characteristics of classical conditioning

There are a number of important features associated with classical conditioning. These include:

● extinction

● spontaneous recovery

● generalisation

● discrimination

● higher-order conditioning

Extinction

Pavlov was interested to find out whether a conditioned response is permanent. He tested this by conditioning a dog to salivate at the sound of a bell by pairing the bell with food. Once the animal was conditioned, Pavlov continued to ring the bell but did not provide any more food. Pavlov found that over time the conditioned response weakened and eventually disappeared altogether. This process is called **extinction**, and it suggests that conditioned responses need not last forever.

Spontaneous recovery

However, Pavlov also discovered that if he waited a while after a response had been extinguished and then presented the conditional stimulus, the conditional response would suddenly reappear. Pavlov called this reappearance of the conditional response **spontaneous recovery**. Spontaneous recovery occurs in a number of species including sheep, rats and pigeons, even after long periods of time have elapsed. The process suggests that to some extent what we learn is never really forgotten.

Generalisation

Pavlov found that once an animal had been trained to respond to a particular conditional stimulus, a *similar* stimulus could also elicit a response. For example, if a dog was trained to salivate to a red light, the animal would also salivate to an orange light because it was similar. This process is called **stimulus generalisation**. A blue light would not cause salivation because it is not similar enough to the red light. Furthermore, the more similar the new stimulus is to the original one, the stronger the animal's response.

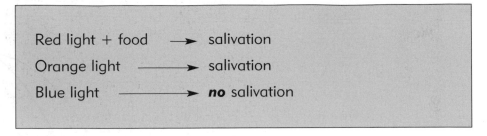

Red light + food   ⟶   salivation

Orange light   ⟶   salivation

Blue light   ⟶   **no** salivation

Stimulus generalisation is a useful process because it means that a response learned in one situation can be transferred to a number of different situations.

Discrimination

Pavlov found that animals could be trained to tell the difference between two very similar stimuli. He referred to this ability as **stimulus discrimination**. In one experiment, he presented dogs with two similar shapes, a circle and an ellipse. The circle was *always* presented with food and the ellipse was *never* presented with food. As a result, the animals learned to salivate in response to the circle but did not salivate in response to the ellipse. Being a curious scientist, Pavlov wanted to see how fine the animal's ability to discriminate really was. Over a number of trials, Pavlov changed the shape of the ellipse so that it began to look more and more like a circle.

For a while the dogs were still able to tell the difference between the two shapes. However, when the shapes were nearly the same, the animals could no longer discriminate between them and began to show signs of distress. Pavlov believed that he had created a nervous disorder in the animals.

Higher-order conditioning

Pavlov showed that once an animal was conditioned to respond to a particular conditional stimulus such as a bell, it was possible to use that conditional stimulus as if it were an unconditional stimulus.

For example, once the animal was trained to respond to the bell, a new stimulus (a black square) was introduced. The new stimulus was repeatedly paired with the bell and after a period of time, the animal would salivate to the black square alone. This process was called **higher-order conditioning** and is demonstrated in the diagram below:

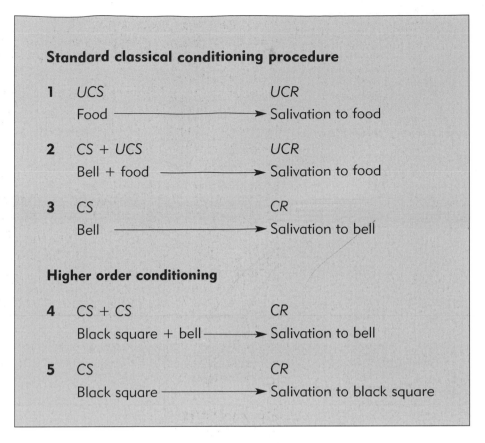

Not surprisingly, the response to the second conditional stimulus (black square) is not as strong as the original conditional stimulus.

Applications of classical conditioning

In 1920, Watson and Rayner carried out an experiment to see if classical conditioning could explain how we acquire emotional responses to certain objects or situations. Their study is described below.

KEY STUDY   The participant used in the study was an eleven-month-old boy called Albert. In the first part of the study, the researchers wanted to see how Albert responded to a loud noise, so they struck a steel bar with a hammer. The noise frightened Albert and he tried to hide his face. The researchers also presented Albert with a number of objects to play with, including a ball of wool, some blocks, masks with and without hair and a white rat. Albert did not show any negative responses to any of the objects.

Several weeks later, the researchers presented Albert with a white rat. When he reached out to touch it, they made a loud noise behind his head. After the loud noise had been repeatedly paired with the white rat, Albert tried to crawl away when the rat was presented on its own.

In the final part of the study, the researchers presented other objects such as a white rabbit, a fur coat and a Santa Claus mask. Albert reacted to all of these objects with fear.

Little Albert learned to fear the rat through classical conditioning. Before conditioning, the rat was a neutral stimulus that caused no fear. During conditioning, John Watson made a loud noise that frightened Albert whenever the rat was near. After conditioning, the rat caused an instant 'fear response' in Albert

During conditioning

Fear

After conditioning

Fear

Questions

1. What evidence is there in the text that generalisation has occurred?

2. In the study, what is being used as the:

   a) unconditional stimulus
   b) conditional stimulus
   c) conditional response

3. Albert was never 'deconditioned'. Suggest one long-term effect that participating in this experiment could have had on his behaviour.

4. Describe one other ethical problem with this experiment.

Source: Watson, J.B., & Rayner, R., 'Conditioned Emotional Reactions', in *Journal of Experimental Psychology*, 3 (1920), pp.1–14

Therapeutic applications of classical conditioning

Watson and Rayner (1920) demonstrated that fears can be acquired through classical conditioning. However, it was left to other researchers to discover how classical conditioning could be used to *treat* phobias or irrational fears. The following techniques are therapeutic applications of classical conditioning.

Counter-conditioning

In 1924, Mary C. Jones worked with a three-year-old boy called Peter who had an irrational fear of rabbits. Unlike Albert, who had been experimentally conditioned to fear a white rat, Peter had acquired his fear naturally. Jones used a process called **counter-conditioning** to remove Peter's fear. This involved presenting Peter with the feared object (the rabbit) but at the same time offering him a pleasant stimulus like food. Peter would be given the food while the rabbit was placed a safe distance away. Over a number of sessions, the rabbit was brought closer and closer, always in the presence of food, until Peter had lost his fear.

Systematic desensitisation

It was not until the 1950s that researchers began to take another look at Mary Jones's work. Joseph Wolpe (1950) expanded her work and

Exposure to the feared object can help overcome phobias ▲

developed a therapeutic technique called **systematic desensitisation**. The therapy depends on three elements:

● training in relaxation
● construction of an anxiety hierarchy
● exposure to the feared object or situation

During the course of the therapy participants are taught how to monitor their own levels of anxiety and how to relax. They are asked to construct an **anxiety hierarchy** which consists of a number of events or situations. The situations are ranked in order of 'least frightening' to 'most frightening'. They are then asked to start at the bottom of the hierarchy and imagine the least frightening situation, or are confronted with it directly. The therapist encourages them to relax. The therapy is based on the assumption that it is impossible to feel relaxed and frightened at the same time. Over a number of sessions participants work through their anxiety hierarchy, until they are able to cope with each situation. For example, someone frightened of spiders may gradually move from a situation in which they tolerate a small spider in a jar in the corner of a room, to one where the spider is actually scuttling over their body.

TRY THIS

Think of something that you are very frightened of. This could include a fear of animals, examinations or injections. Construct an **anxiety hierarchy** for your fear. Place the situation which is *least frightening* at the bottom of your hierarchy (Level 1). Place the *most frightening* situation at the top (Level 5). The situations listed in the other levels should be ranked in terms of how frightening they are for you.

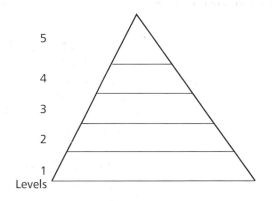

Implosion therapy and 'flooding'

These two techniques assume that if the individual can experience the feared object or situation and nothing terrible happens, the link between the two will be broken. The difference between implosion therapy and flooding is that implosion therapy involves the person *imagining* the feared situation, while flooding involves the person actually confronting the feared situation directly. For example, one of Wolpe's patients had a fear of cars. The flooding therapy consisted of driving her around in a car for several hours until her fear began to subside.

Aversion therapy

Aversion therapy has been used to treat alcohol and drug abuse. The treatment involves giving the individual a drug which, if combined with alcohol, causes vomiting. Aversion therapy is based on the assumption that the unpleasant experience of nausea and vomiting will come to be associated with the alcohol through classical conditioning.

Instrumental conditioning

While Pavlov was investigating the nature of classical conditioning, Edward Thorndike (1898) was studying the nature of **instrumental conditioning**. Thorndike observed the responses of cats in an apparatus called a **puzzle box**.

The cats were placed inside a box, and food positioned outside to encourage them to escape. In order to escape from the box, the cat had to loosen a bolt or pull a string which released a weight to open the door. Thorndike found that initially the cat would engage in random behaviours like scratching and clawing. Eventually, through trial and error, the cat would work out how to get out. On successive trials, the cats took less and less time to escape.

Based on these results, Thorndike developed what he called the **law of effect**. The favourable outcome of getting the food 'strengthened' the escape response. According to Thorndike, any behaviour which was followed by a satisfying state of affairs is likely to be repeated. Any behaviour which is followed by an unsatisfying state of affairs is not likely to be repeated. Thorndike was proposing that learning was not based on an association between two stimuli as Pavlov suggested, but on the consequences of a behaviour.

Operant conditioning

Thorndike's theory was expanded by the American psychologist **B.F. Skinner** (1904–90). Skinner rephrased Thorndike's law of effect using more scientific terms. He disliked the use of terms such as 'satisfying' and replaced them with terms such as 'reinforcement' and 'punishment'. Skinner called his theory **operant conditioning**.

Skinner developed an apparatus (now called a **Skinner box**) which allowed him to observe and record the frequency of the animal's behaviour. The basic Skinner box contains a food dish and a lever.

Skinner found that when a hungry rat was placed in the box, it would engage in random behaviours such as scratching and sniffing. Eventually, purely by accident, the rat would press the lever. At that point, the rat was automatically reinforced with a food pellet. Skinner discovered that if food was presented each time the lever was pressed, the frequency of lever-pressing increased significantly. On the other hand, if a mild electric current was given to the rat when the lever was pressed, lever-pressing decreased significantly. Skinner recognised that he could influence the animal's behaviour by providing either a reward or punishment after a response.

The Thorndike
'puzzle box' ▼

The 'Skinner box' ▼

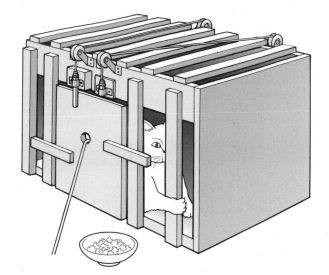

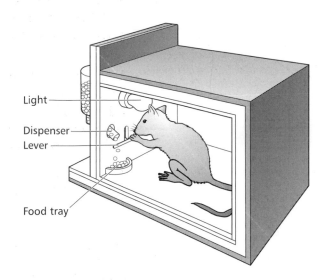

Light

Dispenser

Lever

Food tray

Types of reinforcers

Skinner defined a **reinforcer** as *anything that increases the frequency of a response*. He described different types of reinforcers:

● positive reinforcers

● negative reinforcers

● primary reinforcers

● secondary reinforcers

Positive and negative reinforcers

Positive reinforcement involves presenting something pleasant in order to increase the frequency of a response. For example, if one of your employees has produced record sales for this year, you could reward her with a substantial pay rise.

Negative reinforcement is often confused with **punishment**, but the two things are quite different. Negative reinforcement involves *removing* something unpleasant in order to *increase* the frequency of a response. For example, imagine that your child is begging for a biscuit before tea-time. As a responsible parent, you may refuse to give her a biscuit because it will spoil her appetite. However, the child continues to complain until eventually you give in and hand over a biscuit. At that point the whining stops. Your child has just successfully used negative reinforcement in order to get a biscuit. She has removed the unpleasant stimulus (the whining) when you provided the treat.

Punishment, on the other hand, involves *presenting* something unpleasant in order to *decrease* the frequency of a response. For example, if your child runs out into a busy street, you will want to stop the response from occurring again. You may scold the child so that

THINK ABOUT IT

Can you remember being punished as a child? How did it make you feel?

he/she will not repeat the response. In general, Skinner believed that positive reinforcement was more effective than punishment. There are, of course, a number of negative effects of using punishment.

There are several reasons why punishment may not be effective:

● It can create feelings of anger or fear in the person who is being punished

● Punishment does not help to explain *why* a certain behaviour is unacceptable or tell you what you *should* do.

Primary and secondary reinforcers

Skinner also made a distinction between **primary** and **secondary** reinforcers:

● A **primary reinforcer** is any reinforcer which satisfies an innate, biological need. An example of a primary reinforcer is food.

● **Secondary reinforcers** are learned rather than innate and do not satisfy basic biological needs. Examples of secondary reinforcers include praise, money or applause. Secondary reinforcers acquire their ability to influence behaviour because at some point in time they were associated with a primary reinforcer.

Features of operant conditioning

There are a number of characteristics associated with operant conditioning. Some of the characteristics are the same as for classical conditioning. They include:

● extinction
● generalisation
● discrimination
● schedules of reinforcement
● shaping

Extinction

As in classical conditioning, **extinction** is a procedure which causes a previously learned response to stop occurring. In operant conditioning, extinction occurs when a response is no longer followed by a reinforcer.

Generalisation

If a person is reinforced for responding to a particular stimulus, they are likely to make the same response to a similar stimulus. For example, a pigeon who has been trained to peck at a circle will also peck at an oval shape.

When we said "Try offering your employees a carrot" we didn't mean literally.

Discrimination

As we saw earlier, discrimination involves teaching an organism to tell the difference between two very similar stimuli. To achieve discrimination in operant conditioning, the researcher could present both a circle and an oval to a pigeon. Reinforcement is given only when the pigeon pecks at the circle and never given when the pigeon pecks at the oval figure. As a result, the pigeon will learn to discriminate between the two shapes.

Schedules of reinforcement

Skinner found that reinforcers can be presented according to different schedules or time periods. For example, **continuous reinforcement** occurs when reinforcement is presented every time the desired response occurs. Skinner found that **partial reinforcement** (i.e. reinforcing some but not all of the desirable responses) was also effective. He identified four types of partial reinforcement:

- fixed interval
- variable interval
- fixed ratio
- variable ratio

Interval schedules involve providing a reinforcer after a specified interval or period of time has elapsed. Ratio schedules involve providing reinforcement after a certain number of responses have occurred.

- In a **fixed interval (FI)** schedule, reinforcement is given after a fixed period of time. For example, a researcher may have an 'FI (2)' (a fixed interval of two minutes). This might mean that an animal in an experiment is reinforced for the first correct response after two minutes have passed since the last reinforcement. A fixed interval schedule which is relevant to humans occurs if you are paid your wages on a weekly basis. After a fixed interval (seven days), you receive your reward for working.

- In a **variable interval (VI)** schedule, a response is reinforced after a variable amount of time has passed since the previous reinforcer. For example, a 'VI (15 seconds)' means that the necessary interval of time will vary on each trial but will average out at 15 seconds. Since the animal cannot predict when a reward will come, the rate of responding is relatively low but steady. To take a human example, suppose that instead of sitting a final exam at the end of your course, you had 'spot' examinations that could occur at any time. You might find that your rate of revising was pretty steady because you could not predict exactly when you would be tested.

- **Fixed ratio (FR)** means that reinforcement is given after a fixed number of responses. For example, an 'FR (5)' means that a reinforcer is given after every fifth response. An example for humans would be a salesman's commission. The salesman's salary (the reinforcement) would depend on selling a certain number of products each week.

- **Variable ratio (VR)** means that reinforcement occurs after an average number of responses. Here, the number of responses needed will vary from trial to trial. For example, a 'VR (4)' means that a reinforcement is given on average after every fourth response, but each trial will vary. Gambling machines are based on variable ratio schedules.

Shaping

The technical name for this is the **method of successive approximations**. Basically, shaping is a way of speeding up learning through operant conditioning.

For example, imagine you had to teach a chicken to peck in the left-hand corner of a room. You are not allowed to cheat by putting some grain down in the corner of the room and waiting for the chicken to find it! Instead, you have to wait until the chicken pecks in just the right place and then provide reinforcement.

This process could take a very long time, so one way of speeding it up is to use shaping. You would start by reinforcing any behaviour which is vaguely related to the desired behaviour. Then gradually, you would reinforce only those responses that **approximate**, i.e. are closer to, the desired behaviour. For example, you could divide the area of the room in half and provide reinforcement when the chicken pecked in the left-hand side. If the chicken moved over to the right-hand side, you would not reinforce that response. Then, you could reduce the area so that you

Goal: To train chicken to peck area of room marked 'X'.

Stage 1: Chicken is rewarded when it pecks in shaded area 'A'.

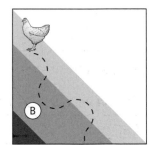

Stage 2: Chicken is rewarded when it pecks in shaded area 'B'.

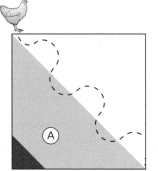

Stage 3: Chicken is rewarded when it pecks in shaded area 'C'.

Stage 4: Reward given only when chicken pecks in 'target area' X.

only provide reinforcement if the chicken is in the left-hand quarter of the room. Finally, you would only provide reinforcement if the chicken pecked in the left-hand corner.

Applications of operant conditioning

Although operant conditioning is based on animal research, there are a number of practical applications for human beings.

Biofeedback

In **biofeedback**, an individual is provided with information about a specific aspect of their physiological functioning such as blood pressure and heart rate. As a result, the person is able to exert some control over these functions. Biofeedback works by using a machine which measures a physiological response and informs the person either through an auditory or visual display about the changes going on in their body. This technique has been used with people who suffer from high blood pressure or from migraine headaches.

Programmed learning

Programmed learning was developed by Skinner as an alternative to the conventional classroom, which Skinner believed was not always the best place to learn. He pointed out that in a classroom setting the teacher has to work very hard to maintain the student's attention and motivation. When students complete a task or assessment, they do not usually get quick feedback because it takes time for the teacher to mark the assessment.

An example of programmed learning methods. Students fill in the gaps in the right-hand column using the 'correct answers' in the left-hand column

▼

In programmed learning, the information to be learned is broken down into very small steps. The material is organised in such a way that the chances of making a mistake are small. This is intended to increase the

Programmed learning module for the topic of operant conditioning	
Correct answers	**Learning frame**
Pavlov B.F. Skinner operant	Another type of conditioning is known as *operant conditioning*. The main theorist associated with operant condtioning is .... The main theorist for *classical conditioning* is .... ; whereas .... conditioning was pioneered by ....
Skinner box reinforcer	Skinner developed an apparatus called a .... which allowed him to record the frequency of an animal's behaviour. If a hungry rat is placed in the box and, by chance alone, presses the lever, the animal is reinforced. Therefore the food pellet is a ....
reinforcement operant	Initially the rat will press the lever only occasionally, but if it continues to receive ...., lever-pressing will increase. When the rat is pressing the lever at a frequent rate, we can say that .... conditioning has occurred.

student's motivation. Typically, the student is presented with information and asked a question about it. Immediate feedback is provided because the student can check straight away to see if their response is right. If they have made a mistake, it is possible to go through the material again until they have understood it correctly. An example of programmed learning is shown on page 67.

Strengths

+ Students can work at their own pace
+ They can get immediate feedback on their performance.

Weaknesses

– Programmed learning is not appropriate for all subject areas.
– Programmed learning can be lonely. Students must work through the material alone and without face-to-face contact with a teacher.

Behaviour modification

The aim of this technique is to increase the frequency of desirable responses and decrease the frequency of undesirable responses. Behaviour modification has been used to control problem behaviour such as aggression and disorders such as phobias. It is based on the assumption that what is learned can be unlearned.

According to Watson and Tharp (1993) there are five basic steps in behaviour modification:

1 Decide which specific response is to be changed. This is called the **target behaviour.**

2 Establish a **baseline rate**; in other words, determine how often the behaviour is occurring before you try to change it.

3 Decide which factors in the environment are **rewarding** the target behaviour, and remove them.

4 Identify **strategies** which will decrease the frequency of the target behaviour and increase the frequency of a more desirable response; observe and record how often the target behaviour is now occurring.

5 **Evaluate** whether the intervention has had any effect; if the target behaviour has not decreased significantly, the factors rewarding the behaviour may not have been correctly identified and the programme may need to be re-designed.

For example, imagine that a teacher is finding it difficult to manage the behaviour of a seven-year-old boy called Matt. Matt is aggressive in the classroom, biting and hitting other children. Using behaviour modification, the steps that could be taken to change Matt's behaviour are shown below:

Steps	Action to be taken	Examples
1	Identify target behaviour to be changed	biting and hitting other children
2	Establish baseline	observe and record how many times Matt bites or hits another child each day for a period of a week
3	Identify reinforcers	teacher should ignore undesirable behaviour and reinforce any desirable responses like sharing
4	Reassess frequency of target behaviour	record the frequency of hitting and biting
5	Evaluate intervention	if frequency of biting and hitting has decreased, intervention is successful

Token economies

A similar technique known as **token economies** has been used with patients suffering from mental disorders in order to try and encourage their social skills. This technique involves rewarding desirable behaviour by providing tokens which can be exchanged for other objects that the individual really wants, such as cigarettes or chocolate or special privileges. Although token economies have been used effectively in hospital settings to encourage patients to take more responsibility for their behaviour, there are a number of problems associated with the technique. Some critics argue that behaviour modification only produces temporary changes in behaviour. There are also ethical issues involved, since the person who receives token economies is at the mercy of the individual providing the reinforcers and so is open to abuse.

Evaluation of the behavioural approach

Strengths
+ Acknowledges the role of the environment on human behaviour.
+ Uses scientific, objective methods like experiments and controlled observation.
+ Has helped to identify principles of learning which apply to both animals and humans.
+ Has developed therapeutic and educational applications for humans.

Weaknesses
− Presents a very mechanistic view of human beings, viewing them as passive receivers of environmental stimuli.
− Ignores emotion, motivation and drives in humans because they are not directly observable.

Summary
● The behavioural approach focuses on how external factors in the environment affect behaviour.

- Two important theories which explain how humans and animals learn include classical conditioning and operant conditioning.
- Classical conditioning involves the organism making an association beween two stimuli (the unconditional and the conditional stimulus).
- There are a number of practical applications of classical conditioning, including systematic desensitisation, flooding and aversion therapy.
- Instrumental and operant conditioning emphasise the relationship between a stimulus situation and whether responses to it are reinforced or punished.
- Both operant and classical conditioning share a number of features, such as generalisation, extinction and discrimination.
- Skinner identified a number of different reinforcers such as positive, negative, primary and secondary reinforcers.
- There are a number of important applications of operant conditioning which include biofeedback, behaviour modification and the use of token economies.

Developmental Psychology

What theories can we put forward to explain our remarkable transformation from helpless infants to fully grown adults? To what extent can we generalise about the way human beings develop? How can we explain the fact that each one of us is unique? Are we born the way we are, or does the environment have a major impact on the way we turn out? This section looks at these issues in relation to several different aspects of development.

8 Attachment and Separation

Most parents love their children, and most children love their parents. Many animals care for their young, and some will even risk their own lives to defend them from predators. This form of caring is what we shall be exploring in this chapter on attachment.

What is attachment?

Attachment refers to a close emotional bond between two people. Kagan et al. (1978) define attachment as an intense emotional relationship that is specific to two people, that endures over time, and in which prolonged separation from the partner is accompanied by stress or sorrow.

Many psychologists believe that the first attachments that we form are very important and can influence the relationships we go on to form in later life. The nature of this early bond between a baby and its carer (often the mother) has been the subject of much study and controversy. In this chapter we will examine how attachments are formed, some theories of attachment, and consider what the consequences may be if such early attachments are not formed.

Forming attachments

The term **sociability** refers to our willingness to interact with other people. There is much evidence to suggest that babies enjoy interacting with others, and so babies are said to be sociable. They show more interest in human beings than other objects from the moment they are born. Newborn babies (**neonates**) will smile reflexively when you stroke their cheek, and within a few weeks of birth babies will smile when they hear a human voice or see a human face (**social smiling**). Ahrens (1954) found that one-month-old babies will smile if shown a picture of just a pair of eyes drawn onto the outline of a face. Later, more details need to be added to elicit a smile, and by five months, all the major features, plus shading to give a 3D effect, are needed to elicit a smile.

Smiling, of course, is precisely the type of reaction that encourages adults to interact with the baby. But even visually handicapped babies of a few weeks old will smile in response to a human voice. Since babies all over the world behave in this way, it is argued that smiling is an **instinctive** (unlearned) behaviour, and that babies come into the world 'programmed' to make themselves attractive to other people.

Trevarthen (1979) described the interaction of young babies with their mothers as **conversations**. Mother and baby take it in turn to make noises or facial or body movements and rarely interrupt each other. Brazelton et al. (1975) asked mothers to withdraw from such activity by being unresponsive to their baby's actions. That is, the mother would 'freeze' for a while, with a blank face and stay quiet, ignoring what the baby did. In response to this, even three-week-old babies became visibly upset and tried to regain their mother's attention. This indicates that babies are active participants in social interactions from a very early age.

The extent to which babies are 'born sociable' is, however, still a matter of debate. Their interest in other human beings may simply reflect the fact that people provide a whole variety of sounds, movement and touch that other objects do not. Some suggest that apparent turn-taking activity in very young babies may possibly reflect cleverness on the part of adults, rather than any inborn abilities of the child. Even so, such activity can help a child to learn that its actions have consequences (e.g. a wiggle and a pause results in a response from the adult). This realisation by the child that what it does *matters* may be crucial to its understanding of itself as a social being – i.e. as someone who is able to influence the environment and other people.

The process of forming attachments

Longitudinal research by Schaffer and Emerson (1964) involved questioning the parents of 60 babies at one-month intervals. The social

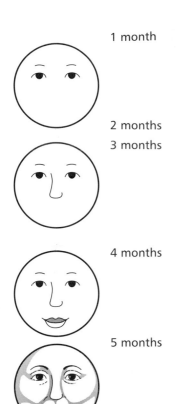

1 month

2 months

3 months

4 months

5 months

6 months

▲

Research by Ahrens showed that babies will smile in response to an oval shape with eye-dots at one month old; more details such as nose and eyebrows are needed to elicit the same response at three months; all facial features are needed at four months; and shading to give a 3D effect is needed by the time the baby is five months old

Young children often show a fear of strangers ▲

behaviour of the children was studied from birth to 18 months of age. The researchers' findings, and those of other researchers such as Mary Ainsworth, suggest that the process of attachment can be divided into a number of phases:

1 **The indiscriminate attachment phase: birth to six months.** The child shows no particular preference and is increasingly sociable with anyone who shows a reciprocal interest in him/her.

2 **The specific attachment phase: seven months to one year**. The child shows a preference for one or two particular carers. Evidence for an attachment bond comes from a number of indicators:

   ● **separation anxiety** – the child shows distress when the carer leaves. Those who protest the most tend to be children whose mothers respond most quickly to their demands and who offer the most interaction.

   ● **stranger fear** – unlike earlier, the child may now show a fear of unknown adults. Interestingly, babies show little fear of unknown children, and the extent of their fear of adults depends on how the adult behaves and where they are. For example, babies tend to show more fear if a strange adult is encountered in a familiar setting.

   ● **social referencing** – the child seeks an emotional response from the carer and can be affected by the adult's mood and emotional state. What upsets the adult may also now upset the child.

3 **The multiple attachment phase: one year plus**. The child forms attachments to a number of other adults and children. By about 18 months, only about 11% of children are attached to only one person. The attachments a child has gradually become less obvious and may only be apparent when the child is frightened or distressed.

The ages given above are only a rough guide and can differ between children. Interestingly, Schaffer and Emerson found that in about a third of cases the main attachment figure was not the mother or primary caretaker, but could be the father, older siblings or some other relative or friend of the family. They also found that different people could be preferred for different things. For example, children would often seek their mothers if they needed comforting and their fathers for rough-and-tumble play. Attachments, therefore, are related not simply to the extent to which carers satisfy physical needs, but also on the *quality* of the interactions – particularly the extent to which a person takes an active interest in the child's happiness and well-being.

Fathers tend to be more physical in their interactions with their children, mothers more verbal ▲

Cultural variations

So far we have looked at the patterns of attachment formation in early infancy. But how far do these patterns vary from country to country and culture to culture?

Ainsworth (1967) looked at Ganda children in Uganda, central Africa, who are carried everywhere by their mothers in a cotton sling, sleep with them, are breast-fed until about two years of age, and are generally kept physically close to the mother and rarely separated. Ainsworth found that Ganda children tended to form attachments with their mothers about two months earlier than children in the West. This shows that the process of attachment is linked to patterns of care.

Children reared in communes in Israel called **Kibbutzim** are looked after by trained childminders (called **metapelets**) for much of the day, while the mother is at work. They spend a few hours each evening with their parents but by the age of one they sleep in separate quarters provided for children. Fox (1977) nevertheless, found that these children form strong attachments with their mothers and therefore that time alone does not account for strong attachments. The children also showed protest when their nurses left them, which indicates that opportunities to form multiple attachments are beneficial to the children in this system.

QUESTIONS

1 Explain the terms:

   a) **attachment**
   b) **sociability**

2 What evidence is there that babies are born sociable?
3 What might be a consequence if babies were not sociable?
4 What three stages in forming attachment bonds were identified by Schaffer and Emerson?

KEY STUDY   Ainsworth and others (1978) used a structured observational study known as the **Strange Situation** to explore the different kinds of attachments that babies can form. In the study, a mother and baby played with toys in a room. After a time, an adult stranger came in, and there followed a series of episodes in which the adults left and returned. As a result the baby and the two adults were sometimes all together; sometimes each adult was alone with the child, and sometimes the child was alone. The baby was observed throughout (using one-way mirrors) to see how it played and responded to the mother and the stranger.

On the basis of this research Ainsworth identified three different kinds of attachment bond:

1 **Type A:** 15% of babies were **insecurely attached**, and described as **anxious–avoidant**. Such babies appeared largely indifferent to their mothers, mostly ignoring them and treating them in a similar fashion to the stranger. The stranger seemed able to supply as much comfort as the mother, and distress was largely caused by the baby being left entirely on its own.

2 **Type B:** 70% of babies were **securely attached**. These babies played happily on their own while their mother, or mother and stranger, were there. They showed distress and played much less when their mother left, and were only partially comforted by the stranger. When the mother returned they immediately sought contact with her, were quickly calmed and resumed playing.

3 **Type C:** 15% of babies were also **insecurely attached** and **anxious–resistant**, i.e. generally more fussy, crying more and exploring less than other babies. They became very upset when their mother left the room and resisted attempts by the stranger to make contact and offer comfort. When the mother did return, the babies behaved ambivalently, appearing to seek comfort and reassurance from them but rejecting comfort when it was offered.

Ainsworth believed that secure attachment was best. Babies who formed secure attachments had sensitive mothers who responded quickly and appropriately to their needs and consistently showed affection. Insensitive mothers misinterpreted the child's needs or imposed their own needs and wishes upon the child rather than responding to the child's desires. Sensitive mothers helped their babies feel more secure, and these babies were more likely to become independent later.

Source: Ainsworth, M.D.S., Belhar, M.C., Waters, E., & Wall, S., *Patterns of Attachment: A psychological study of the strange situation*, (Lawrence Erbaum Associates, New Jersey, 1978)

Questions

1. Give one advantage and one disadvantage of structured observations as a method of research.
2. Suggest an ethical problem for this study.
3. To what extent does the labelling of a child who protests when the mother leaves as 'securely attached' seem reasonable?

Evaluation of Ainsworth's research

Strengths

+ The Strange Situation is generally considered a useful tool for studying a child's emotional development.
+ The classifications developed by Ainsworth have been used to predict future social behaviour. Sroufe et al. (1978, 1983 and 1989) found that two-year-olds rated as insecurely attached were less likely to ask adults for help and became frustrated more quickly if they encountered problems. Sroufe and others also found that children rated as securely attached between 12 to 18 months of age were more confident and outgoing at both 5 and 10 years of age and more enthusiastic about solving problems.

Weaknesses

– Main (1991) found that not all babies fit into the classification system, although many do. For example, Main reports that some babies fall into a fourth category, **insecure–disorganised**. These babies do not show any clear or consistent strategy for coping with attachment-related stress. Main argued that we should think in terms of a range of different kinds of attachments, and not just the three identified by Ainsworth.

– Another criticism is that attachment patterns can change. Vaughn et al. (1980) found that attachments may shift from insecure to secure, and vice versa, depending on family circumstances. These circumstances might include changes in the people available to the child (e.g. new family members may arrive or leave), or changes in the amount of stress a mother may be under. This suggests attachment is not a fixed component of mother-child relationships.

– We should also consider the impact of the baby's personality on the nature of attachments, not just the mother's behaviour on its own. For example, Schaffer and Emerson (1964) found that some babies like to be cuddled more than others. Some may be innately more anxious than others – and so on. Adults may have to adjust the way in which they interact with different children to suit each child, and so maybe no one pattern of interaction is clearly best.

– The Strange Situation has been criticised for being artificial. The stranger had to approach and interact with the child in a prearranged way, and the mother was obliged to leave at certain points. In real life, adults are more flexible and are more likely to adapt what they do according to the child's reactions.

– In a review of research in eight different countries, Ijzendoorn and Kroonenberg (1988) found there were cultural variations in attachment patterns. Secure attachments were most common in all cultures. But Germans have quite a high percentage of avoidant babies (35.3%) and few ambivalent ones (8.1%). This may reflect the fact that German mothers value independent behaviour and may tend to see the securely attached child as 'spoiled'. Japanese families have a high percentage of ambivalent children (27.1%) and few avoidant ones (5.2%). In line with traditional cultural ideals of family loyalty, many Japanese mothers seldom leave their children and foster a strong sense of dependence in them. Being left alone in the Strange Situation often resulted in the Japanese children crying inconsolably. This shows that the Strange Situation may not be a suitable measure of attachment for all cultures. Also, the kind of attachment patterns that are considered to be best may vary from culture to culture.

– The study was also criticised on ethical grounds for the stress it caused some children.

QUESTIONS

1   What **three** types of attachment bond did Ainsworth identify?
2   Can you think of a way to study attachment bonds without causing stress to children?

Childhood attachment and adult relationships

Researchers have been interested to discover the extent to which the quality of childhood attachment bonds can affect adult relationships. It is thought that early relationships lead infants to form **mental models**. These are beliefs and expectations about how important attachment figures behave. These mental models influence how the child goes on to form relationships in later life.

The **Adult Attachment Interview** can be used to discover how adults recall their experiences of childhood. In a review of such research, van Ijzendoorn (1995) found that parents who report happy experiences of being parented themselves, or who have come to terms with earlier unhappy attachment-related experiences, tend to have babies who are securely attached. Parents who view their own childhood attachments as being of little value tend to have babies who are avoidant. Parents who are still preoccupied with, and struggling to please, their own parents tend to have ambivalent babies. This supports the view that children's early relationship with their parents can influence the patterns of parenting they themselves adopt in later life. It also shows that adults who suffered from insecure relationships with their own parents but who mentally work through their difficult childhood experiences can still produce securely attached children of their own.

Hazan and Shaver (1987) wanted to see if attachment theory offered an insight into adult romantic relationships. They asked participants to complete a questionnaire. They found five indicators that suggested that earlier attachment bonds can influence relationships in adulthood.

They asked people which of three attachment styles most closely fitted how they usually felt in relationships. They found:

- 56% of participants described themselves as **secure** in relationships. They found it easy to get close to others, were comfortable about depending on others and being depended upon, and were not often worried about being abandoned
- 24% of participants were **avoidant**. They found it difficult to trust others and became uncomfortable if others got too close to them
- 20% of participants were **ambivalent** in relationships. They found that other people often did not get as close to them as they would like; they often worried that their partners did not really love them, and felt that their desire for close intimacy often scared people away.

This distribution of attachment styles in adulthood (56%, 24%, 20%) is similar to the distribution of attachment styles in childhood. This is what we would expect if early attachment styles continue from childhood to adulthood.

Participants were also asked to complete a 'love scale' in which they were required to rate their most important love relationship along 12 dimensions (e.g. 'happiness', 'obsessiveness', 'jealousy', 'trust'). The researchers found that people with different attachment styles would tend to rate their relationships in different ways:

- **Secure** lovers tended to have more lasting relationships, which they described as 'happy', 'friendly' and 'trusting'
- **Avoidant** lovers reported a fear of intimacy, emotional highs and lows, and jealousy
- **Ambivalent** lovers were more obsessive, had a strong desire for reciprocation and union and experienced extreme sexual attraction and jealousy.

Participants were then presented with different statements about romantic love and asked how far they agreed with them. Again, people with different attachment styles tended to respond differently:

- **Secure** lovers believed in lasting love, saw themselves as likeable and others as trustworthy
- **Avoidant** lovers doubted the endurance of romantic love, believed they didn't need a partner to be happy and felt it was rare to find someone to fall in love with
- **Ambivalent** lovers fell in love easily and often, but rarely found what they would call 'true love'.

Participants were asked about their childhood relationships with their parents. The researchers found that the likelihood of a prolonged separation from either parent did not affect adult attachment styles. Nor were there any differences in adult attachment styles relating to the frequency of divorce or separation of the parents. However, secure participants reported a warmer relationship with, and between, their two parents.

Some participants also completed a scale to measure their feelings of loneliness. Secure participants reported least loneliness. Ambivalent participants had the highest loneliness scores.

Conclusions

This research supports the view that early attachment bonds may have a lasting effect. Early attachment experiences may affect beliefs about yourself and others, and these beliefs in turn may affect your behaviour towards others and the outcome of relationships.

But we should note that the sample comprised 620 participants who responded to a 'love quiz' in a local newspaper, and 108 undergraduates completing the questionnaire as a class exercise. Only the graduates were asked about their loneliness. This sample is not, therefore, representative of the general population. Neither does the finding that attachment styles are distributed in the same way in childhood and adulthood mean that there is *continuity* between childhood and adulthood. Only a longitudinal study could show this. We should also note that people's memories of childhood experiences may be imperfect.

Theories of attachment

Behaviourist theory

For behaviourists, attachment behaviour, like all other forms of behaviour, is the result of learning. Behaviourists provide us with a sort of 'cupboard-love' explanation, arguing that a parent or carer becomes associated with the satisfying of primary needs (e.g. the need for food). Food therefore is a **primary reinforcer**. Since the parent is present when this need is met, the parent becomes a powerful **secondary reinforcer** in their own right, and this is why babies become so attached to their parents (and to their mothers in particular). Children learn to attach to their parents in order to have their needs satisfied. Children are reinforced by stimuli such as food and comfort, and this eventually generalises into feelings of comfort and security for the child whenever the parent is present. The affectionate behaviour children show is also reinforcing to the parent, and so parents attach to their children.

Behaviourists argue babies come to love their mums because they are associated with food and warmth ▲

Evaluation of behaviourist view of attachment

Strengths

+ Behaviourists developed their understanding of primary and secondary reinforcement (which has been applied to attachment theory) using objective, scientific methods.
+ The way adults care for the child undoubtedly influences the formation of attachment bonds.

Weaknesses

– Stages or patterns in the attachment process show the importance of maturational factors (i.e. biological development). The behavioural approach does not consider the role of maturation.
– Attachments are influenced by the quality of the care, the interest adults show, and not just the meeting of primary needs.
– Behaviourists often conducted their research on animals, which may tell us little about humans.
– Other research using animals has pointed to the importance of biological factors in attachment bonding. The work of Lorenz and also Harlow is of particular interest here, and we shall turn to consider their work next.

Konrad Lorenz based his theories on studies of animals in their natural habitat ▼

Biological theories

Konrad Lorenz and imprinting

The theory of **imprinting** was first formulated in early research by the ethologist Konrad Lorenz (1935). **Ethology** involves studying animals in their natural habitat. Lorenz was interested in the way that young ducks and geese followed their mother around soon after hatching. In the course of experiments, he discovered that baby geese would follow any large moving object that they saw soon after hatching, and that after following it around for about ten minutes, they developed such a strong relationship with it that nothing could take its place.

Lorenz encouraged goslings to imprint on him, rather than on their natural mother – and found that having done so, they followed him everywhere, running to him when frightened and becoming distressed when he left them. He also found that goslings could be made to imprint on many different objects, including balls, boxes and flashing lights. Interestingly, fully grown animals sometimes showed a sexual preference for objects or animals of other species on which they had imprinted as babies. This process is known as **sexual imprinting**.

For Lorenz, imprinting reflects genetic programming because:

● it must occur within the first few hours after birth if it is to happen at all
● it happens so quickly when it does
● it does not depend on reinforcement
● it is permanent (once imprinted, animals will not imprint on anything else).

In the normal course of events, imprinting is also useful for an animal's survival. It allows baby animals to learn skills from their parents, such as how to find food, hunt, or escape predators, before they have to fend for themselves as adults.

Evaluation of Lorenz's imprinting theory

Strengths

+ Lorenz's research alerts us to the possibility that early attachment behaviours may be instinctive (i.e. not dependent on learning) – at least in some animals.
+ There is further evidence for the idea that the moments after a child is born can be important for the formation of attachments. Klaus and Kennel (1976) suggested, as a result of experimental research, that mothers who had more hours of contact with their babies shortly after giving birth were likely to form a closer emotional bond with their children, and tended to cuddle and soothe them more than mothers who had briefer contact. At the time, it was common for hospitals to separate mother and baby a few minutes after the birth to allow the mother time to rest and recuperate. Later, hospital practices were changed in the light of their research.

Weaknesses

– However, other researchers have failed to agree with these results. Durkin (1995) found that bonding can still occur even if mothers do not see their babies for days or even months after birth.
– Rapid imprinting really only seems necessary in animals that can move around soon after being born. Human babies are helpless for a long while after birth, and attachments take several months to form. This allows a lot more time for learning to have an influence.

Harlow's work with monkeys

Harlow and Zimmerman (1959) separated infant rhesus monkeys from their mothers soon after birth and raised them in a cage with two substitute or **surrogate mothers**. The surrogate mothers were made of

Harlow's research showed that infant monkeys have a fundamental need for contact comfort as well as food. Here the monkey is seen clinging to the 'cloth' mother, even while being fed by the 'wire' mother

wire mesh. One had a baby bottle attached (meeting the infant's needs for food). The other was wrapped in soft terrycloth but had no bottle. Harlow found that the infant monkeys preferred to spend most of their time clinging to the cloth mother. Since the preference for the cloth mother could not be explained in terms of food, Harlow concluded that baby monkeys, and perhaps humans, have a need for **contact comfort**.

Interestingly, Harlow found that the absence of a terrycloth mother to cling to made it less likely that baby monkeys would explore strange new objects (like a wooden toy spider) placed into their cage. With a soft mother to cling to, baby monkeys typically felt more secure, and would eventually explore new objects. However, a monkey deprived of contact with other monkeys for the first six months or more of its life usually grew up to be disturbed in some way. Such a monkey would have difficulty in relating to other monkeys, and would not play properly, show appropriate mating behaviour, or be a very good parent.

Damage caused by deprivation of less than six months was sometimes reversible, and the monkey might later grow up to behave normally. In such cases, the monkey did not always require the presence of a mother. The presence of other baby monkeys to play with and attach to was enough to enable normal development.

Evaluation of Harlow's research

Strengths

+ Monkeys form attachments more gradually than geese, and so are closer to human patterns of development. Harlow's conclusions may have greater relevance to the topic of human attachment than those of Lorenz. Furthermore, human infants often use their mother (or some attachment figure) as a secure base from which to explore – i.e. they investigate toys and their environment but keep an eye on and may frequently return to, their mother.
+ Harlow reveals that there is more involved in attachments than simply food: contact and comfort are also important.
+ Harlow's research has been beneficial to human babies. Providing a warm, soft environment and stroking premature babies improves their chances of survival.
+ It reveals that social skills and behaviours, play and parenting may be learned by interacting with others when young (in monkeys).
+ It suggests that there may be a **sensitive period** for such learning. A sensitive period is a period during which learning occurs easily, but after which it becomes increasingly difficult. After six months' deprivation, the learning of social skills is unlikely to occur in monkeys. Harlow and others (see Bowlby below) have speculated that humans may be similar, and that we need to form attachments in the first few years of life in order to avoid problems in later life.

Weaknesses

– Monkey development may tell us little about human development.
– Depriving monkeys in this way, and inflicting long-term harm on them, may be considered unethical.

Bowlby's theory

In the 1950s, John Bowlby adapted the idea of imprinting to suggest that human babies act instinctively to form a particular kind of attachment with their mothers (or mother-substitutes) within the first two years of life. The human infant is so helpless that attachment bonding is crucial to its survival. Infants may survive for a while without food or drink, but an isolated infant can die very quickly from exposure or attack by a predator. He argued that, since an infant's best chances for survival lie in being close to a carer, babies have developed genetically programmed behaviours such as smiling, crying, clinging, and gazing to help ensure closeness to a carer and thereby increase their chances of survival. The baby's mother is also genetically programmed to respond to her child.

Bowlby believed that infants have a tendency to form a particularly strong bond with one person (usually, but not necessarily, the mother) and that this bond is different from the bonds formed with anyone else. This special bond is referred to as a **monotropic bond**, because it is focused on just *one* other person. Bowlby accepted that babies form bonds with other people too, but argued that there is a hierarchy of attachments, and that the baby's special attachment bond with one, central caregiver is at the top of the hierarchy. In Bowlby's view, this bond is normally in place by around six to seven months of age – roughly the time that the baby first becomes mobile. Since the baby is now physically able to crawl off and get into danger, attachment behaviours work to keep the baby close to the mother and reduce the dangers that the baby might otherwise face.

Bowlby's maternal deprivation hypothesis

Bowlby believed that it is necessary for the emotional well-being of children to form the type of bond described above, and that children could be psychologically damaged if they were unable to form such a bond, or if the bond was somehow disrupted. In his words, 'mother love in infancy is as important for mental health as are vitamins and proteins for physical health'. In short, the lack of a person with whom to form and maintain a monotropic attachment bond during the child's early years may well result in the child suffering both emotionally and socially, both as a child and later as an adult. This is referred to as Bowlby's **maternal deprivation hypothesis**.

Bowlby came to hold and maintain his views, despite opposition from various quarters, in the light of several sources of evidence. He was aware of the work of Lorenz, and also, later, of Harlow's work. As well as carrying out his own research, he was also aware of research that looked at children raised in institutions who were unable to form monotropic bonds.

Bowlby knew of research by Goldfarb (1943), who compared 15 children who were fostered as infants before 9 months of age, with 15 children raised in a poor orphanage until the age of at least 3½ before being fostered. The children were matched for age, sex and in terms of their mother's education and occupational backgrounds. The children were tested at 3, 6, 8 and 12 years of age. In each case, the children who were fostered early did better in tests of IQ, language skills and social maturity than those fostered later.

Goldfarb believed that the inability to form attachment bonds before the age of three disadvantaged the late-fostered group. But we should note that the early-fostered group may have been brighter to begin with – which is perhaps why they were more readily chosen by foster parents. We should also note that the orphanage provided a poor environment for the children in its care, providing little in the way of physical or social stimulation. This lack of stimulation, rather than the absence of a mother figure with whom to bond, might explain why the children who spent longest in the orphanage performed poorly in later tests.

Children raised in unstimulating and understaffed institutions often show retarded development

Bowlby was also aware of research by Spitz (1945). Spitz had studied children raised in orphanages in South America and found them to be underweight, apathetic and extremely depressed. The overworked staff in these under-resourced institutions could only provide minimal attention and stimulation for the children. Spitz believed that depriving children of an adult with whom to form an attachment bond for just three months could result in depression and emotional damage from which the child might never recover. Once again, though, we must note that, precisely *because* these orphanages were so poor, the children were deprived not only of attachment bonds but also of all sorts of stimulation, toys, games and other forms of social interaction. This might have been as much a factor in the depression and apathy these children displayed as the lack of an adult with whom to bond.

'Forty-four juvenile thieves'

Bowlby himself worked in a clinic in London treating emotionally disturbed adolescents. In his famous 1946 book *Forty-four Juvenile Thieves*, he reported that, of a sample of 44 juveniles at the clinic who had been caught stealing, 17 had been separated from their mothers for a total of 6 months or more before the age of 5. He contrasted this group of 44 thieves with 44 other juveniles attending the clinic who were not delinquents (i.e. had not been convicted of breaking the law). Of these, only 2 had suffered prolonged maternal separation as young children. Bowlby concluded that maternal deprivation could lead to **delinquency**.

Bowlby also found that 14 of the 17 separated children showed no feelings of remorse or guilt for their crimes. They seemed cold and uncaring about others, their own crimes, their victims and even themselves. Bowlby called this condition **affectionless psychopathy** and believed it to be another possible consequence of breaking the bonds between mother and child. He argued that in extreme cases, the lack of a special relationship between a child and its mother could lead to the development of a **psychopathic personality**, i.e. someone who is unable to form relationships with anyone and is unconcerned about the welfare of other people.

Bowlby went on to argue that the full-time employment of the mother could cause lasting damage to children. His views were largely accepted in the 1950s by the **World Health Organisation**. This had a significant influence on government policy, leading to the introduction of forms of social welfare such as child benefit and housing benefit which were designed to help women to stay at home and look after their children. The view that 'a woman's place is in the home' is not one that all women (or men, for that matter) agree with, particularly today.

The timing of Bowlby's work coincided with the end of World War II. During the war, many women had worked in factories and demonstrated they were as able as men to do such work. With many returning servicemen looking for jobs, it was politically convenient for some to use Bowlby's work to claim that the full-time employment of mothers would harm their children.

Today Bowlby's findings are still relevant to issues such as adoption, fostering and day-care. But was Bowlby right?

Evaluation of Bowlby's research

Strengths

+ Bowlby highlighted the importance of meeting children's emotional as well as physical needs.
+ Bowlby drew attention to the poor quality of care in many children's residential institutions.
+ His research had a positive effect on hospital policy.

Weaknesses

- One problem is that Bowlby's sample of 44 delinquents was not representative of all maternally deprived children. To investigate the effects of maternal deprivation, he should have selected a sample of maternally deprived children, and not a sample of delinquents. Not all maternally deprived children become delinquents, and nor, as Bowlby's own research showed, do all delinquents suffer from maternal deprivation.
- As a Freudian, Bowlby naturally concentrated on the first five years of a child's life. This raises the question of how reliable his data was if it depended on memories of events in the distant past. How much of your first five years of life can *you* recall?
- Events after the age of five and other circumstances surrounding the separations can also be important. For example, poor working or living conditions may result in a mother or child being separated because of illness. Ongoing poverty after the age of five and the influence of peer groups may have a greater part to play in creating delinquency than any earlier separation. Rutter (1981) investigated the causes of delinquency in boys aged 9 to 12 years of age and concluded that delinquency was not simply caused by the disruption of the mother–infant bond. Other factors were important, such as the extent to which the child suffered emotional or physical neglect. Rutter found that children raised in poor homes who were subjected to a lot of stress, (e.g. where parents divorce after years of arguing) were more likely to engage in anti-social behaviour.

    — Not all separations are the same. Bowlby has been criticised for failing to distinguish between maternal **privation**, i.e. never having an opportunity to bond in the first place, and maternal **deprivation**, i.e. the disruption of an established bond. Children raised in poor orphanages were victims of maternal privation. Harlow's monkeys were not just maternally privated but socially privated, i.e. they had no-one with whom to interact or bond. It is possible that maternal or social privation in human infants may be more likely than maternal deprivation to result in an affectionless character.

Summary of Bowlby's maternal deprivation hypothesis

● Bowlby believed that children form monotropic attachment bonds, and that disruption of the mother–infant bond in young children could cause lasting emotional damage to them.

● Bowlby was influenced by, and aware of, research on animals which suggested that attachment is an instinctive behaviour needed for survival. Also, work with monkeys and research on children raised in institutions suggested that disruption of the attachment process was damaging. Additionally, Bowlby conducted his own research on 44 juvenile delinquents.

● Bowlby identified delinquency and affectionless psychopathy as possible consequences of maternal deprivation.

● The specific attachment phase identified by Schaffer and Emerson supports the idea that babies often do form a special bond with one other person. However, babies also go on to form bonds with other people too.

● Bowlby was criticised for failing to distinguish between **deprivation** and **privation**; for not adequately considering the impact of the poor environments in the institutional research; for using a biased sample in his own research, and for not considering the different reasons for separation or the impact of events that happened to children after the age of five.

TRY THIS

Match the **terms** on the left to the **definitions** on the right.

affectionless psychopathy	when an established mother-infant bond is disrupted
monotropy	name given to a study conducted by Ainsworth
sensitive period	when a mother-infant bond has no chance to form
maternal deprivation	the time during which learning is most likely to occur
Strange Situation	process of forming one special attachment bond
separation anxiety	inability to care for other people
maternal privation	child protests when attachment figure leaves

Maternal privation

Tizard and Hodges (1989) looked at children raised in an institution with a high staff turnover and a policy of discouraging close relationships between staff and children. The nursery had plenty of toys and provided a generally stimulating environment, but the children had little opportunity to develop a close attachment to any particular adult. Before they were four years old, an average of 50 different carers had looked after the children for at least a week. These children, then, had no chance to form close bonds with an individual carer.

Some of the children were adopted between the ages of two and three, and later went on to form close relationships with their adoptive parents. This indicates that the effects of early privation can be overcome with later care and does not necessarily result in an affectionless character. Interestingly, however, some of the children who were returned to their natural mothers at two or three years of age did not develop as well socially or intellectually as the adopted children. This probably reflected the fact that their mothers were poor and found it difficult to provide the same stimulating environment or time, love and attention as the adoptive parents. We should note, though, that even the adopted children showed some emotional and behavioural difficulties in school, which suggests that early privation can have long-term effects.

An extreme case of maternal privation was reported in a study by Kolochova (1972) of twin boys raised in former Czechoslovakia. The boys were found at the age of seven, having suffered years of abuse from their stepmother since they were 18 months old. They had been raised in an unheated closet, had no social contact with other people, had been poorly fed and regularly beaten. They were unable to walk or stand up straight, had not learned to speak properly, were covered in scars, terrified of adults and were severely intellectually and physically retarded. They did not understand pictures since they had never seen any before. Their development was roughly the equivalent to that of a normal three-year-old.

Following their discovery, the twin boys spent some time in hospital and a school for the mentally retarded before being fostered. The foster home provided a warm and loving environment and the twins made a remarkable recovery. By the age of 11, their speech was normal. By 15 years their IQ was normal. By 20 years they were of above-average intelligence, enjoying good relationships with their foster mother and her relatives, and had experienced their first love affairs. The research shows that the effect of even severe early maternal privation can sometimes be overcome with high-quality care in later life.

We should note, though, that these children did have opportunities to bond with each other, and so the findings are not comparable with those of Harlow in which monkeys were privated of all social contact. Interestingly, Harlow went on to find that exposing privated monkeys to young 'therapist' monkeys who would tend to cling on to them and play more gently than adult monkeys could gradually reverse the damage caused by earlier privation. Similarly, Hartup et al. (1979) found that it was sometimes possible to help withdrawn pre-school children become more outgoing by letting them play with a younger child.

Maternal deprivation: the effects of hospitalisation

In the 1940s, 50s and 60s, James and Joyce Robertson conducted a series of studies of children, mostly aged between 18 months and 3 years, who had been placed in residential nurseries or hospitals for periods ranging from a few days to several weeks. They found that, while institutions usually provided adequately for the children's physical needs, their emotional needs were sometimes poorly catered for, resulting in great distress.

At first doctors and nurses rejected the couple's findings, believing that the children in their care were well looked after. It was only after the Robertsons showed several filmed sequences of the distress suffered by the children in care that the doctors accepted what the Robertsons were saying, and childcare practices were altered.

One of the most famous pieces of film involved a quiet and loving child called John, aged 17 months. John had been placed in a residential nursery for nine days while his mother was in hospital having a baby. His father worked all day but would visit in the evening. There were five other children in the nursery, mostly quite noisy and demanding. The nurses offered John such assistance and comfort as they could, but their attention was often focused on the other children in the group.

Initially John protested at the lack of attention and became angry. But after a few days he was very upset and would often cry. As time went by he seemed to become more despairing. Towards the end of his stay his behaviour changed and he stopped seeking attention from the nurses. He seemed to become emotionally detached. He would mostly ignore his father when he visited and spent a lot of time playing with a large cuddly teddy bear. When his mother returned to pick him up after nine days, John would not even look at her at first. He resisted her attempts to offer comfort and seemed not to want to know her. His mother found it hard to reestablish the sort of relationship with John that had existed before he went into the nursery, and in the months that followed he seemed generally less affectionate, cried more and had more tantrums.

Bowlby worked with the Robertsons, and, as a result of their researches, they concluded that children who are separated from their mothers show a typical pattern of behaviours:

1 **Distress:** a period of protest, anger and upset
2 **Despair:** a period when the child seems to have lost hope and is deeply unhappy
3 **Detachment:** the child becomes emotionally detached and shows no interest in being close to anyone else.

THINK ABOUT IT

John went through all of these stages in just nine days, yet the effects of the separation were long-lasting. What are the implications of this research? How can we explain such findings?

The impact of short-term separations

Some children seem to be better able to cope with separation than others. So what makes a short-term separation traumatic for some children but not for others?

- One important factor in assessing the effect of short-term separation is the *age* of the child when separation occurs. Attachments are usually in evidence from about seven months of age, and this probably links with the child's ability to maintain a mental image of the mother when she is not present. (This is tied to Piaget's notion of **object permanence** – see page 96.) Young children also have poor language skills and may not understand when adults try to explain to them why they are being left or for how long. They may simply feel abandoned and unloved, or blame themselves for the separation. Children between 12 and 18 months of age, when attachment bonds are well established, seem to show the most distress at separation. The greater language and cognitive skills of older children probably help them to cope better, as does the existence of other attachment figures.

- Not all children suffer to the same extent, and those most vulnerable are likely to be unused to meeting new people and to being apart from their mothers, even for short periods.

- Rutter also pointed out that children may not simply be deprived of a maternal attachment figure when entering hospital, but the presence of all loved ones – in addition to the stresses of being in a strange environment surrounded by strange people. Staff rota systems may prevent the child from forming close relationships that would help them cope with the situation.

In the light of considerations such as these, hospital practices have now changed considerably.

- Hospitals encourage staff to form relationships with their young patients.

- Children are treated as outpatients wherever possible.

- Parents are allowed unrestricted visiting to hospitalised children

- Hospitals recognise that, where possible, overnight accommodation should be provided for parents so that they can remain with their children for as long as possible.

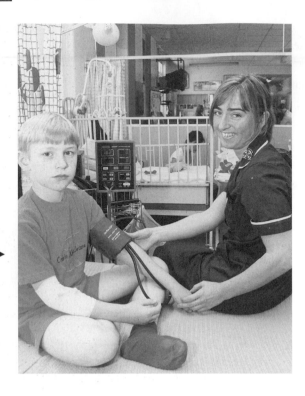

Thanks to pioneering work by Bowlby and the Robertsons, hospitals and other institutions are now much more aware of the emotional needs of young children ▶

● Hospitals also now encourage parents to arrange prior visits so that children are more familiar with the environment when they eventually have to be admitted for treatment.

Maternal deprivation – the effects of day-care

With more and more mothers going to work, it is interesting to know if placing children in day-care centres can affect their development. Belsky (1987) found evidence that children who were often left in day-care centres in the first year of life were more likely to form insecure attachment bonds and be more socially withdrawn and aggressive. However, these effects are difficult to separate from the possible effects of poor-quality day-care centres and the nature of the home environment. Clarke-Stewart (1988) found no ill-effects arising from good-quality day-care. Kagan et al. (1980) compared the social and intellectual development of children attending a day-care centre with those raised at home. The study was longitudinal, following children from just a few months of age up to two-and-a-half. Although there was a large variation among the children, little overall difference was found between the development of the children in the centre and those raised at home. In general, the research suggests that placing children in day-care centres is not likely to harm them, provided that the care they receive is of good quality.

Some conclusions

The evidence suggests that children are resilient and can sometimes overcome quite appalling early experiences if well looked after later on. However, this does not mean that it is not in children's best interests to be able to form attachment bonds early in life. Bowlby did not claim that maternal deprivation inevitably caused later problems – only that such children were at greater risk. We have seen that children are capable of forming multiple attachments, and attachments are not always primarily with the mother. Although fathers typically spend less time with their children than mothers, they do nonetheless form close bonds with their children. While research suggests that fathers spend a higher proportion of their time in play than in nurturing compared to mothers, Field (1978) reported that where fathers become primary carers they are quite capable of interacting in a more gentle, nurturing way.

Delinquency is not explained simply by the disruption of an infant–mother bond, and it appears unlikely that children become affectionless simply as a result of their mothers going out to work. We should note, though, that there is evidence that separating young children from their loved ones, even for a few days, can be potentially damaging to them if such separations are not handled carefully.

Hospitals and other institutions are now much more aware of the emotional needs of young children, and in large part this is due to the work of people like Bowlby and the Robertsons.

Summary

- An attachment is an enduring emotional tie between an infant and a carer.
- Learning theory suggests that attachment bonds are a result of the associations between primary reinforcement and the presence of the caregiver. This is challenged by the work of Lorenz and Harlow.
- According to Bowlby, attachment is instinctive and babies form monotropic attachment bonds. Forming such a bond is important to the future emotional well-being of the child.
- Ainsworth distinguishes between secure and insecure attachment bonds and links these to the behaviour of the mother. Others suggest that the baby's personality also has an impact here. The quality of these bonds can predict later social performance.
- Research shows that even short separations can cause distress and long-lasting damage, but this depends on the age of the child, the formation of other attachments and the circumstances surrounding the separation. Hospital procedures have been changed as the result of the work of pioneers such as the Robertsons.
- Day-care is unlikely to damage children if it is of good quality.
- The adverse effects of even quite severe privation can be reduced with good later care.

9 Cognitive Development

Take a look at these two drawings based on those from the opening pages of *The Little Prince* by Saint-Exupéry.

'Drawing Number One'   'Drawing Number Two'

The six-year-old Little Prince, who was fascinated by jungle animals, showed some grown-ups his 'Drawing Number One' and asked them how much it frightened them. They laughed. Why should they be frightened of a hat? But for the six-year-old, the drawing was *not* of a hat: it was a picture of a boa constrictor eating an elephant – as they realised when the Little Prince showed them 'Drawing Number Two'. The story shows that children and adults have very different ways of seeing and thinking about the world.

The study of cognitive development is concerned with the processes involved in intellectual development, and how thinking develops and improves with age. Young children have a limited understanding of the world. There is much that is confusing and mysterious to them. Adults can reason about the world in more sophisticated ways and can produce complex theories to explain events. Psychologists are interested in how we make this journey from the confusions of childhood to the complex reasoning of adulthood. In this chapter we will examine the hugely influential work of **Jean Piaget**, as well as an alternative theory developed by **Jerome Bruner**.

Piaget's theory of cognitive development

Consider the following facts:

● At the age of seven months, a baby playing with a soft toy will not search for it when someone hides it under a pillow. For the baby, once hidden from view, the toy no longer exists. One year later, however, the baby will watch the toy being hidden and immediately search for it.

Jean Piaget (1896–1980) ▼

- A four-year-old is shown two identically-sized beakers filled to the same level with orange juice. The juice from one beaker is poured into a taller, thinner beaker. When the child is asked, 'Which beaker has more juice?' she points to the tall, thin one. A seven-year-old will recognise that the beakers contain the same amount of juice.

- A five-year-old can learn to walk a couple of streets from home to school, but is unable to trace the same route on paper. A nine-year-old can trace the route on paper, and also give directions without consulting a map. A twelve-year-old can do all this, and also work out other routes and shortcuts to get to school.

These examples all make a simple point. What do you think it is?

The point, first systematically developed by Piaget, is that *our ability to think develops naturally with age*. The nature of the mistakes young children make is interesting, and may provide clues about the course of development. Piaget believed that the reason children appear to think in less sophisticated ways than adults is not simply because they lack the knowledge that adults have. In his view, children think in different ways to adults (a *qualitative* difference in thinking).

Much of Piaget's research involved the method known as the **clinical interview**. This is an open-ended technique in which the questions asked depend on the answers given to earlier ones. Piaget preferred this to asking a set sequence of questions because it helped him to understand the logic of the child – i.e. to understand the world from the child's point of view. In fact Piaget conducted his research on a very small sample of children, including his own.

QUESTIONS

1   Name a disadvantage of the **clinical interview** as a research method.
2   What difficulties might arise from the nature of the **sample** Piaget used?

(Hmm. Plates don't seem to bounce very well)

Piaget believes children learn by experimenting with their world ▲

The processes underlying development

Piaget believed that children are active and learn by doing things. They explore and experiment with their world and thereby gain a better understanding of it. Children's cognitive development, therefore, is helped if they have an environment rich in interesting things to explore. Development is also linked to **maturation** (physical development), and this includes development of the brain itself. This means that children will be unable to think in certain ways until their brains are sufficiently developed to allow them to do so.

Piaget called the basic cognitive structures that we have **schemas** (or **schemata**). A schema is a packet of knowledge or understanding. Schemas can be thought of as 'mental representations', mental moulds, ideas about what things are and how to deal with them, into which we pour our experiences. Schemas are combined in increasingly sophisticated ways as children learn the rules by which the world operates, enabling the child to act more successfully. For example, an infant learns to combine her 'grasping' schema with her schema for 'gazing' in order to pick up a favourite rattle. This combining of schemas is a mental action or **operation**.

Schemas also get changed and added to in order to meet environmental demands. Development is thus a process of adapting, developing, adjusting and refining schemas to cope with an increasingly complex world.

Adaptation occurs through two main processes which continue throughout life:

In order to develop we have to be ready to adapt our ideas about the world

- **Assimilation** involves fitting in new information using the schemas we already have. This extends the range of our understanding but leaves the existing schemas unchanged. Existing knowledge is good enough for the child to understand events, or act successfully. For example, we may use an existing 'grasping' schema to grasp a new object; or we may recognise that a strange fluttering creature is a bird like other birds.

- **Accommodation** involves adjusting to new experiences by radically revising old ideas. For example, in order to grasp an object that is differently shaped to one grasped before, we learn to change the shape of our hand (amend our grasping schema). Similarly we might recognise that a strange fluttering creature is not a bird, but a butterfly (invent a new schema).

For Piaget, the motivation for development comes from *within* and is not dependent on external reinforcement (as the behaviourists would argue – see page 63). The process of adaptation requires the child to keep a balance between what it knows and can do, and environmental demands. When new information cannot be assimilated, a state of imbalance or **disequilibrium** is created which is uncomfortable for the child. According to Piaget, children want to understand their world. This provides the motivation for accommodation, so that sufficient understanding, a state of **equilibrium**, can again be achieved.

Piaget called this process **equilibration**. Children move from a comfortable state of equilibrium in which they understand and can act successfully on the world, to an uncomfortable state of disequilibrium when faced by new problems and challenges. This motivates them to accommodate and thereby re-establish a comfortable state of equilibrium.

For example, a driver faced with a new car can assimilate the car to some extent: he knows what the pedals do and how to steer. But, because some controls are in a different position, he must also accommodate and adjust what he normally does to drive the new car successfully.

TRY THIS

Use the words listed below to fill the gaps in the statements.

- **schemas**
- **accommodation**
- **maturation**
- **equilibration**
- **qualitatively**
- **assimilation**
- **environment**

Piaget believed that children's thinking is .... different to the thinking of adults.

Development is linked to physical development, called .... , and is fostered by an .... rich in things to explore.

Piaget called the basic units of understanding ....

The process of incorporating new information into existing knowledge is called ....

The change that occurs in existing knowledge or experience as a result of coming across new information is called ....

The juggling between old and new knowledge is called ....

Stages of development

Piaget argued that there are four stages of cognitive development. At certain points, schemas get reorganised in fundamentally new ways, enabling children to think about the world in ways that were not possible for them before. New forms of thinking emerge, and mark the boundary between stages. Later stages build on gains made in earlier stages, and the stages are also **universal**, so that everybody passes through the same ones in the same order. Piaget identified rough ages associated with each stage, but these are very approximate. The move between one stage and the next is not sudden, but occurs gradually.

1: The sensory motor stage (birth to nearly two years)

- The world is a confusing place to a young baby. To begin with, children can only understand the world by means of innate reflex mechanisms (e.g. sucking, grasping) and in terms of what they can immediately see or feel. Infants do, however, notice relationships between experiences.

- Children at this stage also appear to gain some concept of **self**. They understand that they have a body which they can control, which is separate from the rest of the world – i.e. they develop the 'me' schema. For example, halfway through their second year, infants with a spot of unscented lipstick on their nose will touch themselves rather than their reflection in a mirror. They also learn that they can sometimes affect the things around them by their actions and enjoy experimenting to find out what they can do and how things behave.

- A major cognitive gain in this stage is what is known as **object permanence**. A four-month-old baby will immediately lose all interest in an attractive toy if it is hidden from view. Piaget believed young babies only realise an object exists while they can see it. A one-year-old child will search for the toy, thereby displaying the concept of object permanence.

- The development of object permanence is linked to the development of **representational thinking**. Children can now represent the world internally and manipulate ideas. This enables them to maintain the idea of an object when it is not in sight. Children of this age will also show separation anxiety and protest when their primary carer leaves. This suggests that attachment behaviours are only possible after the development of object permanence has enabled the child to maintain the idea of the attachment figure in their absence. The child cries in order to hasten the return of the attachment figure (see page 75).

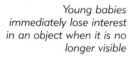

Young babies immediately lose interest in an object when it is no longer visible ▶

- Another sign of representational thinking is that the child begins to acquire **language**. As well as mental images, it can use symbols such as words to name things.

2: The pre-operational stage (2 to about 7 years)

- At this stage, thinking is based on the manipulation of ideas (images, language) rather than reflexes and sensations. Language continues to develop throughout this stage. Representational thinking is also apparent in **symbolic** or **imaginative** play. For example, children can pretend that a hairbrush is a hedgehog. However, mistakes are still made – for example, a two-year-old may try to smell a picture of a flower!

- Thinking at this stage also reveals **animism** – the notion that inanimate objects like dolls or teddy bears are alive. For example, a child may get angry and smack her pram because it 'made her get hurt.' An understanding of which objects are alive and which are not is usually achieved by around four years of age.

- Children believe that all natural phenomena such as lakes, mountains and trees are man-made. Piaget called this **artificialism**. The sky may be blue because 'mummy painted it blue.'

- A well-documented limitation in thinking at this stage is **egocentrism**. This is not the same as 'selfishness' or 'pride', but rather an inability to consider events from another person's point of view. For example, a little boy may genuinely think that Grandma would like a new Tellytubbies video for her birthday because that's what *he* wants. Similarly, a little girl may agree she has a brother but deny that he has a sister.

  Piaget and Inhelder (1956) demonstrated this egocentrism in a classic study known as the **Three Mountains Task**. Children were shown a table-top papier-mâché model of three mountains, each with a distinguishing feature such as a cross, a house or snow on the summit. The child stood at the side of the model to watch the experimenter position a doll at another point to the side of the mountains. Four- or five-year-old pre-operational children were unable to select a photograph showing what the doll could see. Instead they picked the photograph showing what *they* could see.

The Three Mountains Task tested children's ability to imagine a 'point of view' different from their own ▶

- Linked to egocentrism is **moral realism**. When asked whether an action was good or bad, children at this stage do not consider the intention behind it. Instead, they consider things such as how much damage was caused or how much punishment was given. This is because, being egocentric, they cannot imagine the intention of the person responsible for the action (see Chapter 10 *Moral Development*, page *108*).

- Children also have problems with **seriation**. Given several sticks of different lengths, they find it difficult to arrange them in a sequence from shortest to longest.

- Another well-documented finding is that pre-operational children have problems with **conservation**. A four-year-old who is shown similar beakers with equal amounts of water in each will agree that the beakers contain the same amount of water. However,

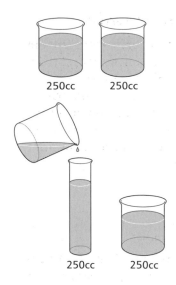

250cc   250cc

250cc   250cc

Children at the pre-operational stage believe that the volume of water is greater after it has been transferred to the taller glass.

Children at the pre-operational stage say that the two rows contain the same number of pennies...

... but also that there are more pennies in the more spread-out, second row .

when the water is tipped into a taller, thinner glass so that the level is higher they will believe that there is now more water. The technical term for this is a failure to **conserve liquid**. It shows that the child does not realise that the amount of something can remain the same even though its appearance has changed.

In a similar way, young children shown equal numbers of counters in two equally-spaced rows will agree that both rows contain the same number of counters. But when an adult adjusts the counters, leaving one row more spread out than the other, young children believe that there are more counters in the row that is more spread out. This is a failure to **conserve number**.

Piaget believed children fail on conservation tasks because they are **centrated**. This means that they can only focus on one aspect of a problem at a time. In the case of the beakers, they focus on the height of the liquid and ignore the width. In the same way, they focus on the length of the row of counters and ignore the spaces between counters, and conclude the longer row has more counters.

3: Concrete operational stage (7 to 11 years)

● By now children are less egocentric and are able to think logically. But their logical reasoning can only be applied to physical objects (hence the term **concrete operations**). They have difficulty manipulating abstract ideas or in reasoning logically about objects which are not physically present. They can now not only conserve, but will usually insist on it: if you tell them there is more water in the tall, thin glass, they will tell you that you are wrong. This is because they have mastered three things:

1   **Identity:** the understanding that something can be the same even though it looks different – for example, that the amount of water is the same, even though the level is higher.

2   **Compensation:** children are no longer centrated, and they can see how changes in one area compensate for changes in another area – for example, how the thinner width of the water compensates for the extra height.

3   **Reversibility:** children can now mentally reverse a sequence of actions – for example, describing a route backwards or mentally tipping water back into the original beaker to confirm that the amount has not changed.

Children's inability to reason in abstract terms is apparent in tasks of the type 'if A is bigger than B and B is bigger than C, which is biggest?' To a young child, it is not clear what A, B or C represent, or in what sense they are bigger than each other, and this causes them difficulties. The sort of thinking that enables a child to reason about such problems belongs to the next stage.

4: Formal operational thinking (11 years onwards)

● By adolescence, children are beginning to be able to reason in abstract terms. In other words, they can reason hypothetically ('What would **x** be like if **y** were like this?'), and not only about objects, but also about topics such as religion, politics and ethics, which are less concrete. They solve problems in a methodical way, as a scientist might do. This type of thinking is described as **formal** because it can focus on the logical form of an argument regardless of its content. Take the following:

1 *If P is true, Q is true*
2 *P is true*
3 *Therefore Q is true*

We can see that the last statement must be true if the first two are true, without needing to know what P and Q represent. In fact, P and Q could stand for a number of different things, e.g.:

1 *If it's raining, I'll take an umbrella*
2 *It's raining*
3 *Therefore, I'll take an umbrella*

Formal operational thinking is the adult form of thinking, and the kind involved in developing scientific or philosophical theories.

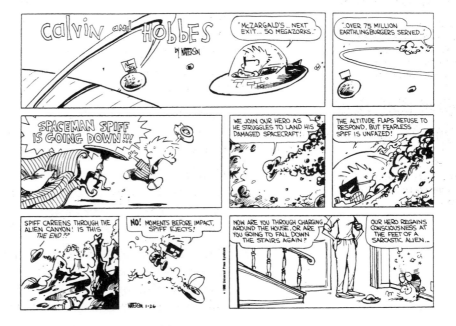

The ability to manipulate ideas, as in symbolic play, is considered by many to be the beginning of true intelligence

Summary of Piaget's stages

● In the early part of the sensory motor stage (0–2 years), infants can only understand the world in terms of what they can immediately see or touch. During this stage, they develop a sense of self and acquire representational abilities (the ability to

Strange how things don't exist for her if they are out of her line of vision

manipulate ideas). This is reflected in the development of object permanence and the beginnings of language.

● In the pre-operational stage (2–7 years) children's thinking involves manipulating images and symbols, and language continues to develop. Children's thinking is egocentric (as shown in the Three Mountains Task), shows animistic thinking, artificialism and moral realism. Children are unable to conserve because they are centrated.

● In the concrete operational stage (7–11 years) children are less egocentric and are able to conserve because they have mastered the concepts of identity, reversibility and compensation. However, they cannot reason in abstract terms yet.

● By the time children reach the formal operational thinking stage (11 years onwards) they are capable of adult, scientific, abstract thought.

TRY THIS

Match the **terms** on the left to the **definitions** on the right:

object permanence	the inability to understand someone else's viewpoint
egocentrism	the ability to mentally reverse a sequence of actions
centration	the belief that objects have an inner life
reversibility	understanding that objects still exist when you can't see them
animistic thinking	the inability to focus on more than one aspect of a problem

Evaluation of Piaget's theory of cognitive development

Strengths

+ Although research has challenged some of Piaget's theories about the age at which children can do things, Piaget was less concerned with the age at which the stages emerged than he was with the order in which they emerged.

+ Young children have an intense, natural curiosity about the world around them. Piaget's theory explains this, since the motivation for development is internal and a result of the child's need to reduce disequilibrium.

+ Piaget's theory highlighted the role of the environment in stimulating intellectual growth. The developing child needs an exciting interactive environment to promote assimilation and accommodation and the ability to think.

+ However we choose to explain it, it certainly seems to be true that young children think differently to adolescents and adults.

Weaknesses

- Bower and Wishart (1972) found that a baby would continue to reach for an object for nearly two minutes after the lights were turned out. This challenged the idea that babies lack object permanence since it suggests they know the object is still there even if it cannot be seen. Instead, it may be that babies may have trouble with concepts like location and movement, and have poor search procedures, which can lead to difficulty.
- A study by Hughes (1975) raised serious questions about Piaget's theory of egocentrism. Pre-operational children aged three to five were shown two intersecting screens and asked to hide a 'naughty doll', first from one 'police doll' and then from two. Almost 90% of the children managed the task even when they had to take two different viewpoints into consideration.

The 'police doll' study by Hughes challenged the view put forward by Piaget that children are unable to imagine viewpoints different from their own

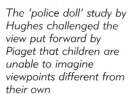
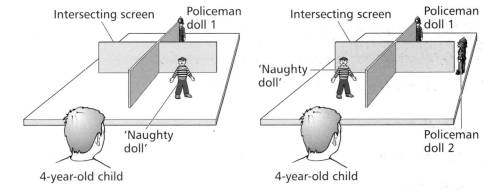

- This research drew attention to another criticism levelled against Piaget: that he had set children tasks which were remote from their experience and too complex for them. Hide-and-seek is a game many children are familiar with, whereas considering models of mountains is not so familiar.
- In a variation on the conservation-of-liquid task, Rose and Blank (1974) left out the first question in the test. Children simply saw water transferred from one of the beakers into a tall, thin beaker and were asked 'Which beaker has more water in it?' In this version of the test it was found that children were more likely to give a conserving response.
- In a conservation-of-number test, instead of an adult deliberately rearranging rows of counters, McGarrigle and Donaldson (1974) used a 'naughty teddy' to rearrange lines of sweets, and found that four- and five-year-olds *were* often able to show conservation of number.
- Donaldson (1978) suggested that when adults asked a question, deliberately changed things and then repeated the question, children might decide that they probably expected a different answer. This implies that the procedures Piaget used could unwittingly lead children into giving wrong answers. Children might also fail number tasks because they had a poor grasp of numbers and could not cope with too many objects at once. When Gelman (1982) presented two rows of just three objects each and then spread out one of the rows,

TRY THIS

Assume you have two beakers containing beads. One beaker contains all red beads. The other beaker contains all yellow beads. There are the same number of beads in each beaker. Take a handful of beads out of the red beaker and put them into the yellow beaker. Shake the yellow jar. Without looking, take back out of the yellow jar the same number of beads that you recently put in and put these back in the red jar.

Question: Are there now the same number of red beads in the red jar as yellow beads in the yellow jar?

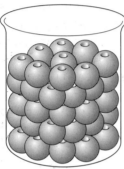

Red beads

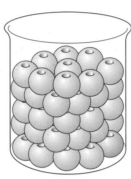

Yellow beads

The answer to this question is 'yes', but people often get it wrong (try it on your friends!). Since you put back the same number of beads, the jars end up with equal amounts. However many yellow beads are in the red jar, that number of red beads must be in the yellow jar. This is an example of a conservation task adults often fail on.

even three- and four-year-olds answered that the rows had the same number of items.

– Piaget underestimated the impact of the social and cultural environment on cognitive development. Cross-cultural studies such as those by Dasen (1994) have shown that cognitive development is strongly influenced by the skills that are valued and encouraged in a particular environment. Aboriginal children, for example, develop concrete operational thinking on visual/spatial tasks critical to locating survival items such as water and food earlier than Swiss children. Conversely, Swiss children develop numerical thinking earlier.

– Elkind (1966) found that many adults only display abstract thought in limited areas of knowledge, and some never show formal operational thought processes at all. This challenges the idea that all the stages, particularly the later ones, are universal.

– Many psychologists believe that Piaget underestimated the abilities of young children and overestimated the abilities of older children (and many adults).

– Meadows (1993) argued that we do, in fact, tolerate much more misunderstanding and gaps in our knowledge than is to be expected if this creates disequilibrium which we are motivated to get rid of.

– The move from one stage to the next, as defined by Piaget, is not clearly definable. People may sometimes fail on one task in a certain stage, but succeed on others. This has led some to question whether the notion of stages is useful, and if development is a more smooth and continuous process than Piaget suggests.

– Concepts like assimilation, accommodation and equilibration are abstract and difficult to test.

Bruner's theory of cognitive development

Bruner (1966) shared with Piaget the conviction that children are **active learners** – that they are constantly busy exploring and interacting with their world and are driven by a fundamental need to understand it. Bruner identified three basic ways or **modes** by which human beings convert their immediate experiences into what he called **cognitive representations**.

These three modes of representation emerge in the following order:

1   **Enactive mode**: this is the first way the child represents its world to itself. The style of thinking here is based on physical action – no use is made of words and images. The enactive mode involves muscle memory or learning, i.e. remembering what it feels like to do things. Objects for the child at this stage have meaning by reference to the actions performed on them – for example, shaking a rattle or grasping a toy. In fact, muscle memory or knowledge stays with us into adulthood: we never forget how to ride a bicycle or throw a ball, and we may use our hands to describe things like a helter-skelter or a corkscrew. This is learning, thinking and remembering by *doing something*.

TRY THIS

Write down on paper how to tie a shoelace for the benefit of someone who knows nothing about tying laces or knots.

Although tying our laces is something we all find very easy to do, *describing* it is actually quite hard. This highlights the importance of muscle memory for all kinds of activities.

2   **Iconic mode**: an **icon** is an image or picture of some sort. In this mode, we use images to stand for events and things in the real world. Children's mental images are based on what they see, hear, taste or touch; these images allow them to think about their world, even though they may not have language to describe it and talk about it. A child may form a mental image of a rattle in thinking about a rattle.

3   **Symbolic mode:** this third level of thinking is not tied to an image, action, or to any particular feature of an event in the environment. A **symbol** is something that stands for something else though it may itself be very different to the thing it stands for. For example, words are symbols. A picture or image of a car represents a car in an obvious way, but the letters C-A-R do not. For Bruner,

symbolic thinking often involves using language, though it takes place inside our heads without us moving our lips. This represents developed adult thought. A child now may use the word 'rattle' in thinking about a rattle (though the *word* 'rattle' doesn't look or sound like the object it describes).

Learning to categorise

One important function of language is to help us to **categorise** our world by saying 'This is a fruit' and 'This is a vegetable' etc. The world is full of different objects. Being able to put objects into categories is essential to help us to simplify and understand our environment.

Kuhlman (1960) showed children abstract shapes and asked them to learn nonsense names for them. Remembering shapes involves iconic thinking and younger and older children could do this equally well. However, when Kuhlman went on to show the children images of things such as an igloo, a dog kennel and a house and asked them to say what they had in common, the results were intriguing. Younger children, limited to iconic thinking, could not answer the question because the pictures all looked different from one another. Older children were able to use the symbolic mode, particularly language, to answer the question. They were therefore able to categorise the images as 'homes' or 'places to live in' (or something similar).

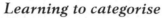

Each of the models above is different, but each belongs to the category 'cars'

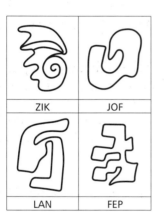

Younger children were able to memorise meaningless iconic shapes like the ones on the left...

...but were not able to group the symbolic pictures on the right into meaningful categories

ZIK   JOF

LAN   FEP

THINK ABOUT IT

How difficult would it be to think about the world if we were unable to put things into categories using language?

Language is also useful for organising our thoughts about the world and considering not only how things are different from each other but also the relationships between them. This was demonstrated in a study by Bruner and Kenney (1966).

KEY STUDY Children aged five to seven were shown an arrangement of glass tumblers placed on a grid on a board in rank order of height and width. When the glasses were taken away, most of the participants managed to replace them correctly. Then the glasses were removed, and one glass was replaced in a different position. The task was to put back the other glasses using the original pattern – only in reverse order.

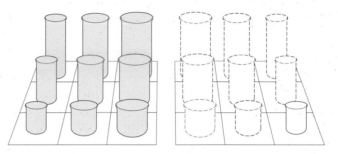

None of the younger children was able to do it: they were tied to an image of how the glasses looked originally. However, of the seven-year-olds, 79% were able to complete the task correctly. They were also able to describe *how* the glasses were different and *why* the rearranged formation should be as it was – for example 'They get wider this way and taller that way'. Because they could use language to describe the pattern, they could perform an abstract mental manipulation of the collection of glasses to repeat the pattern backwards. This shows how language helps us to organise our thoughts and understand the relationships between things

Bruner believed that the emergence of the symbolic mode, particularly in the use of language, enables children to think about the world in powerful new ways. But since earlier modes are useful too, these are still used when appropriate. For example, the iconic mode helps us remember a map, and the enactive mode helps us kick a football.

Questions

1. Why could five-year-olds replace the glasses in the same order but not in reverse order?
2. What type of experimental design is being used here?
3. Give one advantage and one disadvantage of this design.
4. Can you think of any tasks for which the enactive or iconic modes might be more useful than the symbolic mode?

Source: Bruner, J.S., & Kenney, H., *The Development of the Concepts of Order and Proportion in Children: Studies in Cognitive Growth*, (Wiley, New York, 1966).

Comparing Piaget and Bruner

● Bruner places greater importance on language for the development of thinking than Piaget. For Piaget, development is largely driven by maturation, and language skills follow on from developments in thinking. For Bruner, it is important for thinking itself that a child should develop language skills which enable him or her to manipulate ideas in more complex ways.

- Bruner gives more importance to social influences than Piaget. He believes that the skills we learn come from the culture around us and that each culture will transmit skills considered to be important within it (be it hunting or computing).

- Both theories propose that development occurs in a particular order (i.e. are sequential). However, Piaget argued that we leave earlier stages behind as we develop; Bruner argued that earlier modes of thinking are retained.

Cognitive theory and the classroom

- Although Piaget never really considered how his theory could be applied to education, the theory has had an impact on ideas about how children should be taught. Piaget believed that children learn by doing. It follows that teachers should not simply stand in front of a class and lecture, but that education should be child-centred. Children learn more from discovering than by being taught. **Discovery learning** requires children to be given an environment rich in materials to explore in order to help them learn things for themselves.

- Piaget's theory implied the idea of *readiness* in learning: this meant that children cannot learn something until they have acquired the necessary cognitive structures that will enable understanding. Materials and methods used should, as near as possible, match the stage of cognitive development of the child. Younger children should be given 'concrete' materials to play with and explore (e.g. sand, water), and abstract ideas and concepts should not be presented until children's cognitive abilities are advanced enough for them to understand them.

- Piaget's theory reveals that simple pen-and-paper tests may not give an accurate idea of children's development. Children think in different ways. Assessment of children therefore requires more flexible techniques, such as the clinical interview, to enable the teacher to understand the underlying logic of the child.

- Both Piaget and Bruner valued peer-group discussion to help with development. Piaget argued that this would help a child to decentre and see other points of view, and also strengthen emotional development. Bruner argued that it encourages symbolic thinking, and that exposure to more advanced ideas from slightly older peers can improve understanding.

- Like Piaget, Bruner favoured discovery learning in schools. He too believed children learn by doing, and argued that development is helped if a child can use all three modes. Coursework projects in which students have to plan, illustrate and discuss issues with other students would be seen as useful – and Bruner would approve of psychology practicals too!

- Bruner was less concerned than Piaget with the notion of readiness. Bruner believed that, provided we can find an appropriate method, children can be taught aspects of just about anything. He suggested that schools should adopt a **spiral curriculum**, where subjects are introduced and then returned to later at more advanced level. Sunderland (1992) suggested that the same principle could be applied to the topic of 'volume' by initially letting young children play with water and buckets, later introducing concepts like 'more water', 'less water', and later still introducing the word 'volume' and introducing activities to help achieve conservation. Later still, children could be presented with formulae for working out volumes for different objects.

Summary

- Piaget's contribution to psychology was that he was the first to see the child as active participant in his own cognitive development through four sequential stages (sensory motor, pre-operational, concrete operational, formal operational) leading up to full adult abstract reasoning.
- Thinking for Piaget revolved around a number of basic mental processes: assimilation, accommodation and equilibration.
- Piaget's work has stimulated a lot of further research. In general, he is thought to have underestimated the abilities of children. Furthermore, not everyone may reach formal operations, and some psychologists have doubts about the notion of development occurring in stages.
- Bruner accounted for cognitive development in terms of three different modes or styles of thinking: enactive, iconic and symbolic. He saw each mode as progressively more powerful than the last, but also believed that all three ways of thinking have their uses and remain with us as adults.
- Both Piaget and Bruner have influenced the way that children are taught in the classroom.

10 Moral Development

Michigan doctor Jack Kevorkian admitted to helping more than 130 people to commit suicide

Here is a real-life moral dilemma: Michigan physician Jack Kevorkian developed a device to help terminally ill patients kill themselves painlessly. He believed that he was acting out of compassion to end needless suffering. In April 1999 he was sentenced to a minimum of ten years in jail for second-degree murder.

Is it morally right or wrong to help someone commit suicide?

Right and wrong

Morality is to do with our beliefs about what is right and wrong and good and bad. Society teaches us standards and codes of moral behaviour, but people differ in their views of what is right and wrong, and cultures vary in their beliefs too. In studying moral development, psychologists are not concerned with the specific content of any one particular set of standards or moral values. Rather, they are concerned to understand generally how it is that people come to learn and adopt the standards that they do.

Why is this important? One answer is that the insights we gain here may help to tell us how to raise children for the best. They may also tell us where the limits of moral responsibility lie. For example, there is little point in blaming children for wrongdoing if they are not capable of understanding the difference between right and wrong.

Here, as elsewhere, it can be useful to consider moral development in terms of three factors which we can label **A**, **B** and **C**:

A **Affective:** our affections are our moral feelings; they determine whether a behaviour makes us feel good or bad
B **Behavioural:** what we actually do
C **Cognitive:** cognition refers to what we think about something, and whether we judge it to be good or bad

Although different psychologists have focused on different aspects of moral development, we should remember that these three factors are likely to interact: what we think about a certain behaviour will influence how we feel about it, and so influence what we actually do.

The psychoanalytic approach

Freud had a great deal to say about emotions and morality (see pages 46–7). For Freud, the moral component of the personality is the **superego**, which is acquired during the **phallic stage** of psychosexual development (three to five years of age). Before this time, children are **amoral**, i.e. they have no real sense of right and wrong and are motivated by personal pleasure and the desire to please themselves and be happy. During the phallic stage, children develop desires for the parent of the opposite sex and come to resent the parent of the same sex, seeing them as a rival. In boys this is known as the **Oedipus complex**, and in girls it is called the **Electra complex**. These feelings are eventually resolved by a process of **identification** with the same-sex parent. In identifying with that parent the child seeks to be just like them and adopts their ways of behaving and their values and attitudes. This includes sharing their moral values. In this way, boys acquire similar morals to their fathers, and girls acquire morals similar to their mothers.

The superego

The superego has been likened to 'the parent within you.' Behaviour that would please the same-sex parent now pleases the child, and behaviour that would upset that parent now upsets the child. The superego thus has two components:

1   The **ego ideal** which rewards you with pleasant feelings when you are good

2   The **conscience** which punishes you with guilt when you are bad

The superego operates largely in the unconscious mind and is not rational: it operates according to the **morality principle**. This means that it is only concerned with issues of right and wrong and is not concerned with the demands the real world may place on you. For example, if you are forced to steal a loaf of bread to avoid starving to death, the superego may still punish you with guilt for stealing if stealing is something you consider wrong.

The superego (right) ▲
*punishes us with guilt for
wrongdoing*

Evaluation of the psychoanalytic approach

Strengths

+   Childrens' morals are often linked to the moral values of their parents.
+   Psychologists accept that the ways in which children are raised can influence their moral (and other) behaviour.

Weaknesses

−   Freud's theory and concepts have been criticised as unscientific and not testable (see page 53). There is no direct evidence for the superego, or for the Oedipus or Electra complexes.
−   There is little evidence that children are morally mature by around six years of age, but younger children do show some sense of good and bad.
−   Freud predicted that boys should have stronger moral consciences than girls because in his view morals are acquired by identifying with the same-sex parent, and the need to identify is stronger in boys (because of castration anxiety). However, there is little evidence to support the idea that boys are in fact more moral than girls.

– Freud's theory implies that children from single-parent families should have poorer moral development – but again there is no evidence to support this.

– The link between parental behaviour and children's morality can be explained in other ways – for example in terms of learning theory (see below).

The behavioural approach

Behaviourists argue that moral behaviour is acquired by learning, just like other behaviours. They place no emphasis on unconscious forces or stages of development. Behaviours are learned through reinforcement and punishment (see pages 63–7). Behaviourists focus on two main types of learning:

1 **Classical conditioning** is learning by association. Pavlov trained dogs to salivate at the sound of a bell by training them to associate the bell with food. If bad behaviour is punished, then bad behaviour is associated with unpleasant feelings and so will tend not to be repeated. This is described as a **learned avoidance reaction**.

2 **Operant conditioning** is based on the principle that behaviours that are reinforced will tend to be repeated, and those which are not will tend to die out. Skinner trained rats to press a lever for a food reward. In the same way, praise and attention can serve as reinforcers for humans. If we are praised for our good behaviour then we are more likely to repeat such behaviour in future. Unreinforced, bad behaviours should die out.

Behaviourists argue that children learn moral behaviour by being punished for wrong actions (above) and rewarded for good actions (below) ▶

Punishment

Learning theory predicts that punishment is most effective if it is severe and immediately follows the undesired behaviour. In real life this is difficult to achieve. Children may often get away with bad behaviour and so reap some benefit from it, or at least not get caught and punished until later on, in which case their behaviour may have been reinforcing for them in the meantime.

THINK ABOUT IT

- In the early 1980s the US Navy decided to crack down hard on the use of drugs. All officers and senior personnel caught with drugs were dismissed. Lower ranks were fined heavily and dismissed from the service for further offences. After the campaign, tests in 1983 showed that the use of drugs dropped from about 35% to just 3.7%.

  How does this relate to learning theory?

- Assume you are a student away at college and you are short of money for end-of-term celebrations. You ring your parents and ask them for money, and they send you some the next day. If you are short of cash next term, would you be more or less likely to ask your parents if your earlier request had been bluntly refused?

  How does this relate to learning theory?

Although punishment tells children what *not* to do, it does not tell children what they *should* do. Skinner favoured an environment in which behaviour was carefully controlled by positive reinforcement (rewards). In this way he believed we could all learn to be 'good citizens.'

In fact, Hoffman (1972) looked at the ways in which parents disciplined their children, and found that parents who tended to punish children harshly for wrongdoing tended to have children who showed *less* resistance to temptation. Again, this probably reflects the inadequacies of punishment as a means of teaching children.

By contrast, Hoffman found that warm and loving parents who relied mainly on what he called **inductive discipline** tended to have children who were more morally mature. **Induction** means using reason and argument to point out to the child why certain forms of behaviour are wrong and persuading them to change their behaviour because of its unpleasant consequences. Hoffman found that parents who use physical punishment to discipline their children may engender feelings of resentment and hostility, as well as providing a model for the child to imitate when trying to deal with frustrations and unpleasant emotions in later life. This is something that social learning theorists would be keen to emphasise.

THINK ABOUT IT

Do you agree with Skinner that it would be a good idea to have a carefully controlled society in which all behaviours were monitored and good deeds rewarded?

Social learning theory

Social learning theorists such as Bandura (1977) agree that moral and other behaviours are acquired through learning, and that this can involve classical and operant conditioning. However, they are also keen to stress the importance of **modelling**. Children and adults observe the behaviour of people (**models**) around them, and its consequences for the actors. If they observe people being punished for bad behaviour, they are less likely to imitate them. On the other hand, people who are perceived as warm, supportive or powerful are especially likely to be imitated, as are those perceived to be similar to the observers themselves. This highlights the importance of people such as parents and peers as models for children to imitate. The media may also provide a number of models from which children can learn.

As children get older, they are exposed to a wider range of models in an increasing variety of contexts. In the course of this process, their understanding of moral issues becomes more advanced: they learn a wider variety of responses and discover more about the likely effect of these responses and whether they are liable to lead to reward or punishment. In general, children come to **internalise** the standards set for them by models in their environment. This means they come to accept certain ways of behaving as the correct way to behave. It therefore becomes rewarding for them to act in accordance with the moral values practised by those around them.

What people *do* is as important as what they *say*. A parent who physically punishes a child for aggressive behaviour is providing an aggressive model for the child to imitate. Life in the real world offers many moral choices, and models are rarely consistently good or consistently bad. People often benefit from bad behaviour, just as good behaviour often goes unrewarded. In consequence, children themselves may come to show inconsistency in behaviour. What they do depends on what happens to them and what they have seen others do in the past, and what they think is likely to be a consequence of behaving in a

Children often imitate adults – especially their parents ▼

particular way, as well as reflecting internalised standards. This explains why all of us are liable to behave well at some times and badly at other times. The wide variation in our moral standards is a reflection of our very different learning histories.

THINK ABOUT IT

If a father tells his daughter not to smoke but smokes himself, how will this affect the likelihood of the daughter not smoking? Is the daughter more or less likely to smoke if her friends at college are smokers?

Suppose you have two chances to steal money. In one case, you have a chance to steal £5 from a police station. In the other case, you have a chance to steal £1,000,000 with no chance of getting caught. Are you more likely to steal in one case than the other? If so, why? How would social learning theory explain this?

Evaluation of social learning theory

Strengths

+ For better or worse, parents punish and praise their children for their good and bad behaviour in the belief that it will teach them to behave properly. It seems likely that this must have some influence on the child.
+ The differences in people's learning history is a good explanation for the wide variety of moral codes at both the individual and cultural level.
+ Social learning theory provides a good explanation for why people may be inconsistent in their standards, and behave well sometimes but not always.
+ Research suggests that children can develop an understanding of moral rules from TV programmes. For example, *Sesame Street* encourages children to share and cooperate with one another. This supports the idea that models can have an impact on behaviour.

Weaknesses

− The wide variation in people's learning histories means it is difficult to test the theory in the real world. People with apparently similar backgrounds can behave in very different ways. It is tempting to conclude that people's morals must be in some way due to their upbringing, but it is not easy to demonstrate precisely how.
− The theory places little emphasis on the effect on moral development of maturational factors such as the development of the brain and changes in cognition.
− Some researchers have found that moral behaviour is more consistent than learning theory expects, and indeed, that there are age-related patterns in moral development. Piaget and Kohlberg are examples of researchers who believed this, and we will now turn to consider their views.

Peer-group pressure has
a powerful influence on
the behaviour of
teenagers ▶

The cognitive–developmental approach

Cognitive approaches are concerned with how people *think* about moral issues and how they come to judge behaviour to be morally good or bad. We will examine cognitive theories proposed by:

1 Piaget
2 Kohlberg
3 Gilligan

1. Piaget's theory of moral development

Piaget's views on moral development are closely linked to his theory of cognitive development (see pages 92–103). For him, children's ability to think about moral issues is linked to their ability to think in general. Thinking develops in stages, with older children able to think, and so make moral judgements, in more advanced ways than younger children.

As with his work on cognitive development, Piaget mainly used the clinical interview to investigate how children reason about moral issues (1932, 1965). In particular he used two interesting strategies to test children's reasoning about morality: he played games with them and he told them stories. In this way he developed an insight into their understanding of rules, wrong acts, and punishment and justice.

The game of marbles

To gain insight into children's moral development, Piaget spent much time with his sleeves rolled up, playing marbles with children and asking them about the game. He particularly wanted to explore children's understanding of *rules*. Moral behaviour is often rule-governed. In marbles – as in life – the rules are not written down, and children are free to create their own rules and change them if they wish to. This also reflects the adult world, where adults can decide about what they do or do not wish to do. So Piaget played marbles with children, and asked them about the rules of the game, where the rules came from, and if the rules could be changed.

Telling stories

Piaget also presented children with pairs of short stories in which accidents happen or children behave badly, and asked children to judge who was the 'naughtiest' person. An example is given below:

KEY STUDY   Piaget (1932) gave children the following two stories:

John broke fifteen cups by accident ▲

● A little boy called **John** is in his room. He is called to dinner. He goes into the dining room. But behind the door is a chair, and on the chair is a tray with fifteen cups on it. John couldn't have known that all this was behind the door. He goes in, the door knocks against the tray, bang go the fifteen cups, and they all get broken.

● Once there was a little boy called **Henry**. One day when his mother was out he tried to get some jam out of the cupboard. He climbed onto a chair and stretched out his arm. But the jam was too high up, and he couldn't reach it. While he was trying to get it, he knocked over a cup. The cup fell down and broke.

Henry broke one cup while helping himself to jam ▲

Having told the stories, Piaget asked children: 'Is John as bad or guilty as Henry?' and 'If not, which of them is naughtier? Why?' The children were also asked how the naughtier children should be punished. Piaget found that younger children tended to consider John naughtier because he broke the most cups. Older children considered Henry naughtier because he was trying to steal jam.

Questions
1. What is a **clinical interview**?
2. How did Piaget measure moral development in this study?
3. Give one **practical** and one **ethical** problem with using children as participants in research.

Source: Piaget, J., *The Moral Judgement of the Child* (Penguin, Harmondsworth, Middx., 1932) ▲

Piaget also used various other stories. Two were about people who stole bread from a shop – one in order to feed himself, and the other to feed a starving friend. He also told two stories about two boys getting into trouble, one for making a large inkstain while trying to help his father, the other for making a small mess with ink when playing around. Again, children were asked about who was naughtier and the type of punishment they deserved. Based on this research, Piaget put forward his stage theory of moral development.

Piaget's stage theory of moral development

1. The amoral stage
Before around four years of age, children do not understand what 'rules' really are, and are therefore not able to make judgements about breaking them. Children are not yet cognitively able to reason about morality.

2. The stage of heteronomous morality
From around 4 or 5 years to 10 years of age, children develop a good understanding of rules, but they believe rules come from 'outside': from figures of **authority** like older siblings, teachers, parents or even God.

Changing the rules would be likely to upset these authority figures, and so rules are fixed and should be followed. Rules may be interpreted literally. For example, being told you shouldn't kick your sister does not mean you shouldn't slap her!

At this stage, children accept that breaking rules deserves punishment (and generally, the more severe the punishment, the better!). This belief is based on the idea that bad things happen to you because you deserve them for being bad. There is a belief in **immanent justice**, i.e. justice that is inescapable: if you do bad things, one way or another, you will be punished.

Piaget saw children as **moral realists**: that is, as being unable to consider the *intention* behind an action in deciding how good or bad the action was. Instead, children focus on things like the amount of damage that was caused or the amount of punishment given.

3. The stage of autonomous morality

From about ten years onwards children recognise that rules are not so fixed and absolute, but are to some extent arbitrary ways of regulating how people interact. In other words, children recognise that rules are not simply imposed from outside, but have a purpose. Consequently, decisions about whether to break or change a rule are now taken internally, in the knowledge that punishment need not necessarily follow. Rules can be changed if people agree and wish to change them.

In the same way, punishment is now seen as having a purpose: to inform the child that what he or she is doing is wrong. Punishment should be appropriate to the crime, and is not some simple form of revenge.

By this stage, therefore, children have left behind the crude 'moral economics' of the broken crockery in Piaget's story, and moved from moral realism to **moral relativism**. They now recognise that what makes an action moral or immoral is the intention behind it.

For Piaget, underpinning these shifts in moral reasoning are developments in cognition. Importantly, older children are less **egocentric** than younger children. If you are egocentric, you cannot appreciate other people's point of view. Because of this, younger children cannot consider the intentions people have when they do something, nor can they consider why punishment was given: it is just something bad that the wrongdoer deserves. Neither can they consider the social function of rules: rules are just there to be obeyed. The ability to **decentre** and consider different viewpoints is crucial to the development of an autonomous view of morality.

Evaluation of Piaget's stage theory of moral development

Strengths

+ Older children do seem to reason differently to younger children, and psychology owes an enormous debt to Piaget for suggesting that children's moral reasoning is closely tied to the development of their cognitive development generally. This idea, along with his idea that reasoning develops in stages, has been further developed by Kohlberg (see below).

Weaknesses

–   However, Piaget has been criticised for researching only a small number of children (including his own). His use of the clinical interview also depends heavily on subjective interpretation of children's responses.
–   Smetana (1981) found that not all rules are considered in the same way by children. Breaking moral rules, like not hitting or stealing from people, is considered more serious than breaking social or conventional rules like saying 'please' and 'thank you'.
–   The view that all young children are moral realists has also been challenged. Piaget based this view largely on children's reactions to his stories, yet the point about the 'wrongdoer's' intentions in these stories is not always clear. Other researchers, (e.g. Nelson 1980, Youille and Perner 1988), have found that when the stories are made simpler and the intentions clearer, even three-year-olds are capable of considering the intentions behind the actions described.
–   Piaget believed that adult moral reasoning was achieved by around ten years of age. This is linked to his belief that adult thinking (formal operations) emerges at around this time, and that this enables children to reason in abstract terms. However, mature adults may reason about moral issues differently to a ten-year-old child, just as a fifty-year-old may reason differently to, say, a twenty-year-old. Piaget never really explored this possibility.

TRY THIS

Match the **terms** on the left to the **definitions** on the right.

superego	the belief that all wrongdoing will somehow be punished
moral realism	process of observing and imitating the behaviour of others
modelling	involves reasoning with a child about their wrongdoing
inductive discipline	the moral component of the personality, according to Freud
immanent justice	involves failing to consider the intentions behind an action

2. Kohlberg's theory of moral development

Kohlberg accepted much of Piaget's theory, but went on to revise and extend it. Kohlberg (1963) initially studied 10- to 16-year-old boys, testing them using stories involving moral dilemmas. Perhaps the most famous example of such a story is the story of Heinz and the drug:

'Heinz's wife was dying of cancer. A local pharmacist had invented a drug that might save her, but Heinz could not afford it. The pharmacist was charging ten times the amount that it cost him to make it. Heinz explained to him that his wife was dying and asked if he would sell it more cheaply or let him pay later. The pharmacist refused to help. Heinz became desperate, and one night he broke into the store and stole the drug for his wife.'[5]

Having told the story, Kohlberg would then ask the boys a number of questions. For example, was Heinz right to steal the drug? If so, why? What if the person dying was a stranger? Kohlberg was not really interested in whether the boys thought Heinz was right or wrong: he was interested in the *reasons* the boys gave to justify their answer.

He went on to apply this technique to people from many different cultures, and, using their answers to this and other dilemmas, devised his stage theory of moral development.

He proposed that there are three levels of development, with two stages in each level, making six stages in all:

Kohlberg's six-stage theory of moral development

Level 1: **Pre-conventional morality (based on external authority)**

    Stage 1: Child acts to avoid unpleasant consequences (punishment)

    Stage 2: Child acts to gain rewards. You should behave fairly and honour deals

Level 2: **Conventional morality (based on judgements about the expectations of others)**

    Stage 3: Child wishes to please others and be thought of as 'nice' – a 'good boy' or 'good girl'

    Stage 4: Child respects social rules. It is good to uphold the law and do one's duty

Level 3: **Post-conventional morality (based on self-chosen ethical principles)**

    Stage 5: Involves recognising rules or laws may be unjust, and so can sometimes be broken

    Stage 6: Reasoning is based on universal principles which show profound respect for life

---

In general, the stages reveal progression as follows:

- **Level 1** reasoning occurs before children understand rules, when they are guided by the personal costs and benefits of acting in a particular way.

- **Level 2** children understand and follow rules. Judgements are internalised and show respect for others such as parents and society at large.

- **Level 3** children move beyond established rules. Others are seen as having rights and being worthy of respect, even if laws and social conventions do not reflect this. Reasoning in the highest stage involves a recognition of the universal value and dignity of human life.

Kohlberg believed that everyone develops moral reasoning in the same way and progresses through the stages in the same order. The ability to reason about morality is linked to general reasoning ability. As thinking becomes more advanced, we become able to apply this to moral issues, just as we do with other issues. So Stage 1 reflects the egocentric thinking of children, and Level 3 requires the development of formal operational thinking (the ability to reason in abstract terms).

Sometimes we may fail to apply our reasoning abilities fully to moral issues. This is because we may be less advanced morally than we are cognitively. However, the same cannot be true the other way round: we cannot be more advanced morally than we are cognitively.

Once we are able to reason about morality in more advanced ways, we can understand – although we may not accept – the reasoning of those at lower stages. Exposure to moral reasoning in the stage above our own can help us to understand the failings in our current reasoning, and so help us develop the reasoning of the next stage.

For Kohlberg, as for Piaget, it is the *order* of development that is important, rather than the specific age at which advances occur. However, research has indicated that:

- Level 1 reasoning is common up until about 11 years of age
- Level 2 reasoning may last from about 12 to 15 years of age
- Level 3 reasoning develops after this.

Not everyone achieves the higher stages. Most adults are in Stages 3 and 4. Only about 10% of adults attain Level 3 reasoning, and very few people ever achieve the highest stage (Stage 6).

Evaluation of Kohlberg's theory

Strengths

+ Kohlberg's theory has been tested in over 1,000 different studies over a wide range of cultures and age groups, and it has found general support. On average, older people reason at higher levels than younger people, and there are links between moral reasoning and cognitive development.

Weaknesses

− Stage 6 reasoning is so rarely achieved that many psychologists believe it should be dropped from the classification system altogether. More recent versions of Kohlberg's scoring system no longer contain guidelines for assessing it.

- The moral dilemmas in Kohlberg's stories are rather artificial. For example, how many boys have had first-hand experience of caring for a dying wife?
- Fitting people's answers into Kohlberg's classification system is often difficult and involves subjective interpretation by the researcher. Different researchers sometimes code responses differently.
- Not everyone agrees that moral development is best characterised by stages. For example, social learning theorists emphasise that there is much variability in a person's moral behaviour.
- Kohlberg's classification shows a cultural bias. In some cultures, respect for family and elders is seen as the highest expression of morality, yet Kohlberg scores this at a lower level.
- Kohlberg focused on what people *say* rather than what they *do*. In his view, people may behave differently but be in the same stage of moral development depending on how they justify their behaviour. There are two objections to this. Firstly, it seems to tie morality to verbal ability, and it seems unfair to say someone is not morally advanced because they are poor at expressing themselves. Secondly, what people actually do may be considered by some to be a more important element of morality than how well they can justify their behaviour to others.
- Some of Kohlberg's research found that males tend to achieve higher stages of development than females; it may therefore contain a sex bias in favour of males. This is a point made by Gilligan (1982), whose work we shall consider shortly.
- Kohlberg's moral dilemmas mostly focused on wrongdoing, (e.g. stealing). By contrast, Eisenberg et al. (1990) gave children stories in which they could choose between self-interest and helping another person. An example is whether a child should stop to help an injured child when the delay might mean they miss out on the cakes at a party they are going to. These dilemmas, therefore, investigated how children reason about **prosocial** behaviour. Eisenberg identified five levels of prosocial reasoning. Children progress from acting out of self-interest (Level 1) to taking decisions based on respect for the dignity and rights of others (Level 5). This has parallels with Kohlberg's research, though Eisenberg found that children's prosocial reasoning advances slightly more quickly than Kohlbergian reasoning.

QUESTION

According to Freud, boys are more 'moral' than girls. Why was this?

3. Gilligan's theory

Gilligan (1982) argued that because boys and girls tend to be raised differently, they come to reason about moral issues in different ways. Boys are often raised to be concerned with independence and achievement, and so become concerned with issues such as justice.

Girls are raised to be concerned with the welfare of others, and so become more concerned with issues to do with caring.

In Kohlberg's classification, abstract notions of justice score higher than concern for the well-being of family or friends. But, Gilligan argued, females are not inferior to males in their moral reasoning: they just tend to have a different *style* of moral reasoning.

Gilligan interviewed 29 15- to 33-year-old pregnant women, and discussed ethical dilemmas with them, such as whether it would be right to have an abortion. From their responses Gilligan identified three levels of moral reasoning:

1   **Self-interest:** doing what was best for them

2   **Self-sacrifice:** being willing to sacrifice personal interests for the benefit of others

3   **Care as a universal obligation:** balancing personal needs against the needs of others

To translate this into practical terms, a woman in **Level 1** might abort or keep a baby because she would benefit somehow. A woman in **Level 2** would consider the needs of the baby, or perhaps of her parents or boyfriend. A woman in **Level 3** would take a balanced view of her own needs and those of others in deciding what was best for the future.

Gilligan believed that the emphasis in the judgements women make is more to do with people than with abstract rules. This pointed to a fundamental difference between the moral reasoning of men and women.

Evaluation of Gilligan's theory

Strengths

+   Gilligan alerted psychologists to the possibility of gender bias in research, both in the types of questions asked (many of Kohlberg's stories centred around males), and in the way in which findings are interpreted (there is more to morality than concern with rules and justice).

+   Gilligan presented research evidence to support her theory, and further support came from others such as Gilligan and Attanucci (1988).

Weaknesses

−   Other research has challenged the idea of a gender bias in Kohlberg's work. Walker (1984), in a review of evidence, found no overall differences between the scores of men and women.

−   Other researchers have challenged the view that men and women reason differently about moral issues. For example, Clopton and Sorell (1993) found that men and women argue in similar ways when presented with similar problems.

Summary

- Freud emphasised the role of emotions in moral development. The moral component of the personality is the superego, which has two components, the ego-ideal and the conscience. The superego is acquired during the phallic stage of psychosexual development as a result of identifying with the same-sex parent in order to resolve Oedipal conflict.
- Learning theory concentrates on moral behaviour. Behaviours are learned through the processes of classical and operant conditioning and by observing others. Since reinforcement is not systematic, and other people are not always consistent in their behaviour, children may also be inconsistent in their moral behaviour.
- Cognitive theorists such as Piaget and Kohlberg emphasise the importance of thinking in moral development. As cognition develops, so children can make more sophisticated judgements about moral issues. Development is believed to occur universally in an identifiable sequence of stages. Gilligan has alerted us to the possibility of gender bias in the research, but issues here are uncertain.
- Different theorists have focused on different aspects of moral development. No individual theory seems adequate on its own, but together they provide a good basis for thinking about and understanding the ways in which children acquire their morals.

The main approaches to moral development			
	Psychoanalytic approach	*Learning theory*	*Cognitive approach*
Major theorist	Freud	Bandura	Piaget Kohlberg
Main focus	Feelings	Behaviour	Thinking
How morality is acquired	Internalisation of parental values in superego	Classical and operant conditioning: observation and modelling	Orderly sequence of stages
Age of becoming moral	By around five years	Learning continues throughout life	Ongoing process to, and possibly through, adulthood (Kohlberg)
Agents of socialisation	Parents	Adults and peers	People in next-highest stage

11 The Psychology of Sex and Gender

When a child is born one of the first questions we ask is whether it is a boy or a girl. In fact, we are more likely to ask about the sex of the child than the health of the mother or the child.

In one study, 60 new parents recorded the kind of questions that relatives asked when they were told about the birth. Of these, 81% of the first questions asked by relatives related to the sex of the child (Peterson, Reddel, 1984). Clearly, being male or female is an important issue for us all.

Defining terms

Before describing the research on gender differences, it is important to define some terms. Psychologists make an important distinction between a person's **sex** and their **gender**.

- **Sex** refers to biologically-based characteristics which distinguish males and females, including differences in anatomy and hormones.

- **Gender** refers to the psychological and cultural aspects of masculinity and femininity. A person's sense of gender is learned.

- **Gender roles** refer to the patterns of behaviour which are considered appropriate for males and females in a particular society. The term **gender typing** is used to refer to the psychological process by which a person adopts a particular gender role.

- Psychologists are also interested in **gender stereotypes**. These are the beliefs held by a particular culture about the abilities and personality characteristics of males and females.

The table on page 124 summarises these terms.

THINK ABOUT IT

List three common stereotypes which we have about males and females in our society.

| Sex and Gender – terms and definitions ||
Term	Definition
Sex	biologically based characteristics of males and females
Gender	psychological characteristics of masculinity and femininity which are culturally determined
Gender stereotypes	beliefs held about the personality, characteristics and abilities of males and females
Gender roles	culturally defined expectations about appropriate behaviour for males and females
Gender typing	psychological process by which a person acquires the attitudes, values and behaviour considered appropriate for males and females
Gender differences	psychological or behavioural differences between males and females

In Western culture, we are constantly exposed to stereotypical images of femininity and masculinity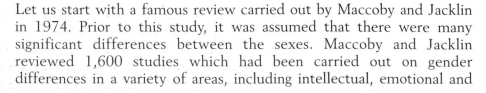

Research on gender differences

We know that there are physical differences between men and women – we don't need to read a psychology book to tell us that! But are there *psychological* differences between the sexes as well? You might assume that there would be an easy answer to this question, but in fact trying to come up with a definitive list of psychological gender differences has proved to be a very difficult task.

There are several reasons for this:

● First, all psychological research is influenced by the **social climate** in which it occurs. The way in which the research is carried out and even the type of questions that are asked are heavily influenced by a culture's values and beliefs at a particular time. Although this is true for all psychological research, it is particularly true for the research on gender differences.

● Secondly, it is much easier to get research published which shows significant differences between the sexes. Studies which find no gender differences (of which there are hundreds) although just as important, are less likely to get published.

● Finally, many of the studies carried out fail to consider how other variables – for example, class and ethnicity – may affect performance.

Let us start with a famous review carried out by Maccoby and Jacklin in 1974. Prior to this study, it was assumed that there were many significant differences between the sexes. Maccoby and Jacklin reviewed 1,600 studies which had been carried out on gender differences in a variety of areas, including intellectual, emotional and social differences. Their conclusion was that there were only four areas where reliable differences between the sexes could be found:

Gender difference	Age difference occurs
Females are superior to males in verbal ability	from adolescence onwards
Males are superior in mathematical ability	from age 12 onwards
Males are superior in spatial ability	from adolescence onwards
Males are more aggressive	by the age of 2–3

Thus Maccoby and Jacklin concluded that there were very few 'well established' differences between males and females. They also pointed out that many of the differences found were actually very small. In fact, of the 30 studies of spatial ability analysed by Maccoby and Jacklin:

- **9** showed differences favouring males
- **2** showed differences favouring females
- **19** reported no significant differences

Since most of the differences did not appear until adolescence, Maccoby and Jacklin suggested that they were unlikely to be biologically based.

Maccoby and Jacklin's conclusions about gender differences were well publicised both in psychology textbooks and in journals. Their work was accepted as a truthful account of how men and women differ. However, their research is not the end of the story.

More recent research using a statistical technique called **meta-analysis** has put Maccoby and Jacklin's work into a somewhat different perspective. The aim of meta-analysis is to summarise the results of many different studies on gender differences.

Meta-analysis involves computing a statistic called d. This value is calculated by finding the difference in the means for males and females on a particular type of task. The difference between the means is then divided by the average standard deviations of the male and female participants. A d value of 0.50 indicates that the means for males and females were half a standard deviation apart.

Although meta-analysis cannot provide us with a simple answer to the question 'are men and women different?' it does take us a little bit closer. What meta-analysis can do is to:

- indicate when a gender difference is **consistently** found across a large number of different studies
- indicate how large the average gender difference is
- estimate how much of the difference between males and females is due to gender and how much is due to other variables.

So, what does the research using meta-analysis reveal about gender differences? According to Janet Hyde and her colleagues (1981, 1984), gender differences are even smaller than Maccoby and Jacklin's research would suggest.

Hyde et al. used meta-analysis to re-analyse the original studies included in Maccoby and Jacklin's review. Their results suggested that gender accounts for very little of the difference between males and females on tasks involving verbal ability. In relation to mathematical ability, spatial ability and aggression, there appeared to be small-to-moderate differences, as shown in the table below:

Adapted from Hyde, J. 'How Large are Cognitive Gender Differences?' in *American Psychologist*, 36 (1981), pp. 892–901

Characteristic	'd' value
Verbal ability	0.24
Mathematical ability	0.43
Spatial ability	0.45
Aggression	0.48

It is worth noting that:

- a 'd' value of 0.20 is considered to be small
- a 'd' value of 0.50 is considered to be moderate
- a 'd' value of 0.80 is considered to be large

These results suggest that gender is a poor predictor of a person's performance on verbal, mathematical or spatial ability tests.

You can see that psychologists have found it quite difficult to decide how – or if – males and females differ significantly from each other. Equally problematic is why these differences occur and whether they are innate or learned. According to one psychologist:

'If sex-linked personality and cognitive traits are innate, then contemporary sex roles are appropriate. If, however, males learn to be "masculine"… and women learn to be "feminine", then the learned roles are subject to change. Women, therefore can be taught to utilise their full intellectual potential (i.e. become mathematicians and scientists) and men, whatever their vocation, can be taught to be nurturant and compassionate.'[6]

Although Birns wrote that statement in 1976, her predictions appear to be coming true. Read the following article from the *Guardian*:

'In 1992, a teacher decided to compare the GCSE results for males and females in her school. She expected to find that girls were under-achieving in areas like maths and sciences. However, what she found was quite different. The results showed that girls were doing as well as, if not better than boys in maths and sciences. In terms of overall results, based on her school, girls were more likely than boys to get five GCSEs at grades A–C.

In summary

- *Sex refers to the biologically-based categories of being male or female.*

- *Gender refers to a person's sense of being masculine or feminine.*

- *Early research suggested that females had greater verbal ability while males were better at spatial and mathematical ability. Males were also found to be more aggressive.*

- *More recent research using meta-analysis suggests that gender differences between males and females are moderate to small.*

'The results from her school were not a "fluke". Statistics from the Department of Education and Employment have shown that this is happening nationally. The statistics suggest that in 1998 41.3% of boys are achieving five or more A–C grades compared with 51.5% of girls. The gap is widest for English, with 59% of girls achieving Grade C or better compared to 41% of boys.'[7]

Psychological theories of gender identity

During the first years of life, children begin to form a sense of who they are, based on the **social categories** they belong to. Being male or female is an example of a social category. Therefore, an important part of their self-concept is the extent to which they see themselves as masculine or feminine. Psychologists use the term **gender typing** to refer to the process by which a person acquires the values, attitudes and behaviour considered appropriate for their sex. Gender-typing is the psychological process by which males and females become 'masculine' and 'feminine.'

There are various ways in which psychologists explain the process of gender identity and gender role development:

1 the **psychoanalytic** approach
2 the **behavioural** approach
3 the **cognitive developmental** approach
4 the **biological** approach

Each approach has a different emphasis. For example, the behavioural approach focuses on external factors in the social environment, while the psychoanalytic approach focuses on the process of identification with the same-sex parent.

1. The psychoanalytic approach

Freud's theory of psychosexual development seeks to explain how a child adopts a gender identity which is consistent with his/her biological sex. According to Freud, gender typing occurs during the **phallic stage** of development when the child is aged 3–5. In general terms, Freud believed that boys become masculine and girls become feminine through identifying with the parent of the same sex. In other words, the child adopts the same-sex parent as a **role model** and **internalises** his or her beliefs and values. However, the nature of the process is different for boys and girls.

As we saw earlier, the little boy desires his mother and sees his father as a rival. The boy fears that his father will castrate him for desiring his mother. This fear of castration is enough to make the boy give up his desire for his mother and identify with his father. It is almost as if the boy realises that he cannot take the place of his father and that they may as well be 'all boys together'. He therefore adopts the father's beliefs and values and decides to be masculine like him.

Freud's description of female gender development is more complicated and perhaps even less convincing. The girl experiences the **Electra complex** and desires the father for herself. However, unlike the boy, she is not motivated by castration anxiety to resolve her Electra complex. As a result, the Electra complex is never fully resolved. According to Freud, penis envy plays an important part in the girl's development, but the girl's identification with the mother will not be as strong as the boy's identification with the father.

Even Freud himself realised that his theory of female development was less than perfect. In one of his lectures he admitted:

> 'That is all I had to say to you about femininity. It is certainly incomplete and fragmentary and does not always sound friendly … If you want to know more about femininity, enquire from your own experiences of life, or turn to the poets, or wait until science can give you deeper and more coherent information.'[8]

Evaluation of the psychoanalytic approach

Strengths
+   Freud believed that children were not born masculine or feminine but acquired their gender identity as a result of identifying with the same-sex parent.

Weaknesses
–   There is little evidence to support the notion of penis envy. Tavris and Wade (1984) present evidence which suggests that penis envy is not necessarily a universal response to seeing a boy's genitals. They describe one young girl's mixed reaction on seeing the genitals of her male cousin: 'Mom, isn't it a blessing he doesn't have it on his face!'
–   There is very little evidence to suggest that young children are aware of the physical differences between males and females. In fact, most young children discriminate between males and females on the basis of hair length or clothing.

2. The behavioural approach
The behavioural approach assumes that gender roles are learned in the same way as any other behaviour. According to this approach, the processes that are important are observation, imitation, reinforcement and punishment. For our purposes, we will divide this approach into two sections, one on the role of reinforcement and punishment and the second on the importance of role models.

Reinforcement and punishment
One way that children learn gender roles is by being rewarded for behaviour which is gender-typical and punished for behaviour which is gender-atypical. Is there evidence to suggest that boys and girls are treated differently? For example, are they rewarded for different kinds of behaviour?

The research evidence supports the idea that boys and girls are treated in different ways. Stereotypes seem to be an important influence here.

Even with young infants, the stereotypes we have about males and females influence how we perceive the behaviour of boy and girl infants. In other words, we expect males to behave in a certain way and females to behave in a different way.

In one study by Condry and Condry (1976), university students were shown videotapes of nine-month-old infants. The infants' responses to a loud buzzer were recorded. When the participants thought the infant they were watching was a male, they described the infant's response as anger. However, when the participants thought the infant was a female, they described the same response as fear. The study suggests that parents expect different types of behaviour from males and females.

A more important question is whether parents treat boys and girls in a different way. The research suggests that parents do in fact reinforce boys and girls for different kinds of behaviour. In order to understand how psychologists have investigated the role of parents in gender typing, read the following Key Study and answer the questions. The answers are given at the end of the chapter.

KEY STUDY

In 1978, Beverly Fagot carried out a naturalistic observation of 24 families. Twelve of the families had sons and the other twelve had daughters. The families were all white and came from middle-class backgrounds. The children were aged between 20 and 24 months.

The parents were told that their behaviour and the child's behaviour were being observed, but they were not told that the researcher was interested in looking at gender differences. The researcher used an observation checklist to record the child's behaviour and the parents' reactions to it. The results of the study are shown in the table on page 130.

Questions
Use the table and the text on page 130 to answer the following questions.

1. What was the total sample size of toddlers?
2. Give one problem with the sample used.
3. Using the table, give three behaviours which parents were more likely to respond positively to in girls compared to boys.
4. How did the parents respond to aggression in their children?
5. Give one example of a behaviour for which parents were more likely to give a negative response to their daughters than their sons.
6. Give one measure of control that the researcher used in the study.
7. What could the researcher conclude about parental reactions to children's behaviour?

	Parental responses to child's behaviour*			
	% Positive response		% Negative response	
Type of behaviour	Boys	Girls	Boys	Girls
Playing with blocks	36	0	0	0
Manipulating objects	46	46	2	26
Transportation toys	61	57	0	2
Rough/tumble play	91	84	3	2
Aggression	23	18	50	53
Climbing	39	43	12	24
Playing with dolls	39	63	14	4
Dancing	0	50	0	0
Asking for help	72	87	13	6
Dressing-up play	50	71	50	6

Adapted from Fagot, B., *The Influence of Sex of Child on Parental Reactions to Toddler Children* (Child Development, 1978)

* *The numbers in the table represent the percentage of occasions in which parents reacted positively or negatively when the child was engaged in a particular behaviour.*

Fagot concluded that parents do reinforce their boy and girl children for different types of behaviour and that this pattern of reinforcement is important in explaining gender differences in adulthood.

Eisenberg et al. (1985) also observed parents playing with their children but did not find evidence that parents rewarded different types of play behaviour. However, parents were more likely to choose gender-typical toys for their children to play with. Parents of boy toddlers tended to choose more masculine or neutral toys, while parents of female toddlers tended to choose more neutral toys.

More recently, Lytton and Romney (1991) carried out a meta-analysis of the research on parental treatment of boys and girls. They found that parents did not treat boys and girls differently in terms of:

● amount of parent-child interaction
● discipline
● encouragement of achievement

However, parents did encourage boys and girls differently in relation to certain activities, and were more likely to provide encouragement when children were engaged in gender-typical activities.

Finally, in relation to punishment, it appears that fathers are more likely than mothers to reinforce gender-typical behaviour, particularly in their sons.

Research evidence suggests that parents tend to choose 'gender-appropriate' toys for their children

So the psychological evidence does suggest that parents reinforce their male and female children differently. But how about teachers? Research in America suggests that in general, boys tend to get more attention from teachers than girls (Sadker and Sadker, 1985). Boys also tend to get more positive feedback from teachers regarding the intellectual or academic quality of their work.

? THINK ABOUT IT

Can you think of a reason why fathers are more likely than mothers to reinforce gender-typical behaviour?

Influence of observation and imitation

Social learning theorists suggest that gender roles are learned through observing and imitating role models – and noticing whether the role model's behaviour is rewarded or punished. Important role models include parents, teachers, peers and characters in films and on television. However, children do not imitate just any model. Research indicates that children are more likely to pay attention to certain models depending on:

- the sex of the model
- whether the model's behaviour is gender-appropriate.

For example, in a study by Perry and Bussey (1979), a group of children watched male and female adult models choose between a number of activities that were gender-neutral. They found that when the children were given a choice of activities, they were more likely to imitate the behaviour of the same-sex models.

However, whether the model's behaviour is gender-appropriate is also important. Masters et al. (1979) asked four- to five-year-olds to choose toys to play with. They found that the children were more likely to choose a toy which was gender-appropriate regardless of the sex of the model.

131

Under-representation of women in jobs such as motor mechanics tends to reinforce gender stereotypes

According to social learning theory (Mischel, 1966), children do not have to be reinforced directly for a particular behaviour; just seeing someone else being rewarded is enough. This is called **vicarious conditioning**. For example, if a girl sees a female television character being punished (or not being rewarded) for being assertive, she may believe that being assertive is not appropriate behaviour for females.

It may also be worth noting that not only are role models important, but the lack of appropriate role models is also important. For example, the absence of female role models in areas like science and engineering is widely believed to discourage girls from entering these traditionally male-dominated fields.

Evaluation of the behavioural approach to gender development

Strengths

+ The behavioural approach emphasises the importance of the social environment on the development of gender roles in children.
+ This approach has also shown that children can learn behaviours through vicarious conditioning. They do not always have to try things out for themselves. They can learn just by observing others.
+ An implication of the theory is that gender typing is not an inevitable process. It occurs because children are rewarded for different types of behaviour.

Weaknesses

– The emphasis on reinforcement in the behavioural approach implies the child plays a passive role in gender typing.
– This approach does not make any predictions about age-related patterns or developmental trends in gender role development. In other words, it does not provide us with a stage theory of gender role development.

3. Cognitive developmental theory

This approach to the development of gender identity is heavily influenced by Piaget's theory of cognitive development. Lawrence Kohlberg (1966) applied Piaget's theory to the area of gender identity, arguing that children try to make sense of their social world in the same way as they make sense of their physical world. Therefore, the child's understanding of gender will depend upon their level of cognitive development. As the child's cognitive abilities mature, their understanding of the social world, including gender, will mature also.

According to Kohlberg, gender development takes place in three stages at each of which the child makes a cognitive judgement about him/herself. The stages are:

● gender identity

● gender stability

● gender constancy

Gender identity (ages 2–5)

The process begins at around the age of two, with the child learning a gender label. A little girl will hear the word 'girl' and begin to associate herself with it. For example, parents will say things like 'Aren't you a clever girl!' or 'Aren't you a good girl!'

By the age of three, most children are able to state accurately whether they are a boy or a girl. Thompson (1975) asked children aged between 24 and 36 months whether they were a boy or a girl. The results are shown below:

Age (in months)	Percentage of children who correctly identified their own sex
24 months	76%
30 months	83%
36 months	90%

During the third year, children generalise gender labels to other people. In other words, they realise that other people are also either male or female. Leinbach and Fagot (1986) found that nearly 50% of children aged two-and-a-half could successfully label the sex of *other* children.

During this stage, children will distinguish between males and females on the basis of superficial characteristics like hair-length and clothes. By the end of it, children can correctly label their own and another person's gender and therefore have achieved gender identity. However, they do not understand that being male or female is based on biological features, or that their gender identity is permanent.

Gender stability (ages 5–6)

During this stage, children become aware that sex is stable over time in that they are able to predict what sex they will be when they grow up. However, they are less aware that sex is stable across different situations. A child at this stage will assume that a change in physical appearance such as a girl wearing boy's clothes implies a change in gender. For example, Emmerich et al. (1976) showed drawings of boys and girls like those below to groups of children aged four to seven:

The drawings were cut at the neck so that the children could be shown all-girl and all-boy pictures as well as a picture of a girl's head with masculine clothes. The children were also shown an all-girl doll called 'Janie' and were asked the following questions:

- Could Janie be a boy if she wanted to be?

- If Janie played with lorries and did 'boy things', would she be a boy or a girl?

- If Janie put on boy clothes, would she be a boy or a girl?

The experimenter would then go through the same procedure using an all-boy doll. They found that the majority of the children thought that Janie could become a boy if she wore boy's clothes or did 'boy things'.

Gender constancy (6–7)

Children at this stage understand that gender is constant over time and across situations. They are no longer fooled by appearances. They understand that gender does not change despite changes in appearance. Gender constancy is thought to be achieved around seven years of age and is related to the child's level of cognitive development.

According to Piaget, children up to the age of seven are in the pre-operational stage of cognitive development and find it difficult to understand that changing the shape of an object does not necessarily change its amount or quantity (see page 98). This inability to conserve can be related to gender development, in that, until the age of seven, pre-operational children do not understand that a person's gender remains constant despite changes in appearance.

Comparison of social learning theory and Kohlberg's theory

There is an important difference between social learning theory and Kohlberg's theory. According to social learning theory, children develop gender-appropriate behaviour because they are *reinforced* for imitating the behaviour of same-sex models. Kohlberg's theory suggests that children acquire gender-appropriate behaviour because they have categorised themselves as male or female and want to do things that are consistent with that self-categorisation. As Kohlberg describes:

> 'Once the boy has stably identified himself as male, he then values positively those objects and acts that are consistent with his gender identity.'[9]

Evaluation of Kohlberg's theory

Strengths

+ Like Piaget, Kohlberg emphasises the role of the child as an active processor of information from both the physical and social world.

+ There is evidence to support Kohlberg's idea that once children have achieved gender constancy, they are more likely to pay attention to the behaviour of same-sex models. For example, Slaby and Frey

(1975) divided children aged two to five into two groups depending on their level of understanding of gender constancy. The children then watched a film of adult models. The film was shown in such a way that male actors were presented on one side of the screen and female actors on the other side. The researchers measured the amount of time the children watched each side of the screen. If (as social learning theory predicts) children were more likely to pay attention to same-sex models, then girls would be expected to pay more attention to the female actors, and boys would be expected to pay more attention to the male actors. However, If Kohlberg's theory was right, children's tendency to attend to same-sex models would depend on their level of gender constancy and the extent to which they categorised themselves as male or female.

The results supported Kohlberg's view. The researchers found that children who were at the higher levels of gender constancy were more likely to attend to the same-sex models than children who were at lower levels. The effect was stronger for the boy children than for the girls.

+ There is evidence to support the view that the child's gender development is related to cognitive development. Research has shown that the child's understanding of gender is related to his or her understanding of conservation of physical objects such as mass and liquids (Marcus and Overton, 1978).

Weaknesses

– Kohlberg's theory says very little about the influence of biological factors on gender development.
– The theory also under-emphasises environmental factors and therefore does not explain the fact that there are cultural variations in gender-role behaviour.

Summary of Kohlberg's stage theory of gender development	
Stage	**Description**
Gender identity	Child categorises him/herself as a boy or girl
Gender stability	Child understands that gender is stable over time, and that boys become men and girls become women
Gender constancy	Child realises gender is constant over time and across situations and is not changed by superficial changes in appearance

In summary

- *Kohlberg believed that a child's understanding of gender is related to their level of cognitive development.*

- *The theory emphasises the active nature of the child who tries to make sense of the social world around them.*

- *According to Kohlberg, gender development occurs in three stages: gender identity, gender stability and gender constancy.*

4. Gender schematic processing theory

Gender schematic processing theory is also part of the cognitive developmental approach to gender typing. This approach developed from the work of a number of researchers including Martin and Halverson (1981), Markus (1982) and Bem (1981).

The theory is based on the assumption that humans have a natural tendency to categorise information. **Schemas** (which are central to

Piaget's theory of cognitive development – see page 92) are internal cognitive structures which help us to impose structure and meaning on incoming information. Schemas develop as a result of past experience and new information being assimilated (fitted into) them. Children have many schemas, including one for gender. These schemas are used to help children understand their culture's definition of maleness and femaleness. Therefore, a **gender schema** contains information about the behaviour and traits which are associated with males and females. Gender schematic processing theory suggests that gender typing arises from two factors:

- the child's natural tendency to organise information, including information about the self
- the way in which the culture defines maleness and femaleness.

How do gender schemas develop?

According to Martin and Halverson (1987), the first gender schema develops between the age of two and three, when the child has achieved gender identity. This first schema involves categorising which objects and activities are appropriate for each sex. So the child distinguishes between 'boy things' and 'girl things'.

The next gender schema to develop is the child's own-sex schema which contains information about the activities appropriate to his/her own sex. This will become an important part of the child's self-concept. Once the gender schemas are formed, they will influence the child's preferences for certain objects and activities. In other words, the child will want to behave in a way that is consistent with what is stored in his or her gender schema.

If children are presented with information which is not consistent with their gender schemas, they are likely to ignore or distort it. For example, Cordura et al. (1979) showed children films which portrayed males and females as both doctors and nurses. When the children were asked at a later date to identify photographs of what they had seen in the film, the majority of children who had seen a male nurse and a female doctor recalled seeing a *male* doctor and a *female* nurse.

Markus (1982) and Bem (1981) suggested that there are differences between the way gender schemas are used in organising new information and the way they are used in thinking about the self. Bem (1981) developed the **Bem Sex Role Inventory (BSRI)** to measure the extent to which an individual is gender-typed (see page 138). The inventory consists of 60 characteristics. Of these, 20 reflect the American definition of masculinity and 20 reflect the American definition of femininity (Bem's research was done in the USA). The remaining 20 characteristics are neutral, i.e. not associated with either males or females.

Each individual is asked to indicate on a seven-point scale the degree to which each characteristic describes them. On the basis of their scores, it is possible to place individuals into one of four categories:

- **masculine-typed**: participants who rate themselves higher on the male characteristics

- **feminine-typed**: participants who rate themselves higher on the female characteristics

- **androgynous**: participants who feel that both masculine and feminine characteristics describe them

- **undifferentiated**: participants who feel that neither the masculine nor the feminine characteristics describe them

A study carried out by Markus et al. (1982) explored whether individuals classed as either masculine or feminine had better recall for words which were consistent with their gender identity. To investigate this, participants were first asked to complete the BSRI in order to assess the extent to which they were gender-typed. On the basis of their scores, the participants were then classified as being masculine-typed, feminine-typed or androgynous. The participants were then asked to recall as many words as possible from the BSRI.

According to the gender schematic processing approach, the predicted results would be that:

- **masculine-typed participants** would recall more of the male words from the BSRI

- **feminine-typed participants** would recall more of the female words from the BSRI

- **androgynous participants** would recall equal numbers of male and female words.

The actual results are shown below:

Adapted from Markus, H., Crane, M., Bernstein, S. and Salidi, M.: 'Self Schemas and Gender' in *Journal of Personality and Social Psychology*, 42 (1982), pp. 38–53.

Mean number of male, female and neutral words recalled			
	Gender-type of participants		
Type of word from the BSRI	**Masculine**	**Feminine**	**Androgynous**
Male	3.42	2.68	3.00
Female	2.60	3.90	3.39
Neutral	2.10	2.09	2.05

QUESTION

To what extent do the results above support the predictions based on gender schematic processing theory?

TRY THIS

Read through the following characteristics. Beside each one put a number from **1 to 7** depending on how well each characteristic describes you (**1** means that the item is never or almost never true; **7** means that the item is almost always true.)

Characteristic	Score	Characteristic	Score
1 self-reliant	....	31 make decisions easily	....
2 yielding	....	32 compassionate	....
3 helpful	....	33 sincere	....
4 defends own beliefs	....	34 self-sufficient	....
5 cheerful	....	35 eager to soothe hurt feelings	....
6 moody	....	36 conceited	....
7 independent	....	37 dominant	....
8 shy	....	38 soft-spoken	....
9 conscientious	....	39 likeable	....
10 athletic	....	40 masculine	....
11 affectionate	....	41 warm	....
12 theatrical	....	42 solemn	....
13 assertive	....	43 willing to take a stand	....
14 flatterable	....	44 tender	....
15 happy	....	45 friendly	....
16 strong personality	....	46 aggressive	....
17 loyal	....	47 gullible	....
18 unpredictable	....	48 inefficient	....
19 forceful	....	49 acts as a leader	....
20 feminine	....	50 childlike	....
21 reliable	....	51 adaptable	....
22 analytical	....	52 individualistic	....
23 sympathetic	....	53 does not use harsh language	....
24 jealous	....	54 unsystematic	....
25 has leadership abilities	....	55 competitive	....
26 sensitive to others' needs	....	56 loves children	....
27 truthful	....	57 tactful	....
28 willing to take risks	....	58 ambitious	....
29 understanding	....	59 gentle	....
30 secretive	....	60 conventional	....

The questionnaire that you have just completed is called the **Bem Sex Role Inventory** (Bem, 1974). In order to find out how masculine, feminine or androgynous you are:

● Add up your ratings for items 2, 5, 8, 11, 14, 17, 20, 23, 26, 29, 32, 35, 38, 41, 44, 47, 50, 53, 56, 59.
● Divide your total by 20. This is your **femininity score**.
● Add up your ratings for items 1, 4, 7, 10, 13, 16, 19, 22, 25, 28, 31, 34, 37, 40, 43, 46, 49, 52, 55, 58.
● Divide your total by 20. This is your **masculinity score**.

Which is higher: your masculinity or femininity score? If your two totals are quite similar, you are **androgynous**, i.e. you have a mixture of masculine and feminine characteristics.

These results do support gender schematic processing theory, in that participants show enhanced recall for words which are consistent with their gender typing.

In another study, Bem (1981) set out to investigate whether gender schemas affect how information is processed. She presented participants with the 60 characteristics which make up the BSRI. Each characteristic was projected one at a time on a screen. The participants had to indicate whether the characteristic described them by pushing two buttons, one labelled 'me' and the other labelled 'not me'. Bem recorded the length of time taken to respond to each characteristic. She found that gender-typed individuals were significantly faster than androgynous individuals in responding to each characteristic. Presumably, gender-typed individuals were using their schemas to help them process the characteristics, and so responded more quickly.

According to Bem, children would be less likely to depend on gender schemas if society did not make such important distinctions between males and females.

Evaluation of gender schematic processing theory

Strengths
+ The BSRI is a useful tool in measuring the extent to which individuals are gender-typed.
+ Like Kohlberg's theory of gender typing, gender schematic processing theory focuses on the child as an active processor of information.
+ Gender schematic processing theory attempts to deal with the ways in which information is processed differently by boys and girls.
+ There is evidence to support the view that children ignore or distort information which is inconsistent with their gender schemas (Cordura et al., 1979). This could help to explain why children persist in believing in sex-role stereotypes.

Weaknesses
− Gender schematic processing theory focuses on the cognitive aspect of gender typing and therefore has very little to say about the emotional and motivational features of gender development.
− The theory also under-emphasises the influence of role models such as parents and peers.

5. The biological approach
The biological approach suggests that gender differences which exist between males and females are the result of biological factors such as genes, hormones or differences in brain structure or organisation. Unlike the behavioural approach, which focuses on the influence of external factors such as reinforcement, punishment and role models, this approach suggests that gender differences are the product of internal factors.

Pre-natal development
When an infant is born, its sex is determined by its external genitalia. If

it has a penis and a scrotum, it will be male and if it has a vagina and clitoris, it will be female. So far, so good. But the child's external genitalia are only one factor making up its biological sex. Several developments will already have taken place before birth which directly influence the sex of the unborn child. These include:

- **the child's chromosomal make-up:** females have two X chromosomes (XX) while males have an X and a Y chromosome (XY)

- **production of the appropriate sex hormones:** although males and females have both types of hormones, males have more androgen and females have more oestrogen and progesterone

- **the development of the child's internal reproductive organs:** ovaries in females and testes in males

- **the development of the child's external genitals:** the vagina and clitoris in females and the penis and scrotum in males

In most cases, all these factors will be consistent. In other words, a person who is genetically female (XX) will have ovaries, will produce progesterone and oestrogen and will have a clitoris and a vagina. However, sometimes things go wrong. For example, there are cases of genetic males (XY) who develop external female genitalia. Some have been studied by psychologists in an attempt to compare the influence of biological factors and the role of socialisation.

Sex-linked traits

If you look at a picture of a person's chromosomes you will see that there are 23 pairs of chromosomes. All the pairs look similar except for the 23rd pair, which consists of two sex chromosomes.

Each pair of chromosomes looks similar except for the 23rd pair ▶

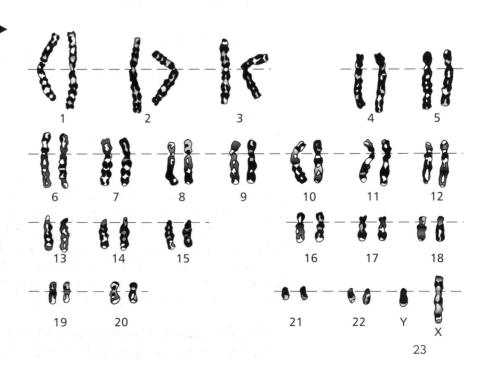

As mentioned above, a female has two X chromosomes while a male has an X and a Y. If you look at the diagram above, you will see that the X chromosome is much bigger than the Y chromosome. The X chromosome also contains more genetic information than the Y chromosome. What implications does this have for men?

The sex chromosomes (particularly the X chromosome) carry genetic instructions which influence a number of characteristics such as blood-clotting and colour vision. Since these genes are on the X chromosome, they are said to be **sex-linked**. Males can only inherit these genes from their mothers, not from their fathers. Since a male only has one X chromosome, if the genes that control these characteristics are defective, the male will be affected. However, if a female has a defective gene on the X chromosome, there is another healthy X chromosome to counterbalance it.

So what is the link between sex-linked traits and gender? Some early research suggests that at least one of the genes controlling spatial ability is carried on the X chromosome and is **recessive** (Harris, 1978). A **recessive trait** requires the presence of two genes. This means that in order for a female to have good spatial ability, she needs to have the spatial gene on both X chromosomes, whereas a male needs only one X chromosome.

Effect of prenatal hormones

Just as sex hormones are responsible for the development of the infant's internal and external genitalia, they may also affect the infant's developing brain, programming it into a male or female pattern. Evidence for the effect of prenatal hormones comes from two sources: animal studies, and case studies of children who have been exposed to abnormal levels of hormones.

1. Animal studies

Animal research on a number of species including rats, rabbits and rhesus monkeys indicates that prenatal hormones can affect behaviours such as:

● aggression
● activity level
● sexual behaviour

For example, Phoenix (1978) injected pregnant rhesus monkeys with the male hormone testosterone. Exposure to the testosterone affected the female infants in a number of ways. The female infants were born with masculine-looking genitalia. The hormone also affected their social behaviour, making them more aggressive and more inclined to take part in rough-and-tumble play than normal female monkeys. The affected females were also more likely to mount other monkeys during intercourse – usually the position adopted by the male monkey.

2. Children exposed to abnormal hormone levels

Other evidence to support the influence of hormones is based on case

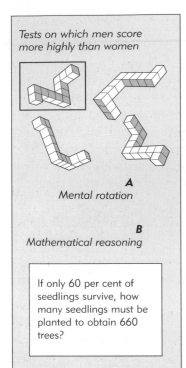

Tests on which men score more highly than women

A
Mental rotation

B
Mathematical reasoning

If only 60 per cent of seedlings survive, how many seedlings must be planted to obtain 660 trees?

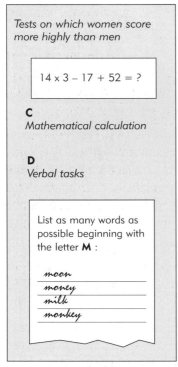

Tests on which women score more highly than men

$14 \times 3 - 17 + 52 = ?$

C
Mathematical calculation

D
Verbal tasks

List as many words as possible beginning with the letter **M** :

moon
money
milk
monkey

Examples of tasks in which men and women show different patterns of ability ▲

A and B above reproduced with permission of Jared Scheidman Design

studies of female infants exposed to excessive amounts of androgens. Female infants may be exposed to excessive amounts of androgens if their adrenal glands function improperly and produce more hormones than normal, or if their mothers are given hormones during pregnancy to reduce the risk of a miscarriage.

Money and Ehrhardt (1972) studied 25 genetic females aged 5–16 who had been exposed to high levels of hormones before birth. Of the 25 girls, 15 had defective adrenal glands. Ten had mothers who were given progesterone (which is chemically similar to testosterone). All 25 girls were born with masculinised external genitalia which were later corrected by surgery. The researchers interviewed both the girls and their mothers. In order to make comparisions, a control group of 25 normal girls was also studied. Compared to this control group, the girls who had been exposed to the hormones:

- had higher levels of physical activity
- preferred boys as playmates
- preferred boys' activities

In a similar experiment, Imperato-McGinley et al. (1979) studied a group of 18 genetic males who had suffered from a disorder which meant that their prenatal testosterone had not influenced the development of their male genitalia. As a result, the boys had been born looking like girls and were also raised as girls. However, at puberty, their testosterone had 'kicked in' and they had developed male genitalia.

Even though they had all been reared as girls, 16 of the 18 boys changed their gender identity at puberty and adopted a male gender role. According to the researchers, the boys were able to do this because their prenatal testosterone had already masculinised their brain. The researchers concluded that biology was more influential in developing male gender identity than environment.

Sex differences in the brain

Recent research indicates that there is little difference in the verbal and mathematical skills of men and women. But men and women do show different patterns of ability on certain types of tasks.

For example, on average men perform better on:

- spatial tasks which involve mental rotation (see example **A**)
- tasks which involve navigating their way through a route
- tasks which involve mathematical reasoning (see example **B**)

Women on average perform better on:

- tasks involving mathematical calculations (see example **C**)
- verbal tasks which involve finding words beginning with a specific letter (see example **D**)
- recalling landmarks from a route

For example, Galea (1991) asked participants to follow a route on a table-top map. Although men learned the route more quickly and made fewer errors, women were better at remembering the landmarks once they had been learned.

Silverman and Eals (1991) asked male and female participants to study a complex drawing which contained a number of objects. The participants were then presented with a second drawing which contained additional objects. The participants were asked to cross out any objects which were not present in the original drawing. They were also asked to circle any objects which had moved to a new position. Women performed better than men on this task.

One way to explain these differences is to compare the functions of particular areas of the brain in males and females. Previous research evidence has supported the view that in most people, the left hemisphere is responsible for language and the right hemisphere is responsible for spatial ability. One suggestion has been that women are left-hemisphere-dominant and men are right-hemisphere-dominant.

A more recent explanation is that males and females differ in the degree to which they use their hemispheres. For example, Bennett and Shaywitz (1995) gave male and female participants a number of tasks and scanned their brain activity using magnetic resonance imaging (see page 425). When carrying out a verbal task, males showed activity at the front of the left hemisphere. However, women participants showed signs of activity in their left *and* right hemispheres.

Other evidence which suggests that women and men vary in terms of hemispheres comes from research on the incidence of speech disorders or **aphasias**. Research has shown that speech disorders are more frequent in men than women after damage to the left hemisphere.

It has been argued that differences in men and women may be due to the **corpus callosum**, a thick bundle of nerves which allows the right hemisphere to communicate with the left hemisphere. Evidence suggests that the corpus callosum is larger in women than men. This could mean that in women, the two hemispheres communicate more effectively.

However, more recent research by Kimura (1992) provides a different explanation. Kimura found that women were more likely than men to suffer speech disorders when the *front* part of the brain is damaged. In men, speech disorders occur more frequently when the *rear* part of the brain is damaged, as shown in the table below.

Incidence of speech disorders resulting from brain injury		
	Front part of brain	*Rear part of brain*
Females	65%	12%
Males	29%	60%

According to Kimura, the reason that speech disorders occur in men after damage to the left hemisphere is not due to speech being based in

- *A number of factors make up the biological sex of a child. They include chromosomal make-up (either XX or XY), the production of appropriate sex hormones and the development of internal and external genitalia.*

- *Sex-linked traits are carried on the X and Y chromosomes. Examples of traits which are sex-linked are colour blindess and haemophilia. There is some evidence to suggest that spatial ability is sex-linked.*

the left hemisphere. Instead, Kimura points out that when there is restricted damage within a hemisphere, it is more likely to affect the back of the brain than the front. Damage in the rear part of the brain affects men more than it does women. Kimura concluded that men and women's brains are organised differently. She suggested that this is due to the influence of sex hormones early in life.

Evaluation of the biological approach

Strengths

+ The biological approach focuses on how the biological differences between males and females (chromosomal differences, hormonal differences) could account for gender differences.

Weaknesses

- Researchers are still not entirely clear how hormones affect and are affected by behaviour (Jacklin 1989)
- Some of the research on the effect of sex hormones is based on animal research. It is not clear how easy it is to generalise that research to humans.
- It is very difficult to measure hormone levels in humans before birth, and therefore hard to determine their effect on gender development.
- The biological approach plays down environmental influences on gender development and does not explain cultural variations in gender roles.

Summary

- There are a number of ways of explaining how children acquire the values and behaviour considered appropriate for their sex (called gender typing).
- The psychoanalytic approach focuses on identifying with the same-sex parent.
- The behavioural approach emphasises the role of observation, imitation, reinforcement and punishment.
- Cognitive developmental theory suggests that gender typing is linked to the child's cognitive development.
- The biological approach emphasises the influence of genes, hormones and differences in the structure and organisation of the male and female brain.

Overview of approaches to gender typing			
Approach	*Leading theorist*	*Key factors*	*Age/stage*
Psychoanalytic	Freud	Identification with the same-sex parent and successful resolution of the Oedipus and Electra complexes	occurs during the phallic stage (ages 3–5)
Behavioural	Mischel	Emphasises observation, imitation, reinforcement and punishment that children receive for gender-appropriate behaviour	focuses on the influence of role models, particularly same-sex models
Cognitive developmental	Kohlberg	Child strives to make sense of the social world; gender development is thought to be related to cognitive development	gender identity (2–5) gender stability (5–6) gender constancy (6–7)
Gender schema processing theory	Martin, Halverson, Markus, Bem	Child uses gender schemas to process information from their social world	No stages given
Biological	None	Gender differences are due to genes, hormones or differences in brain structure/ organisation	No stages given

12 Theories of Personality

Have you ever filled in a personality questionnaire in a magazine to find out what kind of personality you have? The word **personality** is part of our everyday language. We often say that someone has a 'great' personality, or that someone we don't like has 'no personality' – but what does the term mean to a psychologist?

Defining personality

According to Burnham (1930):

> 'What personality is everybody knows: but nobody can tell.'[10]

You may not be surprised to hear that psychologists have found it very difficult to agree on a precise definition of personality. There are at least two reasons for this:

- Personality is an internal, hidden quality which cannot be directly observed. Instead, we observe a person's behaviour and make assumptions about their personality based on their behaviour
- How personality is defined depends upon the psychologist's approach. Psychologists from the psychoanalytic approach have very different views about personality from humanistic psychologists.

A straightforward definition that we can agree to use is from Carole Tavris (1995). Tavris defines personality as the:

> 'distinctive and stable pattern(s) of behaviour, thoughts, motives and emotions which characterise a person.'[11]

This definition suggests that personality consists of the thoughts, actions and emotions which make each one of us a unique individual. Including the word 'stable' in the definition implies that while our moods may change rapidly within a short period of time, our personality remains broadly the same.

In this chapter we will look at the ways in which personality develops and how psychologists from different approaches have tried to define and measure the psychological construct we call 'personality'.

The development of personality

Any parent will tell you that although new-born infants may look alike, their personalities are very different! Some are generally happy and easy-going, while others are very restless and irritable. Since these temperamental differences are obvious at such an early age, they are unlikely to be the result of environmental influences. Many psychologists believe that differences in temperament are inherited and may be relatively stable throughout a person's life.

So what is the relationship between personality and temperament? The term **temperament** is used to refer to *general behavioural dispositions which are present in infancy and influence the way a person reacts to the environment*. Psychologists are interested in temperament for a number of reasons:

● Temperament can influence an infant's relationship with its carers
● Temperamental differences can develop into stable personality traits.

Studies of temperament

One of the earliest studies of temperament was carried out by Thomas et al. (1977). The researchers carried out a longitudinal study of 136 children from infancy to adolescence, observing each child's behaviour and conducting interviews with the mothers. On the basis of the descriptions of the child's behaviour, the researchers were able to identify the nine different aspects of temperament shown below:

1 activity level
2 regularity of hunger and sleep
3 extent to which the child was distracted by environmental stimuli
4 how the child responded to a new object or person
5 adaptability
6 attention span
7 intensity of emotional reaction
8 intensity of stimulation needed to cause a response
9 quality of mood

Each child was rated **high**, **medium** or **low** on each of the nine aspects, and the researchers were able to produce a behavioural profile for each child. On the basis of the profiles, the researchers were able to categorise the children's temperaments into one of three types:

● **easy** children

● **difficult** children

● **slow-to-warm-up** children

Easy children, who made up 40% of the sample, were able to adapt to new experiences and were generally happy. **Difficult** children (10% of the sample) were fussy and tended to withdraw from new experiences. Difficult children also showed intense reactions. **Slow-to-warm-up**

An easy child ▲

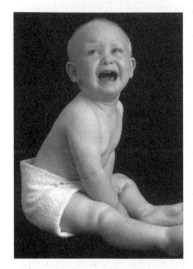

A difficult child ▲

A slow-to-warm-up child ▲

children made up 15% of the sample. Initially these children withdrew from new situations, but eventually they adapted to them. However, they tended to respond to stimuli with low levels of intensity.

The profiles of the other children in the sample (about a third of the total) could not be placed into any one of the three types.

What are the practical implications of this research? One suggestion is that parents should use parenting styles which match the child's temperament. For example, difficult children may need patient parents who respond to the child in a consistent way. Easy children may thrive with a variety of parenting styles. Slow-to-warm-up children need to be able to adjust to change at their own pace and so may benefit from encouragement mixed with patience.

Buss and Plomin's temperamental model

Buss and Plomin (1984) identified three **dispositions** or temperaments:

- **activity**: general level of energy

- **emotionality**: intensity of the child's emotional reaction

- **sociability**: tendency to want to be with other people

Buss and Plomin carried out a number of twin studies in which parents were asked to rate their children according to the three temperaments. The research included both identical twins (**monozygotic** twins) and fraternal twins (**dizygotic** twins). They found that identical twins (i.e. twins who shared the same genes) were more similar in their levels of activity, emotionality and sociability than fraternal twins. The results suggested that heredity played an important role in determining the level of these three characteristics.

Inhibited and uninhibited children

Studies carried out by Kagan et al. (1991) suggest that an important temperamental difference between infants is the degree to which they are **inhibited** or **uninhibited**. Research in developmental psychology has shown that infants who are passive and cautious in new situations develop into adults who are shy and somewhat anxious. According to Kagan's research:

- inhibited children are controlled, restrained, may cling to parents in new situations and are slow in exploring new objects or toys

- uninhibited children are more confident in new situations and in exploring new objects; they also tend to play in a more spontaneous way than uninhibited children.

Kagan found that inhibited children are not frightened of everything. Their anxiety is *specific* to new environments, unfamiliar people and challenging situations. Kagan refers to this as **anxiety to novelty**. Kagan and his colleagues also suggest that these differences in temperament have a biological basis. For example, uninhibited and inhibited children show a number of physical differences at birth, including body build and

▲ *An 'inhibited' child is reluctant to explore a new environment*

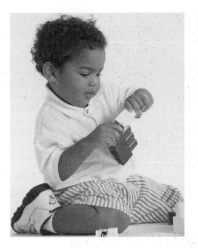

▲ *An 'uninhibited' child is keen to sample new experiences*

In summary

- *Temperament refers to general behavioural dispositions which are present in infancy and affect how the person responds to the environment.*

- *Thomas and Chess (1977) found that most children could be categorised as difficult, easy or slow-to-warm-up.*

- *Buss and Plomin (1971) identified three temperaments: activity, emotionality and sociability. They found that identical twins were more similar in temperament than fraternal twins.*

- *Kagan et al. (1991) suggested that children differ in terms of how inhibited or uninhibited they are.*

- *Temperaments can often develop into stable personality traits*

susceptibility to allergies. Infants who in the first few days of life show an increase in pupil dilation and heart rate when presented with unfamiliar stimuli are more likely to be identified as inhibited children. They are also more likely to have problems sleeping and are more irritable than uninhibited children.

These differences in temperament do seem to be stable over time. Reznick et al. (1986) measured how children responded to unfamiliar situations when they were 21 months old and again when they were aged 4. Finally, when the children were five and a half years old, their behaviour was observed in a number of situations. The researchers were particularly interested in:

- the children's activity level
- how likely they were to approach or play with new toys
- how often they looked at the experimenter
- how likely they were to explore a new environment

The researchers found that children who were inhibited at 21 months and age 4 showed the same pattern of behaviour at age 5.

Type and trait theories of personality

Type theories of personality

The idea that people could be divided into 'types' goes back to the time of the early Greeks. A **type** can be defined as one of a limited number of categories that a person may belong to. These categories are usually independent of each other – i.e. you can belong to only one category. Hippocrates, who lived around 400 BC, believed that people could be classified into one of four temperament types:

Temperament type	Characteristics
Choleric	Irritable
Phlegmatic	Calm, easy-going
Melancholic	sad or depressed
Sanguine	optimistic

According to Hippocrates, a person's 'type' depended on the balance of the **four humours**. These humours were bodily fluids and included blood, phlegm, yellow bile and black bile. For example, a melancholic person had too much black bile. The idea behind such a type theory is that a person fits into one or other category.

THINK ABOUT IT

Think of people that you know. Could any of them be classified as **choleric**, **phlegmatic**, **melancholic** or **sanguine**?

Body types

Another example of a type theory was proposed by Sheldon (1942). Sheldon believed that a person's personality was related to their **body type** or physique. According to Sheldon, there were three body types:

- endomorphy
- mesomorphy
- ectomorphy

The characteristics of each body type are shown below.

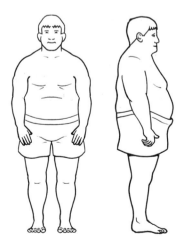

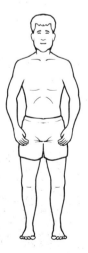

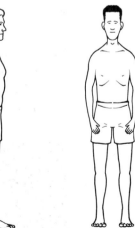

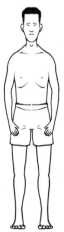

Endomorphs are soft and round and put on fat easily

Mesomorphs are strong and muscular

Ectomorphs are thin and lightly muscled

Very conveniently, Sheldon also suggested that there were three corresponding temperament types:

- **viscerotonia**: being easy-going, loving food and comfort
- **somatotonia**: enjoys physical activity and likes to take risks
- **cerebrotonia**: being inhibited and somewhat restrained.

The body types were related to the temperament types as follows:

Body type	Corresponding temperament type
Endomorph	Viscerotonia
Mesomorph	Somatotonia
Ectomorph	Cerebrotonia

Sheldon's research involved assessing the temperament type and body type of over 200 men. However, his sample was limited to white male university students, and was not representative. It is also possible that Sheldon biased the ratings of his participants because he knew the aim of the study.

Type A and Type B personalities

A more recent example of a type theory is the work by Friedman and Rosenman (*1974*) on **Type A** and **Type B** personalities. Friedman and Rosenman were not psychologists but cardiologists working with heart patients. They noticed that a lot of patients who had suffered heart attacks had similar personalities.

Friedman and Rosenman found that **Type A** personalities tended to have three personality characteristics in common:

- being competitive and achievement-oriented
- having a sense of urgency and always being in a hurry
- feeling angry and hostile

In contrast, **Type B** personalities had lower levels of competition, were less worried about time and had less hostility. The researchers found that a Type A personality was more than twice as likely to suffer a heart attack as a Type B personality.

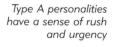

Some people are able to cope comfortably with a number of different tasks simultaneously

Type A personalities have a sense of rush and urgency

Evaluation of type theories

Strengths

+ The idea of categorising people into types can be very appealing because it is a simple and neat approach to personality.

Weaknesses

– Other psychologists like Hampson (1988) have pointed out that categorising a person as being one type or another is somewhat artifical in that most of us differ in the degree to which we possess a certain trait. Also, being forced into one category or another oversimplifies the complexity of human personality and does not allow for people who may have characteristics of several types.

TRY THIS

Answer the following questions with **Yes** or **No** to see if you have a tendency towards a **Type A** personality.

Questions	Your response
● Do you tend to do more than one thing at a time?	....
● Do you often urge others to hurry up and finish what they are saying?	....
● Do you 'play to win' at games?	....
● Do you get impatient if you have to wait in a queue?	....
● Do you tend to get involved in lots of projects at the same time?	....
● Do you have a strong desire to get on in life and impress people?	....

If you answered **Yes** to most of these questions you may have the characteristics of a **Type A** personality.

In summary

- *Type theories of personality attempt to place people in a limited number of categories.*

- *Sheldon suggested that personality was related to the individual's body type or physique. He identified three temperament types: viscerotonia, somatotonia and cerebrotonia.*

- *Friedman and Rosenman identified Type A and Type B personalities.*

Trait theories of personality

According to trait theories the fundamental building blocks of personality are **traits**. For example, when we say that Bhavna is 'friendly' or that Chris is 'aggressive', we are using traits to describe their personality. A trait is defined as *a relatively stable and enduring aspect of personality*. A person's traits predispose him/her to behave in a certain way.

The idea behind trait theories is that a person's personality is simply a combination of traits. Unlike type theories, which aim to place individuals in one category or other, trait theories suggest that we all share the same kinds of traits, but that some of us have more of a particular trait than others. Therefore differences in personality are due either to differences in the number of traits that a person possesses or the way in which traits are combined.

The trait approach to personality is based on two assumptions:

- that personality characteristics are relatively stable over time

- that an individual's personality remains consistent in different situations.

Allport's trait theory

One of the first psychologists to emphasise the trait approach to personality was Gordon Allport (1897–1967). Allport believed that the only way to study personality was to focus on each individual's unique traits. For this reason he is referred to as an **idiographic** theorist.

Allport believed that the best way to study personality was to use personal documents such as diaries and letters. He published a series of letters written by a woman called Jenny in which she describes her relationship with her son Ross. Some of the letters are written to Ross's friends. Allport presented his students with parts of these letters and asked them to provide a description of Jenny's personality. (An activity using two of Jenny's letters appears on page 154.)

Traits and dispositions

Allport believed that traits were the building blocks of personality. He identified and described three different types of traits which he categorised in order of importance to the person:

- In some cases, one particular trait can be so dominant that almost all of a person's behaviour can be traced to it. These traits Allport called **cardinal** traits. However, Allport believed that most people do not have cardinal traits.

- Allport's second type were **central** traits. In order to understand what he meant by this, make a list of the traits which you think best describe your personality. You should be able to list between five to ten traits. Allport would argue that the traits that you have listed are your central traits. Central traits are the traits which 'stand out' in a person's personality and influence their behaviour in a variety of settings.

- Finally, **secondary dispositions** are less consistent traits which may only apply in certain situations. For example, we may have a central trait of friendliness which is expressed in our behaviour. However, we may also have a secondary disposition of being arrogant which we may display in some situations but not in others.

TRY THIS

In order to understand Allport's approach, read the following parts of Jenny's letters. After you have read them, write down five characteristics which you think describe Jenny's personality.

Letter 1

'Ross brought this same woman and her brat to my house one Sunday evening and I was angry and told him if he ever brought any more prostitutes to my house I would have them both arrested. Anyone short of a fool would know what she was at one glance...

Letter 2

'Anyway, I am firmly convinced that I am "through" and ought to step out. I have done all, of any use, that it is possible for me to do in this world. Whether it was for good or bad it is over and done and nothing can change it now ... I should step out, but am a coward. To suppose that Ross needs me now would be a joke...'

After you have written your list of characteristics, compare them to the list at the end of the chapter which was based on a computer analysis of Jenny's letters.

1 How accurate were you at describing Jenny?
2 Describe one **advantage** and one **disadvantage** of using personal documents to study someone's personality.

Source:
Allport, G.W., *Letters from Jenny* (Harcourt Brace Jovanovich, New York, 1965)

▲

Evaluation of Allport

Strengths

+ However, Allport's work has made psychologists appreciate that understanding personality is a very complicated issue since all individuals are unique.

Weaknesses

– Many psychologists have criticised Allport's idiographic approach to personality since it focuses on the individual but tells us very little about people in general.
– Mischel (1968) has argued that traits do not predispose us to behave in certain ways. Psychological research has shown that individuals show very little consistency in their behaviour across different situations.

Other trait theorists: Cattell and Eysenck

Although both Raymond Cattell and Hans Eysenck can also be considered as trait theorists, they are different from Allport in two important ways:

- Cattell and Eysenck prefer the **nomothetic** approach to personality
- They both use **factor analysis** in their research.

The **nomothetic** approach to personality is concerned with discovering general laws of personality rather than focusing on the uniqueness of each individual. This can mean that it is easier to apply the results to people in general.

Cattell and Eysenck used **factor analysis** to help them identify the basic traits of personality. Factor analysis is a mathematical technique which helps to determine 'what goes with what'. The best way to think of factor analysis is as a sophisticated type of correlation which helps to identify relationships between different factors. Cattell and Eysenck use factor analysis to help them reduce large amounts of complex data into a simpler form.

Cattell (1905–) was originally trained as a chemist, and this has influenced his approach to personality. For Cattell, 'science demands measurement' and the study of personality demands the type of objective measurement used in science. Regarding personality as a complex structure of traits, Cattell's goal has been to try and identify the basic elements of personality in much the same way as a chemist would try and identify the basic elements of a compound.

Cattell began by trying to determine how many personality traits there are. This was not easy since earlier psychologists had identified literally hundreds of different traits. Clearly, there needed to be some agreement about which traits were most important, so Cattell grouped together those traits which were related to each other and separated those traits that appeared to be independent. He then used factor analysis to help identify the basic structure of personality.

'L', 'Q' and 'T' data

Cattell used three different types of data:

- '**L**' or **life record data** includes school reports, employer references and ratings of the person by family or close friends. It provides information about the person's behaviour based on other people's observations.

- With '**Q**' or **questionnaire data**, the person describes their own behaviour or feelings through a questionnaire or interview. 'Q' data provides a measure of how the person sees him/herself.

- '**T**' or **objective test data** involves recording the person's behaviour in a controlled situation such as a laboratory experiment and observing how they respond. It could involve taking physiological measurements such as heart-rate.

A school report is an example of 'L' data ▲

A job interview will provide 'Q' data ▲

A laboratory experiment or controlled test provides 'T' data ▲

Using these three types of data, Cattell was able to identify two types of traits which he called **source traits** and **surface traits**.

● **Surface traits** may be responses to certain items on a questionnaire or specific behaviours. They are usually traits that other people can see or observe. For example, if you see someone smiling and chatting at a party you can assume that they have a surface trait of being sociable.

People seen chatting at a party may be assumed to have the surface trait of being 'sociable' ▲

● **Source traits** are more difficult to describe since they cannot be directly inferred from behaviour. Source traits are the factors which shape and direct our behaviour and may interact with each other to form surface traits. Cattell identified 16 source traits which he believed were the primary personality factors. The **16PF** or **Sixteen Personality Factors** questionnaire was developed by Cattell to measure these major source traits.

The 16PF has important practical applications – for example, in business it is widely used for helping managers select employees. Cattell also developed over 100 profiles describing the ideal traits for various jobs, including nurse, teacher and airline pilot (see page 158). The 16PF has also been used in clinical psychology for diagnosing people with certain behavioural problems.

Evaluation of Cattell

Strengths

+ Cattell emphasised the importance of trying to measure personality in an objective way. This makes his theory easier to test.
+ The 16PF is a successful psychometric test which has been used in industry for selecting employees.

Weaknesses

− Cattell has not been entirely successful in identifying the major traits of personality. He may have overestimated the number of personality traits. More recent research has suggested that there are not sixteen but five basic personality traits. Cattell has responded to this criticism as follows:

TRY THIS

Listed below are Cattell's **16 source traits**. In order to appreciate how the **16PF** works to produce a personality profile, place a dot in each box according to how much of each factor you think you have. When you have finished, join up the dots. This will create your own personality profile. Just in case you are not sure what all the words mean, some of them are defined below.

Low score								***High score***
Description								*Description*
Reserved	☐	☐	☐	☐	☐	☐	☐	Outgoing
Less intelligent	☐	☐	☐	☐	☐	☐	☐	More intelligent
Emotional	☐	☐	☐	☐	☐	☐	☐	Stable
Submissive	☐	☐	☐	☐	☐	☐	☐	Dominant
Serious	☐	☐	☐	☐	☐	☐	☐	Happy-go-lucky
Expedient	☐	☐	☐	☐	☐	☐	☐	Conscientious
Timid	☐	☐	☐	☐	☐	☐	☐	Venturesome
Tough-minded	☐	☐	☐	☐	☐	☐	☐	Sensitive
Trusting	☐	☐	☐	☐	☐	☐	☐	Suspicious
Practical	☐	☐	☐	☐	☐	☐	☐	Imaginative
Forthright	☐	☐	☐	☐	☐	☐	☐	Shrewd
Self-assured	☐	☐	☐	☐	☐	☐	☐	Apprehensive
Conservative	☐	☐	☐	☐	☐	☐	☐	Experimenting
Group-dependent	☐	☐	☐	☐	☐	☐	☐	Self-sufficient
Uncontrolled	☐	☐	☐	☐	☐	☐	☐	Controlled
Relaxed	☐	☐	☐	☐	☐	☐	☐	Tense

Definitions

Expedient   doing whatever is most suitable or most advantageous, perhaps disregarding rules

Tough-minded   being able to rely on yourself and being realistic about things

Conservative   respecting traditional values

Source:
Cattell, R., 'Advances in Cattellian Personality Theory' in Pervin, L.A., *Handbook of Personality* (Guildford Publications, New York, 1990). Reproduced with permission.

'... psychologists find 16 factors too many to learn about. One of the first tasks in a course on personality should be to learn the names and natures of these 16PF source traits. If psychology students balk at this, one might remind them that medical students learn hundreds of new names, that chemists know over 100 elements and that astronomers have discovered a nameless number of galaxies. Where do psychology students come from who find 3 or 4 factors all they can use to describe personality?'[12]

Personality profile of Canadian airline pilots based on Cattell's 'Sixteen Personality Factors' questionnaire ▶

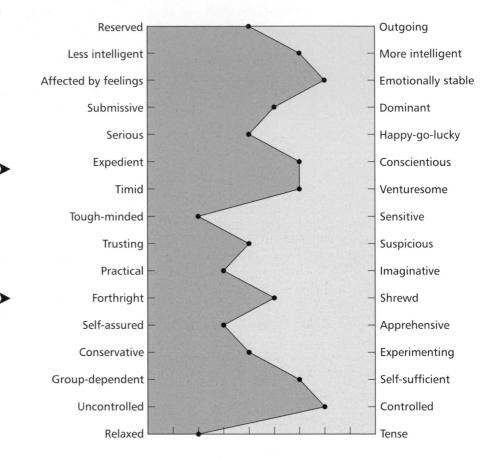

Source: Weiten, W., & Lloyd, M., *Psychology Applied to Modern Life: adjustment in the 90s*, 4th edn (Wadsworth Publishing). Reprinted with permission. ▶

Reserved		Outgoing
Less intelligent		More intelligent
Affected by feelings		Emotionally stable
Submissive		Dominant
Serious		Happy-go-lucky
Expedient		Conscientious
Timid		Venturesome
Tough-minded		Sensitive
Trusting		Suspicious
Practical		Imaginative
Forthright		Shrewd
Self-assured		Apprehensive
Conservative		Experimenting
Group-dependent		Self-sufficient
Uncontrolled		Controlled
Relaxed		Tense

Eysenck's theory of personality

Like the trait theorists described above, **Hans Eysenck** (1916–98) was concerned with discovering the underlying structure of personality. However, Eysenck believed that there is a **genetic basis** to personality and that individual differences in personality have a physiological dimension. Eysenck argued this case for nearly 40 years, and recent research seems to lend support for his theory.

Unlike Cattell, who suggested that there are 16 major source traits, Eysenck proposed just three basic dimensions of personality:

● **extraversion–introversion** – the degree to which a person is outgoing and sociable or quiet and reserved
● **neuroticism** – refers to being anxious or moody
● **psychoticism** – refers to being aggressive or hostile

For Eysenck, the units of personality are arranged in a hierarchy. At the bottom is the **specific response level**. This refers to an act or response that occurs in a single instance. For example, if you observe someone being very lively and energetic at a social gathering, this could just be 'one-off' behaviour. However, if the person is *always* the life and soul of a party, then it is reasonable to talk of a habit or habitual response – the second level in the hierarchy.

If you also know that this person is lively and outgoing at work as well as at parties, you may assume this person is exhibiting the trait of liveliness. In Eysenck's model, this is known as the **trait level**.

Finally, Eysenck believed that certain traits are often associated with other traits – for example the trait of liveliness may be linked with sociability and impulsiveness. Together, these traits make up a **dimension**, or **supertrait**, of personality known as **extraversion**.

Each level of Eysenck's hierarchy provides us with a different kind of information. Level 1 is usually very specific, while Level 4 is very general.

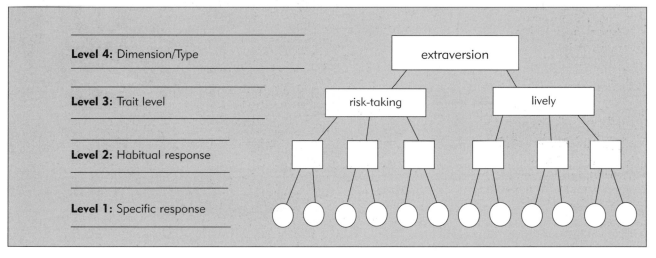

Don't be confused by the fact that Eysenck refers to extraversion as a 'type' in the diagram above. He was not using the word in the same way as a type theorist – i.e. to suggest that people fit into an 'extraversion type' or 'neurotic type'. Instead, he believed that we all have varying degrees of each of these dimensions within our personality.

What shaped Eysenck's outlook?

How did Eysenck arrive at the idea that personality is made up of three dimensions or types? During World War II, Eysenck studied 700 soldiers who were suffering from mental disturbances. He had access to detailed case studies of each patient. He selected items from the case studies such as symptoms and personal background, and subjected them to factor analysis. On the basis of the factor analysis, he isolated two factors, each of which consisted of a number of traits. These two factors he named **extraversion–introversion** and **neuroticism**. He later added the third type, **psychoticism**.

Eysenck argued that extraversion–introversion and neuroticism were independent of each other. In other words, someone who scores high on extraversion could score high or low on neuroticism. The diagram below shows the different traits associated with extraversion–intraversion and neuroticism.

Traits associated with extraversion and neuroticism ▶

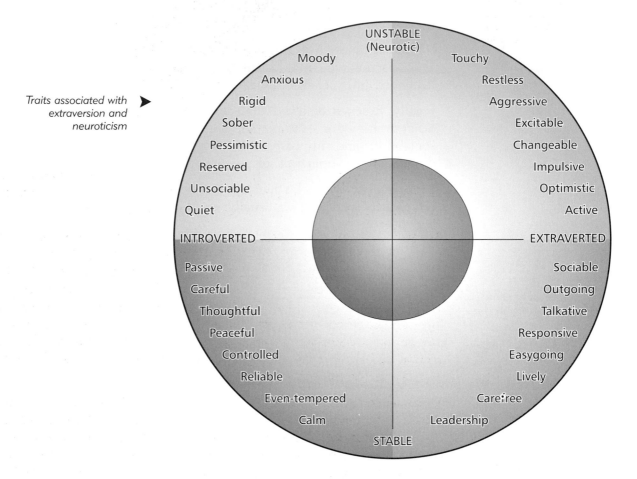

In effect, Eysenck is saying that extraversion–introversion and neuroticism are two independent dimensions of personality. But what determines a person's level of extraversion–introversion? According to Eysenck:

> 'Personality is determined by a large extent by a person's genes … while environment can do something to redress the balance, its influence is severely limited.'[13]

Eysenck believed that there is a physiological basis for extraversion–introversion, and that extraverts and introverts differ from each other in the level of functioning of a part of the brain called the **reticular activation system (RAS)**. The function of the RAS is to activate higher parts of the brain. The RAS is not a specific brain structure. It is a brain system whose cell bodies are located in the brain stem and project to many parts of the cortex.

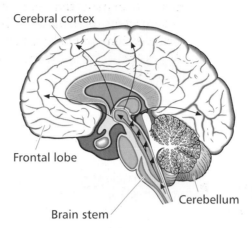

Cerebral cortex

Frontal lobe

Brain stem

Cerebellum

Diagram of the human brain, showing how the cell bodies of the RAS project to different areas of the cortex ▶

The RAS helps to maintain concentration and alertness. When we feel awake and perky, our RAS is functioning at a high level. When we feel tired and lacking in energy, the RAS is functioning at a low level.

According to Eysenck, introverts have higher levels of RAS functioning than extraverts. This has several implications. First, it means that introverts should be able to concentrate for longer periods than extraverts. Secondly, since introverts have a high internal level of arousal, they may avoid situations in the external world which might 'over-arouse' them. Introverts are said to be 'stimulus-shy'. Extraverts on the other hand are 'stimulus-hungry'. Since their internal level of arousal is low, extraverts need to seek extra stimulation from the external environment.

This may sound reasonable enough – but is it true? Is there any research evidence to support Eysenck's theory? Stelmack (1990) found that extraverts and introverts did not show any differences in brainwave activity when asleep or at rest. However, when exposed to stimulation such as loud music, introverts were more likely to become aroused.

Other studies have been carried out to see if extraverts and introverts differ in their levels of concentration. One approach was to ask participants to carry out **vigilance tasks** in which they had to maintain their attention for long periods of time. Claridge (1967) asked extraverts and introverts to listen to a long series of numbers and press a button whenever they heard three odd numbers in a row. Claridge found that introverts were more likely to spot the odd numbers and were also more physiologically aroused.

But what about the other dimensions of personality, such as neuroticism? Eysenck also believed that there is a physiological basis for neuroticism which involves the **autonomic nervous system (ANS)**. The autonomic nervous system controls internal organs such as the heart, bladder and stomach. For example, if you come across something that really frightens you such as a spider or snake, your heart may start to pound as your body prepares for 'fight or flight'. This is your ANS at work. According to Eysenck, people who score high on neuroticism tend to have strong emotional responses to the things that happen to them. This may be because their autonomic nervous systems respond quickly and strongly to situations.

Harvey and Hirschmann (1980) used Eysenck's Personality Questionnaire to measure extraversion and neuroticism. Participants were shown colour slides of people who died violently and their heart-rates were recorded. The researchers found that participants who had the highest heart-rate were:

- participants who scored low on extraversion
- participants who scored high on neuroticism

The results support the idea that people with high scores on neuroticism tend to have strong emotional responses to stimuli.

What is psychoticism?

As early as 1952, Eysenck had referred to the need to add a third dimension of personality. However, despite this, Eysenck admitted that there is less research on psychoticism than on the other dimensions of personality.

There has been a great deal of debate about the nature of psychoticism. Eysenck described a person who scores high on psychoticism as:

> 'solitary, not caring for people … he may be cruel and inhumane … he is hostile to others and aggressive even to loved ones …'[14]

Even more debate has centred on what *causes* psychoticism. Early research suggested significant differences in psychoticism between males and females. Females tended to show lower levels of psychoticism at all ages. Eysenck proposed that the physiological basis for psychoticism could be hormonal differences, in particular the male hormone, testosterone. However, more recently it has been suggested that the breakdown of certain neurotransmitters and enzymes may have an important part to play.

Research with 58 male participants showed that impulsivity and aggressiveness were negatively correlated with the activity of a particular enzyme called monamine oxidase. The question 'Do you often do things on the spur of the moment?' produced the following type of answers among the participants:

Source: Schalling, P., Edman, G., Asberg, M. and Oreland, L., 'Platelet MAO Activity Associated with Impulsivity and Aggressivity', in *Personality and Individual Differences*, 9 (1988), pp.597–606

Enzyme levels of participant	Percentage answering Yes
Low levels	83
Intermediate levels	41
High levels	8

In summary

- *Trait theorists believe traits are the building blocks of personality and predispose people to behave in certain ways.*

- *Allport identified three different types of traits: cardinal, central and secondary dispositions.*

- *Cattell used 'L', 'Q' and 'T' data to study personality.*

- *Cattell used factor analysis to identify 'source traits' and 'surface traits'.*

- *According to Cattell, there are 16 different source traits which can be measured using the 16PF.*

- *Eysenck identified three dimensions of personality: extraversion–introversion, neuroticism and psychoticism.*

The results indicate that low levels of this particular enzyme are associated with high levels of impulsivity. Eysenck concludes that psychoticism may be related to levels of the enzyme and/or levels of testosterone.

Although the discussion about the nature and origin of psychoticism seems somewhat vague, research has indicated that the 'P' scale (the part of the Personality Questionnaire that measures psychoticism) has its uses. According to Davis (1974) the 'P' scale is very good at identifying a whole range of antisocial people and evaluating their levels of aggressiveness, emotionality and impulsivity.

Evaluation of Eysenck

Strengths
+ According to more recent research, Eysenck identified at least two of the major dimensions of personality, including extraversion–introversion and neuroticism.
+ Eysenck had some success in arguing the physiological basis of personality, especially for extraversion–introversion.
+ Like Cattell, Eysenck tried to study personality in a scientific, objective way. He attempted to bring aspects of experimental psychology into the study of personality.
+ Eysenck's work has functioned as a heuristic device, i.e. it has stimulated an enormous amount of research by other people.

Weaknesses
– Other research suggests that the relationship between extraversion–introversion and task performance is more complicated than it appears. Factors such as the time of day when the task is performed and the type of task have also been found to be important variables.

The five-factor model of personality

In the previous section we saw how different psychologists have tried to describe the structure of personality by identifying basic traits. Cattell believes that 16 factors are necessary to describe personality, while Eysenck maintained that there are three dimensions of personality. More recent research seems to suggest that there are just five factors of personality, often referred to as the **Big Five**. The problem is that different psychologists have all identified slightly different factors. Hence psychologists may refer to the five-factor model as '*Which* Big Five' or '*Whose* Big Five'! However, out of this confusion some sort of consensus appears to be emerging.

The five-factor model represents an attempt to integrate previous trait theories of personality. The model consists of five broad dimensions of personality. Within each dimension are more specific traits or facets which define each dimension. Although the first 'Big Five' model was proposed in the 1960s (Tupes 1961; Norman 1963), the most popular version is by McCrae and Costa (1989). The table below shows the five dimensions as well as some of the facets, or more specific traits, associated with each dimension:

Factor	Dimension	Facets
1	Extraversion	talkative, sociable
2	Agreeableness	warm, good-natured
3	Conscientiousness	dependable, ethical
4	Neuroticism	anxious, insecure
5	Openness to experience	non-conforming, imaginative

Support for the 'Big Five' comes from many studies carried out in different countries. Also, longitudinal studies carried out on both men and women suggest that these traits are stable in a person over time. But how does the 'Big Five' model compare to the models developed by Eysenck and Cattell?

According to Eysenck, the five-factor model does not represent an improvement upon his own three–factor system. However, a closer look at the two models shows there is some overlap. For example, Eysenck's dimensions of extraversion and neuroticism are similar to Factor 1 and Factor 4.

Where do Cattell's 16 personality factors fit in? Again, there is some overlap. Cattell's factors of 'being suspicious', 'shy', 'affected by feelings', 'apprehensive' and 'tense' are similar to some of the traits covered by the factor neuroticism. Cattell's factors of 'reserved' and 'happy-go-lucky' are similar to traits covered by the factor extraversion.

So a close comparison between previous models and the 'Big Five' model does reveal some similarities.

Theorists such as Cattell and Allport argue that traits are relatively stable qualities which predispose people to behave in certain ways. In the late 1960s, the concept of a trait came under some criticism from behaviourists. Firstly, it was argued that traits are not directly observable. Secondly, behaviourists argued that situations were more important than traits in determining behaviour. They produced research evidence to show that people did not behave in a consistent way in different situations.

However, the 'Big Five' model seems to have re-established the importance of traits in the study of personality. According to one psychologist:

> 'traits are not only alive and well, they are beginning to take their rightful place at the very heart of psychology as a science.'[15]

● *The 'Big Five' model of personality suggests that there are five factors or dimensions of personality: 'extraversion', 'agreeableness', 'conscientiousness', 'neuroticism' and 'openness to experience'.*

● *There is overlap between the five-factor model and the traits identified by Cattell and Eysenck.*

Evaluation of the 'Big Five' model

Strengths

+ The 'Big Five' model has produced a useful synthesis (pulling together) of earlier theories.

+ The five-factor model has several important practical applications for clinical psychology. It has been suggested that measuring a person on the five factors should be the first step in carrying out a psychological assessment. Also, the five-factor model may be helpful in diagnosing certain personality disorders. Finally, knowing a person's position on the five factors can help predict the likelihood of success in therapy. For example, a person who scores low on the factor of 'agreeableness' may be less willing to co-operate with a therapist, and therapeutic progress may be slower as a result (McCrae, Costa, 1989).

Weaknesses

– There is still disagreement about the nature of the five factors. The last factor, 'openness to experience', has stimulated much debate. Other researchers have labelled this factor 'culture' or 'intellect'.

– Not all the research supports the five-factor model. Some researchers claim to find more than five factors, others less.

The humanistic approach to personality

The humanistic approach to personality developed in the 1950s as a reaction against behaviourism and the psychoanalytic approach. The humanists felt that psychology had been dominated for too long by these two approaches and that it was time to focus on the more positive aspects of human nature. Humanism promised to be a progressive **third force** in psychology, emphasising our potential for personal growth.

The main theorists associated with the humanistic approach are:

● Abraham Maslow (1908–70)
● Carl Rogers (1902–87)

Unlike Freud, who believed that human beings were dominated by instinct, humanistic psychologists have a very positive view of human nature. Humanism is based on the following assumptions:

● **Personal growth:** humanistic psychologists reject the idea that our sole concern is to satisfy our immediate needs. Instead, we are motivated towards becoming the 'best' that we can be and have an innate need to fulfil our own potential. This idea is expressed by the term **self-actualisation**.

● **Personal responsibility:** Humanists believe that each of us has the power to decide our own actions and determine our own destiny.

● **Focus on the 'here and now':** Unlike the psychodynamic approach which emphasises the importance of past experiences, humanistic psychologists prefer to focus on the present. They believe that we should learn to live our lives as they happen and not be imprisoned by our past.

Maslow's Hierarchy of Needs

Abraham Maslow's key contributions to humanism are his emphasis on the healthy personality and his theory of the **hierarchy of needs**.

Consider for a moment the needs of a person in today's society who has a secure job and no financial worries. This person may be concerned about 'where their life is going' and 'what it all means'. They may go to art-appreciation or creative writing classes in order to be intellectually stimulated. Compare them with someone who has no job and is worried about where their next meal is coming from. Maslow pointed out that these two people have quite different needs.

Maslow identified two different types of needs or motives. The first type he called **deficiency needs**. These are the result of a *lack* of some necessary object like food, water or shelter. Secondly, there are **growth needs**, such as the need to satisfy our intellectual or cognitive needs and fulfil our own potential. The key point is that growth needs can only be satisfied if deficiency needs are (at least partially) met first.

Maslow organised the different types of needs into a hierarchy or pyramid like the one shown below. He believed that needs lower down in the hierarchy had to be met before needs higher up could be satisfied.

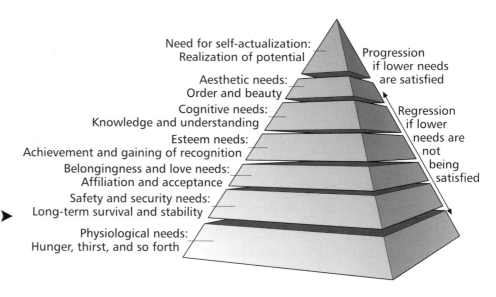

Maslow's Hierarchy of Needs

Maslow was also interested in studying the nature of the healthy personality. He believed that people who had very healthy personalities were self-actualisers.

In an attempt to identify examples of 'self-actualised' personalities, Maslow carried out interviews and studied the biographies of historical figures, including Albert Einstein, William James and Abraham Lincoln. Some of the characteristics which self-actualisers are supposed to have include being problem-centred (as opposed to self-centred), being concerned for the human race, having 'peak experiences' and having strong moral and ethical standards. (Peak experiences, according to Maslow, involve a sense of wonder and a feeling of unity with the universe).

TRY THIS

How do you know whether you are a self-actualiser or not? To see how self-actualised you are, read the following statements. For each statement, indicate the extent to which the statement describes you. Use the following scoring method:

1 if you completely disagree with the statement
2 if you disagree somewhat
3 if you agree somewhat
4 if you completely agree with the statement

Statements   *Score*

 1   I am not ashamed of any of my emotions.   ....
 2   I feel I must do what other people expect of me.   ....
 3   I believe that people are basically good and can be trusted.   ....
 4   I can be angry at people I love.   ....
 5   It is essential that other people approve of what I do.   ....
 6   I find it difficult to accept my own weaknesses.   ....
 7   I can like people without having to approve of them.   ....
 8   I am frightened of failure.   ....
 9   I avoid analysing or simplifying complex things.   ....
10   It is much better to be yourself than to be popular.   ....
11   I am not dedicated to any particular aim in life.   ....
12   I can express my feelings even if they result in undesirable   ....
     consequences.
13   I do not feel responsible to help anybody.   ....
14   I worry about being inadequate.   ....
15   I am able to give love because I am loved.   ....

Scoring

To obtain your self-actualisation score:

● Add up the scores you have given for items 1, 3, 4, 7, 10, 12, and 15.
● For the rest of the items you need to reverse the scoring method. So if you have **disagreed** with any of the remaining items, instead of giving yourself a score of **1**, give yourself **4** (1 = 4, 2 = 3, 3 = 2, 4 = 1).
● Add up the total for all the items. The result is your self-actualisation score. The higher the score, the more self-actualised you are supposed to be.

Adapted from Jones, A., & Crandell, R., 'Validation of a Short Index of Self-Actualisation', in *Personality and Social Psychology Bulletin*, 12, (1986) pp.63–73

Evaluation of Maslow

Strengths

+ Maslow emphasised that psychology should also include the study of healthy personalities. Many previous theorists, such as Freud, had tended to focus on people with emotional problems.
+ Maslow , like Allport and other idiographic theorists, focused on the subjective experience of the individual.
+ Maslow's Hierarchy of Needs has been used in management theory as a means of understanding how to motivate employees.

Weaknesses

– Critics have argued that Maslow's Hierarchy of Needs is very difficult to test scientifically.
– Critics have also pointed out that Maslow's concept of self-actualisation was based on what *he* thought healthy personalities should be like, and that his theory is somewhat subjective.

Rogers's theory of personality

Rogers is probably best known for the development of **client-centred therapy,** which is a method of treating people with emotional problems. Like Freud, Rogers developed his theory of personality out of his clinical experiences with his clients (notice that Rogers called them *'clients'* while to Freud they were *'patients'*). However, unlike Freud, Rogers did not develop a stage theory of personality development. Instead, he was interested in how the evaluations we receive from other people (such as parents) influence our self-concept and development.

The **self** is one of the most important concepts in Rogers's theory. According to Rogers, the self is made up of all the feelings, beliefs and thoughts that we have about ourselves. It refers to how we see ourselves as individuals and in relation to others. Rogers also defined the **ideal self**, which is our perception of what we feel we *should* be like.

The 'Q' sort

Rogers found that at the beginning of therapy many of his clients exhibited a difference between their self and ideal self. He used a technique called the **'Q' Sort** to measure the difference between the two.

The 'Q' Sort consists of 100 cards with statements printed on them – for example, 'I am friendly', or 'I am moody'. The person is asked to sort the cards into nine different categories, according to how accurately the statement on the card describes them. For example, if the statement on a card is 'extremely uncharacteristic' of them, they place the card in the Category 1. If a statement is 'extremely characteristic' of them, they place the card in the Category 9. They continue sorting until all the cards are placed into one of the nine categories. Then the cards are shuffled and the person is asked to sort the cards again in relation to their ideal self. Finally the differences can be examined.

TRY THIS

In order to appreciate what Rogers meant by the terms **self** and **ideal self**, read through the following characteristics.

1 Place a tick in **Column 1** if that characteristic describes you.
2 When you have finished, go back through the list and put a tick in **Column 2** beside each characteristic you would *like* to have.

		Column 1	Column 2
1	Anxious		
2	Clever		
3	Artistic		
4	Moody		
5	Hard-working		
6	Brave		
7	Emotional		
8	Attractive		
9	Sociable		
10	Ambitious		

The items that you have ticked in the Column 1 represent how you see yourself, while the items in the Column 2 represent your ideal self. How well does your self-concept match your ideal self?

Adapted from Byrne, P., and Kelley, L., *An Introduction to Personality*, 3rd edn (Prentice-Hall, Englewood Cliffs, N.J., 1981)

How then does our sense of self develop? Rogers believed that humans are born with two important needs or motives. First, he argued – like Maslow – that humans have a need to **self-actualise** or reach their full potential. Secondly, humans have a need for **positive regard** from others. Positive regard means being loved and respected by the people who are important in our lives.

So far so good. We are all born with a need to self-actualise and receive positive regard from others. But where does it go wrong? Why aren't we all wonderfully self-actualised?

Rogers argued that distortions in the self-concept occur because many people grow up without receiving unconditional positive regard. Children may feel that they will not be loved and approved of unless they behave in a way that meets their parents' expectations.

Consider the following conversation between a therapist and a client who as a child did not receive unconditional positive regard.

> **Client**: 'I don't remember my parents actually praising me for anything. Even when I did really well at school, they made me feel that it wasn't good enough. I never really felt that I was special to them as a person. They seemed to have such clear expectations of me. If I didn't meet those expectations, I felt I didn't deserve their love.'

> **Therapist**: 'So you felt that as a child you couldn't do anything right no matter how hard you tried.'

> **Client**: 'That's right. And being an adult hasn't really changed anything. When I went to college, I really wanted to study English but to please my father I took a business course. He believed that I needed to study something so I could get a proper job. And now I'm stuck in this boring job which I hate! I need to discover for myself what I really want. I don't want to spend the rest of my life trying to please other people!'

THINK ABOUT IT

How might Rogers explain the situation?

Rogers would say that in an attempt to win her parents' love and approval, this client has tried to become the person her parents wanted her to be. As a result, she lost touch with her own needs and desires.

Rogers described another problem which may limit our ability to become self-actualised. According to Rogers, we experience anxiety when we are presented with information which is not consistent with our own self-concept. For example, I see myself as an easy-going and likeable person. However, one day I overhear some of my colleagues saying how difficult and moody I am. This information conflicts with the view that I have of myself. (Of course, my colleagues have got it wrong!) According to Rogers, I may use one or more psychological defences (like denial) to deal with my anxiety. Although such strategies may be useful in the short term, they create a gap between a person's self-concept and reality. The bigger the gap, the more likely it is that the person will show some sign of unhappiness and maladjustment.

The smaller the gap between the person's self-concept and reality, the less likely they are to have experiences which do not fit with it.

Can anything be done for people who have a distorted self-concept or who grow up without receiving unconditional positive regard? Rogers believed that client-centred therapy might help to put things right. What the therapist needed to do was to provide a supportive environment to encourage the person's self-development – rather like a gardener transplanting a sickly plant into more fertile soil.

A client-centred therapist would help the client by:

- **providing unconditional positive regard:** the therapist should be non-judgemental, encouraging the client to 'open up' and talk freely without fear of rejection.

- **providing empathy:** the therapist must be able to perceive the world as the client sees it and let the client know that his/her feelings have been understood.

- **being genuine:** the therapist must not put up a professional front: he or she must show the client that it is best to just 'be yourself'.

Evaluation of Rogers

Strengths
+ Rogers's method of client-centred therapy has proved to be an effective way of dealing with psychological disorders and has provided an important alternative to psychoanalysis.
+ Rogers has pointed out the importance of positive regard for human beings.

Weaknesses
- Many of his concepts are vague and difficult to measure.
- Rogers's theory was based on observations of his clients during therapy. It is difficult to know how far we can trust the self-reports they made to Rogers during their therapeutic sessions.
- Some critics have accused Rogers of being too optimistic about human nature.

The cognitive approach to personality

Have you ever come away from a party or social situation, and discovered afterwards that your memory of it was totally different from everybody else's? How is that people can experience the same situation and yet come away with such different impressions?

The theory of **George Kelly** (1905–67) goes some way towards providing an explanation.

Kelly's personal construct theory
Like Rogers, Kelly focuses on the *subjective experience* of the individual. However, even though Kelly did not see himself as a cognitive psychologist, his theory of personality has been one of the starting points for the cognitive approach to personality. Kelly believed that differences in personality and behaviour were due to the different ways in which people perceive and process the information around them.

Kelly believed that we have a need to predict and control the things that happen to us. When we cannot predict what is going to happen, we may experience anxiety. For example, think about how you might feel before a job interview when you don't know who will be on the interview panel or what type of questions you may be asked. That level of uncertainty can be very nerve-wracking. So, according to Kelly, we are motivated to make sense of the world so that we can predict and control events.

How can we do this? According to Kelly, we act like scientists. Scientists tend to form **hypotheses** (testable ideas) about the world. Next they test out these hypotheses and, if they don't work, they change them.

Now, this may be true for scientists, but what about ordinary people like you and me? Kelly argued that in order to understand a person's personality, we must understand how they make sense of the world around them. He used the term **personal constructs** to refer to the cognitive structures which we use to interpret the world around us. The best way to think of constructs is to consider them as transparent 'goggles' or templates through which a person sees the world. According to Kelly:

> 'Man looks at his world through transparent patterns or templates which he creates and then attempts to fit over the realities of which the world is composed. The fit is not always very good. Yet without such patterns, man would not make any sense of the world.'[16]

Naturally, the constructs I use will be different to the ones you use. Therefore the way in which I perceive a situation will also be different. Kelly described constructs as **bipolar** – that is, they have two opposite extremes (e.g. aggressive–unaggressive).

The structure of constructs

Kelly saw personal constructs as being organised in a hierarchy, with the most important ones at the top and the less important ones at the bottom. **Superordinate** constructs are the most important ones, but they may include other lesser important constructs called **subordinate constructs**. For example:

Superordinate construct	good/bad
Subordinate constructs	trustworthy/not trustworthy honest/dishonest

To help identify the constucts we use to make sense of the world around us, Kelly developed the **Role Construct Repertory Test (Rep Test)**.

First, the candidate is asked to list 15 people who have played an important role in their life – for example, father, mother or close friend. The person is then asked to consider three of these people at a time and to find a way in which two of them are similar to each, and different from the third.

The following activity is a much shortened version of the original test.

TRY THIS

Beside each statement, write the name of the person who fits that role. For example, write down the name of your mother, or the person who has played the part of mother in your life. Do not use any name more than once.

	Role	**Name of person**
1	Mother	....
2	Father	....
3	Brother	....
4	Sister	....
5	A teacher you liked	....
6	A teacher you disliked	....
7	Your partner/boyfriend,girlfriend	....
8	A person who for some unexplained reason dislikes you	....
9	A person you feel sorry for	....

- Now consider three of these people at a time.
- Describe how two of them are alike but different from the third.
- Put your description of how two of them are alike in **Column 1** and how the third one is different in **Column 2**.

	How two are alike	*How the third person is different*
People to consider	*Column 1*	*Column 2*
2, 5, 7 (e.g. your father, a teacher you like, a partner)	....	....
1, 8, 3	....	....
4, 5, 9	....	....

In summary

- *Kelly believed that differences in personality and behaviour were due to differences in personal constructs. Personal constructs are like templates or goggles through which we perceive the world around us.*

- *Kelly developed the Repertory Grid Test to identify an individual's personal constructs.*

The Rep test has been useful in identifying how complex or simple a person's constructs are. A person with a complex system of constructs is able to maintain a clear distinction between different constructs and is able to put people into lots of categories. A person with a simple system of constructs has a less elaborate system and the differences between constructs are not so clear-cut.

Evaluation of Kelly's theory

Strengths

+ Kelly was one of the first psychologists to attempt to adopt a cognitive approach to personality.
+ The Role Rep Test has been useful for therapists in that it gives some idea of how clients perceive the world around them.

Weaknesses

– Some of the concepts used are very vague. For example, trying to define what a personal construct is can be quite difficult. Kelly believed that personal constructs influenced behaviour. But if they cannot be defined accurately, how can we expect to prove that they influence behaviour?

Summary

- Temperament refers to certain patterns of behaviour or dispositions that are present in infancy. These dispositions can develop into stable personality traits.
- Type theories of personality attempt to place people in different categories. Examples of type theories include Sheldon's body types and 'Type A' and 'Type B' personalities.
- Trait theories assume that a personality is simply a combination of traits. For example, Allport identified three different types of traits while Cattell identified 16 personality traits.
- Eysenck believed there were three basic dimensions of personality: extraversion–introversion, neuroticism and psychoticism.
- More recently it has been suggested that personality is made up of five broad dimensions called the Big Five.
- Other approaches to personality include the humanistic approach (e.g., Maslow, Rogers) and the cognitive approach (e.g. Kelly).

Answers to 'Try This' activity, page 154 ('Jenny's letters')

According to computer analysis, the central traits of Jenny's character are as follows:

- aggressive
- need to be independent
- possessive
- likes to be seen sacrificing for others
- needs to be accepted by others

How did your list compare to the computer analysis?

13 Abnormal Development

In many ways, it is the differences between people that make life interesting. We are all unique individuals, shaped by a complex interaction of genetic and environmental factors. But where does 'difference' end and **abnormality** begin? What do we mean by 'abnormal behaviour' and how do we decide who is and who is not 'abnormal'?

Defining 'abnormality'

There are a number of different ways of defining abnormality. Take the case of Richard Thompson. In 1986, at the age of 54, Richard Thompson was evicted from his 'home' in San Diego, along with all his belongings. His belongings were not particularly unusual and included shirts, trousers, dozens of shoes, several bibles, a toolchest, deckchairs, an outdoor barbecue, birdcages, and two pet rats. However, Richard's 'home' for the previous nine months was extremely unusual. Rather than living in day-care centres and psychiatric units, Richard had made his home in a sewer in the centre of San Diego.

THINK ABOUT IT

How would you define the term 'abnormal behaviour'?

Unfortunately for Richard, the city did not allow people to live in sewers. But how extreme was his behaviour really? Let us consider it in the light of different criteria for defining abnormality:

1. Deviation from the statistical norm

By this definition, behaviour is judged to be abnormal if it is *rare* – i.e. if it occurs infrequently within the general population. Living in sewers is certainly rare (among people, at least), so Richard's behaviour could be considered abnormal. So would 'hearing voices'. But so too would living in a monastery, or selling a million books or records – thousands of the people listed in the Guinness Book of Records satisfy this criterion. It is not clear, either, just how rare the behaviour must be, or how far it must deviate from the norm, in order to be labelled abnormal. One person's 'abnormality' might be another person's 'eccentricity'. This way of defining abnormality, then, has its limitations.

2. Deviation from social norms

By this definition, behaviour is considered abnormal if it does not conform to *social rules*. Most people's behaviour is to some extent governed by the standards and values of the society in which they live. So behaviour which breaks certain laws or conventions may be judged abnormal. Indecent exposure, murder, alcoholism – all these may be seen as examples of abnormal behaviour. Richard's preference for living in a sewer would be seen as abnormal by this criterion too.

A problem with this definition, however, is that abnormality is defined in terms of other people and what they consider appropriate, and not in terms of any particular problem that the 'abnormal' person may have. It may therefore be used as a means of social control, and result in certain people trying to impose their standards on others. For example, someone who is homophobic may label homosexuals as abnormal, and use this as an excuse to discriminate against them.

Dress or customs that might shock or offend in one country or culture may be perfectly normal in another ▼

There is also the difficulty that social norms vary over time and across cultures. Thirty years ago, most men in Britain would have considered it highly inappropriate to wear an earring or a pony tail, but today both are widely accepted. For a woman to walk down the street naked from

the waist up may break social norms in Britain but not in some other cultures. The fact that social norms can and do change over time and cross-culturally raises difficulties for this definition of abnormality.

3. *Maladaptiveness*

By this criterion, behaviour is seen as abnormal if it results in physical or psychological harm either to the person behaving in that way or to other people. Violent or abusive people would fall into this category. So too would people who cannot wash or feed themselves, for example, or people with phobias that prevent them from being able to live a normal life or function within society.

This definition has some advantages. Certain forms of mental illness such as schizophrenia, or mania, may not necessarily cause psychological distress to the sufferer, but they can mean that sufferers are unable to look after themselves, or to function socially, and they can sometimes cause harm to others.

But again, labelling someone 'abnormal' may result in others discriminating against them or trying to control (or 'treat') them – and this can seriously affect their human rights. Just because a person's behaviour may offend or alarm other people, it does not mean that they do not have a right to behave in the way they do. And even if they are doing something that may prove harmful to them, provided it does not harm anyone else, don't they have the right to do it? What about people who enjoy dangerous sports? The fact that Richard lived in a sewer had no bad effects on others. He liked the privacy it offered and in some ways it may have been just what he needed.

So far we have seen that each of the three criteria for judging

QUESTIONS

1 Under which of the definitions above might the following people be considered abnormal?

a) a rapist
b) a smoker
c) a genius

2 Psychiatrists are a group of people who are relatively uncommon in society. They may sometimes keep patients imprisoned against their will, and force them to take drugs that have unpleasant side-effects. Should psychiatrists be considered abnormal?

abnormality has its limitations. Perhaps an answer is to use a mix of different factors to help us to decide whether a person or their behaviour is abnormal. One such approach comes from Rosenhan and Seligman (1984), who suggest seven factors we can use to help us judge behaviour.

These are:

1 **Suffering:** whether the person is in distress
2 **Maladaptiveness:** whether the person's behaviour makes their life more difficult rather than helping them
3 **Irrationality:** whether or not the person can communicate with others in a way that is reasoned and comprehensible
4 **Unpredictability:** whether the person's behaviour seems under their control, or is bizarre and unexpected by that person and other people
5 **Vividness and unconventionality:** whether the person has experiences which others do not have, or experiences things more intensely
6 **Observer discomfort:** whether other people find it upsetting to watch what the person does
7 **Violation of moral and ideal standards:** whether the person frequently behaves in ways that society considers to be morally wrong

The sensitive consideration of a mixture of factors may be a more sensible approach to defining abnormality than simply using just one, crude definition as described previously.

QUESTIONS

Do you think Richard Thompson should be labelled as abnormal using the seven criteria above?

The mental health criterion

An alternative strategy is to try and understand abnormality by contrasting it with normality. Jahoda (1958) identified a number of criteria associated with mental health, and suggested that the extent to which someone should be judged as abnormal depended on the extent to which they failed to meet the criteria identified. The criteria include:

1 The absence of mental illness
2 The ability to act independently
3 An accurate perception of the world
4 The ability to cope with stress
5 The ability to maintain interpersonal relationships
6 Positive self-esteem
7 Continuing growth and development as a person

This approach to abnormality, however, has problems of its own. The first criterion is negative and not particularly helpful until we know what 'mental illness' means. People's perceptions of the world differ, which raises difficulties for the third criterion. We all have times when life seems to be getting on top of us, when relationships break down, or when we feel bad about ourselves. It appears that, using these criteria, most of us could be seen as mentally ill.

Today, mental health professionals generally tend to use the **maladaptive** definition of abnormality. This generally follows a clinical assessment involving:

- **clinical interview:** gathering information about relevant life events
- **psychological tests:** for example, personality tests
- **neurological tests:** checking for possible brain damage or abnormalities in the functioning of the body

Once it is apparent that someone is behaving in a way that is abnormal, and is possibly in need of help, the next task is to diagnose what is wrong with the person and what sort of help they are likely to need.

Historical approaches to abnormality

The question of how to explain and treat people with behavioural disorders goes back thousands of years. In Ancient Egypt and in the Christian church, disorders were sometimes explained in terms of possession by evil spirits or demons. This had the consequence that sufferers were sometimes 'treated' by making them suffer to the point where the 'demons' could tolerate no more and opted to leave the body. Often flogging and starvation were seen as appropriate treatment for victims. Sometimes sufferers of disorders underwent **trepanning**, a procedure in which a hole was made in the top of the skull to create an exit through which the evil spirit could leave the body. 'Witches' were sometimes blamed for causing disorders in people, and the torturing and burning of 'witches' was supported by the Pope and Church.

The ancient Greeks believed that mental disorders were the result of an imbalance in the body's 'humours'

The ancient Greeks considered that disorders were a result of an imbalance in the body fluids or **humours**. Hippocrates suggested that an excess of black bile made a person melancholic (pessimistic, unsociable); too much yellow bile made a person choleric (excitable, aggressive); too much phlegm made a person phlegmatic (calm, unresponsive); and too much blood made a person sanguine (easy-going, overly cheerful). Treatment for these conditions consisted of various drugs, purgatives and exercises designed to restore the balance of the bodily fluids.

In the period following the French Revolution, the French reformer Pinel used **moral therapy** to treat disturbed people. Pinel argued that his patients had lost the power to reason as a result of too much stress. He believed in treating them with respect and dignity, in as stress-free an environment as possible, in order to help them recover their powers of reason. He achieved a high success rate with this approach.

We can see, then, that the way in which disorders are thought about influences the kind of labels that are attached to sufferers – and the kind of treatment that is thought to be appropriate.

Classifying mental disorders

People may show a wide variety of abnormal behaviours. If psychologists wish to be able to understand and study these, they need to develop a *shared vocabulary*. That is, if a psychologist in one part of the country wishes to talk about something called 'schizophrenia' with a psychologist in another part of the country – or indeed a psychologist in a different country – then both psychologists need to have a common understanding of what is meant by the term. Once this shared vocabulary has been established, it becomes much easier to share information and make progress in understanding the cause of the disorder, how it is likely to develop and the best form of treatment. What is needed, then, is a **classification** system.

Psychologists need to have a means of classifying mental disorders

One of the first comprehensive classification systems was developed by the German psychiatrist Kraepelin (1896), who suggested that there were 18 different types of mental disorder. Kraepelin's work was important because it influenced the development of the classification systems which are used today. Different countries have developed their own classification systems. Two major classification systems in use today are:

- **DSM–IV:** 'DSM' stands for the Diagnostic and Statistical Manual, and 'IV' denotes it is the fourth version (the manual has been significantly updated a number of times in the past). This manual is mainly used in the USA.
- **ICD–10:** 'ICD' stands for International Standard Classification of Diseases, Injuries, and Causes of Death, and '10' means it is the tenth version of the manual. This system is mainly used in Britain and the rest of Europe.

In practice, there is a good deal of overlap between the two systems, although the American system has more categories than the European one. Both systems are continually revised and updated. For example, the DSM was first published in 1952 and classified 60 types of mental illness, whereas the most recent version identifies around 300 different mental disorders. The earlier versions of DSM tended to consider disorders as if they were entirely the result of internal processes within the individual (i.e. what was wrong with them). Both DSM and ICD are now described as **multi-axial**. That is, assessment has broadened to consider a variety of different kinds of factors that need to be considered when seeking to understand a disorder. These different kinds of factors are listed in the report, each class of factor representing an axis for consideration.

For example, DSM-IV has five axes. The first two simply list the symptoms of different disorders that the psychiatrist must consider. The other axes list further sorts of information the psychiatrist must also consider in making a diagnosis. These are:

- **Axis III:** the person's general medical condition
- **Axis IV:** any social or environmental stressors
- **Axis V:** how well the person is currently functioning at home and at work.

In summary

- *There are different ways of defining abnormality.*

- *Historically, abnormality has been linked to evil spirits or demons, an imbalance of bodily fluids, or exposure to stress.*

- *A first step towards gaining a proper understanding of mental disorders is the development of a classification system.*

- *Two main classification systems for mental disorders in use today are DSM–IV in the USA and ICD–10 in Europe.*

Armed with this information, the psychologist is in a better position to try to assign the person to a specific category or type of mental disorder. Once the person is given a diagnosis (such as anorexia or depression), the psychologist can decide upon an appropriate treatment.

Problems of diagnosis

Despite the detailed and elaborate classification systems we looked at above, the diagnosis of mental disorders can be very difficult. We shall discuss some of these difficulties below.

Reliability

One problem is to do with the **reliability** of diagnosis. Diagnosis is only reliable if it is consistent and if different psychiatrists can agree about what is wrong with someone. Even using these classification systems, psychiatrists can often disagree. Beck (1962) found that the overall level of agreement between 4 psychiatrists who interviewed 153 patients was just 54%. New York psychiatrists in 1972 were twice as likely to diagnose schizophrenia in a patient as their counterparts in London. Dumont (1987) found that clinicians still disagree with each other about patients.

KEY STUDY

Rosenhan (1973) arranged for himself and seven other 'normal' people to present themselves to different psychiatric hospitals in five different states in the USA, and to try to gain admission by saying they could hear voices saying the words 'empty', 'hollow' and 'thud'. Once accepted into the hospital, each person was to behave in a normal way, and to stop claiming to hear voices. All eight people were admitted to hospital, and all except one were diagnosed as schizophrenic. They remained hospitalised for periods ranging from 7 to 52 days (19 days on average).

While in the hospitals, not one of these 'pseudo-patients' was judged by the staff as sane. Interestingly, many of the other patients suspected that they were fakes, and some suspected that Rosenhan and his team of impostors were checking up on the hospital. Rosenhan asked his experimenters to take notes to record their experiences as patients. Initially this was done secretly, but it soon became clear that no one much cared, and so note-taking came to be done quite openly.

The study found that the hospital staff often interpreted the behaviour of the pseudo-patients to fit the context. If the pseudo-patients discussed their situation with staff in a rational way, they were reported to be using 'intellectualisation' defences. One experimenter's note-taking was described in the nursing notes as 'patient engages in writing behaviour', as if this was a result of his psychiatric disorder – though he was never asked about why he was writing. When, with the help of partners and colleagues, the pseudo-patients were finally released, the diagnosis was 'schizophrenia in remission'. In other words, it was never acknowledged that these people were sane, and indeed the label implied that they had been sick and might become ill again.

Rosenhan concluded that it is often hard to distinguish insanity from sanity. The labels given to people in hospitals exert a strong influence on how others interpret their behaviour. Hospitals are also often run in a way that discourages meaningful contact between patients and staff, and the frequent administration of drugs often convinced staff that their patients were ill and were receiving appropriate treatment.

Questions

1. What effect does labelling someone as mentally ill have, according to Rosenhan?
2. Does this research raise any ethical issues?
3. What research design is being used in this study?
4. Give one advantage and one disadvantage of this design.

Source: Rosenhan, D.L., 'On Being Sane in Insane Places', in *Science*, 179 (1973), pp.250–8

In a follow-up to this research, Rosenhan told members of a teaching hospital about the study he had conducted. He warned that, over a three-month period, some pseudo-patients might try to gain access to the hospital. Each member of staff was asked to rate every new patient according to whether or not they believed them to be an impostor. During the three-month period, 193 patients were admitted, 41 of whom were thought to be impostors by at least one member of staff, and 23 were suspected to be impostors by at least one psychiatrist. All were genuine patients.

These studies led Rosenhan to conclude that the diagnosis of mental disorder is unreliable, and that psychiatrists were often unable to make an informed judgement about who was or was not ill. He also concluded that diagnosis is often not valid, since sane people were being diagnosed as disordered.

Validity

In order to be **valid**, a diagnosis must be accurate – i.e. the patient must be suffering from what they are said to be suffering from. One difficulty here is that disorders such as schizophrenia may present a wide variety of different symptoms. One person diagnosed as schizophrenic may show some of these symptoms, and another person diagnosed as schizophrenic may show a different set of symptoms. In other words, it is possible for people with different symptoms to be diagnosed as having the same illness. Because of this, some have argued that the classification systems are just guesswork and do not represent scientific knowledge.

Szasz and the 'myth' of mental illness

Szasz (1961) argued that the whole concept of 'mental illness' is a myth. The term 'ill' implies something physically wrong. You *can* have something physically wrong with your brain, which is a physical object, and Szasz would prefer to use terms like 'brain disease' here. The mind, however, is not a physical entity and so cannot be 'ill'. If people have something physically wrong with them, they should be classified as having a physical illness. But where people show no physical disorder, they should be described as having a 'problem with living'. Such people may, for example, have difficulties in communicating with others, or they may have ideas that others find unusual or do not understand.

To label someone as ill may result in the person believing that there is nothing they can do about their condition: nothing is their 'fault', since they are sick. This may result in their denying any personal responsibility, and failing to look for other ways of living that would improve the quality of their lives. Also, doctors who see a patient as 'sick' may be tempted to treat them with drugs rather than try to help them find better ways of coping. Both DSM and ICD use the term 'mental disorder' rather than 'mental illness'. However, the title 'ICD' refers to a classification of *diseases*, and the assumption behind both systems is that the 'mentally disordered' have a physical, medical problem.

Labelling

Giving a **label** to a collection of symptoms may lead to overdiagnosis (as in the Rosenhan study) and it may also **stigmatise** a person – that is, it can negatively affect the way in which other people think of them and behave towards them. If you have 'flu, you are described as a person who has 'flu. If you have schizophrenia, you are not simply described as someone who has schizophrenia but as 'a schizophrenic'. To be labelled in this way often implies something deeply meaningful about the sort of person you are – and are likely to go on being. People may respond to you in more negative ways once the label is applied. Rosenhan referred to this as the 'stickiness' of diagnostic labels.

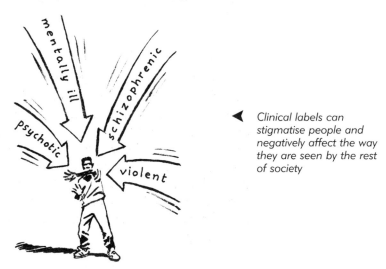

◀ *Clinical labels can stigmatise people and negatively affect the way they are seen by the rest of society*

Social and political implications

Just as the use of clinical labels can have significant negative consequences for the sufferer, the decision to stop using a stigmatising label can have a significant positive effect. For example, 'homosexuality' was eventually dropped from DSM-III, with great positive effect on public attitudes.

Subcultural differences in diagnosis

Within any society there are likely to be a number of identifiable smaller social groups or subcultures based on gender, age, social class, etc. Research indicates that a person's chances of developing a mental disorder depend to some extent on the groups that they belong to. Hill (1998) quotes the following:

- In the UK, women are about 40% more likely to be admitted to mental hospital than men, and are around twice as likely as men to suffer from depression and neuroses.

- Schizophrenia is 2–8 times more common in the lower socioeconomic groups of society than the higher.

- In the UK, admission to mental hospitals increases by 30% from the 55–64 to the 65–74 age bracket.

- Between 1985 and 1990 the rate of admissions to mental hospitals increased by around 65% for 10- to 14-year-olds, and by 21% for 15- to 19-year-olds.

- In the USA, higher rates of mental illness have been found in first-generation Hispanic immigrants. In the UK, children of Afro-Caribbean immigrants are ten times more likely than native white children to develop schizophrenia as adults.

To understand these differences, we clearly need to look at a number of different factors. These include:

- **biological influences**: examples here include hormonal fluctuations caused by menstruation, childbirth, or the menopause; the onset of senile dementia; the results of stress experienced in pregnancy; the exposure of immigrants to unfamiliar viruses

- **environmental influences**: examples here include: material deprivation (no money, poor housing, etc.) among the lower socio-economic classes; increased isolation and financial hardship in old age; increased stress or lower self-esteem in females as a result of social discrimination that pushes women to adopt roles that have less status or power than males; increased stress among ethnic groups as a result of racial discrimination, or the need to cope with different cultural values and social expectations

- **diagnostic bias**: examples here include the 'social drift' to lower socioeconomic groups following mental illness (i.e. the problems experienced by people with a history of mental illness in coping with life or finding acceptance among higher socioeconomic groups); age, ethnic or gender stereotyping (for example, viewing older people as 'prone to mental disorder' may render them more likely to be labelled 'mentally ill'); the assumption that the behaviour of the white population should be considered 'normal' and that deviations from these norms by other ethnic groups are 'abnormal'.

Cross-cultural differences

Some mental disorders appear to be universal – that is, they occur in all societies. Nevertheless, there are major differences in the reported rate of occurrence between cultures, as well as within cultures over time. Schizophrenia is a prime example. Although it is one of the most common disorders in the world, the form in which it appears varies across cultures, from intense suspicion of others in Nigeria, to auditory hallucinations in Europe. Onset can also be related to culture-specific factors: for example, in different countries sufferers variously report feeling 'possessed by evil forces', being the victim of 'witchcraft', or simply being 'under stress'. At one time, psychiatrists in the USA diagnosed four times as many people suffering from schizophrenia as British psychiatrists.

Some mental disorders appear to be culturally relative, i.e. unique to a particular culture. For example:

- **TKS or Taijin Kyofusho:** this is a social phobia found in Asia, especially Japan, that is characterised by a morbid fear of making eye-to-eye contact, blushing, giving off an offensive odour, having an unpleasant or tense facial expression, or having trembling hands. *Taijin kyofu* in Japanese means 'fear of interpersonal relations', and it is the third most common psychiatric disorder reported among Japanese college students. It is also more common in males than in females.

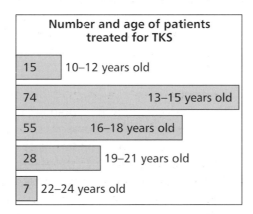

Number and age of patients treated for TKS	
15	10–12 years old
74	13–15 years old
55	16–18 years old
28	19–21 years old
7	22–24 years old

- **Witiko syndrome:** among the Algonquin Indians in Canada, the Witiko, a man-eating monster, is an important mythological figure. Sufferers believe that they are possessed by the Witiko spirit and become increasingly obsessed with the craving for human flesh. In their desperation to escape the cannibalistic urges, they may become suicidal.

- **Latah:** in the Malay language *latah* means 'ticklish'. Latah usually affects females and involves apparently uncontrollable imitative behaviour. Victims copy the movements and speech of others and are liable to act in completely uncharacteristic ways, e.g. uttering obscenities.

In summary

- *The diagnosis of mental disorders is still unreliable. Psychiatrists often disagree about the nature of mental illness.*

- *Rosenhan believed that diagnosis is neither reliable or valid and that it is impossible to tell the sane from the insane.*

- *Szasz believed that mental illness is a myth. People either have physical problems or 'problems with living'.*

- *Clinical labelling can have a stigmatising effect on the sufferer.*

- *There are subcultural and cross-cultural variations in the incidence and symptoms of mental disorders. This highlights the importance of environmental influences in the development of disorders, and also the strong possibility of cultural biases both in diagnosis and in classification.*

TKS or Taijin Kyofusho is a social phobia commonly found in Japan but rarely encountered in the West ▶

Theoretical models of abnormality

The different approaches within psychology all offer different explanations for mental disorders. The psychologist's choice of model influences the way in which research is conducted, the way findings are analysed, and the kind of treatment patients are offered.

Let us consider five major approaches to abnormality.

1. The medical model

This approach is based on the view that abnormal behaviour is a consequence of a physical problem or fault within the brain. This is the dominant approach in the field. It finds expression in terms such as 'illness', 'treatment', 'cure' and 'mental hospital'. Unlike psychologists, psychiatrists must be qualified doctors, and will often treat patients with drugs or by making other physical interventions such as **electro-convulsive therapy (ECT)** in which the patient is given a quick electric shock to the brain, or surgery such as **lobotomy**.

In the film 'One Flew Over The Cuckoo's Nest' Jack Nicholson (left) played a patient forcibly lobotomised by hospital authorities because of his 'troublesome' behaviour

Strengths

+ Some drugs have proven invaluable with severely disturbed patients. For example, anti-psychotic drugs have revolutionised the treatment of schizophrenics who were otherwise untreatable. Likewise, ECT and even surgery can have their uses as last-resort treatments.

+ In many cases researchers have identified physical abnormalities that are related to certain disorders. For example, some cases of schizophrenia are believed to result from an excess of the neurotransmitter dopamine in the brain.

Weaknesses

– Treatments often have unpleasant side-effects and some drugs may be addictive.

– The focus on biology may overlook the impact of environmental influences on the development of a disorder.

– The belief that mentally ill people are helpless victims of a physical condition may mean that they and those around them take no responsibility for their condition and so do not seek positive ways of improving their lifestyle.

2. The psychoanalytic model

The assumptions of the psychoanalytic model are that mental disorders are caused by conflicts between different components of the personality such as the id, ego and superego (see page 46–7). These conflicts lie buried in the unconscious mind. The recommended treatment involves psychoanalysis and the use of free association and dream analysis. Freud believed that some degree of psychic conflict was inevitable for all of us, and therefore some abnormality is also inevitable and beyond conscious control.

Strengths

+ Psychoanalysis, in one form or another, is widely practised, and many practitioners firmly believe that their techniques are effective.

+ The therapy addresses the whole person, seeking to reorganise the personality and get at the deep, underlying causes of abnormal behaviour, and not just the surface symptoms.

Weaknesses
- The theory is criticised as unscientific and impossible to test.
- Therapy is very time-consuming and expensive.
- There are other, quicker and cheaper alternative treatments for many disorders. For example, desensitisation techniques developed by behaviourists may quickly cure a phobia without the need to look for the deep underlying cause for the fear (if there is one).

3. The behavioural model

The behaviourists take the view that abnormal behaviour, like normal behaviour, is learned (see Chapter 7, *The Behavioural Approach*, page 54). They refuse to accept that behaviour may be prompted by unconscious forces, and argue that abnormal behaviour should be treated using techniques such as desensitisation and aversion therapy.

Strengths
+ Many of the techniques developed by behaviourists have proven to be very effective in dealing with abnormal behaviours (particularly phobias). They are also relatively quick and inexpensive.
+ Token economy systems (see page 69) have been found to be useful in improving the behaviours of even severely disturbed patients.
+ Behaviourist theory is derived from systematic research in the laboratory and claims to be scientific.

Weaknesses
- Much of the behaviourists' research was done on animals, and cannot necessarily be generalised to humans and their problems.
- Behaviourist therapy has been criticised for addressing the symptoms of a disorder rather than its underlying causes. As a result, it is claimed, curing a person of a fear for one object may simply result in a person developing a fear for something else (this is referred to as **symptom substitution**).
- Behaviourist techniques also sometimes raise ethical questions. For example, introducing a token economy system in an institution may involve imposing conditions upon people without their consent.

4. The humanistic model

Humanists such as Rogers (1951) and Maslow (1968) take a positive view of people, believing that we possess free will and a drive towards self-actualisation (see pages 165–171). For them, problems within the personality arise when our path to self-development is blocked and we are forced to make choices we are not really happy with. Sometimes we may even try to convince ourselves that we really are happy with our lives when in fact we are not. This gives rise to anxiety and makes us feel that our lives are unfulfilling – which makes us unhappy. In other cases we may set ourselves impossibly high standards in trying to live up to what we think others expect of us – and again this causes unhappiness.

For the humanists, treatment must be client-centred: therapy should be conducted in a warm, supportive environment in which the person is free to discuss and explore their feelings. In this way they can come to a better understanding of themselves and make choices that are more likely to make them happy.

Strengths

+ Unlike Freudian theory, which tends to dwell on the past, humanistic theory focuses more on the present day and on conscious motives.
+ The approach is positive in that the emphasis is on the individual's ability to make positive choices to change their life for the better.
+ The emphasis on free will means that people are encouraged to take responsibility for their life and the lives of those around them.
+ The humanistic approach is person-centred and focused on the individual. People are not labelled and the theory avoids the problems of stigmatising.

Weaknesses

− Humanist theory is unscientific. Notions like self, self-actualisation, etc., are abstract and impossible to test.
− Not everybody is able to change their life for the better. What about a homeless person with no money or job prospects? How helpful is it to suggest they are responsible for their own plight?
− Some philosophies believe happiness is best achieved by reconciling ourselves to the world and coming to terms with ourselves as we are, rather than struggling to change ourselves and the world around us.

5. The cognitive model

Cognitive psychologists such as Ellis (1962) and Beck (1963) emphasise the thinking that occurs between stimulus and response. They see emotional problems as the result of illogical or **disorganised thinking**. So, for example, people suffering from depression may believe that the world is a hopeless place, that nothing good ever does or will happen, and that they are powerless to do anything about it. Therapy involves highlighting the inconsistencies in this way of thinking, showing them that things are not as bleak as they believe, that good experiences can happen, and that they are able to change their lives for the better.

Strengths

+ Research (e.g. by Gustafson, 1992) has revealed that many people suffering from depression or anxiety do display negative thinking.
+ Cognitive behavioural therapy has been found to be effective with some forms of depression and anxiety disorders.

Weaknesses

− It is not clear whether faulty thinking causes or results from mental disorder.
− It is difficult to highlight inconsistencies in thinking to a patient whose thought-processes are too disorganised to reason with.

In summary

- *The medical model looks for physical causes to symptoms*

- *The psychodynamic approach is to explore the patient's unconscious conflicts through techniques of psychoanalysis*

- *The behavioural approach sees abnormal behaviour as learned.*

- *The humanistic approach believes that people's problems are often caused by their having an unrealistic view of themselves. Humanists advocate techniques such as client-centred therapy.*

- *According to the cognitive approach, mental disorders arise as a result of faulty thinking. Cognitive psychologists aim to help people to understand the inconsistent and irrational nature of their thinking and change it for the better.*

Eating disorders

So far we have considered what we mean by abnormality, how abnormal behaviours are classified and how different schools of psychology approach the problem of treating abnormal behaviour. Now let us try to develop a deeper understanding of abnormality by exploring one particular class of disorder, that of eating disorders.

In the UK, as in many other rich nations, we are all exposed to a large number of advertisements for food products, restaurants, sweets and chocolates, on TV and in the media generally. It seems virtually impossible to turn on the TV without seeing a show about cookery. Bookshops also contain a wide variety of books on cooking – and, at the same time, a large number of books about dieting.

Sharing a meal can be a way of promoting and maintaining friendships ▲

Clearly, we need to eat in order to live. But for those of us fortunate enough to be living in the richer societies of the West (and East), food is more than just a means of survival. It is a source of physical pleasure and a source of comfort when we are stressed; shared meals can also be a way of promoting 'togetherness' and friendships. At the same time, Western culture, like many cultures, promotes images of beauty that are associated with being slim. Media images of heroes and heroines, pop stars and models are dominated by slender people. The general view seems to be that it is 'bad' to be fat and 'good' to be slim. To be seen as someone who is 'fat' is to risk being teased and rejected by others, which may lead to low self-esteem and feelings of loneliness and guilt. Given these mixed messages, it is not altogether surprising that people develop eating disorders.

THINK ABOUT IT

Take three minutes to list as many food-related advertisements as you can think of. What does the list tell you about the extent of your exposure to food-related images, and about peoples' attitudes to food?

Types of eating disorders

Let us consider the two most common forms of eating disorder: **anorexia** and **bulimia**. Although the two are different, they share some common features. Both are characterised by severe disturbances in the individual's eating patterns. Sufferers of either disorder may show a preoccupation with food, but whereas a bulimic may often maintain normal body weight despite frequent food 'binges', an anorexic may read cookery books, talk about food, and cook for others, while at the same time literally starving herself (or himself) to death.

Anorexia nervosa

The earliest written account of anorexia was published by Richard Morton in 1689. Morton called the condition 'nervous consumption'. He described an 18-year-old patient who showed a number of symptoms including severe loss of appetite and cessation of periods. According to Morton, the young girl resembled a 'skeleton only clad with skin.' The young girl refused to take the medication that Morton offered and three months later she died.

Later, in 1874, the British psychiatrist W. Gull introduced the term 'anorexia nervosa'. Gull observed that anorexia tended to occur among young females.

It is clear from both these reports that anorexia has been recognised for hundreds of years as a disorder. However, in the past ten years it has received increased attention.

The symptoms of anorexia nervosa

One of the main symptoms of anorexia nervosa is the sufferer's refusal to maintain a minimal body weight. To be diagnosed as anorexic, the person's body weight must be at least 15% below their expected weight based on age and height. Other symptoms include an intense fear of gaining weight, which does not decrease even when the sufferer is actually losing weight. Horne et al. (1991) found that 75% of people with anorexia also show a distorted body image. Despite being very thin, they continue to see themselves as being heavier than they really are.

The self-esteem of individuals who suffer from anorexia depends on their being thin. Weight loss is considered to be a great achievement and a sign of self-control. Gaining weight is seen as a failure.

Lack of food brings with it a number of other physical changes besides weight loss. For example, women with anorexia often stop having periods (**amenorrhea**). The blood-pressure and body temperature of anorexics may also be lowered, and they may suffer from a slowed heart-rate, constipation and dehydration. About 20% of sufferers have a single episode and recover. About 20% continue to be affected and may need hospitalisation. About 60% have recurring episodes over a number of years. The disorder is extremely dangerous and can be fatal. About 5% of anorexic girls die from weight loss (Hsu, 1986).

A key factor in eating disorders is the distorted self-image of the sufferer

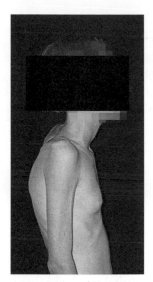

About 5% of anorexic girls eventually die from weight loss ▲

The majority of individuals who suffer from anorexia (90–95%) are female. Anorexia is considered to be a disorder of childhood because it is most likely to occur during early-to-late adolescence. The onset of the disorder is often associated with stressful life events.

According to the DSM-IV (see page 180) patients who suffer from anorexia can be divided into two subtypes:

- **Restricting type:** these are people who lose weight through dieting, excessive exercise or fasting

- **Binge/purging type:** people who regularly engage in either 'binge eating' or 'purging' or both (purging is achieved by using laxatives or self-induced vomiting).

Research based on 105 anorexic patients indicated that 53% lost weight through fasting (restricting type) while the remaining 47% lost weight through binge-eating/purging (Sue, Sue, 1991). Research also suggests that people who binge-eat or purge tend to be more extraverted, while people who lose weight through dieting or fasting tend to be more introverted.

Bulimia nervosa

Bulimia nervosa is characterised by **binge eating** followed by measures to prevent weight gain. A **binge** involves consuming a large amount of food in a very short period of time. Although the type of food eaten varies, it is usually high in calories, soft and can be eaten very quickly. Bulimics tend to be ashamed of their eating problems and usually try to conceal their symptoms. As a result, bingeing usually occurs in secrecy. The need for secrecy may sometimes leave a bulimic socially isolated. During a bingeing session, the person often experiences a loss of control and after the bingeing session experiences guilt. In order for a sufferer to be diagnosed with bulimia nervosa, the bingeing must occur on average at least twice a week for a period of three months.

Bulimics may sometimes turn to food as a source of comfort when they are going through a stressful time, and eat a lot of high-calorie food even though they are not hungry.

Like anorexics, people suffering from bulimia are often afraid of gaining weight and tend to overestimate their body size. They also use a variety of methods to prevent weight gain, including self-induced vomiting or the use of laxatives. This again is damaging to various organs in the body. However, unlike anorexics who are below their normal body weight, individuals with bulimia usually maintain a normal body weight.

Bulimia is more common than anorexia. According to one study, as many as 2–4% of the general population suffers from bulimia (Kendler et al. 1991). The disorder is also more common among females than males. Bulimia nervosa usually occurs in late adolescence or early adulthood.

What causes eating disorders?

As mentioned earlier, anorexia and bulimia have many of the same features, and this has led some psychologists to suggest that they may have similar causes. As you might expect, the different approaches in psychology offer different suggestions as to the nature of the disorders.

1. The psychoanalytic approach

According to the psychoanalytic approach, anorexia may represent an unconscious conflict about becoming sexually mature. Freud believed that eating could be a substitute for sexual expression. Therefore, if a person refuses to eat, this may indicate a fear of sexual activity. This is confirmed by the fact that depriving the body of food means that menstruation stops and the body does not develop into a feminine shape.

Bruch (1979) suggested that anorexic girls are trying to hold back maturity because they do not want to take on the responsibilities associated with being an adult woman in modern society. Girls may also unconsciously equate being fat with pregnancy, and so refuse to gain weight out of an unconscious fear of becoming pregnant.

Strengths
+ Some girls who suffer from eating disorders have suffered sexual abuse as children. It is hypothesised that, for such people, self-disgust or rejection of their bodies as they approach sexual maturity may play a part in the disorder.

Weaknesses
− Fear of pregnancy does not explain the 5–10% of anorexics who are male.
− Freudian theory is unscientific and cannot be directly tested.

2. The biological approach

One biological explanation suggests that there could be a genetic predisposition towards anorexia. Research suggests that if one twin is anorexic, the chances of the other twin having anorexia is much higher among identical twins (55%) than non-identical twins (7%) (Holland et al., 1984). The evidence for a genetic basis for bulimia is not as strong. Kendler et al. (1991) compared the incidence of bulimia in identical and non-identical twins. The researchers found that in cases where one twin had been diagnosed as bulimic, 23% of identical twins and 9% of non-identical twins were also diagnosed as bulimic.

Some have suggested that anorexia may be caused by a physiological dysfunction. One biological explanation focuses on the role of the **hypothalamus** (see page 414), which is the part of the brain that controls eating and sexual activity. Other recent research has focused on the neurotransmitter **serotonin**. Serotonin induces feelings of being satiated (i.e. it suppresses feelings of hunger), so perhaps a biological condition that increased the effect of serotonin may also reduce a person's desire to eat.

Strengths

+ Evidence for the role of the hypothalamus in influencing hunger is derived from experimental research, often using laboratory rats.

Weaknesses

- Post mortems on anorexics do not show any damage to this region of the brain.
- Even if eating disorders could be linked to abnormalities in the hypothalamus, it would still not be clear whether abnormal functioning of the hypothalamus was a cause of anorexia or whether the emotional distress associated with anorexia affects the hypothalamus.
- It is not clear why a condition that increases the effect of serotonin should be more prevalent in females than males.
- The approach ignores environmental influences. Research on twins or family members is not conclusive evidence for a genetic basis to a disorder. Family members share similar environments, twins especially. Poverty also tends to run in families, but is not genetically inherited.

3. The behavioural approach

The behavioural approach suggests that anorexia could be similar to having a weight phobia. Generally, weight loss in females is greeted with positive reinforcement (unfortunately, hardly anyone gets reinforced for putting weight on). Losing weight then becomes a habit. When girls start to become too thin, the concern and attention that parents show is also reinforcing, and so they continue to deny themselves food. It is possible that some girls seek to exert control over their families by using their eating disorder as a 'weapon' to ensure they remain the centre of attention even though they are now growing up and expected to be more independent.

Strengths

+ The notion that starvation results in increased attention from parents is intuitive, and supported by evidence. Bemis (1978) reports that self-starvation can often have a distressing effect on parents, and some teenagers may sometimes use this as a weapon against them. Minuchin (1978) suggested that not eating may help divert attention towards the child and away from other conflicts within the home. In this way, starvation is an attempt to preserve family unity.

Weaknesses

- In itself this does not explain why eating disorders should be so much more common among females than males.

4. The humanistic approach

This approach links eating disorders to an individual's need to achieve and maintain a sense of identity. In a family in which the child is rigidly controlled by the parents, the choice of eating or not eating is at least one aspect of life over which the child can exert control. Starvation is an indication that the child's life is not entirely controlled by others. Being thin, therefore, is a sign of self-control and independence.

Media images link female attractiveness with being thin ▲

Strength
+ A number of psychologists agree that adolescence can be a period in which children, confronted with bodily changes and changes in social relationships, struggle to achieve a sense of personal identity.

Weakness
– Again, in itself, this does not explain the greater incidence of the disorder among females.

5. Cognitive and socio-cognitive approaches

Cognitive approaches see eating disorders as the result of faulty thinking. Anorexics often display a highly distorted body image, believing themselves to be fat when they are in fact painfully thin. One possibility is that they have internalised repeated media messages linking female attractiveness with being thin. They have therefore come to believe that the thin models that they see in the media are 'normal' and that their own bodies are unacceptably fat. An alternative explanation from Agras et al. (1974) is that anorexics fail to properly identify hunger pangs, and so do not eat when they need to. Not eating then becomes a habit.

Strengths
+ Anorexia appears to be more prevalent in industrialised countries where there is an abundance of food and where attractiveness is linked to being thin.
+ The cognitive approach helps to explain why so many anorexics are female. Many commentators agree that the abundance of media images linking female desirability with being thin must have an impact on girls' sense of self-worth and on their idea of the 'ideal figure'.
+ Leon et al. (1989) reported that around 75% of teenage girls have either been on diets or are dieting, while boys rarely attempt to lose weight. This is understandable if the ideal male body-image is considered to be fairly big and strong, while the ideal female body-image is seen as slim. The findings, therefore, indicate that some form of restriction on food intake is not rare. Indeed, it is the norm for teenage girls.
+ Cultural norms may also play an important role in bulimia. Women may respond to social pressure to be thin by excessive dieting. Many women who develop bulimia have a history of going on strict diets. When the diet fails, they feel a loss of control and often end up bingeing. Then guilt sets in, they become worried about weight gain, and so purging follows the bingeing.

Weaknesses
– Not all anorexics display a distorted body image. Some recognise how thin they are and agree that it is unattractive. It is simply that they do not want to eat. They also know that their condition is life-threatening, and are as puzzled as everyone else by their condition.

Summary

- Anorexia nervosa is a life-threatening disorder characterised by extreme weight loss. It affects mainly adolescent girls.
- Bulimia nervosa involves bingeing and purging and, again, mostly affects young women. Sufferers may look outwardly normal and healthy.
- The psychoanalytic approach explains anorexia in terms of an unconscious fear of adult responsibilities or sexuality.
- Biological approaches suggest there may be abnormalities in the hypothalamus, or in the brain's sensitivity to serotonin.
- Behavioural approaches suggest losing weight is reinforcing because it results in increased attention from others.
- Humanistic approaches suggest eating disorders may reflect a need to demonstrate some independence as part of developing a sense of identity.
- Socio-cognitive approaches point to the distorted body image of anorexics and suggest this faulty thinking may arise as a result of societal pressures on women to be slim in order to be considered attractive.
- As ever, no one approach is likely to offer an adequate explanation on its own, but taken together they help us to gain a fuller understanding of the nature of the disorder.

Cognitive Psychology

Cognition involves acquiring, storing, retrieving and using knowledge. As you read these words you are carrying out a number of cognitive processes: perceiving and attending to the letters on the page; interpreting the letters as forming words and sentences; using your memory and your capacity to understand language. Studying cognition involves trying to understand these mental processes. Psychologists want to know how our minds *work*. They have made good progress towards this in recent years, but there is much that remains mysterious and unknown.

14 Visual Perception

Can we really believe ▶
our eyes?

We see a world full of objects of different shapes, sizes and colours. Some objects are moving and some are still. Some are near and some are far. All of this information is available to us – in the blink of an eye. Seeing seems effortless. Yet the processes involved are highly complex and far from being fully understood. In this chapter we will explore some of these processes and consider how far they are innate or learned.

What is perception?

Visual perception depends on the presence of **light**. Objects reflect light, either from the sun or an artificial source, and this light is what our eyes detect. The black circle in the middle of our eyes, the **pupil**, is simply a hole that lets light in. Too much light can be painful, so the

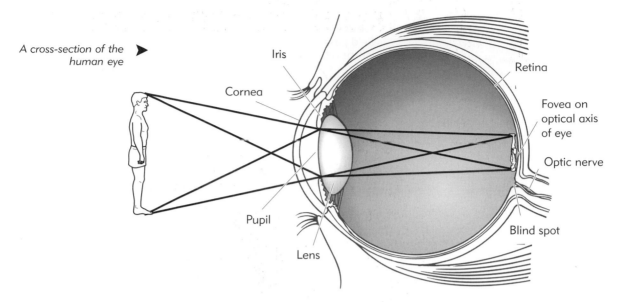

A cross-section of the human eye ▶

Iris

Cornea

Retina

Fovea on optical axis of eye

Optic nerve

Pupil

Blind spot

Lens

coloured area around the pupil, the **iris**, expands and contracts, making the pupil wider or smaller to control the amount of light that is admitted. In bright light our pupils are small to prevent hurt. In the dark they are wide, to let in more light to help us see.

Behind the pupil is a **lens**. This is a small sac of clear fluid that can change shape to focus light onto the back of the eye. If the light comes from an object that is close to us, it has to be bent more sharply to bring it into focus. The lens therefore becomes more compressed when we are looking at near objects, and more expanded when we are looking at more distant objects. This adjustment of the lens is called **accommodation**.

At the back of the eye is an array of millions of light-sensitive cells called the **retina**. When light falls onto these cells they send messages to the brain. There are two basic sorts of cells in the retina:

● **rod cells** are not found at the centre of the retina but towards the edges. They are used for night vision, and see in black and white.

● **cone cells** detect colour and are used in good lighting conditions. The cells are mostly at the centre of the retina, particularly at a region called the **fovea**. It is this region of the eye that can detect details most sharply. In poor lighting conditions, it is best to look slightly to the side of an object to let the rod cells detect it, since cones are not good at detecting objects when light levels are low.

The cells in the retina send messages to the brain via the **optic nerve**. Half of the information received by each eye goes to the opposite half of the brain. The nerves carrying this information cross over at a junction called the **optic chiasma**. Each eye sends information received from the left visual field to the right half of the brain, and vice-versa. This means that if you shut one eye, or one of your eyes is damaged, both halves of the brain can still receive information about both the left and the right visual scene.

Cells in the retina send messages to the brain via the optic nerve ▶

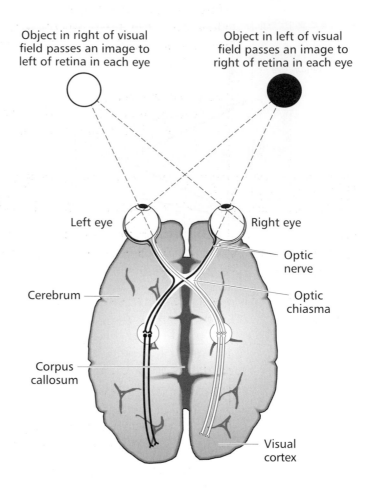

Object in right of visual field passes an image to left of retina in each eye

Object in left of visual field passes an image to right of retina in each eye

Left eye

Right eye

Optic nerve

Cerebrum

Optic chiasma

Corpus callosum

Visual cortex

A region of the brain towards the back of the head called the **visual cortex** is responsible for making sense of the information received by our eyes. The information is carried along the optic nerve in the form of electrical impulses. It is the job of the visual cortex to interpret what these electrical impulses mean.

Interpreting visual data

In order to understand the process of perception it is important to remember that the image on the retina is flat, (i.e. two-dimensional). It is also upside-down. Not only this, but as we have already seen, information from the right goes to the left half of the brain, and vice-versa. Clearly, therefore, although seeing does not involve conscious effort, a huge amount of work has to be done by the brain in order for perception to take place. Furthermore, the images of the world around us that each eye receives keep changing as lighting and viewing conditions change. Despite this, the world that we actually perceive seems to be relatively stable. This phenomenon is referred to as **perceptual constancy**, and it shows that there is more involved in visual perception than simply the images in our eyes.

Perceptual constancy

How does the brain maintain this image of relative stability? The process is a difficult one but becomes clearer as we consider some examples.

Shape constancy

Shape constancy refers to the way the shape of an image in our eyes may change, but its perceived shape in our mind remains the same.

TRY THIS

Hold an object (say, a book or pen) in front of you, and move it around. As you do so, the image that the object makes in your eyes keeps changing. Does the object appear to keep changing shape?

In fact, the object probably appears to retain the same shape. This demonstrates **shape constancy.**

Colour constancy

The perceived colour of objects remains the same even when lighting conditions change. What we see depends on the light that enters our eyes. This light frequently changes, as when the sun comes out (or goes in), or we go outdoors (or indoors), or turn lights on or off.

Despite these frequent changes in lighting, the intrinsic colour of the objects we see does not appear to keep changing. This is because our brains do not rely solely on the light from the particular object that we are looking at in order to work out its colour, but also on the light from surrounding objects. Often, when there is a change in the light falling on an object, there is also a change in the light falling on the surrounding objects. Our brain therefore makes an overall comparison and decides that the colours are still the same.

Location constancy

Objects appear to stay in the same place even though the images in our eyes may change as we move around. For example, if you move your head to the right, all the images in your eyes change, but the objects you see around you are perceived as staying in the same place. This is because the brain once again uses information from the surroundings and background (called **configuration change**) to help interpret the

THINK ABOUT IT

Have you ever sat in a train waiting in a station while another train next to you starts to pull away? In this situation it is often hard to tell at first which train is moving. Can you suggest why this happens?

In summary

- Perceptual constancy means our perceptions stay constant even though viewing conditions, and so the images in our eyes, change.

- Shape constancy means things are perceived as having the same shape even when viewed from different angles.

- Colour constancy means things look the same colour even when lighting conditions change.

- Size constancy means objects are perceived to be the same size no matter how near or far away they are.

- Location constancy means stationary objects are perceived as remaining still as we move around.

data it receives from our eyes. As the images change, the brain decides that it is more likely that the perceiver has moved to the right, than that everything else has moved to the left. The result is that the world, and the objects in it, are perceived as staying in the same place. Of course, the brain also has information from the muscles and the body's sense of balance to tell it about the person's position and movement in space.

Size constancy

Objects appear to stay the same size even though the size of the images they make in our eyes change as the objects either get nearer or further away.

As people move away from us they make a smaller image in our eyes. Yet we do not usually perceive them as shrinking – just getting further away. Neither do they appear to be growing as they come towards us, just getting closer.

This is because, in deciding how big things are, our brain uses not just the size of the images in our eyes, but also information about distance. This allows us to make a mental adjustment and see things at their correct size. This is referred to as **size constancy scaling**. A small image close up is therefore probably a small object (e.g. an ant). But a small image a long way away may be perceived, once your brain has scaled up to allow for the distance, as a big object (e.g. a building, hill or tree).

In the left-hand drawing the two figures are perceived as being the same size because the brain allows for the distance between them. In the right-hand drawing, the figure on the left appears much larger than the tiny seated figure ▶

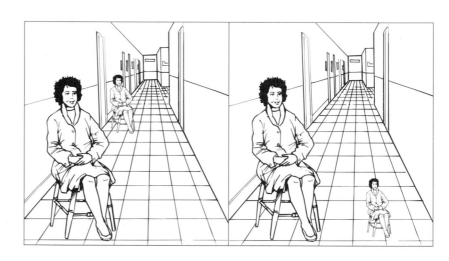

TRY THIS

Look out of your window at the houses, and cars in the street. Do they look to be normal size? Or do they appear to be tiny, perhaps objects smaller than your hand?

Usually we see them as normal size. But if you hold your hand close to your eyes it will block them from view. This is because, close up, your hand forms a big image in your eyes, but distant objects make a smaller image, so that the image of your hand completely covers them.

Perceiving distance

To apply size constancy scaling properly, our brains must be able to work out how far away things are. But if the images inside our eyes are flat (2D), how is this achieved? How is the third dimension of depth or distance worked out?

It is thought that our brains use a number of clues, or **cues**, in the flat images in our eyes to work out how far away things are. Some of these cues are available in a single image (i.e. are present even in just one eye). These are called **monocular cues**. Other cues require the use of both eyes, and these are called **binocular cues**.

Monocular cues

A characteristic of monocular cues is that they still give us information about depth or distance, even when we are looking with only one eye open.

Monocular cues to depth or distance are as follows:

1. Decreasing size

This refers to the size of the image in the eye. The further away things are, the smaller the image they make. So a house which makes a small image is probably far away. The smaller the image is, the further away it probably is.

2. Height in the horizontal plane

Think of the image in the eye as a painting or photograph. There are clues to distance in how high up the picture an object is. For example, assume the line of the horizon cuts across the middle of the image or scene being observed. As objects on the ground move away from us, they move up the image and towards the horizon.

Similarly, objects above the horizon appear to move down as they get further away. (Of course, for objects in the air like birds or planes, there is the added problem that they may be flying at different heights, but all things being equal the principle still applies, i.e. a bird will move down towards the horizon as it flies away from you). So the height of an object in the visual field (the **retinal image**) helps us decide how far away it is.

In the diagram B appears further away than A, and Y appears further away than X. This is because of their relative height on the picture plane.

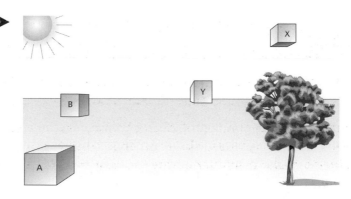

TRY THIS

Look at the ground through a window. Concentrate on a patch of ground near to you, and 'touch it' by placing your finger on the windowpane. Keep your finger there, and repeat the exercise while looking at a piece of ground further away. Notice that, the further away you look, the higher the point on the window that you look through.

3. Gradient of texture

Texture refers to the grain of a surface. Textures get more compressed with distance. Look at these pictures:

The more compressed the texture, the further away things are likely to be. In A, evenly spaced lines make the surface seem flat, while B and C give an appearance of slope or distance. ▶

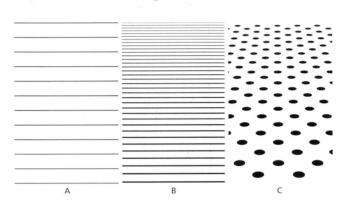

Notice how an impression of depth is created by the way in which the textures become compressed or denser towards the top of the pictures.

4. Linear perspective

Parallel lines get closer together as they get further away. The parallel lines of a road or railway track converge as they recede into the distance.

Parallel lines meet at infinity ▶

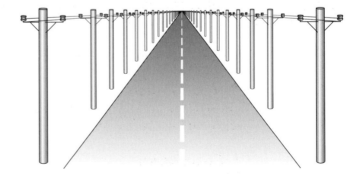

5. Clarity

Quite simply, the nearer things are, the *clearer* they are. With distance details become more obscure. This is because air molecules scatter light. The more air molecules a particle of light has to travel through, the more scattered and diffused it becomes, and the darker and fuzzier the object will appear.

6. Overlap

If Object A blocks your view of Object B, then A must be closer than B.

If A blocks your view of B, then A must be closer than B

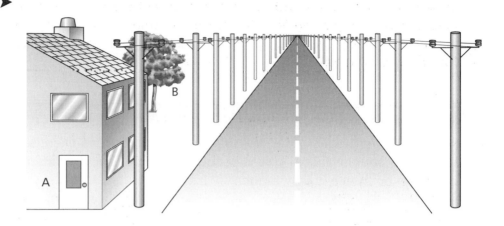

7. Motion parallax

Nearer objects move more quickly across the visual field. In a car on the motorway the nearby verge seems to whizz by, while the trees in the distance appear to pass by more slowly. Meanwhile, distant objects like the sun or moon (if visible) will seem to be relatively stationary and will appear to follow you, because they are such a long way away.

TRY THIS

Stand facing the wall of a room and hold your finger up at arm's length. Now move your head from side to side, so that your finger moves from left to right relative to the wall. Notice how far your finger appears to move, and then repeat the exercise with your finger close to your nose. Notice that your finger appears to move more when it is closer to your eyes. This demonstrates motion parallax.

Binocular cues

Unlike monocular cues, **binocular cues** only work if you are looking with *both* eyes.

1. Convergence

When we look at distant objects, both eyes face straight ahead. But when we look at close objects, our eyes have to swivel inwards (**converge**) in order to focus on them. (This is why we go 'cross-eyed' when we try to look at the tip of our nose.) The muscles used to swivel our eyes convey information to the brain which can be used to help in judging distance. The more our eyes have to be turned inwards, the closer the object that we are looking at.

2. Binocular disparity

This refers to the **disparity** (or difference) between the images in each eye. Because our eyes are set slightly apart they each receive a slightly different image. The closer things are to us, the bigger the difference between the images in each eye. Again, this is information the brain can use in judging distance.

TRY THIS

Hold your finger up at arm's length and open and close each eye in turn. Your finger will appear to 'bounce about'. This is because each eye sees it from a slightly different angle. Now bring your finger closer towards you and repeat the exercise. Notice that your finger appears to bounce more. This is because, being closer, the difference between the images in each eye is now bigger.

The information which the brain receives from the overlap in the images of both eyes can be very important to us. Most predatory animals such as tigers, eagles and humans, have eyes in the front of their head. This is because they need to be able to judge distances very well in order to catch their prey. Non-predatory animals have less need for such accurate depth perception and a greater need for all-round vision to detect predators. As a result their eyes are usually farther apart (i.e. on the side of their head).

TRY THIS

Hold two pens horizontally with their points facing each other, one in each hand, at nearly arm's length, and about a foot apart. Try to touch the points together, first with one eye shut, and then with both eyes open. What does this tell you about the importance of binocular vision?

Visual illusions

An **illusion** is a perceptual mistake. Illusions occur when we misinterpret a stimulus, or have trouble seeing something for what it truly is. (Note that this is not the same as an **hallucination**. Hallucinating involves seeing something when there is nothing there at all – i.e. no stimulus causing the perception.)

Gregory (1966) argued that illusions occur because our brains make guesses about what we are looking at. This is usually a very rapid process which happens unconsciously. When we look at something, our brains use the knowledge that they have stored over a lifetime to help us decide exactly what it is we are seeing. The ability to use past learning greatly increases the power of the perceptual system and helps to explain why perception is usually so accurate and fast. Sometimes, however, we encounter unusual situations in which past learning is not appropriate, and this leads us into error.

Distortions

We have seen that we normally use information about distance to help us decide how big something is. If we draw shapes on paper we can include cues to distance, even though the drawings are necessarily flat (two-dimensional). This can give rise to what Gregory calls **distortions**. In distortion illusions, the wrong use of cues to distance mislead us into thinking that something is bigger or smaller than it really is.

In the **Ponzo illusion** the higher horizontal line wrongly appears longer than the lower one. Gregory argued that this is because the two outside lines provide linear perspective cues suggesting something like a track receding into the distance. The higher line is therefore wrongly interpreted as further away than the lower line. Size constancy scaling (see page 202) results in an expansion of the higher line and we (wrongly) scale it up to allow for the 'extra' distance.

In the **Müller-Lyer illusion**, the line in the outgoing fins wrongly appears longer than the line in the ingoing fins. Gregory argued that the fins suggest depth, in that they produce shapes on the retina similar to the shapes produced by the inside corner of a room (outgoing fins), or the outside corner of a building (ingoing fins). An inside corner recedes away from us; an outside corner sticks out towards us. The line in the outgoing fins is therefore interpreted by our brains as further away, and again it gets scaled up to allow for this 'extra' distance.

The above distortions are a consequence of wrongly adding depth to a drawing (which is flat). The **Ames Room** (see page 208) is a distortion that arises as a consequence of not adding in depth when we should.

An Ames Room is constructed in such a way that the back wall slopes, but the slope is disguised so as to make the observer think it is a 'normal' flat wall. One person in the room is therefore further away than the other, and so creates a smaller image. However, since the people appear to be the same distance away, scaling is not applied as it should be, and so one person seems much bigger than the other.

One naturally occurring illusion is that the moon looks bigger when it is lower in the sky – the so-called **moon illusion**. This may in part be because, when it is lower down and nearer the horizon, it is interpreted by our brains as being further away than when it is overhead due to its height in the horizontal plane. As a consequence, it is scaled up by the brain to allow for this 'extra' distance.

Ambiguous figures

An **ambiguous figure** is a figure that can be interpreted in more than one way, so that the brain is not sure what to make of it. Gregory argued that ambiguous figures are a result of patterns occurring in the eye that have two or more equally likely explanations. As a consequence, when the brain tries to guess what it is that we are seeing, it cannot decide which guess is best.

The Ponzo Illusion

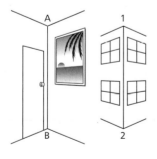

In the Ponzo illusion, the higher bar wrongly appears longer than the lower one. ▲

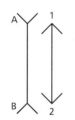

The Müller-Lyer Illusion

In the two sets of drawings above, the verticals A–B and 1–2 are the same length, but A–B appears longer in both cases. ▲

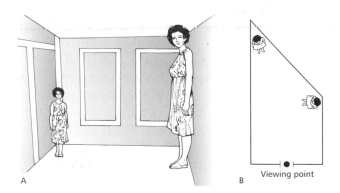

The unusual shape of the Ames Room tricks the brain into not allowing for the effect of distance and depth ▶

Viewing point

The **Necker Cube (below)** creates uncertainty about whether the marked face is at the front or the back. If we stare at it for a while it will suddenly switch from one perspective to the other. This is because our brains first try one possibility and find it works, then try out another possibility and find that works just as well, and so cannot decide which alternative is best.

Is the marked face of the Necker Cube at the front or the back? ▶

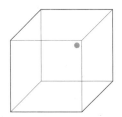

Other famous ambiguous figures include the old/young woman ('Leeper's Lady'), and the two faces/vase figure ('The Rubin Vase'):

Visual ambiguity: 'The Rubin Vase' and 'Leeper's Lady' ▶

Fictions

Look at the figure on the left. This figure is called the **Kanisza Triangle**. Many people claim to be able to see a white triangle in it, although in fact there is no triangle there. Gregory believed that this is because our brain makes a guess at what we are looking at and decides that it is very unlikely that the shapes are arranged in the way they are, and much more likely that there is a white triangle blocking our view. Once the brain has decided that that is what we are looking at, then that is what we see.

The Kanisza Triangle ▲

Gestalt principles

Evidence from visual illusions such as the Kanisza Triangle and the two faces/vase figure above tends to support the views of **Gestalt** psychologists of the 1930s. Gestalt psychologists argued that the brain is wired up in such a way that it automatically imposes organisation on incoming information in particular ways. Unlike Gregory, the Gestalt theorists argued that this tendency to organise information does *not* depend on learning, but is an **innate** (inborn) capacity of the mind.

1. Figure-ground relationships

When we open our eyes, we see a world of objects. To interpret the world we must be able to separate one thing from another and distinguish an object from its surroundings. The **figure** refers to the object seen. It appears to be a solid unit that has its own coherence and boundary, and is separate from the **ground**, which is more formless and provides the background against which the object is seen. The two faces/ vase figure provides an example of this process. We see either two black faces against a white background, or a white vase against a black background.

2. Closure

This refers to our tendency to fill in the gaps in incomplete figures. In the Kanisza triangle we close up the shapes to make three black circles and a triangle with a black border, and this is what leads to the perception of a white triangle. The principle of closure has also been used to explain why we often struggle with the nine-dot problem.

```
●   ●   ●

●   ●   ●

●   ●   ●
```

In the nine-dot problem we are asked to join up all the dots using not more than four straight lines and without taking our pen off the paper. (The solution is on page 220.)

3. Proximity

When asked to describe the figure below, people often report seeing three pairs of circles.

OO   OO   OO

Gestalt psychologists argued that there is no logical reason why we should see things in this way. In all possible worlds there are other alternatives, e.g.

209

or perhaps:

B

That is, we could view the figure as made up of two middle pairs with odd circles outside (**A**), or two groups of three circles (**B**). Our tendency to see it as three pairs shows that we organise the scene according to how close together (or proximate) the circles are.

4. Similarity

This refers to our tendency to organise a scene according to how similar items look.

In the figure below, for example, many people describe seeing *columns* of figures.

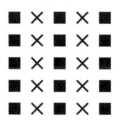

However, when the figure is tipped on its side…

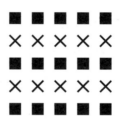

many people report seeing *rows* of figures.

5. Continuation

Many people describe the figure below as a *cross*.

Again, Gestalt psychologists have suggested that there are logical alternatives to this interpretation, e.g. connected 'V' shapes:

A cross, though, is the interpretation that requires the fewest breaks or changes in direction of the lines, and it is this, the simplest organisation, that we opt for.

A basic principle of Gestalt psychology is that the *whole is greater than the sum of its parts*. This means that we cannot fully understand something just by looking at the 'bits' that make it up. Once we have looked at the bits, the whole still eludes us. In the same way we cannot understand a symphony by examining every note individually. We have to listen to the whole symphony to understand it properly and respond to it.

Wertheimer (1912) demonstrated this principle using the **phi phenomenon**. This can often be seen on the illuminated signs on fairground rides, where flashing lights seem to move back and forth or round and round in a circle. If we look at the 'bits' here, all we have are stationary lights flashing on and off in turn. But the (whole) perception includes the impression of movement – something we would not discover just by looking at the individual parts.

A general criticism of the Gestalt approach to visual perception is that, while it may demonstrate some interesting facts about shapes on paper, it may not tell us a lot about perception in the real world. Additionally, not everyone agrees that the organising principles identified by the Gestalt school are innate. As we have seen, Gregory is more keen to emphasise the role that learning has to play, and we will consider this issue shortly in looking at perceptual development

TRY THIS

Match the **terms** on the left to the **definitions** on the right.

motion parallax	region of the brain which interprets visual data
visual distortion	a binocular cue to distance
visual cortex	an illusion in which something appears the wrong size
size constancy	a monocular cue to distance
convergence	the distinction between an object and its surroundings
location constancy	why things don't look smaller as they move away
figure/ground relationship	why stationary objects don't appear to move when we do

Some factors affecting perception

By now it should be clear that perception is a complex business. To complicate matters further, what we see is influenced by a wide variety of other factors. Some are listed below, but you should remember that these may sometimes operate together, and so should not be considered to always be working independently of each other.

Attention

What we see or notice often depends on how we look at objects or what we attend to. A police officer, trained to notice what people look like, will usually be able to give a better description of a stranger seen briefly than those of us who are not so trained.

Some things are more likely to grab our attention than others. In particular, a *strong* stimulus like a loud noise or a bright light is likely to be noticed. Things that are *moving* are more likely to be noticed than when they are still (as when you suddenly notice a tiny spider when it scuttles across the floor).

Perceptual set

The term **set** refers to our 'readiness to perceive'. Our expectations can affect what we notice and how we choose to interpret it. Sprinters on the starting blocks will ignore distractions and are not likely to dive for cover when the starting gun is fired. They are focused on a particular sound (of a pistol being fired) and have decided to interpret it as a signal to start running, rather than as a potential assassination attempt. The *context* in which something is seen, then, can affect *what* is seen:

TAE CAT   A 13 C 12 13 14

In the examples above, the middle figures are the same but may be interpreted differently depending on the context.

Motivation

Our perceptions may also be influenced by our needs. Sandford (1936) found that if he showed people ambiguous shapes on a screen, as time went by and people got hungrier, they were more likely to interpret the shapes as having a connection with food. Gilchrist and Nesberg (1952) deprived people of food and drink for up to eight hours and found that, as time went by, pictures of food and drink were seen as brighter than pictures of non-food objects. Of course, advertisers would love you to be hungry when walking around a supermarket!

Reward and punishment

Schafer and Murphy (1974) showed people two face drawings, A and B, and asked them to learn to name the faces. Whenever A was shown, people were rewarded by being given money. Whenever B was shown, they were punished by money being taken away. Then both faces were shown together. People more readily reported seeing A than B. This indicates that reward and punishment can influence perceptual set, and that we may sometimes be readier to notice things associated with rewards than with punishments.

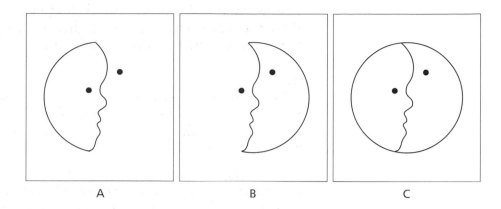

Research by Schafer and Murphy using these face motifs showed that reward and punishment can influence perceptual set

Source: Cassells, A., & Green, P., *Perception* (BPS Open Learning Unit, 1991) © The British Psychological Society. Reproduced with permission

A   B   C

Emotion

Freud suggested that we may sometimes not notice, or remember, things which we do not like or which make us anxious. He claimed that, without being aware of doing it, we sometimes push anxiety-provoking information into our unconscious mind. This is called **repression** (see page 225)

McGinnies (1949) flashed individual words on a screen too quickly to be recognised and gradually slowed the presentation until people could correctly report the words. He found that people took longer to recognise anxiety-provoking or taboo words like 'penis', 'bitch', 'filth' than neutral words like 'apple', 'river' or 'broom'. He argued that this was evidence for **perceptual defence** – in other words, that we try not to see things that we do not like. However, critics have pointed out that people might simply want to be a bit more sure before calling out taboo words to avoid embarrassment if they are wrong.

To sum up so far:

- We can make a distinction between **perception** and **sensation**. Visual sensations are the patterns of light and dark detected by the light-sensitive cells which make up the retina in the back of our eyes. Visual perceptions are what we see as a result of the work that our brains do on those flat, constantly changing images. Our brain translates those images into perceptions of a stable, three-dimensional world of objects. This is the world of our everyday experience.

- **Perceptual constancy** refers to the fact that our perceptions of things like shape, size, colour and location remain stable despite changes in viewing conditions and consequent changes in the patterns in our eyes.

- **Size constancy** requires accurate depth perception. It is believed the brain works out how far away things are by using various monocular and binocular cues contained in the flat images in our eyes.

- Perception is a matter of **interpreting visual data**. Our brain usually does this very quickly and accurately. Gregory argues that the perceptual system is so powerful because our brains use past learning about the world to help in interpreting present data. However, there are times when past learning is applied inappropriately, and this can generate visual illusions.

- **Gestalt psychologists** argue that our brains automatically impose organisation on visual data. We are wired up to process visual information in particular ways, and this is not dependent on learning. They cite principles like proximity, similarity, continuation, closure, and figure–ground relationships as evidence of inborn organising tendencies of the brain. They argue that the whole is greater than, or different to, the sum of its parts. The extent to which these principles are innate (inborn) is disputed by some.

- Perception can be affected by a number of factors including **perceptual set, motivation, and emotion**. This also shows that perception is a complex process, and there is more involved than simply patterns in our eyes. The extent to which our perceptual abilities are innate is the focus of the next section.

Perceptual development

If newborn babies (**neonates**) can do something straight away, the ability must be innate. But some abilities may take a little while to emerge. This could be because they depend on **maturation** (i.e. physical development). Babies' brains and the muscles in their eyes continue to develop after they are born. In general, the earlier an ability appears, the more likely it is to be innate, and the longer it takes to appear, the more likely it is to depend on learning. Of course, one difficulty is that babies cannot tell us what they can see. Researchers therefore have to use the baby's behaviour as a guide.

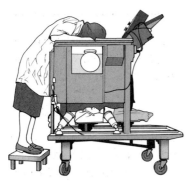

The perception of form and faces
Fantz (1956) devised a viewing chamber (left) to find out what babies can see and like to look at. The research technique was based on the idea of **preferential looking**. If a baby was shown two things and continuously preferred to look at one thing rather than another, Fantz concluded that the baby must be able to tell the difference between them, and secondly, that the baby had a perceptual bias towards some things rather than others.

Fantz's viewing chamber for investigating infant perception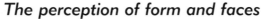

Fantz showed pairs of different patterns to babies and timed how long they looked at each pattern. He found that babies preferred to look at complex patterns rather than simple ones.

Fantz also wanted to discover if babies had an innate preference for human faces. Since babies depend utterly on human carers, their survival could depend on their ability to recognise and respond to human faces. Fantz timed how long babies would look at (a) a drawing of a normal face, compared to (b) a drawing of a face in which the

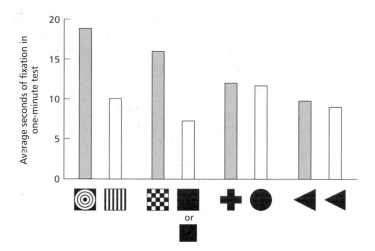

features were jumbled up; and (c) the outline of a face in which the top region was shaded in and the bottom region was left blank. He found that even babies as young as four days old preferred to look at the picture of a normal face. From this he concluded that a preference for looking at a human face is innate.

Fantz timed how long babies would look at each of the 'faces' shown on the right ▶

The perception of depth or distance

Are we born with the ability to see how far away things are? This was investigated by Gibson and Walk (below).

KEY STUDY

Gibson and Walk (1960) devised an apparatus called a **visual cliff** to see if babies could detect depth. The visual cliff is a glass-topped table, with a check pattern fixed to the underside of one half of the glass, and fixed to the floor beneath the other half of the glass. There is therefore a visual drop, but the baby cannot fall since the glass top prevents it.

Babies as young as six months were placed in the middle to see if they would crawl over the 'deep' side. Gibson and Walk found that most babies refused to cross over the deep side, even when encouraged to do so. Other research has shown that newly-hatched chicks and kittens whose eyes have just opened also refuse to go over the deep side. Gibson and Walk concluded that depth perception is innate. Blindfolding one eye did not encourage babies to cross over the deep side. Neither did increasing the size of the square checks patterned on the floor. The researchers concluded that the babies were using motion parallax (a monocular cue) to perceive depth. As the baby moved, the checks immediately beneath the glass moved more rapidly across their field of view than those on the floor.

The 'visual cliff' experiment by Gibson and Walk ▶

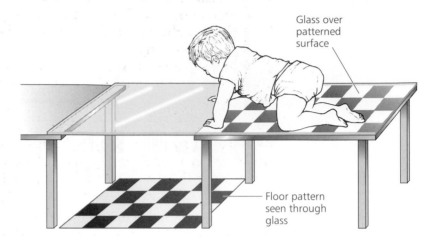

Glass over patterned surface

Floor pattern seen through glass

However, since babies do not crawl before they are around six months old, it is possible they could learn to perceive depth in this time. Campos et al. (1970), though, found that even two-month-old babies showed a drop in heart rate (indicating interest) when placed on the glass over the deep side, which supports the idea of depth perception being innate.

Questions
1. What was the result of blindfolding one of the baby's eyes?
2. What was the purpose of increasing the size of the checks on the floor?
3. Give two practical problems of conducting research on babies.
4. Identify two ethical issues raised by the use of babies in research.

THINK ABOUT IT

In psychological experiments involving babies, food is not considered a suitable 'reinforcer' – although it is widely used as a reinforcer in animal experiments. Why do you think this is?

Size constancy
We know that the perception of distance is involved in the perception of size. But is size constancy innate? Bower (1966) trained babies aged between 40 to 60 days to look at a 30cm cube placed 1 metre away. He did this by rewarding the baby every time it looked at the cube. The reward used was a 'peek-a-boo', i.e. an adult would pop their head up from behind a screen, say 'peek-a-boo' and then hide again. Babies like this, and will repeat behaviour for a peek-a-boo reward.

Once the baby was conditioned to the cube, Bower replaced this with three other stimuli:

1 **A 30cm cube at 3m** (same-sized cube, 3 x distance: image therefore one-third the size of the original)
2 **A 90cm cube at 3m** (3 x bigger cube, 3 x distance: same-size image as original)
3 **A 90cm cube at 1m** (3 x bigger cube, same distance: image therefore three times bigger than original)

The stimuli were presented in a counterbalanced order for four 30-second periods each, and the time the baby spent looking at them was recorded. If size constancy is learned we would predict that babies would prefer to look at (2), the cube producing the same-size retinal image, since the young babies had not had time to learn size constancy. In fact, the babies preferred to look at (1), the same actual cube, even though the extra distance reduced the image size. This suggests that some ability for size constancy is, in fact, innate.

The Gestalt principle of closure
Bower (1977) trained two-month-old babies to respond to a black wire triangle with a black iron bar across it.

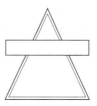

The babies were then tested with four different stimuli to see which they would prefer:

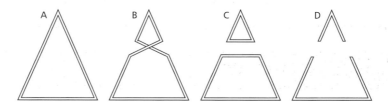

Bower found that babies preferred the complete triangle. This indicates that they had realised that there was a complete triangle partially hidden beneath the iron bar in the original stimulus. This supports the idea that closure is an innate feature of the perceptual system as Gestalt psychologists argued.

Cross-cultural research
If, despite living in different environments, everybody throughout the world sees things in the same way, this would suggest that learning is irrelevant and that our perceptual abilities are entirely innate. But there is much evidence, from cross-cultural research, to support the idea that learning is also important for the development of our perceptual abilities.

Turnbull (1961) studied pygmies living in dense jungle in the Congo. Turnbull took one pygmy out to a plain and showed him a herd of buffalo in the distance. He asked the pygmy what he could see. The pygmy replied that he could see some strange insects. He refused to believe Turnbull when he told him they were buffalo, and was amazed when Turnbull drove him up to the herd and the 'insects' magically changed into buffalo before his eyes. The pygmy had obviously not developed size constancy for objects at a great distance – presumably because in a dense forest there is no opportunity for surveying objects or animals over great distances. The story shows, therefore, how size constancy can be developed and refined through learning.

Segall et al. (1963) studied the extent to which different cultures are fooled by visual illusions like the Müller-Lyer illusion (see page 207). They found wide variations in susceptibility to such illusions between different cultures. One African tribe, the Batoro, who live in open country, were very likely to be fooled by the illusion. Another tribe, the Bete, who live in jungle, were unlikely to be fooled by the illusion. The very fact that there are such differences supports the idea that the environment, and so learning, has an influence on our perceptions.

Segall et al. put forward the **carpentered world hypothesis** to explain cross-cultural differences, arguing that in Western-type cultures we are exposed to many straight lines, because our built environment is usually made up of corners, edges and right angles. Since these are cues to depth in our environment, we interpret them in the same way when we see them in drawings. This is why Westerners may be fooled by illusions such as the Müller-Lyer illusion, since depth is interpreted in a drawing which is flat (2D). Tribes like the Batoro also use vertical lines to estimate depth, as when a distant tree provides a focal point to estimate distance. But in other cultures where straight lines are not cues to distance, they are not interpreted as such in drawings, and so scaling is not used inappropriately to generate illusions. It should be noted that not all research supports this hypothesis, which remains controversial.

Hudson (1960) tested a variety of African cultural groups with drawings and found that they often failed to interpret depth properly in the drawings. He concluded that many people in such cultures were unable to see depth in pictures. Subsequent research has found that the more depth cues that are used in a drawing (for example, texture gradient), the easier it is for people from such cultures to properly interpret them. Furthermore, critics have pointed out that the pictures used in research often satisfied Western artistic conventions, but different cultures use different conventions, which may account for the findings. In the same way, Westerners may find it difficult to properly interpret drawings by Tsimshian Indians of British Columbia, which are stylised to be ornamental and show particular characteristics of objects rather than to represent them as a photograph might. Again, though, we find that cultural experience, and so learning, can have an impact upon our perceptual abilities.

QUESTIONS

Can you describe:

1   Two studies that show that perceptual abilities are innate?
2   Two studies that show that perceptual abilities are influenced by learning?

Evaluation

In general, in perception as elsewhere, the nature-nurture debate is not an either/or question. How we see the world is a reflection of *both* our biological inheritance *and* the ways in which that inheritance has been shaped and influenced by environmental factors.

We may be born with certain basic abilities, like the ability to distinguish an object from its background, track it as it moves, understand that some objects are further away than others etc. Some of these abilities may be developed and refined with further learning, or they may deteriorate if they are not used. To go beyond these basic abilities, and understand just what it is that we are looking at, and what the implications of what we see are for us, seems likely to depend on learning.

Summary

- Visual perception is a very complex process; it involves the brain interpreting patterns in the eyes. Perceptual constancies, gestalt principles of organisation, factors which affect perception (like emotion), all indicate just how complex perceptual processes are.
- Of course, babies are learning about seeing from the moment they are born, and so discovering the true extent of innate abilities is difficult. In general the earlier an ability appears the more likely it is to be innate.
- Research with babies indicates that the ability to perceive things like figure-ground relationships, the principle of closure, the perception of depth, and size constancy may be innate, at least to some limited extent.
- Cross-cultural research has shown that learning also has an important part to play in the development of human perceptual abilities.

Solution to the 9-dot problem (page 209)

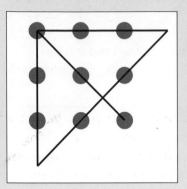

The reason people often find the task difficult is because they mentally 'close up' the dots to form a square and then try not to draw outside this square. The drawing itself, however, is not a square.

15 Memory

Memory can be defined as *the retention of information or learning*. Our memory contains everything we know about ourselves and our world. Just think for a moment how important memory is. If we couldn't remember anything, how could we possibly survive?

Since memory is so important to us, it is not surprising that psychologists have spent many years studying it and trying to understand it. Among the questions psychologists ask about memory are:

- how *much* can we remember?
- how *accurate* are our memories?
- why do we *forget* things?
- how can we *improve* memory?
- Can we construct a *theory* of how memory works?

We are still a long way from knowing all there is to know about memory, but this chapter will explore some of the ideas that have been developed so far.

Could YOU survive without a memory? ▲

Memory is reconstructive

Few of us can remember much, if anything, of what happened to us before the age of three or four. This is called **childhood amnesia**. It is probably linked to the fact that in very early childhood our brain is still developing. Can you remember potty training, or taking your first steps, or uttering your first sentence? Some people claim that they *can* clearly recall events from their second, or even first year of life, but research

Childhood amnesia means most of us find it hard to recall our very early years ▶

suggests that these 'memories' are more likely to be **reconstructions** based on family stories, imagination, photographs, etc. As a child, the Swiss psychologist Jean Piaget claimed to have a clear memory of his nurse defending him from a would-be kidnapper when he was just two years old. It was not until he was fifteen that he discovered that this 'memory' was actually a story his nurse had made up.

THINK ABOUT IT

Can you think of an event or incident which you thought you had experienced, but which turned out to be something you had dreamed, imagined or confused with something else? What does this tell you about the nature of memory?

Eyewitness testimony

Research shows that our reconstructions of past events can be influenced by the way in which people ask us questions about them – in other words, that what we remember may change according to how we are asked. Loftus and Palmer (1974) showed people a film in which two cars were involved in an accident. Afterwards, some of the people were asked how fast were the cars going when they hit each other. Others were asked the same question, but with a slight change of wording. Instead of 'hit', the researchers used the words 'smashed into'.

As expected, the estimate of speed that people gave varied depending on the question they were asked. The average estimate for the term 'smashed' was 41 mph, whereas the average estimate for the word 'hit' was just 34 mph.

One week later all the participants were asked: 'Did you see any broken glass?' although there was no broken glass in the film. Of the 'smashed' group, 32% said they remembered seeing broken glass in the film, compared to just 14% of the 'hit' group.

In a similar study, Loftus and Zanni (1975) showed a group of people a film of a car accident. Afterwards, some were asked 'Did you see a broken headlight?' Others were asked, 'Did you see the broken headlight?' Notice the word '*the*' implies that there *was* a broken headlight. Sure enough, those who were asked the question using the word '*the*' rather than the word '*a*' were much more likely to report seeing a broken headlight – even though there wasn't one! Both of these studies reveal that the way in which we remember events can be affected by the way in which we are asked about them.

THINK ABOUT IT

Consider the case of a witness in a murder trial who is being cross-examined in a courtroom. What difference might it make if the lawyer were to ask, 'Did you see *the* knife?' instead of 'Did you see *a* knife?'

Eysenck (1998) argued that research reveals that misleading information is most likely to affect memory for *trivial* details (like broken glass). Crucial information or central details, like the presence of a gun, are less likely to be distorted.

Recognition of faces

Many people think that a violent criminal would probably be better remembered than a non-violent one. Loftus, in fact, found that the presence of a gun at a crime often served to distract attention away from the face of the criminal, resulting in the criminal being less well remembered. Shapiro and Penrod (1986) analysed 128 research studies on the identification of faces. They found that we are better at remembering faces from our own ethnic group than from other groups. It is not certain why this is so. One suggestion is that the facial features that are most useful for distinguishing between people (such as hair- or eye-colour, or shape of mouth) may differ between groups. However, we tend to concentrate on the features we usually use to distinguish between members of our own group, even when these are not so suitable for discriminating the faces of members of another group.

Stereotypes

An important consideration, linked to the reconstructive nature of memory and eyewitness testimony, is that stereotypes and prejudices can distort recall. Buckhout (1974) showed a group of white participants a drawing in which a casually dressed white man holding a razor threatened a smartly dressed black man on a train. Half of the participants wrongly remembered the black man as holding a razor. Duncan (1976) showed people a video of a discussion between two men (both actors). The discussion became heated, and at one point one man pushed the other one, and then the screen went blank. The behaviour was the same, but the race of the person pushing or being pushed varied in different versions of the film. Duncan asked participants to describe the push, choosing from a rating of 'playing around', 'dramatising', 'aggressive behaviour' or 'violent behaviour'. He found that more people were likely to classify the push as 'violent behaviour' if it was given by a black person, and this was especially likely if the victim of the push was white.

Schemas

Bartlett (1932) investigated the ways in which our memories can change, using a North American Indian folk-tale called 'The War of the Ghosts' (see activity on page 224). Sometimes he read the story to a person and asked them to recount it to another person, who then had to repeat it to someone else – and so on. Sometimes, the same person was asked to recall the story after different intervals – a week later, a month later, etc. This technique of repeatedly recalling information is called **serial reproduction**. The purpose was to observe how the story changed in the re-telling.

Bartlett chose to use 'The War of the Ghosts' deliberately because people who lack the appropriate cultural background find certain parts

Mrs Smith, are you quite sure this is the man you saw?

Eyewitness testimony can be unreliable ▲

of the story quite difficult to follow. He found that people would impose their own meanings on the material. As a result, unusual material was particularly likely to get dropped or changed to become more conventional. This shows that remembering is an active process. Past learning can affect how we interpret information and remember it. Bartlett called the ideas that we hold about the world **schemata**. Our prior learning, our schemata, can influence the memories that we form and what we remember.

TRY THIS

Read through 'The War of the Ghosts' once only, then, without referring back to it, write down as much of the story as you can remember.

'One night two young men from Egulac went down to the river to hunt seals. While they were there, it became foggy and calm. They heard war-cries and thought "Maybe this is a war party". They escaped to the shore and hid behind a log. Now canoes came up and they heard the noise of paddles and saw one canoe coming up to them. There were five men in the canoe and they said: "What do you think? We wish to take you along. We are going up the river to make war on the people." One of the young men said "I have no arrows." "Arrows are in the canoe," they said. "I will not go along. I might be killed. My relatives do not know where I have gone. But you," he said, turning to the other, "may go with them."

'So one of the young men went but the other returned home. And the warriors went on up the river to a town on the other side of Kalama. The people came down to the water and they began to fight and many were killed. But presently the young man heard one of the warriors say: "Quick, let us go home: that Indian has been hit." Now he thought, "Oh, they are ghosts." He did not feel sick, but they said he had been shot. So the canoes went back to Egulac and the young man went ashore to his house and made a fire. And he told everybody and said, "Behold, I accompanied the ghosts and we went to fight. Many of our fellows were killed and many of those who attacked us were killed. They said I was hit and I did not feel sick." He told it all and then he became quiet. When the sun rose he fell down. Something black came out of his mouth. His face became contorted. The people jumped up and cried. He was dead.'

Now write down as much as you can remember.

How did you do?

Most people find that they come up with something much shorter than the original. Sometimes they miss out material altogether, and sometimes they change parts of the story. Nevertheless, people still often manage to produce a story of some sort.

This shows that remembering is an *active* process. We may add, delete or change information in order to reconstruct the material in a way that makes sense to us.

Of course, at an everyday level our memories are usually quite accurate. We are not often confused about what happened yesterday, or how to catch a bus. But memory is not like a videotape. It can contain distortions or incorporate information in a way that is not reliable. This can happen even though the memory seems to be, to the person holding it, very clear and unambiguous. For example, the police know that eyewitnesses can sometimes give very different accounts of an event; the fact that someone is convinced that they can recall things clearly does not guarantee that their memory provides a true account of what happened.

Forgetting

Our tendency to forget things is one of the most annoying aspects of memory. But it is possible that some forgetting is essential if memory is to be truly useful. If everything we had ever done or learned was available to us constantly, competing for attention in our conscious mind, life would be extremely complicated.

THINK ABOUT IT

Think of a simple activity like eating a sandwich. How many possible memory associations could this everyday experience trigger off? What does this tell you about the importance of forgetting?

Repression

Psychologists believe that we forget things for a number of different reasons. One reason suggested by Freud is **repression**. Freud argued that sometimes events that we find upsetting, or that make us anxious, are pushed out of consciousness into our unconscious mind and memories for these events are no longer available to us. This is referred to as the **theory of motivated forgetting**, and may be used to explain, for example, why someone who has been abused as a child may be unable to recall details of how and when the abuse took place: the painful memory is buried in their unconscious mind.

Freud's theories are not accepted by all psychologists and have met with some criticism (see Chapter 6, *Freud and Psychoanalytical Theory*). But we should note that if repression does occur, it does not explain all forgetting. For example, it does not easily explain why we forget emotionally neutral or pleasant things and remember some bad things which we would prefer to forget. It also fails to explain why we forget more as time goes by.

Two theories that explain why we forget more as time goes by are those of **decay** and **interference**. Let us consider each of these in turn.

Decay

According to this theory, memories simply fade away over time if they are not used. Clearly, some memories are more resistant to decay than others. For example, once we have learned how to ride a bike, the memory seems to stay with us; on the other hand, a list of facts and figures learned the night before an exam is likely to fade quite rapidly. Yet the common experience of having our memory 'jogged' by someone or something shows that often the facts we are looking for *are* still stored in our memory somewhere – it is just that they can be hard to find.

THINK ABOUT IT

Have you ever had to wrack your memory to think of a name or word? It is sometimes called the **tip-of-the-tongue** phenomenon. Often the memory will eventually come back – although usually too late to be useful! What does the tip-of-the tongue phenomenon tell you about the nature of memory?

Interference

Another reason for forgetting is **interference**. According to this theory, we forget information because it gets buried among all the other information we have in our heads.

There are two types of interference that psychologists distinguish:

● **Proactive** interference occurs when *old* information prevents you from remembering *new* information. For example, you can remember a woman's maiden name, but not her married one.

● **Retroactive** interference occurs when *new* information prevents you from remembering *old* information. In this case, you can remember the woman's married name but not her maiden name.

QUESTION

Imagine you go to a party and are introduced to a woman called Mandy. Shortly afterwards you are introduced to a woman called Wendy. A bit later you see Mandy again but say 'Hello Wendy' by mistake. Is this **proactive** or **retroactive** interference?

Jenkins and Dallenbach (1924) asked two groups of people to learn lists of nonsense syllables. One group learned the list late at night, just before going to bed. The other group learned the list early in the morning, just before going about their normal daily activities. The groups' recall was tested after intervals of one, two, four or eight hours (the late-night group were asleep and had to be woken specially).

In the experiment it was found that the daytime group forgot more than the sleepers. This suggests that it is not just the passage of time, but what happens *in* that time that can influence forgetting. One suggestion is that since the waking group were receiving more information during the day, this new information resulted in increased interference and so poorer recall of the list.

Damage to the brain

Some forms of forgetting are caused by shock, injury or damage to the brain. Different sorts of brain damage can result in a wide variety of different forms of forgetting. Two that have been identified are:

1   **Retrograde amnesia:** this can result from injury or accident. Typically, sufferers lose their memory of the accident and of a period of time before it. However, memories may slowly return. The ability to learn new things is not usually impaired unless there is accompanying brain damage.

2   **Anterograde amnesia:** this may result from injury or illness, especially if a region of the brain called the **hippocampus** is damaged. In anterograde amnesia the victim is unable to learn anything new, but old memories, i.e. from before the damage, are still intact. Milner and Scoville (1957) reported the case of H.M., who suffered from epilepsy and underwent brain surgery to remove part of his hippocampus. As a result H.M. never came to recognise his new doctors or nurses, would re-read books and magazines without knowing he had just read them, could not keep track of time or TV programmes or remember simple sequences of events. Clearly the condition was a severely disabling one.

Increasing forgetfulness can also be a symptom of **Alzheimer's Disease (senile dementia)**, which causes cells in the brain to degenerate and die. With an increasing elderly population, this is becoming an ever more common problem. However, Alzheimer's is not a normal part of the ageing process and most of us can expect to grow old without suffering from Alzheimer's or any serious memory impairment.

In summary

● *Work by Loftus and Bartlett shows that memory is reconstructive. This means that while memory is often reliable, it isn't always.*

● *We can forget things for different reasons. Reasons for forgetting include repression, decay, interference, and shock or damage to the brain.*

TRY THIS

Match the **terms** on the left with the **definitions** on the right.

proactive interference	when memories just fade with time
repression	when you cannot recall an accident
anterograde amnesia	old learning hinders recall of recent learning
decay	you know you know it but you can't recall it
retroactive interference	when you are unable to remember new things
the tip-of-the-tongue phenomenon	new learning hinders recall of old learning
retrograde amnesia	burying memories in the unconscious

Improving memory

The amount of information that we store in our heads is huge. Most of our memories are accurate – otherwise we could not function. Yet we have seen that memory is sometimes unreliable and that we can forget things for a number of reasons. So is there anything we can do to improve memory?

Organisation

One thing that helps us remember is to *organise* information. Bower et al. (1969) gave two groups of people lists of words to remember (each group received 4 sets of 28 words, making 112 words in total). The lists were the same for both groups, but one group was given the words in an organised, hierarchical manner (see below), while the other group was given the same words selected randomly. The group that received the lists in an organised form remembered 65% of the words, whereas the group that received the words in a random order only remembered 20% of the words. This shows that organisation can improve recall.

An example of an organised hierarchy of words, as used by Bower et al.

Bower, G.H., Clark, M., Lesgold, A. and Winzenz, D.,'Hierarchical Retrieval Schemes in Recall of Categorised Word Lists,' in *Journal of Verbal Learning and Verbal Behaviour*, 8 (1969), pp.323–43

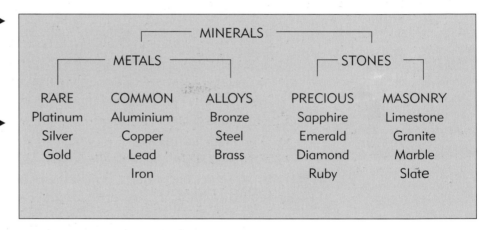

The act of imposing organisation on information gives it meaning – and that makes it easier to recall. A sentence is easier to recall than a meaningless jumble of words. Information about an exam topic (or any other subject) is easier to learn if we understand and can make sense of the material, rather than if we simply try to learn it parrot-fashion without understanding.

TRY THIS

Imagine you have to learn the list of words below. Can you think of anything you could do to help you remember?

- horse
- onion
- sheep
- copper
- cow
- silver
- potato
- gold
- carrot

Did you come up with anything? If so, what does this tell you about memory?

Cues

Another thing that we can do to aid recall is to provide **cues**. Cues are like little 'this way' signs that guide us through information and help us find the exact material we are looking for. Tulving and Pearlstone (1966) asked people to read lists containing a mixture of words from particular categories (types of animals, types of furniture, etc.). When tested in free recall, one group had to write what they could remember on a blank sheet of paper. The other group was given paper with category headings for the words in the list ('animals', 'furniture', etc.). The group with the headings recalled more than the group with a blank sheet of paper. This shows how the category headings served as cues and thereby improved recall.

Sometimes, simply being back in the context or environment where the original learning took place can provide cues that improve recall – a phenomenon known as **context-dependent recall**. Godden and Baddeley (1975) conducted an experiment in which divers were required to learn lists of words either on land or underwater. When tested, the divers' recall was best if they were in the environment where the original learning took place, i.e. if the list was learned underwater it was recalled better underwater compared to on land. In the same way, we might find that if, as adults, we return to the neighbourhood where we grew up, memories of childhood events may return to us as we travel around the once-familiar streets, and childhood haunts.

Of course, actually returning to the original context may not always be possible, but it may be possible to reconstruct the context mentally, i.e. to **imagine** yourself back in the same situation.

It can be easier to remember material if you return to the environment in which it was first learned

Cognitive interviews

The usefulness of cues in helping recall explains why the police often use what are called **cognitive interviews** when questioning witnesses. The technique involves asking them to recall everything they can, leaving nothing out, including even small details that may seem unimportant. Witnesses may be asked to recall things in reverse order or to describe what they think other people could see; they are also encouraged to recreate the *external* context (including lighting conditions, smells) and the *internal* context (how they felt) at the time of the incident. Sometimes they may revisit the scene of the incident to help recreate their mood state at the time. The aim is to provide as many retrieval cues as possible to jog their memory for something important. In a laboratory study, Geiselman et al. (1985) found that cognitive interviews produced 40% more correctly remembered details than standard police interviews.

THINK ABOUT IT

Given what you have just read about context-dependent recall, where do you think would be the best place for students to sit their exams?

Research supports the idea that physical or mental state can be a retrieval cue. This is called **state-dependent recall**. Mayer et al. (1990) report that you are more likely to remember happy events when you are feeling happy compared to when you are feeling sad, (though this is not always the case). Similarly, Overton (1972) reports that, when sober, a person may sometimes forget what they did when they were drunk, but remember it when they are drunk again.

Being unable to remember something because we are now in a different state or context is referred to as **cue-dependent forgetting**. We have seen that providing cues can be a good way to improve memory. This underpins a distinction between **recognition** and **recall**:

- a **recognition test** simply asks if you have come across a particular thing before. The very act of hearing about or seeing the item before you (the one asked about) acts as a retrieval cue. This jogs your memory, and makes the process of recognition easier.
- a **test of recall** is usually harder than a recognition test: it involves trying to remember things with the minimum of cues to help you.

TRY THIS

Write down the names of **all** the students in your class. How easy did you find it?

Suppose instead that someone **reads** a list of names to you and asks you which names belong to people in your class. Would this be easier or harder than the first task? Why?

In fact, the second task is probably easier for most people. This is because it is a test of **recognition** rather than **recall**.

Visual imagery can help recall ▲

Imagery

Other methods that have been found to improve recall involve the use of **imagery**. Bower (1972) asked people to remember word pairs consisting of unrelated nouns such as 'horse/table'. He found that people remembered the word pairs more easily if they were asked to form a mental image in which the objects in each pair were interacting in some way. Constructing a mental image was therefore a better way of trying to recall something than simply trying to memorise the words.

Mnemonics

A **mnemonic** is a device designed to improve recall. Many mnemonics use **rhymes and rhythms** – as in 'Thirty days hath September'. Another way is to use **acronyms** by making words from initial letters, e.g. 'NUT' stands for 'National Union of Teachers.'

THINK ABOUT IT

You may be surprised at how many mnemonic devices you already know. Try and list as many as you can. Are there any others that you may have invented for yourself?

I certainly won't forget that in a hurry!

The 'keyword method' uses imagery linked to words as a mnemonic device ▲

One mnemonic device which involves the use of imagery is known as the **keyword method**. This can prove useful in learning a foreign language. For example, suppose you are trying to learn the French word *escargot*, which means 'snail'. Using the keyword method, you would focus on some part of escargot which you can turn into a retrieval cue. You might, for example, pick out the 'car' segment of the word. Then using 'car' as a keyword you might imagine you are in a car on the motorway when a giant snail in helmet and goggles goes zipping past you at 100mph. The idea is that, when you next come across the word *escargot*, you will be cued back to this mental image and thereby remember that it means 'snail'.

Another technique using imagery is the **method of loci**. This involves using a place or route that you know well – for example, the route to school, or to the pub, or even a route through your house – and forming links between points on that route and things you want to remember.

For example, if you want to memorise a shopping list of bread, bacon and other food items, you might use a route through your house as a way of suggesting cues. You could begin by opening your bedroom door and seeing loaves of bread in a great pile on the landing; the stairs you go down are sticky and bendy underfoot because they are made of strips of bacon – and so on. The secret is to make a real effort to create vivid images in your mind's eye. To remember the list, all you then have to do is to mentally walk through your house.

One final mnemonic device is the **pegword number system**. This is particularly good for remembering lists of items in a particular order. To use this method you have to start by learning the 'pegs'. To make things easier, these can be based on well-known rhymes. For example:

1. bun   **2.** shoe   **3.** tree   **4.** door   **5.** hive
6. sticks   **7.** heaven   **8.** gate   **9.** line   **10.** hen

Once you have learned the peg words the next step is to link them to the list of items you want to remember. You do this by forming mental images (and remember, the weirder the images, the better!).

Let's invent the following list of words to remember:

1. hat   **2.** taxi   **3.** stone   **4.** boat   **5.** socks
6. chair   **7.** bottle   **8.** gun   **9.** table   **10.** dress

You start by taking the first pegword ('bun') and form a mental image that links it to the first word in the list ('hat'). Perhaps you could imagine that you are wearing a big sticky bun as a hat, and you can feel the icing dripping into your eyes and messing up your hair.

Continue forming links in this way for the rest of the list. (So, the 'taxi' that comes for you is a big, smelly, motorised 'shoe' on wheels. The 'tree' you picnic under has leaves of 'stone' – and so on. Try and finish the list using images of your own). Again, you must try to picture the images in your mind. Then, to recall the list, you simply have to recall the peg words, and the peg words will cue you to the items you wish to remember.

In summary

- *Organised material is easier to recall than information presented at random.*

- *Providing people with cues (e.g. category headings) helps recall.*

- *The context in which information is learned can act as a cue to recall.*

- *Internal emotional state can also act as a cue to aid memory.*

- *The fact that cues are present in recognition explains why a recognition test is usually easier than a test of recall.*

- *Mental imagery (e.g. 'horse/ table') can help recall.*

- *Mnemonic devices that use imagery to provide cues are the keyword method, the method of loci, and the pegword number system.*

QUESTIONS

1 Why is recognition easier than recall?

2 What is a cognitive interview, and why is it useful?

3 What could you do to help you remember the friends and teachers you had as a child?

4 Describe a mnemonic device that might help in learning a foreign language.

5 From all you have read so far, suggest three ways in which you could improve your recall of psychology.

Models of memory

So far, we have looked at how memory can sometimes fail, the reasons why we forget things and ways in which memory can be improved. But can we build on these topics to put forward a *theory* of how memory works?

As we have seen, we sometimes forget things quite quickly. For example, if we look up a telephone number in the directory we are likely to forget it almost imediately unless we keep repeating it to ourselves. On the other hand, some information – such as our telephone number or bank PIN number – is easy to recall and no longer has to be rehearsed, even though we may have had to do this at first when it was new to us. This has led some people to claim that there are different types of memory, and that we should distinguish between memory for new information that will be quickly forgotten, and memory for other information that will last for a long time. Such a distinction is made in the **two-process model of memory** put forward by Atkinson and Shiffrin (1968).

The two-process model (Atkinson and Shiffrin)
This model distinguishes between **short-term** memory (**STM**) and **long-term** memory (**LTM**).

- Information that is attended to is initially held in **STM**. This memory store is short-lived, and information held in it will quickly be forgotten. However, it is possible to prolong the life of the store by **rehearsal**: for example, repeating a new phone number to yourself in order not to forget it.

- With enough rehearsal, information gets transferred to **LTM** which can hold information for a long time. So, if the phone number is important, and you repeat it to yourself often enough, it will get transferred to LTM. At this point you can stop repeating it, because the information will be available to you when needed. We can represent this model in the diagram shown below:

The two-process model distinguished between short-term and long-term memory ►

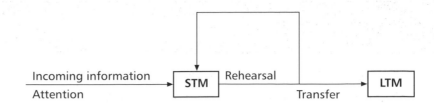

Incoming information → STM — Rehearsal → LTM
Attention   Transfer

The two-process model has been very influential, and many psychologists have tried to understand the different characteristics of these two memory stores. One obvious question is *how long* information can be stored in them. Information in LTM may sometimes be lost quite quickly – perhaps after a few minutes. But information in LTM can last for a very long time. Elderly people often have a clear memory of events that happened in their childhood. The duration of LTM can therefore be anything from a few minutes to a lifetime.

The duration of STM, however, is thought to be much shorter. Peterson and Peterson (1959) found that if people are prevented from rehearsing information they can forget it in just a few seconds. They gave people **trigrams** to recall. A trigram is a series of three consonants, (e.g. PXF). Participants had only to remember one trigram at a time. However, the participants were prevented from rehearsing the trigrams by making them count backwards in threes from some number immediately after the trigram was shown. Peterson and Peterson found that 90% of information was forgotten in just 18 seconds using this method.

Some memories may last a lifetime ▲

The task below provides an insight into the **capacity** of STM (i.e. *how much* information can be held in it). Although the first number is easy to recall, the second number is just too long for most people. In fact, most of us will probably want more time to rehearse the number, because we *know* that we will forget it straight away. This shows that STM can only hold a *limited* amount of information. However, so far as we know, LTM has no such limits. Certainly we have never come across anyone whose memory was so full that they were unable to learn anything new. LTM is therefore generally considered to have an *unlimited capacity*.

TRY THIS

Quickly look at the following number once – then immediately cover it up and try to write down as much of it as you can remember.

39625

Now do the same for the next number.

7483629153689247

How did you do? You probably found the first number fairly easy to remember, but the second one was just impossible. What does this tell us about STM?

Research supports the idea that STM can hold about seven units of information. So it is not surprising that we have trouble remembering long numbers. Miller (1956) estimated the capacity of STM to be '7 plus or minus 2' (i.e. between 5 and 9) **chunks** of information. A 'chunk' is 'a meaningful unit of information'. For example, it could be a letter, a word, a phrase, a single number, or a string of digits. This explains why remembering a string of letters is harder like this:

RA–CBB–CGP–OUS–ACI–A

than like this:

RAC–BBC–GPO–USA–CIA

The letters are the same in both lists, but they are easier to recall in the second list because they are grouped into meaningful units. We can think of STM, then, as having about seven 'slots' available in which to put information. Just how much information goes into a slot depends, in part, on how effectively we can organise (or chunk) it.

THINK ABOUT IT

Can you think of a way to 'chunk' the following numbers to aid recall?

106619452001

Coding

A final difference between STM and LTM has to do with **coding**. Coding refers to the way in which information is assigned to our memory. Research suggests that information in STM is stored according an **acoustic code** – i.e. by how things sound – whereas LTM often codes according to meaning (**semantic coding**) .

When trying to remember a telephone number we usually repeat it to ourselves, and this involves acoustic coding and rehearsal, since we are remembering the sound of the numbers. We do not usually try to hold an image of the numbers on the page in our minds (visual coding), or to impose any meaning on the numbers (semantic coding).

Conrad, (1963) asked people to remember lists of six consonants shown visually, (e.g. 'HRBMSK') and found that the errors they made were often similar in sound to the correct answer. For example a 'B' might be incorrectly recalled as a 'P'. The study, therefore, confirmed that acoustic coding may be important in STM.

However, if you try to remember, say, the content of this chapter, or of a school or college lecture, it is not the exact words that you try to recall so much as the *meaning* of the words (i.e. what it was about). So the meaning of things seems to be important in LTM.

Kintsch and Buschke (1969) asked people to recall long lists of words after a delay of several minutes. They found that people often made errors by recalling words with a similar meaning to the correct word, e.g. recalling 'quick' instead of 'fast'. This suggests that semantic coding is important in LTM – and of course we have already seen how recall can be improved by imposing meaning on material.

Acoustic interference in STM

Further evidence for different coding by STM and LTM comes from a study by Baddeley (1966). He found that in *immediate* recall words that *sounded* the same were hard to remember. This is because of **acoustic interference**. Different-sounding words with similar meanings were quite easy to remember immediately, because meaning is less important in STM, so there was little interference. After a *delay*, however, the similar meanings created difficulties in recall, showing that meanings are important in LTM.

TRY THIS

Quickly read the following short lists of words to someone. Immediately after reading each list of five words, ask them to try to write down the list.

a) mad, cap, cat, map, cad   b) mat, can, map, mad, cat
c) cap, map, mat, man, can

Now do the same with the following lists:

a) big, wide, huge, tall, great   b) broad, tall, long, big, large
c) wide, large, long, great, high

What do the words in the first list have in common? What about the words in the second list? Which list did your friend remember best? What does this reveal about STM?

We should note, though, that not *everything* we need to remember can be given a verbal meaning. When we try to recall a face , our aim is not to remember its meaning, but its appearance. And we have also seen how the use of imagery can be a powerful aid to memory. Because of this, LTM is often thought to find visual coding useful too. Sometimes appearance is important for recall. Note that both STM and LTM can use a variety of codes, (after all, chunking in STM involves imposing meaning). In general, however, STM and LTM seem to prefer to do things in slightly different ways:

	STM	*LTM*
Capacity	5–9 chunks	Unlimited
Duration	Approx. 18 seconds	Few mins. to a lifetime
Coding	Acoustic	Semantic/visual

The central claim of the two-process model of memory is that there are different kinds of memory, STM and LTM. Not everyone accepts this, but before we look at an alternative approach, let us look at some further evidence in support of the STM/LTM distinction.

The serial position effect

Research by Murdock (1962) and others has revealed a typical pattern that emerges when people recall lists. If people are given long lists of words to remember, and then allowed to recall them in any order, a fairly consistent finding is that people remember most words from the beginning and end of the list, and forget most of the words in the middle. This is known as the **serial position effect**. In other words, the likelihood of an item in a list being remembered depends on its position in the original list. Information at the beginning and end is more likely to be remembered than information in the middle.

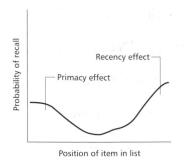

According to the serial position effect, the likelihood of an item being remembered depends on where it occurs in a list.

It is suggested that this happens because material at the end of the list is still there, fresh, in STM and this is often remembered first. To get into STM it will have had to **displace** (push out) items already in STM since STM has a limited capacity and will already be full. This tendency to remember the most recent items is known as the **recency effect**.

The reason why material at the beginning of a list is often well remembered too is that it goes into a fresh memory store, where it does not have to compete with existing items, and it has more time for rehearsal. This means it has a better chance of being transferred to LTM and therefore of being recalled later on. This tendency to recall the first or earlier items in a list is called the **primacy effect.**

TRY THIS

The **serial position effect** is a well-documented finding that you can easily test for yourself. Simply write out a list of around 15 words and read the list to some friends. Tell them that when you have finished they must try and recall as many of the words as they can in any order they like. Then check how many of the first five words in your list are remembered, how many of the middle five, and how many of the last five are recalled.

The point about this finding is that it can be explained by reference to the two-process model. The **primacy effect** reflects **LTM** and the **recency effect** reflects **STM**. This ability to explain a common finding about memory provides support for the model.

Evaluation of the two-process model

Strengths

+ The two-process model of memory has been very influential and has provided a widely used framework for study. It helps to explain the findings from research into the serial position effect.
+ It helps explain some kinds of memory problems like anterograde amnesia. A sufferer can hold a conversation (STM is OK) but cannot recall new learning (LTM is damaged).

Weaknesses

– The research is often artificial. It usually involves learning meaningless lists. Also, the people tested are often aware they are in an experiment, which may affect what they do.

– Rehearsal is not always needed to transfer information to LTM. Jenkin (1974) found that people could remember material even though they were not expecting to be tested on it and so felt no need to rehearse it.

– STM is more complex than the model shows (see **The working memory model** below).

– The model does not distinguish sufficiently between different kinds of LTM (see **Varieties of LTM** below).

– The model does not take sufficient account of different ways of rehearsing. Some theorists believe that it is *how* we rehearse information that is important (see **levels of processing** below).

The working memory model

Baddeley and Hitch (1974) argued that STM contains the ideas we are currently considering in our conscious mind. As such, we should think of immediate memory as a much more active system, and one that can deal with information in different ways. They developed the **working memory model**. This comprises a **central executive** and three interlinking **subsystems**.

The most important component is the central executive which deals with many different types of information, and is involved in complex tasks like solving problems and deciding what to do next. The subsystems each deal with information in their own particular way. They include:

● the **articulatory loop**: a verbal or subverbal rehearsal loop characterised as the *inner voice*

● the **visuo-spatial scratch pad**: deals with information in terms of how it looks and is characterised as the *inner eye*

● the **primary acoustic store**: deals with information in terms of its sound and is characterised as the *inner ear*.

At any one time, the subsystems may be used for different tasks. For example, when driving, you may recall the next track on your cassette tape (primary acoustic store) while remembering the best way to negotiate the next bend (visuo-spatial scratch pad). Sometimes the subsystems may combine on a task. For example, you may look up a telephone number (scratch pad), repeat it subverbally so as not to forget (articulatory loop), and the sound of this rehearsal is then also held in the acoustic store.

Baddeley (1981) believed there are further subsystems to be identified and argued that one of the goals of research should be to discover as many of them as possible. The model is good in that it reminds us that immediate memory is used in different ways and that sometimes we can be doing more than one thing at a time. However, exactly how the central executive performs the complex tasks that it does is still pretty much a mystery. This, Eysenck (1986) believed, is probably the greatest weakness of the model.

Varieties of LTM

We know that some memories are more likely to be forgotten than others. Memories for some details of psychology are more likely to be forgotten than memories for motor skills (like how to ride a bike). Also, brain-damaged sufferers of anterograde amnesia (see page 227) can often still learn new motor skills, though they may not be able to recall that they have learned them. This has led researchers to consider that there may be different *kinds* of memory in long-term store.

Procedural and declarative memory

Cohen and Squire (1980) suggested we can distinguish between **declarative** memories and **procedural** memories.

- **Declarative memory** is to do with 'knowing *that*'. It includes the vast range of information that we know and can easily tell other people about ('declare') – like knowledge of your psychology notes, and where the local pub is.

- **Procedural knowledge** is knowledge of *how to do* things, ('knowing how'), like how to ride a bike. This is not knowledge that is easy to share verbally since it is not open to conscious introspection. If someone asks you how to ride a bike, you can tell them to sit on the saddle and pedal, but that doesn't capture it. They are still likely to fall off. It is only through repeated practice that they will come to know how to ride a bike.

Episodic and semantic memory

Tulving (1972,1985) also distinguishes between procedural memory and *two* broad types of declarative memory, **episodic** and **semantic** memory:

- **Episodic** memories are memories for particular life events (things that you have done or that have happened to you)

- **Semantic** memories are memories for concepts, rules (including the rules of language) and general knowledge of the world.

Broadly, knowing how to catch a bus involves semantic memory (there are rules about queueing, signalling, paying, etc.). If you remember catching the bus this morning, then that involves episodic memory.

Both kinds of memories are closely interlinked in everyday remembering. Clearly, much semantic memory is acquired through personal experience. At the same time, our general understanding of the world helps us to make sense of, and remember, the experiences we have. Cohen (1984) argued that it is declarative memory that is damaged in amnesiac patients. This distinction between episodic and semantic memory helps us to explain why some amnesiac patients may lose personal information about themselves and events that have happened to them (episodic memory), but still know how to speak or read and get dressed (semantic memory).

Flashbulb memories

Some episodic memories, particularly of personal experiences that evoke a strong emotional response, may be recalled with great clarity. These may include not only the key event itself, but also trivial details surrounding it, like where we were at the time, what other people may have been doing, saying or wearing. Memory for hearing about the death of Princess Diana may be such a memory for some people. Brown and Kulik (1977) referred to such memories as **flashbulb memories**. They believed that two main determinants for such memories were:

1 a high level of surprise
2 emotional arousal

Surprising events which evoke strong emotions are potentially dangerous. The ability to remember these events and the details surrounding them may be important. The capacity for flashbulb memories may therefore be useful for survival. Such memories may reflect increased rehearsal on our part of such events, either in conversation with others or silently on our own.

Interestingly, there is a deal of research to show that flashbulb memories are not always accurate (though they often are). For example, Neisser and Harsch (1992) asked college students how they had learned of the explosion of the space shuttle *Challenger* (in which seven astronauts died) on the morning of the event. The researchers found that three years afterwards, not one student could recall entirely accurately how they heard the news, and a third of them were wrong.

Explicit and implicit memory

Graf and Schacter (1985) distinguished between **explicit** and **implicit memory**:

- **Explicit memory** involves the *conscious* recollection of information and is used in tests of recognition or recall. Declarative memory usually involves explicit memory.
- **Implicit memory** involves *unconscious* memory. Information that we cannot consciously recall can nevertheless affect what we think or do. Procedural knowledge involves implicit memory.

One test for implicit memory was devised by Ebbinghaus (1885). He gave himself lists of nonsense syllables to remember, like 'GOK', 'RUJ', etc. He found that when he came to relearn a list that he once knew but could no longer recall, this was much easier than learning a new list that he had never seen before. This means that something of the original memory must still have been present, even though he could not consciously recall it.

Tasks such as *word-stem completion* also reveal implicit memories. Here, people are asked to read lists of words ('chair', 'table', etc.). Later they are given word-stems such as 'CHA–' and asked to complete them with the first word that comes to mind. Even though participants may show poor recall or recognition of the earlier lists, they are more likely to complete the word stems with words from those lists than are control participants who were never shown the lists to begin with.

In summary

- *Procedural memory is 'knowing how'.*

- *Declarative memory is 'knowing that'.*

- *Semantic memory involves general concepts and rules.*

- *Episodic memory involves particular life events.*

- *Flashbulb memory involves very vivid memory for a particular event.*

- *Implicit memory cannot be consciously recalled but affects behaviour.*

- *Explicit memory involves conscious recall or recognition.*

THINK ABOUT IT

What relevance does Ebbinghaus' discovery about the relative ease of relearning material have for students?

Levels of processing

Although the two-process model of memory has been widely influential, an alternative approach has been put forward by Craik and Lockhart (1972) called the **levels of processing** approach. Craik and Lockhart place less emphasis on different kinds of memory and argue that whether we remember information or not depends more on what we do with it, and more particularly how we *process* it, when we first come across it. The more work we do on it, the more deeply we process it, the longer we will remember it.

For verbal material, Craik and Lockhart identify three levels of processing:

1 **structural**: what a word *looks* like
2 **phonetic:** what a word *sounds* like
3 **semantic:** what a word *means*

The structural level is the most shallow, and semantic processing is the deepest level. The deeper the level used, the more likely something is to be remembered.

KEY STUDY

Craik and Lockhart asked people to look at lists of words. They did not tell them it was a memory test. People were simply shown words and asked to answer different questions about the words.

Three sorts of questions were asked, each involving different ways of thinking about the words.

1 For some words participants were asked questions such as:

   Is the word in capital letters? (Note that this required people to consider what the words looked like).

2 For other words, they were asked questions such as:

   Does the word rhyme with _____ ? (Note that this required people to consider what the words sounded like).

3 For other words, they were asked questions such as

   Would the word fit into the following sentence...? (Note that this required people to consider the meaning of the words).

Afterwards the participants were unexpectedly asked to recall all the words. As the graph below shows, Craik and Lockhart found that recall was best for words that involved considering their meaning (semantic processing), and worst for words that simply asked about what they looked like (structural processing).

Craik and Lockhart found semantic processing to be most effective ▶

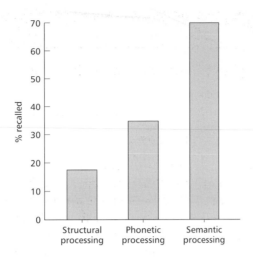

Source: Craik, F.I.M. & Lockhart, R.S., 'Levels of Processing: a framework for memory research', *Journal of Verbal Learning and Verbal Behaviour*, 11 (1972), pp.671–84

Questions

1. What is the independent variable in this study?
2. What is the dependent variable in this study?
3. What is the advantage of having an *unexpected* test of recall?
4. According to the graph:
   a) Approximately what percentage of semantically processed words were correctly recalled?
   b) What percentage of structurally processed words were recalled?

Evaluation of the levels of processing approach

Strengths

+ The major strength of the levels of processing approach is that it forces us to recognise that there are lots of different ways of dealing with information. The two-process model simply talks of 'rehearsal', but the levels of processing approach emphasises that there are different kinds of rehearsal (i.e. different ways of processing information).

+ The approach can be applied to material other than lists of words. For example Karlin (1974) and also Sporer (1996) have found that asking people to look at pictures of faces, and then to decide whether the person shown appears honest or not, can improve recognition later. This indicates that the more work we do with information the more likely we are to remember it.

Weaknesses

− The theory appears to be based on a circular argument. If something is well remembered it is deeply processed, and if it is deeply processed it is well remembered. There does not seem to be an independent way of assessing depth of processing. Baddeley (1990) argues that this severely limits the usefulness of the theory.

Some conclusions

We have seen that memory is very complex and that we can sometimes distort or forget information for different reasons. We have also seen that there are various techniques we can use to improve memory.

There is some dispute about just how our memories work. For all its importance to us, our understanding of memory is quite poor. One problem is that many studies have focused on the learning of lists in the laboratory. The real challenge is to understand memory in the context of everyday life. Memory does not operate in a vacuum. What we attend to and how we interpret what we see are linked to past learning and so to memory. We study memory as a separate topic simply to make things easier for us. In real life, things like attention, perception and memory are not so easily separable.

Summary

- Memory is reconstructive. While our memories are accurate most of the time, they are not 100% reliable, and people can have different memories of the same event. Memories that may seem very clear can nevertheless be false.
- Although memories can go back many years, we also forget a lot of information – often quite quickly. We can forget for a number of different reasons including decay, interference, repression, or amnesia caused by illness or injury.
- There are various ways to improve recall. These include organisation of material, providing appropriate cues and using various mnemonic devices like the keyword method, the peg word method or method of loci.
- **The two-process model** of memory suggests that we have different kinds of memory: a short-term memory store used to recall information from the recent past, and a long-term memory store that holds information about things that happened some while ago. These stores are thought to be different in terms of how they code information, their capacity and their duration.
- A different approach to memory is called the **levels of processing approach**. According to this, how well we remember information depends on how deeply we process it in the first place. Three levels of processing are identified: processing according to appearance (**structural**), sound (**phonetic**), or meaning (**semantic**).

16 Measured Intelligence

Intelligence is a word we use in everyday conversation. We say this person is more (or less) intelligent than that person. Despite this, psychologists are divided on what the term means, and whether we can actually measure intelligence. This chapter looks at the techniques that have been developed to test and measure intelligence. It also considers research into the impact of genetic and environmental factors on the development of intelligence.

Intelligence and ability

What is intelligence? ▲

Intelligence can be thought of as a *general capacity*, or the ability to solve a *wide variety* of different problems. Nevertheless, people can be good at doing some things and bad at doing other things. Some psychologists believe we have certain specific abilities, and that, rather than a *general* capacity to cope with everything, intelligence involves different capacities to solve specific sorts of problems. Keep this in mind as we consider how tests were developed to measure intelligence.

THINK ABOUT IT

How intelligent is, say, a nuclear physicist who is socially inept?

The development of intelligence testing

The first intelligence tests were developed by Binet and Simon at the beginning of the twentieth century. At the time, the French government was introducing schooling for all children, and wanted to be able to identify children who might need extra help to succeed. By testing children of different ages they were able to establish what tasks a child of a particular age could usually perform. This provided an indicator of the **mental age** of the child. A mental age of ten meant a child could solve most of the problems that the average ten-year-old could solve. It is therefore possible to have a mental age below or above your actual (chronological) age.

A bright 8-year-old could have a mental age of 10 if they were able to do what most 10-year-olds could do. A 10-year-old could have a mental age of 8 if they were able to do what most 8-year-olds could do but could not do what most 9- and 10-year-olds could do.

IQ tests

The notion of mental age was used by Stern (1871–1938) to develop the idea of **IQ**. IQ stands for **intelligence quotient**, and it expresses the relationship between mental age and actual age as follows:

$$IQ = \frac{\text{Mental age} \times 100}{\text{Actual age}}$$

So the bright 8-year-old mentioned above would have an IQ of:

$$\frac{10 \times 100}{8} = \mathbf{125}$$

The first IQ test was developed by Terman (1916) at Stanford University in the USA and was known as the **Stanford-Binet test**. Using the concept of mental age, Terman tested people to see what level of age-graded problems they could solve. The test was designed around the performance of white children from middle-class backgrounds.

By age	a child should be able to:
3	• Point to objects that serve various functions such as 'goes on your feet' • Name pictures of objects such as 'chair', 'flag' • Repeat a list of two words or digits – for example 'car', 'dog'
4	• Discriminate visual forms such as squares, circles and triangles • Define words such as 'ball' and 'bat' • Repeat 10-word sentences • Count up to 4 objects • Solve problems such as 'In daytime it is light; at night it is _____.'
6	• State the difference between familiar items such as 'bird' and 'dog' • Count up to 9 objects • Solve analogies such as 'an inch is short; a mile is _____.'
9	• Solve verbal problems • Solve simple arithmetic problems such as 'If I buy 4 cents' worth of candy and give the storekeeper 10 cents, how much money will I get back?' • Repeat 4 digits in reverse order
12	• Define words such as 'skill' and 'muzzle' • Repeat 5 digits in reverse order • Solve verbal absurdities such as 'One day we saw several icebergs that had been entirely melted by the warmth of the Gulf Stream'. What is foolish about that?

Sample tasks from the Stanford–Binet Test

© Society for Research in Child Development, INC

This test has been updated several times, and is now based on data from people of many different racial and socio-economic backgrounds. It is designed to measure the intelligence of children between 3 and 16 years of age. The concept of mental age is no longer used. Instead, a person's performance is compared to that of other people of the same age. An IQ of 100 is still average, and if a child solves more problems than his or her peers, (i.e. other people of the same age), he or she has an IQ above 100.

A widely used test for adults was devised by Weschler (1939), called the **Weschler Adult Intelligence Scale (WAIS)**. This has also been updated several times, and it, too, is designed (as are many other tests produced nowadays) in such a way that the average score for adults who take the test is 100. The tests are also designed so that it is rare for people to score below 70 (subnormal intelligence) or above 130 (genius).

The process of constructing a test so that most people from a particular group can be expected to achieve a certain score, and so that you get a certain range of scores in the test, is called **standardisation**. That is, tests are standardised on a group, so that most people in the group will score **x** (usually 100), and few people in the group will get very low scores and few people will get very high scores.

Pen-and-paper tests

The tests discussed so far are individual tests, in that they need someone to sit with the person being tested and ask them to do things. More recently, a number of pen-and-paper tests have been developed which simply involve giving people a series of questions that they must try to complete within a particular time. These are obviously easier to use, in that a lot of people can be tested at the same time. The eleven-plus exam was a form of intelligence test used to determine whether a child was intelligent enough to benefit from attending a grammar school. These schools aimed to prepare pupils for university. About 80% of children 'failed' the test and went to secondary modern schools, which were less academic.

Criticisms of IQ testing

Validity

One criticism of IQ tests has to do with their validity. A test is only **valid** if it measures what it says it does. The items in many pen-and-paper IQ tests often tests things like:

- vocabulary, or verbal reasoning, e.g.:

  'What is the odd one out among sheep, cow, duck, pig...'

- mathematical reasoning:

  'What is the next number in the sequence 2, 5, 11, 23...'

- visual–spatial abilities:

  'Mentally rotate a figure'/'Find a shape embedded within another shape'

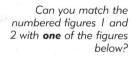

Can you match the numbered figures 1 and 2 with **one** of the figures below?

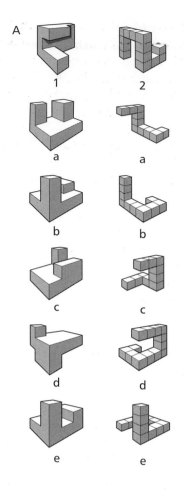

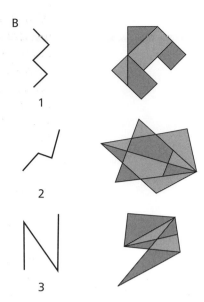

Can you find shapes 1, 2 and 3 embedded in the shapes on the right?

Extract from an IQ test ▼

Q1 Write down the **largest** of these figures:
1 2 3 4 5 6 7 8 9

Q2 Write down the **middle one** of these figures:
1 2 3 4 5 6 7 8 9

Q3 *Late* means the opposite of:
1 appointment
2 early
3 behind
4 postponed
5 immediate

Q4 *Big* means the opposite of:
1 tall
2 large
3 place
4 small
5 high

Q5 What number comes next?
1 4 7 10 13 ?

Q6 What number comes next?
2 4 8 16 32 ?

Q7 *Fish* is to *swim* as *bird* is to:
1 man
2 fly
3 walk
4 aeroplane
5 sparrow

Q8 *Low* is to *high* as *bad* is to:
1 evil
2 red
3 try
4 good
5 right

Q9 Add the largest two figures together and divide the total by the smallest figure:

3 2 5

Ability in these areas is often important in schools, and IQ test scores are quite good predictors of school performance, giving a correlation of about +0.60. However, this does not mean that IQ tests necessarily provide a good measure of intelligence, any more than any other type of school grading. We should remember that for most of human history, people lived as hunters and gatherers of food. The ability to manipulate words, numbers or shapes on bits of paper had little part to play in the daily struggle for survival. These abilities are important in modern, industrial societies; but so are other abilities such as social intelligence (the ability to understand and get along with other people). In other cultures, and in other times, the abilities measured by IQ tests would be much less significant. This is why some psychologists believe that IQ tests should simply be seen as a way of measuring certain abilities, and why we should always remember that people have other skills which these tests do *not* measure. For example, IQ tests are not particularly good predictors of how **creative** someone is (see Chapter 17, *Problem-Solving and Creativity*).

Cultural bias

The tests are also **culture-biased**, in that they are only useful in testing people who belong to the same group as the people who were used in designing the test originally. If a test is constructed so that this particular group of people score an average of 100 on the test, people in other groups may not score in the same way. Our ancestors would score very poorly on such tests, but they were not any less intelligent than we are. How would we fare if asked to survive in their world?

In the USA research has found that, on average, blacks and Hispanics score less well than whites on most IQ tests. Some psychologists, such as Jensen (1968), have argued that these findings indicate that black people are genetically inferior to whites in terms of intelligence. However, we should immediately note that, because of the spread of scores in both black and white populations, there is a great deal of overlap between the two groups. In other words, many black children obtain higher scores than many white children.

Notions of intelligence are often culturally biased

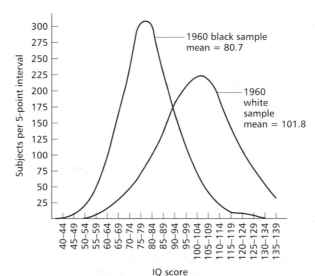

Comparative IQ scores for a sample of 1,800 black schoolchildren in the USA and a sample of white school children. The graph shows that many black children actually scored higher than many white children

Adapted from Kennedy, van der Reit and White, 1963, © Society for Research in Child Development, INC

We must also note that the actual test items used are not equally suitable for people from different cultural backgrounds. For example, take the vocabulary test given earlier:

'Find the odd one out from sheep, cow, duck, pig…'

Many people might pick 'duck', because it is the only bird. However, someone from a different culture might pick 'cow' or 'pig', because in their culture eating these animals might be forbidden on religious grounds.

Some researchers have argued that blacks and Hispanics (people of Spanish origin) speak a different English **dialect** from that of the white middle class. That is, they may sometimes use different words, or use the same words but with different meanings. This puts Blacks and Hispanics at a disadvantage in understanding test instructions, and in solving problems that test word-use and vocabulary.

Adrian Dove (1968) has illustrated this with his own humorous example of a 'culturally biased' test. A sample of test items from the **Dove Counterbalance General 'Intelligence' Test** (The 'Chitling' Test) is given below. The test is based around Black American culture and language. How well would you do on this?

Extract from 'Dove's Counterbalance General "Intelligence" Test' ▶

Q1 Cheap chitlings (not the kind you purchase at a frozen food counter) will taste rubbery unless they are cooked long enough. How soon can you quit cooking them to eat and enjoy them?

A   45 minutes
B   2 hours
C   24 hours
D   One week (on a low flame)
E   1 hour

Q2 A 'handkerchief head' is:

A   a cool cat
B   a porter
C   an Uncle Tom
D   a preacher

Q3 A 'gas head' is a person who has a:

A   fast-moving car
B   stable of 'lace'
C   'Process'
D   habit of stealing cars
E   long jail record for arson

Q4 'Hully Gully' came from:

A   East Oakland
B   Fillmore
C   Watts
D   Harlem
E   Motor City

Q5 If you throw the dice and a seven is showing on top, what is facing down:

A   seven
B   snake eyes
C   boxcars
D   little Joes
E   eleven

Q6 T-Bone Walker got famous for playing what?

A   trombone
B   piano
C   'T-flute'
D   guitar
E   'Hambone'

Genes and environment

Differences in IQ test scores may also reflect environmental factors, rather than genetic ones. We will turn to this shortly when we come to look at the nature-nurture debate on intelligence.

Another factor worth considering here is the different rates at which children's intelligence develops. A major criticism of the eleven-plus exam (see above) was that it did not allow for the fact that some children develop more slowly than others. All children of about 11 years of age were tested and sent to different kinds of school on the basis of the test results. It was therefore possible – and quite common – for children to be labelled 'unintelligent' at the age of 11 simply because they were late developers. Girls tend to develop faster than boys, and it is interesting to note that the scoring for this exam was changed to help boys because girls were doing better. Despite addressing inequalities of gender, however, no attempt was made to address inequalities arising from class background or ethnic group.

'Culture fair' tests

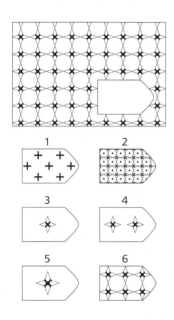

An item from the 'culture fair' Raven Progressive Matrices Test

To design a truly **culture fair** test, i.e. one that is fair to people from all cultures, is probably impossible. How well a person scores in a test must depend to some extent on their knowledge and experience – even down to the language they use and how familiar they are with using a pen and paper. One attempt to produce a culture fair test is the **Raven Progressive Matrices Test**. It contains no verbal items. People must complete a picture by choosing from a number of other pictures. Even so, it has been found that people with more education tend to score higher on the test than those with less education (Anastasi, 1988).

Reliability

IQ tests, like other tests, should be **reliable**. A test is reliable only if it gives consistent results. Early research indicated that IQ tests were quite reliable. For example, in a longitudinal study of more than 250 children, scores obtained by children at the age of 6 years were strongly correlated with scores obtained from the same children at the age of 18 years (Honzik et al., 1948). However, the figures were based on *groups* of people, and so did not show how the IQs of individual children may vary over time. McCall et al. (1973) examined the scores of 140 children who had been tested regularly from 2½ years of age to 17 years. They found that more than half of these children varied in their scores over the years, and that the average range of variation was 28.5 points! In other words, while IQ scores may be fairly stable for some children, they can vary greatly for other children.

The fact that scores can vary in this way probably reflects the importance of things like environmental influences, and the emotional and motivational state of people tested. In other words, it seems that in an IQ test, as in any other kind of test, how well you do can depend very much on how you happen to be feeling on the day.

Labelling

There are also difficulties that can arise as a result of **labelling**. Labelling theory argues that when you put a label on someone – e.g. you could label them as 'unintelligent' – this has consequences for them. It can affect how they see themselves, and how they behave, and also affect the way in which other people think about them and treat them.

For example, if your school labels you 'unintelligent', you may decide that since the school does not value you very highly, the school itself is not worth much. You therefore reject its values, refuse to do the work set and skip lessons. As a result you fail your exams – at which point your teachers will say, 'See? We always said you were unintelligent.' This is an example of a **self-fulfilling prophecy**. It shows that the labels that are put on people, and the predictions made for them, may come true simply *because* the labels were put on them and the predictions were made.

Applications of IQ tests

IQ tests can be used in a variety of ways, some positive, others less so. One major way in which IQ tests are used is for selection and recruitment. We have already seen that exams like the eleven-plus were used to select children for grammar-school entry. They can also be used for **banding** pupils within a school. Tests can also be used in selecting people for jobs and have been used in this way by the Civil Service for a long time. In the USA the first pen-and-paper IQ tests were used to select recruits into the army. In the 1920s they were used to select immigrants to be allowed into America. Not surprisingly, the tests were heavily culture-biased and many immigrants performed badly on them. The British Army nowadays also tests recruits using computer programs and touch-sensitive screens.

Another major use for IQ tests is for **diagnosis** (remember that Binet's original tests were for this purpose). These tests are sometimes individual tests as well as pen-and-paper tests. They are not designed to measure general intelligence but to identify particular areas in which people may have difficulties (e.g. in reading) so that they can be helped.

In summary

- *Psychologists disagree about what intelligence is, and how best to measure it.*

- *IQ tests usually measure verbal, mathematical and spatial skills. IQ stands for 'Intelligence Quotient'.*

- *Like all psychometric tests, IQ tests must be reliable and valid. Tests are not always reliable and may be culture-biased.*

- *IQ tests have been used for selection purposes and for diagnosis.*

- *Certain groups of people may be 'labelled' on the basis of their test score. This labelling can have negative consequences for them.*

QUESTIONS

| Explain the terms: | **1** Reliability | **2** Validity | **3** Culture bias |

The nature-nurture debate

This debate arises because psychologists wish to explain why it is that some people seem to be more intelligent than others.

On the **nature** side of the argument, psychologists believe that people are born the way they are and that intelligence is a matter of heredity.

On the 'environment' or **nurture** side, it is argued that the circumstances in which people are raised, their living conditions, family, peer group, school and life experiences can all contribute to how intelligent they are. Our intelligence depends on what happens to us from the moment we are conceived.

The case for heredity

Twin studies

Twins are useful in studies of heredity because identical (monozygotic) twins, or MZs, have the same genes. If two identical twins differ in intelligence, it must therefore be as a result of environmental factors. (Fraternal [dizygotic] twins, or DZs, are no more alike than brother and sister, sharing just 50% of their genes.)

A number of studies have compared the IQs of MZs who have been reared separately from each other. The results of some of the early research are given below. The numbers quoted show the correlation or concordance between IQ scores. The closer the number is to 1 the better the correlation. A score of 0 would represent no correlation at all.

Researcher	*MZs reared together*	*MZs reared apart*	*DZs reared together*
Newman et al. (1937)	0.91	0.67	0.64
Shields (1962)	0.76	0.77	0.57
Erlenmeyer Kimling and Jarvik (1963)	0.87	0.75	0.53
Burt (1966)	0.94	0.77	0.55

Evaluation of the case for heredity

Strengths

+   This research shows that the IQ of identical twins reared apart is more similar than the IQ of fraternal twins reared together. It suggests, therefore, that genetic similarity is more important than the environment in determining IQ and so supports the case for heredity.

Weaknesses

–   Burt is thought to have made up some of his data, and so Kamin (1977) suggests we should discount his research.
–   Kamin also points out that different studies have used different IQ tests. Newman tested adults using a version of the Stanford Binet test that had not been standardised on adults.
–   High correlations between MZs reared together could reflect the fact that identical twins share a uniquely similar environment. For example, they may wear the same clothes, be in the same class at school, receive identical birthday presents, etc. This is not the case for most brothers and sisters.

- When twins are separated, the agencies that place them may try to find foster families that are as similar as possible to their natural families, and so their environments may not be so different after all.
- If genes were entirely responsible for determining IQ, the correlation between MZs reared apart or together would be +1. The fact that this is not so points to the importance of environmental factors.
- Correlations do not tell us about cause and effect. It is possible that similar-looking people produce similar responses from others, and so to some extent create similar environments for themselves.
- In some cases, twins were not separated until several years after they were born, and so shared similar early environments.
- In some cases, 'separated' twins were raised by close relatives, often visiting each other and even going to the same school. Their environments were, therefore, very similar.
- More recently, Plomin (1988) reviewed a large number of twin studies and concluded that genetics accounted for about 50% of the variance in IQ. This is a high figure, but it does still leave a strong role for the environment in determining IQ.

Professor Plomin believed the research showed that genetics accounts for about 50% of variance in IQ. However a happy, stimulating home environment can still have an important part to play in determining intelligence.

Adoption studies

Researchers have compared the IQ of adopted children with the IQs of both their biological and adoptive parents. The hypothesis here is that if a child's IQ is closer to that of their biological parent than that of their adoptive parent, this would support the influence of genes in determining intelligence. This is because the child shares half their genes with each of their biological parents, and shares no genes with their adoptive parents. On the other hand, if the child's IQ is closer to that of their adoptive parents, this would be evidence in favour of environmental influence. Research of this kind – for example by Skodak and Skeels (1949) and Horn (1983) – has found that childrens' IQs correlate more highly with that of their biological mother than their adoptive mother. This supports the case for genetics.

We should note, though, that other researchers, e.g. Schiff et al. (1978), Dumaret (1985), have found that children born into poor or uneducated families who are adopted by richer, better-educated families, tend to have higher IQ scores than their siblings who remain with their natural mother. This shows that the environment in which children are raised can affect their IQ. Similarly, Scarr and Weinberg (1976) found that black children adopted by white parents of an above-average socio-economic status made substantial gains in IQ (16 points on average). They argued that differences in IQ scores are explained more readily by differences in social class than differences in race, and that a middle-class Euro-American environment helps children develop the necessary skills to do well on IQ tests.

Family studies

Since we know how genetically similar relatives are, if we find that similarity of IQ increases as genetic similarity increases, this would provide evidence in support of the idea that IQ is influenced by genes. Bouchard and McGue reviewed 111 family studies, and some of their results are given below:

Family relationship	*Correlation*
MZs reared together	0.85
MZs reared apart	0.67
DZs reared together	0.58
Siblings reared together	0.45
Siblings reared apart	0.24
Parent/child reared together	0.38
Parent/child reared apart	0.22
Cousins	0.15

This research, therefore, provides strong evidence for some genetic basis to intelligence. As genetic similarity increases, so does similarity of IQ. However, we should note that MZs reared together are more similar than MZs reared apart. This is also true of siblings reared together and apart and shows that environment also has an impact on IQ.

The case for environmental influence

The effects of social class

Children from poorer families tend to have lower IQ scores. There are a number of possible reasons for this. It could be that the poor are naturally less intelligent. Then again, factors such as poor health or living conditions, poor diet or nutrition, poorly educated parents, a lack of books and mental stimulation and more stressful life events may all contribute to a lower IQ score.

Sameroff and Seifer (1983) identified 10 such risk factors, and in a longitudinal study, tested children from different backgrounds at the ages of 4 and 13 years. They found a strong negative correlation between the number of risk factors to which a child was exposed, and their IQ. That is, as the number of risk factors increased, so the child's IQ decreased.

Research by Sameroff indicated that poor home environment (measured in terms of 'risk factors') could adversely affect a child's IQ

KEY STUDY

Skeels (1966) studied 25 children of low IQ who, for the first two years of their life, were raised in a rather poor American orphanage which provided little by way of mental or social stimulation. Thirteen of these children were then sent to another institution (a home for the mentally retarded) which provided much better stimulation, with more toys to play with and more interaction with adults and older children. By the age of three and a half, these children had made great gains in their IQs. By contrast, the IQs of the children who stayed in the original orphanage had fallen.

Skeels followed these children into adulthood and found that the children who had remained in the orphanage tended to be intellectually subnormal and unable to look after themselves. Many of the children who were sent to the better institution, however, were of normal intelligence, and had completed school; many were married and had jobs. This shows that the environment in which people are raised can have a dramatic effect on their IQ scores.

Questions

1. What is the difference between longitudinal research and cross-sectional research?
2. Give one advantage and one disadvantage of each.
3. What form of research is involved in the above study?
4. What are the implications of this study for the ways in which we raise our children?

Source: Skeels, H.M., 'Adult Status of Children with Contrasting Early Life Experiences' in *Monographs of the Society for Research in Child Development*, 31 (3), 1966

Intervention programmes

In the 1960s the view that intelligence could be affected by the environment led the US government to introduce **compensatory education** programmes. It was felt that the reason many poorer children were doing badly at school was because of their disadvantaged background. The education programmes cost the government some 17 billion dollars, and aimed to compensate pre-school children for their disadvantages, so that all children could start their education on an equal footing.

One such programme was called **Operation Headstart**, which first ran as an eight-week programme in the summer of 1965, and later developed into a full year's pre-school programme. Children from poorer homes were given free medical checks and provided with an educational programme aimed at increasing their chances of success when they started school. Children received different types of enrichment depending on the type of programme. Some emphasised basic skills and others encouraged children to be more sociable and co-operative. In some cases teachers would go to the childrens' homes; in other cases, children were taken to a nearby building.

Initially, children seemed to benefit from these programmes, showing gains in IQ and improved school performance compared to children who did not receive the programme. These gains, however, turned out to be short-lived, and after a couple of years any improvements had disappeared. This led to disillusionment with such programmes.

But these criticisms turned out to be premature. Later assessment showed that the children who went through the programmes were:

- more likely to complete their schooling
- more likely to want to succeed academically
- less likely to get into trouble with the police, become pregnant, or to require state benefits

The results of the programmes are difficult to assess, but one estimate is that for every dollar spent on the programme, six dollars were later saved in terms of the costs of welfare, policing and the courts and other special educational programmes. It would appear from this that the programmes were worthwhile. However, we should remember that they were not specifically aimed at increasing IQ. Some researchers believe IQ tests have a class or culture bias. We should also bear in mind that enrichment for just one year before school begins is hardly likely to compensate for the ongoing disadvantages of poverty once school starts. In other words, the disadvantages of a poor home background remain ever-present and may hinder educational achievement or intellectual growth.

In general, the research indicates that where these programmes managed to encourage the parents to take an active interest in their childrens' schooling, then the programmes tended to be more successful.

QUESTIONS

What are:

1) Two studies supporting the case for a strong genetic component to intelligence?
2) Two studies supporting the case for the importance of the environment?

Nature or nurture?

The evidence we have looked at supports the idea that both heredity and the environment have a part to play in determining intelligence. But it is not an either/or question. Biology does not operate in a way that is divorced from the environment. Your genes may provide you with a certain intellectual *potential*, but how you actually turn out depends on a whole host of environmental factors, ranging from whether your mother smoked or took drugs while you were in the womb, to the education of your parents, your living environment and many other things besides.

In practice it seems impossible to pull apart the relative influences of heredity and the environment to say which contributes more to measured IQ. It is the interaction of the two that we can observe and measure. Hebb (1949) argued that asking whether environment or heredity contributes more to intelligence is like asking which contributes more to the area of a rectangle, its length or its width? We should also bear in mind the point raised at the beginning of this chapter: that many psychologists question whether IQ tests are capable of measuring some general capacity that can be called intelligence in the first place.

Summary

- Twin studies strongly suggest genetic factors do influence IQ scores, but their findings are difficult to interpret. The fact that MZ twins vary in their IQ scores suggests that genetics is not everything.
- Adoption studies offer some support for the genetic view, but the finding that adoption into wealthy, well-educated families can boost IQ also shows that environmental factors are important.
- Family studies suggest that both genetics and the environment have an impact on IQ scores.
- Longitudinal research indicates that the impact of environmental factors can be very considerable.
- Sameroff has identified risk factors associated with poorer intellectual development. This may help explain class differences in IQ scores.
- Intervention programmes to compensate for adverse environmental factors turned out to be more valuable than people originally thought. However, they could not fully address the disadvantages of ongoing poverty that children suffered.

17 Problem-solving and Creativity

Everyday life faces us with many problems ▲

For better or worse, our daily lives are full of problems to solve. We not only have to deal with problems at work or school, but how to manage our money, how to treat other people, what clothes to wear, where to go on holiday, how to get to different places… The list is endless.

This chapter looks at some of the research and theories of how people solve problems. We should note that here, as elsewhere, research has often involved setting people problems in a laboratory. Psychologists still have much to learn about the ways in which people solve the everyday problems that they encounter in real life.

Problem-solving strategies

Let us invent a problem. Suppose you are looking for a particular book in a library. How could you go about finding it? There are different strategies that you could use. For example, you could rush about randomly picking out one book after another until you find the one you are looking for. This is called an **unsystematic search**. It involves checking possible solutions to the problem in an unsystematic way. If the library only has three books this method is as good as any, but in a big public library it could take you a very long time indeed.

We can already see that we have a choice of strategies, depending on the nature of the problem to be solved. The more books there are to choose from, or generally, the more possible solutions or choices there are to be considered, the bigger the **problem space** is said to be. With a large problem space, unsystematic searches may take an awfully long time – but they can be useful if the problem space is small.

Even systematic searches can take a long time if the problem space is large ▲

A different way of looking for the book would be to take each shelf in the library in turn and search through them from left to right. This is called a **systematic search**. Again the strategy might be useful if there were only three small shelves to look at, but it could still take a long time in a large public library. Even a systematic search may be time-consuming when there is a large problem space. However it at least avoids looking at the same wrong books more than once, and so it should often be quicker than an unsystematic search.

Note that both of the strategies above will find the book eventually (if it is there). An eventual solution to the problem is guaranteed. It just might take a very long time. Strategies that guarantee finding the answer eventually are called **algorithms**. Research suggests, however, that most human problem-solving is not like this. We rarely have the time or the patience to work through every possible alternative in solving problems, even if we know what all the alternatives are. Instead, we (very sensibly) use past knowledge to help us find the solution more quickly.

For example, given a long anagram like 'SIFTIULECFID', we would probably use our understanding of what words look like, what letter combinations are likely or unlikely, to help solve the problem quickly, rather than try out every possible combination of letters until we find the solution. In searching for the book in a public library, we would probably use our knowledge of libraries to look at the catalogue – or ask a librarian.

Heuristic strategies

When we use past learning as a shortcut to finding a solution, the strategies involved are called **heuristic strategies**. Heuristic strategies are 'rules of thumb' that help us get answers quickly. Much human problem-solving is of this sort. But while heuristic strategies are often very useful, they can lead us into error. Unlike algorithmic strategies, heuristic strategies do not guarantee finding the right solution.

For example, it is theoretically possible that someone could try out likely combinations and still not solve the anagram above, and so have to resort to a systematic search to solve it. In the same way, if the library book we are hunting for is hidden on the wrong shelf, then using the catalogue or librarian to help us might lead us to conclude that since the book is not where it is supposed to be it is not in the library at all – so we would stop looking and never find it. We shall consider some different heuristic strategies below.

Analogies

To solve a problem by **analogy** simply means using a method that has worked for you before on a similar problem.

For example, if directory enquiries were helpful the last time you forgot a friend's telephone number, then they might be worth trying when you find you have forgotten another (different) friend's telephone number. However, remember: this is a heuristic strategy, and so it does not guarantee the answer. So, for example, your friend might be ex-directory.

In a similar way, children can be helped to learn to read by using analogies. The sound '-*at*' in 'cat' is similar in 'bat', 'hat', 'sat', 'mat' etc. But again the strategy can lead us into error. Consider the sound '-*eight*', as used in 'weight' and 'height'. Using analogy this time would result in mispronouncing one of the words.

Before reading on, consider the following problem.

TRY THIS

Water lilies on a pond double in area every 24 hours. From the time that the first water lily appears to the time that the lake is completely covered takes 60 days. On what day is the lake half covered?

Backward search

The easiest way to solve some problems is to consider where you end up (or want to end up) and work backwards. In this case, if the lake is covered in 60 days and the area covered by lilies doubles in size every day, the lake must be half covered after 59 days.

This approach can be especially useful when the end-point is clear but the starting point is difficult or presents too many possible alternatives. Tracing through some maze drawings, for example, is often easier if you work backwards from the finishing point. Retracing your steps to look for an item you have lost is an everyday example of a **backward search**.

Means-ends analysis

In a study of problem-solving methods, Newell and Simon (1972) asked people to solve a number of different problems and to report out loud what they were thinking about as they tried to solve them. (Note that this method of research does have limitations. It cannot reveal unconscious thought processes, since, by definition, people are not aware of them and so cannot report them. Also, the need to give a verbal report while solving a problem is an *additional* problem, which might influence how people go about solving the first problem.)

Newell and Simon discovered that one of the main heuristic strategies that people employ to solve a variety of problems is **means-ends analysis**. Simply, this involves considering where you are now (your **current** state), and where you want to be (your **goal** state), and then systematically reducing the distance between the two. This is done by breaking the problem down into a number of stages or **subgoals**, and then working through each subgoal in turn until the goal state is achieved (and the problem is solved). This is particularly useful if the problem is complex.

The Tower of Hanoi

A famous problem that can be solved in this way is the **Tower of Hanoi** puzzle. A simple version might involve three disks and three pegs as below; more complex versions involve more disks.

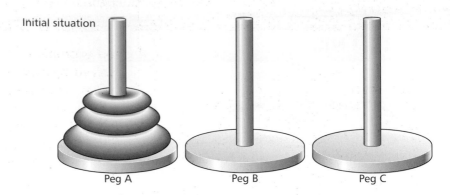

Initial situation

Peg A   Peg B   Peg C

The disks must be moved from Peg A to Peg C. Only one disk may be moved at a time, and no disk may be placed on a disk smaller than itself.

In solving this problem, it is possible to generate a number of **subgoals**. The largest disk must end up on Peg C first. So moving Disk 3 to Peg C is a subgoal. This cannot be achieved in one move, so this generates further subgoals. Disks 1 and 2 must be removed from Peg 1 to begin with, and, looking forward, they will both have to end up on Peg B (to leave space on Peg C for Disk 3). This in turn requires Disk 2 to be placed on Peg B before Disk 1 – so the first move must be to place Disk 1 on Peg C, then Disk 2 to Peg B, then Disk 1 to Peg B, then Disk 3 to Peg C. Now our initial subgoal is completed, and we are close to solving the problem. (The final solution is at the back of this chapter). We can see, then, that both forward and backward searches are used in means-ends analysis.

Means-ends analysis can be applied to a wide variety of problems – even completing psychology coursework! For example, try breaking the problem into smaller problems. What steps do you need to work through to complete your project? Possibilities here include:

1 Decide on a topic of interest
2 Think of some questions you would like to investigate
3 Research the topic area to firm up a question for research and get ideas for how you could carry it out
4 Decide how best to conduct the research
5 Conduct the research
6 Analyse your findings
7 Write the report

By working through each of the subgoals in turn the problem can be solved – and since the subgoals are smaller than the overall problem, tackling them one at a time seems a bit less scary. If some subgoals still seem a bit difficult, you simply generate further subgoals. For example 'Write up the report' could be broken down into:

a) Write an introduction
b) Write a 'method' section... *etc.*

TRY THIS

A good example of a problem that can be solved by means-ends analysis is the **Cannibals and Missionaries Problem**. The object is to get three missionaries and three cannibals across a river in a boat that can only carry a maximum of two people at a time. To travel across the river in either direction someone must be in the boat to row it. If cannibals outnumber missionaries on either side of the river, they will eat the missionaries.

The problem above can be solved in 11 moves, and the answer is at the end of this chapter. You might like to know people most often get stuck about halfway through. At some point you must bring a missionary back from the other side of the river. Research indicates that people often trip up when they have to apparently move *away* from the goal state to solve the problem.

Factors affecting problem-solving

We have said that people often use heuristic strategies to solve problems. This involves using past learning. While it is generally very helpful to do this, it can, sometimes make problem-solving more difficult or lead us into error. One example of this is what is known as **problem-solving set**.

Problem-solving set

To have a 'set' way of thinking about things means that you think about them in a particular way. This may make it difficult to spot other, different ways of approaching the task or problem. A good example of this is provided by Luchins (1942) and his water-jug problems. One such problem is shown below.

KEY STUDY Luchins asked his subjects to imagine that they have three jugs, each of a different, specified size, and that they have to use these three jugs to obtain a specified amount of water. A series of eight problems is given in the table below. The first seven of these problems can be solved using the formula **B − A − 2C**, i.e. fill Jar B, take out the volume of Jar A, and then take out the volume of Jar C twice. The fact that the early problems can all be solved in the same way establishes a problem-solving set.

Problem	Capacity of jars			Required volume
	A	B	C	
1	21	127	3	100
2	14	163	25	99
3	18	43	10	5
4	9	42	6	21
5	20	59	4	31
6	23	49	3	20
7	15	39	3	18
8	28	76	3	25

Luchins found that 95% of people, presented with Problem 8 on its own, could solve it quite easily (A – C), but only 36% of people solved it if they had attempted the previous seven problems first. This is because the mental set established in the earlier problems made solving the eighth problem harder, since the earlier procedures were no longer appropriate.

Luchins also found that people often missed easier solutions to Problems 6 (A – C) and 7 (A + C) for the same reason.

Questions
1. Why did solving the previous seven problems make it harder for people to solve the eighth problem?
2. Suggest an ethical problem for this research.
3. If you wished to replicate this study on students in your school:

   a) how would you obtain a sample that was representative?
   b) how far would you be able to generalise your results?

Source: Luchins, A.S., 'Mechanisation in Problem-Solving. The Effects of Einstellung' in *Psychological Monographs*, 54 (1942), p.248

Functional fixedness
Another type of mental set is **functional fixedness**. If you think about an object as something with a particular use (or function), this may blind you to other ways of using the object. Duncker (1945) gave people matches, a candle, and a box containing drawing pins. The people were asked to attach the candle to the wall in such a way that the wax did not drip onto the floor below.

Duncker found that people tried various solutions, such as glueing it in place with molten wax or pinning the candle directly to the wall, but few people thought to solve the problem by pinning the box to the wall and using it as a platform on which to place the candle. Duncker argued that people were 'fixated' on the box as a container, and this prevented them from realising it could have a different use (as a platform). He found that if people were given the same objects but the box was

empty, i.e. the drawing pins were supplied separately, the likelihood that people would use the box as a platform increased. He argued this was because they were now less fixated on the box as a container, and so were more open to seeing that it could be used as a platform.

Creativity

Creativity refers to a particular approach to problem-solving, though exactly what the term 'creativity' means is difficult to pin down. The hallmark of a creative thinker is the ability to go beyond the usual way of thinking about things and to come up with new and different solutions.

Unlike some of the problems discussed earlier, many problems in real life are open-ended, i.e. they either do not have clear endpoints or solutions, or if they do, it is not clear at the outset what those solutions might be, or how best to achieve them. If the goal state is not clear – for example, if you are asked to design the perfect supermarket, or write a poem – you cannot easily use techniques like means-ends analysis to take you to the solution. You have to invent your own solutions or ways of tackling the problem. Many instances of artistic or scientific innovation are examples of creative solutions.

The creative process

To try and find out how people arrive at creative solutions, researchers have interviewed creative people including artists, scientists, writers and poets. Ghiselin (1952) concluded that people who arrive at creative solutions often go through three stages:

1   There is an initial period of **preparation**. This involves doing a lot of work on a problem, getting a feel for it and struggling with it to try and find a solution.

2   There then follows an **incubation** period. A person may shelve the problem for a while, having made little progress on it. They stop consciously thinking and worrying about it.

3   After a while, a solution to the problem may occur to the person 'out of the blue'. This is referred to as **illumination**. Often they claim to have no idea where the answer came from – it just suddenly struck them. This raises the interesting idea that a

The 'Aha!' experience. A sudden recognition of how to solve a problem

person may be still doing 'unconscious work' on a problem that they believe they have put to one side.

In some ways this is similar to the Gestalt view that some problems can be solved through a sudden flash of **insight**. In this view, seemingly unrelated components of a problem can sometimes be reorganised and made to fit together in new ways to generate a solution.

TRY THIS

Metcalfe (1986) gives the following example of a problem where the answer appears suddenly rather than creeping up slowly:

> *A stranger approached a museum curator and offered him an ancient bronze coin. The coin had an authentic appearance and was marked with the date 544 BC. The curator had happily made acquisitions from suspicious sources before, but this time he promptly called the police and had the stranger arrested. Why?*

If you are stuck on this problem, think carefully about the date on the coin.

(The solution to this problem appears on page 268.)

Cognitive style

Cognitive style refers to the way in which people solve problems. Hudson (1966) analysed the ways in which schoolchildren approached their schoolwork and distinguished between **convergent** and **divergent thinking**. Convergent thinking is more focused, logical, and involves following a series of steps to arrive at the 'right answer'. Divergent thinking is looser, more illogical, involves looking at things from different angles and may generate a variety of different solutions to a problem.

For example, Hudson asked children to think of as many uses as they could for a brick.

- **Convergent** thinkers were likely to suggest using it for building a wall, as a paperweight, etc. They were limited to conventional ideas.

- By contrast, **divergent** thinkers were likely to generate many more possible solutions, because they came up with unusual ideas like using it as a bookend, or to make ripples in a pond, etc.

Hudson found that convergent thinkers were more likely to prefer subjects like science and maths, whereas divergent thinkers tended to like 'arts' subjects like history and English. This is not meant to imply that one cognitive style is any 'better' than the other. What enables us to deal successfully with a wide range of problems is our ability to adopt both styles of thinking. Hudson believed, however, that divergent thinkers might tend to do less well in education or in tests like IQ tests where unconventional answers may simply be seen as wrong.

A concept developed by De Bono is that of **lateral thinking**, which is similar in many ways to the idea of divergent thinking. Lateral thinking involves taking a mental step sideways, or coming at a problem from an unusual angle. De Bono has developed courses for teaching lateral thinking, which involve challenging conventional ways of looking at problems and breaking up mental set.

An example is De Bono's solution to dealing with factories which pollute rivers. He suggested that all such factories should be located downstream. This would result in the polluters themselves suffering most from the pollution they caused. According to De Bono, this might motivate them to do something about it.

Clearly divergent thinking and lateral thinking are closely associated with the idea of creativity. In order to solve problems creatively you need a degree of mental flexibility and a willingness to think in unconventional ways.

Brainstorming

Brainstorming is a technique which can be used by groups of people to generate inventive and new solutions to problems. It is widely used in business as a way of encouraging creativity and counteracting people's tendency to give 'safe' suggestions that do not expose them to the risk of ridicule from colleagues.

Osborn (1957) has suggested six basic rules for a good brainstorming session:

1 People should come up with the most wild and imaginative ideas that they can. It is easier to tame crazy ideas than to make dull ideas exciting.

2 People should come up with as many different ideas as possible. The more ideas there are, the bigger the chance of hitting on something useful.

The technique of brainstorming is often used in business to help find creative solutions to problems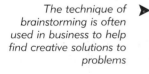

3   No ideas should be criticised during the session itself. Ideas can be evaluated later. People should not be distracted by having to defend their thinking.

4   Group members should not be afraid to spark off, build on and adapt the ideas of others. An odd idea may be useful if combined with or modified by other ideas.

5   A record should be kept of all the ideas generated. Even the smallest comment may turn out to be useful.

6   The session should be run by an experienced leader. This person should not dominate but should encourage everyone to participate and help generate the right atmosphere.

Measuring creativity

Many researchers who study intelligence and creativity believe that they are two different things (Monroe, 1988). The type of ability measured in IQ tests is what Hudson would refer to as convergent thinking. Here, the questions usually have only one answer which is either right or wrong. Creativity tests usually involve questions which have no 'right answer'. Items in such tests may include:

● **'Unusual uses' test**: e.g. *'Think of as many uses as you can for a fork'*

● **Fable completion**: here you are given the start of a story and have to invent the ending

● **Picture construction**: e.g. *'Make as many pictures of real-life objects as you can within a minute using a circle'*

● **'Generation of consequences'**: e.g. *'What would happen if you woke up tomorrow to find everyone was just 10cm tall?'*

A well-known test for creativity is **Guilford's (1967) Divergent Productions Tests**. Examples of items from the test are shown on the left.

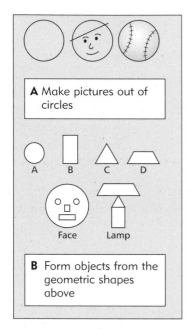

A Make pictures out of circles

A   B   C   D

Face   Lamp

B Form objects from the geometric shapes above

Guilford's Divergent Productions Test is often used to measure creativity ▲

There are many different kinds of item that can be included in tests of creativity. Generally they are scored in terms of the fluency, diversity and originality of the responses. In other words, participants are scored according to how many original ideas they can come up with and how quickly they can produce these ideas. Another type of test, the **Remote Associates Test** designed by Mednick and Mednick (1967), involves giving people lists of three words – e.g. 'gem', 'wall', 'stepping' – and asking them to find an associated word that would provide an appropriate connection with these three (e.g. 'stone'). What is evaluated here is the appropriateness of the solution.

Needless to say, deciding just how novel, appropriate or unusual a response is in such tests is not an easy matter, since it must depend to some extent on the subjective judgement of the scorer. Evaluating a creative solution is difficult, in part precisely because it is something new and different, and because creative solutions often address problems for which there is no, one right answer. What, for example, is a 'good' painting or poem?

Compared to IQ tests, therefore, creativity tests are hard to score objectively. Research shows that scores are only weakly correlated with scores on IQ tests. As with all psychometric tests, creativity tests just give a 'snapshot' view. That is, they show how candidates perform 'on the day', but not necessarily how creative they might be on another day in another place. There is also not much evidence to show that scores on creativity tests are related to how creative people actually are in the real world.

TRY THIS

Match the **terms** on the left to the **definitions** on the right.

convergent thinking	a strategy that guarantees finding the right answer eventually
means-ends analysis	a strategy for generating inventive solutions in a group
algorithmic strategy	logical, focused thinking style that looks for one right answer
heuristic strategy	solving a problem by breaking it into sub-problems
divergent thinking	a rule of thumb, quicker strategy – may not find the answer.
brainstorming	a more illogical thinking style that seeks a variety of answers

Summary

- Algorithmic strategies to problem-solving guarantee the right answer but may take a long time to find it
- Heuristic strategies are often quicker, but may fail to find the right answer. Research suggests most human problem-solving is like this. Heuristic strategies include problem-solving by analogy, backward search, and means-ends analysis.
- Problem-solving can be affected by things like set and functional fixedness.
- Problems requiring creative solutions may offer no obvious way to begin, and the shape of the final solution may be unclear at the outset.
- The creative process may sometimes involve three steps: preparation, incubation, and illumination.
- Hudson distinguishes between convergent and divergent styles of thinking. De Bono's notion of lateral thinking, taking a mental sideways step, is similar to divergent thinking.
- Brainstorming is a technique for getting creative responses from a group.
- Creativity tests measure the fluency and originality of peoples' responses, but creative answers are difficult to evaluate.

1. Solution to Tower of Hanoi puzzle (page 260)

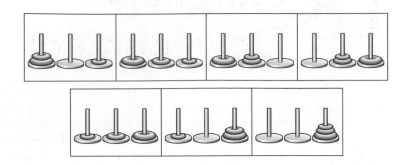

2. Solution to missionaries and cannibals problem (page 261)

Step	Action
1	Move 2 Cannibals, R to L
2	Move 1 Cannibal, L to R
3	Move 2 Cannibals, R to L
4	Move 1 Cannibal, L to R
5	Move 2 Missionaries, R to L
6	Move 1 Cannibal, 1 Missionary, L to R
7	Move 2 Missionaries, R to L
8	Move 1 Cannibal L to R
9	Move 2 Cannibals, R to L
10	Move 1 Cannibal, L to R
11	Move 2 Cannibals, R to L

3. Solution to coin puzzle (page 264)

The coin cannot be authentic since the time-period 'BC' was not created until centuries later.

4. Creative solutions to the 9-dot problem (page 209)

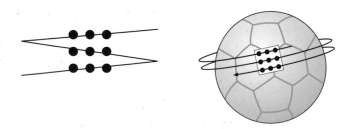

18 Language Development

If you have ever tried to learn a foreign language, you probably found that it took a lot of time and effort. Yet children learn their native language without any direct instruction and without ever consulting a dictionary or grammar book. What is even more remarkable is that they become a fluent speaker of their language by the time they are four or five years old!

How do they do it? And what exactly do children 'learn' when they learn language?

What is language?

Most psychologists would agree that language involves using sounds, signs or symbols to communicate with others (Crystal, 1987). Psychologists would also agree that learning a language involves a lot more than just learning vocabulary. It also involves learning the 'rules of language'. These rules are called **grammar**. Once you know the rules of a language, it is possible to create an infinite number of sentences.

In general, there are three different kinds of rules that a child has to learn in order to use language:

- **Sound combinations (phonological rules):** a child must learn which sound combinations are acceptable for a particular language. For example, in English, the sounds '*pb*' do not occur together but '*pa*' does.

- **Meanings of words or phrases (semantic rules):** a child must learn the rules which deal with the meanings of words or phrases. For example, children learn that the following two sentences mean the same thing even though the structure of the sentences is different.

  'The dog chased the cat.'
  'The cat was chased by the dog.'

- **Rules for combining words into sentences (syntactic rules):** grammar also involves learning how to combine words in the right order to make sentences. There are certain rules which determine the order of words within sentences. For example in English we might ask, 'Where is Michael going?' but we wouldn't ask, 'Is Michael going where?'

How do psychologists study language development?

One of the earliest ways of studying language development involved using **parental diaries**. This was a technique used by a number of different researchers, including Piaget, in studying language development. Parents are asked to keep a written record of their child's use of language, including their first words and sentences.

More recently, studying language development has become easier with the development of recording instruments such as tape recorders and video cameras. As a result, psychologists use the following methods to study language development:

- **Naturalistic observation** involves collecting samples of the child's language when the child is in a familiar setting. A good example is Roger Brown's work with Adam, Eve and Sarah (see Key Study, page 271)

- **Controlled observation** involves bringing the child into a more controlled environment like a laboratory which has been converted into a playroom. The psychologist might also observe the child through a one way mirror.

- **Experimental tasks** involve giving the child a task to perform which allows the researcher to observe the child's ability to use and understand language. A good example is a study carried out by Berko (1958), who was interested to see at what age young children understand the rule for using plurals and past tenses. She showed children drawings like the ones shown below.

This is a wug.

Now there are two of them.
There are two _____.

This is a man who knows how to rick.
He is ricking.

He did the same thing yesterday.
What did he do yesterday?
Yesterday he _____.

If the child understands how to make plurals, he/she will supply the correct word which is 'wugs'. If the child understands about the past tense, he/she will say 'ricked'.

THINK ABOUT IT

Why do you think it was important to use words the child had not heard before?

A good example of a naturalistic observation study is described below.

KEY STUDY   In 1973, Roger Brown and his colleagues carried out a study on the language development of three children using naturalistic observation techniques. The researchers visited the three children in their homes and recorded the conversations between the parent and the child for at least two hours per month. The way in which the researchers measured language development was by finding the child's **mean length of utterance (MLU)**. This measure is based on the number of meaningful units or **morphemes** found in the child's language.

For example, the word 'talk' consists of one meaningful unit or morpheme, but the word 'talking' consists of two meaning units ('talk') and ('-ing'). Although the measure is not perfect it does give the researcher some idea of the complexity of the child's language.

The researcher compared the language development of three children, Adam, Eve and Sarah. The graph below shows the rate at which the children acquired language.

Graph showing rate of language acquisition among three children, Adam, Eve and Sarah, measured in terms of Mean Length of Utterance (MLU). MLU is calculated by taking the total number of utterances in a sample and dividing by the number of words or morphemes

Source: Brown, R., A First Language: The early stages (Harvard University Press, Cambridge, Mass., 1973) © 1973 The President and Fellows of Harvard College. Reprinted with permission

The researchers identified several interesting characteristics of language development:

- Although the pace of language development varied among Adam, Eve and Sarah, the nature of their speech in any one stage was very similar.

- Learning how to add endings to words occurs in a *specific order*. For example, children learn how to add '-ing' to a verb (e.g. 'singing') before they learn to form plurals ('dog-s').

- The first sentences that children utter are usually very short and contain only the most important words.

- Even when children are asked to imitate an adult's simple sentence, they leave out minor parts of speech like 'an', 'the'. This suggests that the child selects key words in the sentence.

- Parents (particularly mothers) play an important role in helping children acquire language. In nearly a third of the interactions between mother and child, the mother expanded the child's speech and helped to 'fill in the gaps'. It was argued that this encouraged the child's language ability because the mother was providing examples of speech which were just above the child's current level of performance.

Questions

Use the text and the graph to answer the following questions.

1. a) Is the study carried out by Brown and his colleagues a cross-sectional or longitudinal study?
   b) Explain your answer.

2. Use the graph to answer the following questions:
   a) At what age did Adam show a MLU of 2.50?
   b) Which child showed the fastest rate of acquiring language?
   c) What was Sarah's MLU at 38 months of age?

3. The researchers used mean length of utterance (MLU) to measure the child's level of language development. Can you think of a problem with using this measure?

4. a) Give one advantage of using naturalistic observation to study language development in children.
   b) Give one advantage of using experimental tasks to study language development.

Source: Brown, R., *A First Language: The early stages* (Harvard University Press, Cambridge, Mass., 1973)

Brown suggested a model of language development which consisted of five stages and was based on the number of MLUs in the child's speech. This model is explained below. Stage 1 begins when the child's language has passed a mean length utterance of 1.0 and ends when the child has achieved an MLU of 2.0.

In summary

- *Language involves learning to use sounds, signs or symbols to communicate with others.*

- *Learning to speak a particular language involves learning the rules for combining sounds, the appropriate order for combining words into sentences and the meaning of words or phrases.*

- *Psychologists have studied language using a variety of methods such as naturalistic observations, controlled observation and experimental tasks.*

- *Brown's study suggested that, although children vary in terms of the rate of their language development, most follow the same sequence in acquiring language.*

Brown also analysed a number of independent studies of children in different countries such as Japan, Finland and Germany. He found that similar patterns of language development occurred in Stage 1 children regardless of the language they were learning. This suggests that this development could be universal.

Stages of language development

Although most children are 12 months old before they utter their first word, language development really begins at birth. For example, research has shown that infants are responsive to speech from birth. In a study by Butterfield and Siperstein (1972), infants were allowed to suck on a special nipple which triggered certain types of sounds. Newborn infants sucked faster on a dummy which turned on recorded speech than they did to listen to rhythmic sounds or other instrumental music. The study showed that infants seem to prefer speech sounds to other sounds.

1. The pre-linguistic stage (0–12 months)

All normal infants are capable of producing sounds at birth. As any new parent will tell you, infants are particularly good at crying. Crying is a reflexive response to any type of discomfort such as hunger or pain. Infants also make other sounds when sucking or swallowing.

At around 6–8 weeks of age infants begin to produce a new sound. These sounds tend to be vowel sounds (like 'ooo', 'aaa'). These sounds are usually made when the infant is in a relaxed state and are called **cooing**, because they sound like the noise that pigeons and doves make.

By 7 months of age (25–30 weeks), infants begin to **babble**. The infant usually adds a consonant sound (like 'b', 'g') to the 'cooing' sounds they have been producing. The result is an utterance like 'bababa', 'gagagaga'. During the babbling period infants will also make other sounds such as blowing bubbles and gurgles. Although parents may get very excited and are convinced that their child is talking, babbling is not usually meaningful speech. As a result psychologists call this early stage of language development the **pre-linguistic stage**. Research has shown that all infants sound the same at this stage, whatever their language environment. Deaf children also coo and babble.

2. First words (12–18 months)

During this stage infants begin to produce meaningful speech. At around 12–13 months of age, they usually produce their first word such as 'bena' for 'Ribena' or 'Dada' for 'Dad'. Although they can only produce one word at a time, these words can often be interpreted as expressing a whole idea. As a result, psychologists tend to refer to these one-word utterances as **holophrases**. For example, the child may say the word 'shoe' and point to a shoe on the floor. This could mean 'that is my shoe' or 'give me the shoe'. Each word may have a variety of meanings, so the child's gestures and the context are important in interpreting what they are trying to express.

So what sort of words do children learn first? In 1973, Nelson followed the language development of 18 infants as they learned their first 50 words. She found that the majority of first words – 65% in fact – were words which referred to people or objects, such as 'Mummy' or 'doggie'. She found that 13% of first words tended to be *action words* like 'go' or 'look'.

3. Two-word sentences

By 18 months, children begin to produce simple sentences which consist of 3–4 words. Psychologists believe that children begin to understand grammar during this phase. This process is usually divided into two stages called Stage 1 and Stage 2 grammar.

Stage 1 Grammar

In Stage 1 grammar, children produce very simple, short sentences. Essential words (such as nouns and verbs) are included, but other parts of grammar (such as adding '-ed' to a verb to indicate the past tense) are left out. These early sentences are often referred to as **telegraphic speech** since they are similar to the sentences used when sending a telegram, where every word costs. Research has shown that children also use telegraphic speech when they are asked to imitate others. For example, if a child is asked to repeat the following sentences, this is how they would respond:

Adult's sentence	Child's response
'This is Mummy's bag.'	'Mummy's bag.'
'He's going out.'	'He go out.'

Stage 2 Grammar (30 months plus)

This stage begins as soon as the child starts to use plurals ('dogs') and the past tense of verbs such as 'walked'. As we saw in the Key Study on page 271, Brown (1973) found that, although children may differ in terms of the age at which they acquire certain parts of speech, all children tend to acquire them in the same order. For example, children learn to add '-ing' to a verb ('running') before they learn to add '-s' to a word to make it plural ('shoes').

Once children have learned how to use a **grammatical marker** such as adding '-ed' to a verb to make it past tense, they tend to over-generalise this rule and apply it to all verbs ('I go-ed to the shop.') Parents' attempts to encourage the child to use the appropriate verb endings are usually to no avail, as the following conversation shows:

Child: My teacher *holded* the baby rabbits and we patted them.
Adult: Did you say your teacher *held* the baby rabbits?
Child: Yes.
Adult: What did you say she did?
Child: She *holded* the baby rabbits and we patted them.
Adult: Did you say that she *held* them tightly?
Child: No, she *holded* them loosely.[17]

Learning to ask questions

Being able to change a statement into a question normally takes three steps which adults do automatically. Children, however, seem to learn each step at a time. For example, children's earliest questions usually consist of two to three words and they simply raise their voice at the end of the sentence ('daddy eat?'). The child may also add a 'wh-' word to the beginning of the sentence ('What daddy eat?').

In the second stage, child is able to use the correct form of the verb ('What Daddy is eating?') but as you can see, the word order is still not quite right.

In the third and final stage, the child is able to put words in the right order so that their question sounds very similar to an adult's: 'What is Daddy eating'?

By the time the child is four or five years of age, he or she will have mastered the main rules of grammar. However, children continue learning the more complex aspects of grammar until the age of ten or eleven.

Theories of language development

So far, we have considered what children learn during language development. Now it is time to consider the various theories of language development. We will look at four main theories which attempt to describe the processes by which children develop language:

- Skinner's theory of operant conditioning
- Social learning theory and the role of imitation
- Chomsky's theory of transformational grammar
- Lenneberg's biological perspective

Skinner's theory of operant conditioning

In 1957, Skinner published a book called *Verbal Behaviour* in which he argued that children learn language just like they would learn any other behaviour, through the process of reinforcement and shaping (see Chapter 7, *The Behavioural Approach*). Infants produce a number of spontaneous sounds. Parents and other adults selectively reinforce any sound which resembles human speech. Since only certain sounds are rewarded, the infant is more likely to repeat those sounds. Through reinforcement, the infant learns which sounds are appropriate to their language, and how those sounds are combined to make words. According to Skinner, the child's speech is reinforced in various ways:

- through the child imitating the speech of others and receiving approval
- through the child uttering certain sounds and being reinforced by getting what he/she wants (e.g. the word *'bena'* results in a drink of Ribena)
- through the child producing correct verbal labels (called **tacts**) for certain objects

What Skinner is suggesting is that children learn to speak grammatically in order to be able to communicate their needs to others. For example, a child may ask, 'Could I have a drink please?' which would be rewarded by being given a drink. But is Skinner's theory an appropriate way of describing how children acquire language?

Evaluation of Skinner's theory of language development

Strengths

+ Skinner's theory recognises environmental influences on language. Parents do play an important role in the child's language development. Research has shown that parents adjust their own speech to match the child's level of understanding, giving rise to a form of language called **parentese**). For example, Snow (1972) compared the language directed by parents to two groups of children who differed in age. One group was aged two and the other group was aged ten. She found that the speech directed at the younger children was usually made up of short, simple sentences and involved repetition. So parents, other adults and even other children do play an important part in language acquisition.

Weaknesses

− Skinner's theory does not explain how children learn language so quickly. Reinforcement of sounds into words and words into sentences would be a slow process and yet children acquire language very rapidly.

− If Skinner is right, parents should reinforce grammatical speech and ignore or discourage ungrammatical speech. However, research does not support this. For example, when Brown et al. (1969) recorded conversations between children and their mothers, they found that mothers were more likely to give approval if a statement was *true* than if it was *grammatically correct*. For example, if a child said 'Teddy sock on' and showed her mother a teddy bear with a sock on it, the mother would provide reinforcement. However, if the child said, 'Look, Teddy is wearing a sock' and showed the mother a teddy with no sock, the mother would correct the child.

− Skinner's theory does not consider the active role of the child in learning language. Children can be very creative in the type of sentences they produce, yet Skinner's theory presents them as passive receivers of reinforcement.

Social learning theory and the role of imitation

This theory suggests that children learn to speak by copying or imitating the speech they hear around them. Imitation undoubtedly plays a part in learning sounds and vocabulary. Imitation also explains how children acquire certain accents. However, imitation alone does not provide a complete explanation of language acquisition. There have to be other processes at work to help children learn language.

Evaluation of social learning theory

Strengths

+ Imitation does play a vital part in the acquisition of accent and vocabulary.

Weaknesses

- Children produce sentences that they are unlikely to have heard from adults (e.g. 'allgone sticky').
- When asked to imitate adult speech (e.g. 'This is Mummy's bag'), children tend to reproduce the statement in a way that fits their own current level of understanding (e.g. 'Mummy bag').
- Furthermore, the errors that children make in their speech (called **errors of growth**) suggest that there is more to acquiring language than just imitation. A child may initially imitate correctly (e.g. 'I ran'), but later make a mistake, (e.g. 'I *runned*). This shows children are not just imitating, but are trying to understand the rules of language. In this case, the child has learned the rule for past tense but has not yet learned that there are important exceptions to the rule.

Chomsky's theory

Problems with both Skinner and social learning theory led Noam Chomsky (1959) to develop an alternative theory. Chomsky is a linguist, rather than a psychologist. Linguists are people who study the structure of language and the rules which govern it.

In 1959, Chomsky published a very critical review of Skinner's theory. He argued that:

- since operant conditioning is based on animal research, it cannot provide an appropriate explanation of how humans learn language
- the process of reinforcement does not explain how children acquire grammmar or the rules of language.

Chomsky believed that learning language involves a great deal more than simply being rewarded for certain verbal responses. It means learning the **rules of grammar**. The rules of grammar as described in the beginning of this chapter allow children to understand the difference in meaning between sentences that may look very similar. For example:

'Jill hit the ball.'
'The ball hit Jill.'

According to Chomsky, these rules cannot be learned through imitation and reinforcement alone.

Since children are able to learn grammar so quickly, Chomsky believes that children are **pre-programmed for language**. For example, children may have an innate ability to:

- distinguish between speech sounds (e.g. parent talking) and non-speech sounds (e.g. parent sneezing)
- understand how language is structured.

For example, children may 'know' that sentences are made up of certain slots or units. These slots can be filled by more than one word as shown in the example on page 278.

```
                    ┌──── Sentence ────┐
Noun phrases                    Verb phrases
Birds                           eat seed.
The small grey birds            have eaten the seed.
```

Children may also 'know' that these slots can be moved around, so that sometimes, although the order of the words is different, the meaning is the same. At other times, the order of the words may be the same but the meaning is different. Chomsky demonstrated this point by giving examples of ambiguous sentences (sentences which can be interpreted in two different ways). Although the following sentences have the same word order, they could have different meanings.

Sentence order	Meaning
Visiting relatives can be boring.	Going to visit relatives can be boring
Visiting relatives can be boring.	Relatives who come to visit can be boring.

Such examples led Chomsky to suggest that language is organised on two different levels. The first is called the **surface level** and refers to the actual order of words or phrases within a sentence. The second level is called **deep level** and refers to the underlying meaning of the sentence. As Gross (1996) has pointed out, when we hear a sentence, we do not process the surface level of the sentence: we process the meaning, or the deep level, of the sentence:

> 'When we hear a spoken sentence, we do not "process" or retain the grammatical structure, the actual words or phrases used (i.e. the surface structure) but instead we transform it into another form, which more or less corresponds to the meaning of the sentence (deep structure). This understanding or knowledge of how to transform the meaning of a sentence into the words that make up the sentence and vice versa (i.e. transformational grammar) is what Chomsky believes is innate…'[18]

Therefore, according to Chomsky, processing language depends on the ability to transform deep structures into surface structures, and vice versa.

But how does this work? According to Chomsky, children have an innate system called the **Language Acquistion Device (LAD)** which helps them interpret the language they hear.

Children listen to the speech around them and they look for regularities or patterns. The child will make guesses or hypotheses about the rules which govern language. Initially, these guesses will be very simple ones. But over time with repeated exposure to language, the child's guesses about the rules of language will become more advanced. However, the child needs more than this to process language. This is where **linguistic universals** come into play. According to Chomsky, all languages have certain features in common. For example, all languages are made up of vowels, consonants, nouns and verbs. Chomsky believed that children have innate understanding of these linguistic universals, and that this helps them 'hook into' the language they hear and begin the task of making sense of it.

Chomsky's theory has generated a lot of debate. Is there any evidence to suggest that humans are 'pre-wired' for language as he suggests?

Evaluation of Chomsky's theory

Strengths

+ Chomsky believed that all humans have the same language acquisition device. This helps to explain why, regardless of the language they are learning to speak, all children go through the same stages of language development at roughly the same age.

+ The idea that children are pre-programmed for language explains how children acquire the complicated rules of grammar so quickly and at such an early stage of cognitive development.

+ Chomsky's theory also accounts for the creativity of children's language. Some of the errors of growth that children make in their language may be due to the fact that they discover a rule (e.g., how to use the past tense of a verb) and then over-generalise its application.

+ There is evidence to support the idea of innate language ability. For example, very young infants are able to tell the difference between different speech sounds. Eimas et al. (1971) found that infants were able to distinguish between similar sounds like 'b' and 'p' at a very early age.

Weaknesses

− Chomsky's theory focuses on what the child knows or understands about language. It is hard to study what children understand because it is not possible to ask them directly.

− Research by Bard and Sachs (1977) emphasises the importance of social interaction in acquiring language The researchers were interested to see how Jim, whose parents were both deaf, learned language. Despite being exposed to spoken language from the radio and television, Jim's speech was significantly below average. However, at the age of four he received intensive speech therapy and his language improved rapidly. The study suggests that just being exposed to language is not enough; children need social interaction.

Lenneberg's biological perspective

In 1967, Eric Lenneberg, a biologist, offered a different approach to language development. Like Chomsky, Lenneberg believed that language ability is innate. However, Lenneberg is interested in the role that biological maturation plays. The term **maturation** is used to refer to biologically scheduled development which has little to do with learning or experience. For example, most children learn to sit up, crawl and walk at about the same age and this development is relatively independent of experience. According to Lenneberg, language is influenced by maturation rather than specific learning experiences:

'Why do children normally begin to speak between their 18–28th month? Surely it is not because all mothers on earth initiate language training at that time. There is, in fact, no evidence that any conscious and systematic teaching of language takes place, just as there is not special training for stance or gait.'[19]

Lenneberg suggested there is a critical period for language acquisition. The term **critical period** suggests that, in order for an event or experience to have an effect, it must occur within a specified period of time. According to Lenneberg, language is acquired between the ages of two and puberty. Very few children are able to produce words before the age of 18 months, despite the fact that the child's vocal cords are in good working order. There is no specific environmental event which triggers language, and children clearly do not make a conscious decision to speak. Instead, the trigger which initiates language is a biological one and is related to development of the brain.

As Lenneberg points out, at birth the brain weighs just over 300 grams. By the age of two, the brain weighs over 1,000 grams. During this period of time, nerve cells within the brain are making connections with each other.

After puberty, learning a language becomes more difficult. According to Lenneberg:

'After puberty...the brain behaves as if it had become set in its ways and primary, basic skills not acquired by that time usually remain deficient for life.'[20]

Lenneberg believes this is mostly due to **brain lateralisation**. For most people, language ability is located in the left hemisphere of the brain. However, at birth there is little difference in the functioning of the two hemispheres. Specialisation (e.g. localisation of language in the left hemisphere) appears to be a gradual process which starts at the age of around two. Lenneberg believes this process is completed by puberty.

Evidence from brain-damaged patients supports Lenneberg's notion of a critical period. If children under the age of two experience severe trauma to the left hemisphere of the brain, their speech will usually develop normally. This may be because the right hemisphere takes over language. As the child gets older, the chance of recovering from brain damage decreases. Furthermore, if adults suffer brain damage to the left hemisphere, they may be unable to regain the power of speech.

Evaluation of Lenneberg's Theory
Strengths
+ There is evidence to support the role of maturation in language development since all children seem to pass through the same stages at roughly the same time.
+ Further evidence to support a critical period of language development comes from case studies of children who have experienced early deprivation. For example, Isabelle (Mason, 1942) was found at the age of six and a half, having been raised in a single room by a

mother who was unable to hear or speak. As a result, Isabelle had not been exposed to language. However, once removed from the deprivation and given special training, she was able to acquire normal language. This could be due to the fact that Isabelle had not passed the critical period for developing language.

Weaknesses

- However, other case studies of severe deprivation do not support Lenneberg's theory. Genie was found at the age of 13 and was past the age of puberty. Like Isabelle, she had spent most of her life alone in a small room. She was physically restrained and was unable to move about. If she made any noise, she was punished.

When Genie was found, she was unable to speak and understood very little language. However, after extensive training, her vocabulary began to increase signficantly. As Gross (1996) points out, although she never learned to speak fluently, the fact that she was able to acquire any language at all questions the notion of a critical period.

Teaching animals to talk

Are human beings the only species that have language? What are the differences between human language and the ways in which animals communicate? There are two ways in which researchers have tried to answer this question:

- by identifying the key features of language and comparing animal communication systems with human language to see how they measure up
- by attempting to teach non-human animals to use language.

As Aitchison (1983) points out, we already know that some animals such as mynah birds and budgies can be trained to talk. We also know that animals use signals in the wild. For example, Struhsaker (1967) showed that vervet monkeys use alarm cries to warn each other of danger. Furthermore, the cries used are different depending on whether the danger comes from a snake, an eagle or a leopard. Does this constitute language?

Comparing animal communication with human language

Charles Hockett (1963), a linguist, identified a number of characteristics of language. These include:

- the use of vocal cords to make sounds and a hearing mechanism to receive them
- the ability to use language spontaneously
- taking turns in conversations
- the fact that language is learned or transmitted from one generation to the next
- the ability to refer to things which are not physically present (called **displacement**)
- the use of symbols to repesent an action or object
- the ability to produce an infinite variety of messages.

According to Aitchison (1983), human language possesses all of these features, while animal communication has some, but not all of them.

THINK ABOUT IT

Which features of language does vervet monkey communication lack?

- Most animal communication lacks displacement because the communication is usualy dependent on a particular context or situation. For example, the vervet monkey would not signal to say that he had seen a snake two days ago.
- Most animals lack the ability to produce an infinite variety of messages. Animals tend to have a limited number of signals, and a particular signal always means the same thing.
- Finally, only some animals are able to use symbols to refer to objects or actions, as we will see in the next section.

Teaching language to non-human animals

Early attempts

In 1931, a baby chimpanzee was 'adopted' by two researchers, Kellogg and Kellogg. They treated Gua as if she were human. She wore nappies and was fed and bathed. Although she was constantly exposed to human language, she never learned to speak. She was however, able to understand the meaning of as many as 70 words.

A similar attempt was carried out by Hayes and Hayes (1947) on another female chimpanzee called Viki. Despite several years of training, Viki learned to speak only four words; 'cup', 'up', 'papa', 'mama'.

One reason why these early attempts to teach chimpanzees to talk failed was because chimpanzees do not have the appropriate vocal organs to allow them to make human sounds.

Washoe

The Gardners (1966) decided to try a different approach. They raised Washoe, a female chimpanzee, as if she was a deaf human child, using **American Sign Language (ASL)** to see if she could acquire language rather than be taught to speak. During her waking hours, Washoe had human companions who used the ASL signs when communicating with her and with each other. With this exposure, Washoe soon learned individual signs such as 'sweet' or 'berry' and later began to combine signs to make basic sentences similar to those of a young child. She was able to sign for objects that were not physically present and to initiate conversations with her trainers by asking questions and making requests. After four years in this environment, Washoe had learnt 132 signs, including verbs ('go', 'hug', 'tickle'), colours and nouns ('brush', 'drink').

This chimp trained by the Gardners (see below) is using sign language to say the word 'friend'

Washoe also used signs to communicate to her adopted son Loulis, who learned more than 80 signs. There are many hours of video recordings of Loulis using signs, in the correct context, to his mother and to other chimpanzees in his home, even when no humans were present.

Sarah

In 1966, the Premacks began to teach Sarah, another female chimpanzee, to use language. Their approach was very different to the one used with Washoe. Unlike Washoe, who was constantly surrounded by humans, Sarah lived in a cage. She was taught to communicate by manipulating plastic tokens of different shapes and colours on a magnetic board. Each plastic token represented a word or action.

The Premacks used operant conditioning techniques with Sarah, including positive reinforcement when she made the correct response. Over time, Sarah learned the meaning of over 100 words and was able to respond to basic commands such as 'Give Mary banana'. She was also able to understand more abstract commands such as 'if/then'. For example, Sarah was shown an apple and a banana and told, 'If banana, then chocolate.' Sarah would take the banana in order to get the chocolate. However, despite her level of understanding, Sarah did not tend to initiate conversations with her trainers or spontaneously produce new sentences. Learning to respond to different arrangements of tokens is a bit like learning a complicated board game. The Premacks accepted that this did not show that Sarah had any understanding of grammatical rules.

Lana

Lana, like Sarah, was trained in a controlled environment (Rumbaugh, 1977). She was taught to communicate by using a keyboard. Each key had a symbol on it which represented a word. In order to help Lana understand word order, each word had a different background colour.

To help Lana understand word order, each word had a different background colour. The symbol for 'Lana' was a solid circle inside a diamond on a purple background.

Yellow	Purple	Blue	Purple	Red
Query	Tim	Give	Lana	Milk
Query	Tim	Give	Lana	Apple
Please	Machine	Give		Coke

Lana's keyboard was also connected to a vending machine so that if she made a correct request for something like a drink, she could get it immediately. Lana learned over 100 symbols. Like Washoe and Sarah, once she learned a symbol like 'more' she was able to generalise it to other situations ('more drink', 'more bread'). Lana was also able to refer to objects not physically present. One morning when her trainer was late with her milk, she requested, 'Tim put milk in machine'.

Koko

Penny Patterson (1979) taught language to Koko, a female gorilla, also using American Sign Language. After five years of training, Koko had a working vocabulary of over 375 signs. Koko's use of language was creative. She was able to combine signs together to make novel utterances which she had not been exposed to before. For example, Koko signed 'white tiger' to describe a zebra and 'me cry there' when she was shown a picture of a gorilla in a bath. In one incident she bit her trainer. Days later, when she saw the mark on Penny's arm, she signed, 'sorry bite scratch. wrong bite.' When Penny asked her why she bit, Koko signed, 'because mad'. It certainly appeared that Koko was using language in a meaningful way. The only difference between Koko's system of communication and human language was that her communication lacked any structure or word order.

Nim Chimpsky

Nim was a male chimpanzee trained by Terrace (1979) and named after the linguist Chomsky (see above)! Nim was able to acquire a number of signs. When Terrace first described Nim's use of language, it appeared as if Nim's language was structured. For example, Terrace found that when Nim used two signs together which included the sign for 'more', he tended to put the sign for 'more' at the beginning of the sentence. However, closer inspection revealed that many of the other words used by Nim were not ordered in any way. It seemed that Nim simply had a preference for putting 'more' at the beginning of a sentence. Also, Nim did not increase the length of his utterances and he did not initiate conversations with his trainers.

Terrace also analysed videotapes of other chimps such as Washoe who had been trained to communicate. He argued that these chimps were being cued by their trainers and therefore were not really using language in any meaningful sense.

Kanzi

Savage-Rumbaugh (1990) decided to use a more naturalistic approach to make the animal's learning more like the way children learn. Kanzi, a male bonobo, was raised in a large forest which formed part of a primate centre. Kanzi was never caged and explored the forest with his human trainers. The trainers used a keyboard or lexigram to communicate with Kanzi. This consisted of 256 shapes, with each shape representing a word. Unlike the other apes who had to be taught the symbols, Kanzi learned by watching his trainers point to the symbols as they spoke. As a result, Kanzi learned both the symbol and the spoken word.

Kanzi's language acquisition was different from the previous apes studied. He began by understanding the spoken word first and then learning the symbol. During the first three years of his life, his understanding of spoken English was limited to individual words and basic sentences. However, by his fifth year, he was able to respond to more complex requests. At ten years of age, Kanzi had over 200 words. However, what was even more impressive was his level of comprehension. The researchers gave Kanzi a number of requests (310

Using a 'lexigram' or keyboard as shown here, the chimpanzee Kanzi was able to communicate with a human trainer

in total). In order to ensure that he was not being cued, the requests were given by someone in another room and the researchers with Kanzi wore earphones so that they could not hear the instructions. Kanzi was able to respond correctly to requests such as 'Can you go to the colony room and get the telephone'. In fact, his success rate was 298/310. Although his capacity for understanding language is greater than his ability to produce language on the lexigram, Kanzi was able to say:

> 'when he is going to be "good" or "bad", what he has just eaten or where he is headed while travelling.'[21]

Evaluation of animal studies

Strengths

+ On the basis of the research it does appear that some primates can learn to use and combine signs and symbols. Kanzi has also shown the ability to understand spoken words.
+ The animal studies may help researchers to understand how language has evolved in humans.

Weaknesses

− Teaching primates to use language raises some ethical concerns. For example, when Washoe grew too big to remain in the Gardners' caravan, she was moved to a primate centre. The change from having constant human company to living with other monkeys could have been stressful for her.
− Terrace (1979) has argued that the achievements of the apes has been exaggerated. He quotes an example from Washoe's training when she apparently signed 'waterbird' when she saw a bird near the river. According to Terrace, Washoe was simply making the signs she had been taught to make when shown a bird and water separately.
− It is difficult to compare the results of the different studies because researchers used different methods of training. Some of the animals were raised in a controlled environment (Sarah and Nim) while others experienced a more natural environment.
− Although the primates' ability to communicate looks impressive, their communication does not fully resemble human language despite extensive training.

SUMMARY			
Animal	Researchers	Training method	Achievements
Gua (chimp)	Kellogg, Kellogg (1931)	reared like a human infant; tried to teach her to speak	never learned to speak but understood the meaning of 70 words
Viki (chimp)	Hayes, Hayes (1947)	used operant conditioning to teach her to speak	could produce four very similar words
Washoe (chimp)	Gardner, Gardner (1966)	used American Sign Language; reinforced correct responses	learned 132 signs and could combine signs, did initiate conversations with trainers
Sarah (chimp)	Premack, Premack (1966)	used plastic tokens to communicate; lived in a controlled environment	learned the meaning of over 100 words; could respond to basic commands but did not initiate conversation
Lana (chimp)	Rumbaugh (1977)	used symbols on a keyboard; lived in a controlled environment	learned over 100 symbols
Koko (gorilla)	Patterson (1979)	American Sign Language	learned 375 signs, can combine signs together and produce novel utterances
Nim Chimpsky (chimp)	Terrace (1979)	controlled environment	learned many signs, but did not initiate conversations with trainers
Kanzi (bonobo)	Savage-Rumbaugh (1990)	reared in primate centre, used a lexigram, trainers spoke when pointing to symbols	understands 200 words, can respond to complicated requests

Social Psychology

Like it or not, people play an important part in our lives. Life without other people is almost unthinkable. This section is concerned to introduce you to research and theory in several topics concerned with how individuals and groups can influence each other.

19 The Development of Social Relationships

Affiliation

What is affiliation? Psychologists use the term **affiliation** to describe the tendency for humans to seek out the company of other people and to form associations. Affilation usually involves co-operating and forming friendships with other people.

Making friends

Developmental psychologists are interested in **peer interactions**. A child's peers are other children who are similar in age, cognitive ability or other characteristics and who are on an 'equal footing' with them.

Research suggests that even young infants will respond to the presence of a peer. Vandell and Mueller (1980) found that by two months, infants will look at a peer. As they get older their interactions with peers increase as shown below:

Do you feel a natural human desire to affiliate with me and form a close personal bond characterised by trust and commitment?

No, but I'll have that rusk, thanks

Age	Type of interaction
3–4 months	Infants will touch and explore one another
6 months	Infants will smile and make vocal sounds to one another
8 months	Infants who are crawling will follow one another
12 months	Infants engage in social behaviour such as laughing

As children get older, they are able to have more meaningful interactions with their peers. Although friendship is related to affiliation, it is not quite the same thing. For example, we may associate with lots of people, but not all of them will be our friends. The term **friendship** means a close association between two people, usually characterised by trust and commitment. According to research, by the time children are 4–5 years of age, 3 out of 4 will have a close relationship with another child (Howes, 1989).

How do children's friendships differ from the attachments that they make with other people such as parents? Children's friendships are not as enduring or as exclusive as their attachment to their parents. Also, their interactions with their friends are on a more equal basis. Research has shown that adults' actions towards children usually consists of either nurturing or controlling behaviour. Children's actions towards adults are usually about seeking comfort or offering submission.

However, there are some similarities between children's friendships with each other and their attachments to parents. Children invest emotional energy into both types of relationship. Also, separation from friends can create the same sense of loss that children feel when they are separated from parents.

Functions of friendship

Children's ability to deal with the social world develops as a result of having close relationships with others. Psychologists believe that friendships serve a number of important functions. For the developing child, friendships provide:

- companionship and opportunities for stimulation

- a context for acquiring basic social skills such as cooperation and management of conflict

- emotional support in new or threatening situations

- a means of gathering and sharing information and learning new skills

- a model or template for subsequent relationships.

What happens to children who are not successful at forming relationships? ▲

But what are the consequences for children who are *not* successful in making close friendships? Research suggests that a significant number of children who are referred to child guidance clinics have experienced difficulties in peer relationships. These children have fewer and less stable friendships than children who show no behavioural difficulties. Studies have also indicated that children who are rejected by their peers at an early age are at greater risk of suffering from anxiety and depression (Rubin, Mills, 1988). The following Key Study demonstrates how peer relations can influence a child's social adjustment at school.

KEY STUDY

The aim of the study was to investigate the role that peer relations play in children's adjustment to school. The researchers believed that close friendships with classmates could make children feel more secure and better able to cope with new and unfamiliar situations. The study investigated how a child's position within their peer group affected their experience of school.

The sample consisted of 125 children from 4 different schools. The average age of the children was 5 years. The children came from white middle-class families. The researchers obtained parental consent to carry out the study.

Each child was interviewed by the researcher. During the interview, children were shown photographs of all the peers in their class and asked to name 3 classmates that they liked to play with, and 3 classmates that they did *not* like to play with. Children were also asked to point to the picture of their 'best friend'. Teachers were then asked to identify who each child's 'best friends' were. On the basis of this data, the children were divided into four categories:

- **popular** – rated favourably by their peers
- **average** – generally accepted by peers
- **neglected** – usually ignored by peers
- **rejected** – rated unfavourably by their peers

The researchers gave the children a number of psychological tests to measure their perceptions of school, their level of anxiety about school and their academic performance. The results are shown below.

Attitudes towards school	Nature of peer group interactions				Explanation
	Popular	Average	Neglected	Rejected	
Level of anxiety	−0.44	−0.50	−0.22	1.39	Higher the number, the more anxiety experienced
Perceptions of school	0.86	0.54	0.70	−2.20	Higher the number, the more positive child felt about school
Academic performance	0.45	0.37	0.61	−1.70	The higher the number, the better the academic performance

(Numbers represent the scores on each psychological test)

Questions

Use the text and the table to answer the following questions:

1. How did the researcher determine the child's friendship patterns?

2. a) Describe one problem with the sample used in the study.
   b) Describe how the researcher could overcome this problem.

3. Why did the researcher use children from four different schools?

4. What evidence is there in the study that the researcher had considered ethical issues?

5. Use the table to answer the following questions.

   a) Which group of children showed the highest level of anxiety?
   b) Which group had the most favourable perception of school?
   c) Which group had the lowest score on academic performance?

Source:
Ladd, G.W., *Having Friends*, 'Keeping Friends, Making Friends and Being Liked by Peers in the Classroom: predictors of children's early school adjustment', in *Child Development*, 61 (1990), pp.1081–100

TRY THIS

Think back to the type of friendships you had when you were in junior school. List **three** factors that were important in those friendships:

1
2
3

Next, think of the friendships you have **now**. List three factors which are important in those friendships.

1
2
3

What does this suggest about the nature of friendship?

Stages of friendship development

Like adult relationships, children's friendships go through stages, with a starting point, middle and an end. Early research (Selman, Jaquette, 1977) suggested that there were five stages in the development of friendships. Selman and Jaquette interviewed 225 people between the ages of 4 and 32. The participants were asked about their understanding of friendship. The researchers identified the following stages:

Level	Age	Description
Level 0: Momentary physical playmate	Around 3–7 years	A friend is the person the child is playing with at the time
Level 1: One-way assistance	Around 4–9 years	A friend is someone who is there to help you but there is no sense of helping being a two-way process
Level 2: Fairweather co-operation	Around 6–12 years	Friendship is now seen as a two-way relationship but the friendship may end if there is conflict
Level 3: Intimate, mutual sharing	Around 9–15 years	Sense of intimacy develops, friends share secrets and the relationship continues despite minor conflicts
Level 4: Autonomous interdependence	Around 12–adult	Friendships grow and change; although friendships are important there is a need for other relationships

More recent research such as Levinger (1986) has focused on some of the factors that influence the development of friendships:

1 **Propinquity or physical proximity:** children are more likely to become friends if they live in the same neighbourhood or go to the same school

2 **First encounters:** children's first encounters usually occur when they are are engaged in activities. At this point the friendship is very superficial

3 **Build-up:** if children are getting along well, they are likely to communicate more and will attempt to settle any conflicts which may arise. However, friendships are still not very stable during this time

4 **Continuation:** interactions between the children become more stable and there is a growing sense of commitment

5 **Deterioration:** friendships may deteriorate because of disagreements or children may simply drift apart. Deterioration does not always mean that the friendship ends

6 **Endings:** in fact, friendships usually end when children no longer have interests in common and cease to depend on one another.

From pre-school to adolescence, children tend to form friendships with other children of the *same sex*. Opposite-sex friendships are relatively rare. Although romantic relationships develop during adolescence, most teenagers still prefer same-sex 'best friends'.

Affiliation in adults

Adults form associations with each other for many of the same reasons that children form friendships. Other reasons why adults affiliate include:

- anxiety reduction
- social comparison
- information-seeking.

Reducing anxiety

Being with other people can help reduce our levels of anxiety. Several studies have shown how affiliation can reduce stress. In one experiment **(Amoroso, Walters, 1969)**, participants were told they were taking part in an experiment on 'learning' and that they would receive electric shocks. They were also told there would be a delay before the experiment began. One group of participants had to wait alone. A second group of participants waited with three other people but were not allowed to talk to one another. These three people were in fact confederates of the experimenter.

The researcher found that participants who waited with others had lower heart rates and expressed less anxiety than participants who waited alone. It seems that the mere presence of other people can help us cope with anxiety.

Social comparison

Have you ever been unsure about your own reactions to a situation and felt great relief when you discovered someone else felt the same? If you are unsure about your emotional reactions, you may want to check them out by comparing them to someone else's. In a very similar study to the one described above, participants were told that they were going to receive painful electric shocks (Schachter 1959). They were also told that there would be a slight delay before the experiment began. They were given the option of:

- waiting alone
- waiting with other people who were also involved in the experiment
- waiting with other people who had nothing to do with the experiment

Schachter found that the majority of the participants (60%) preferred to wait with others who were involved in the same experiment. None of the participants wanted to be with people who were not involved in the same situation. If the participants simply wanted to wait with others as a distraction, then anyone would do. However, the participants preferred to be with others who were undergoing the same experience. This suggests that social comparison was the motive. Being with other people who are undergoing the same experience provides an opportunity to compare reactions.

Seeking information

When we are faced with a new or threatening situation, we may seek out other people who are knowledgeable to help us cope. Kulik and Mahler (1989) studied cancer patients who were waiting to have surgery. Based on Schachter's research we might expect that patients would prefer to be with people who were also waiting for the operation. However, Kulik and Mahler found that, given a choice, the participants preferred to be with someone who had already had a similar operation rather than another person waiting to have the operation. Presumably, this was because the person could tell them what to expect.

Research therefore suggests that being with other people can have a number of beneficial effects. But what happens to adults who do not affiliate with others? Studies have shown that adults who are socially isolated are more likely to experience depression and anxiety and to have higher mortality rates.

Interpersonal attraction

In the previous section we saw that we may seek out the company of other people because we want to compare reactions, or because the presence of other people can help to reduce stress and anxiety. However, there are times when we seek out the company of specific people because we are attracted to them. So how do romantic relationships develop and why are we attracted to some people and not others?

In summary

- *Affiliation refers to the tendency to seek out the company of other people and form associations with them.*

- *Friendship is a close association between two people characterised by trust and commitment.*

- *Friendships serve a number of important functions for children and adults, such as providing companionship and emotional support.*

- *Affiliation provides a means of social comparison and may help us cope with threatening situations.*

Source:
Rubin, Z., *Liking and
Loving* (Holt, Rinehart &
Winston, NY, 1973)
▼

Most psychologists would agree that **liking** and **loving** are different emotions, even though they both play a part in friendships, as well as in romantic relationships. In order to show the difference between liking and loving, try the following activity. You will need to think about your closest or best friend and your closest romantic partner.

TRY THIS

Using the scale, respond to each of the statements below.

1 ········· 2 ········· 3 ········· 4 ········· 5 ········· 6 ········· 7
strongly agree　　　　　　　**generally agree**　　　　　　　**strongly disagree**

In the 'best friend' column enter the number on the scale which reflects your feelings about your best friend. In the 'romantic partner' column enter the number on the scale which reflects your feelings about your closest romantic partner.

Scale 1	Best friend	Romantic partner
_____ is a very likeable person.		
I think _____ is a well-balanced person.		
I think _____ is a responsible person.		
I trust _____ 's judgement.		
I admire ____.		
It is easy for ____ to gain other people's respect.		
Totals		

Scale 2	Best friend	Romantic partner
It would be hard for me to be without _____.		
____'s well-being is very important to me.		
I could forgive ____ almost anything.		
I can tell _____ anything.		
I would do almost anything to make ____ happy.		
Whenever I am lonely, I would prefer to be with _____.		
Totals		

Add up the totals for your best friend and your romantic partner for both Scale 1 and Scale 2.

Psychologists have found that most people have similar scores on Scale 1 for their best friends and their romantic partners. However, on Scale 2, the scores for romantic partners tend to be higher than the scores for best friend. How did your scores compare to this? What factors do you think characterise love?

Liking is characterised by feelings of affection and trust. Loving is a more intense emotion characterised by intimacy and commitment.

Factors affecting the development of relationships

Psychologists have identified a number of factors which influence whether we become attracted to another person. Five of these factors will be considered in some detail. These include:

- physical proximity
- exposure effect
- similarity
- physical attractiveness
- complementarity of needs

Physical proximity

This is about being in the right place at the right time. Before you can form a friendship or relationship with someone, you need to have access to them. Research has shown that one of the most important predictors of whether two people become friends is their geographical nearness to each other. For example, you are more likely to marry someone who lives in your neighbourhood, attends your college or university or works in the same place.

TRY THIS

Draw a picture of the seating arrangement in your psychology class. It doesn't matter if the seats are in rows, in a circle or in a 'horseshoe' shape. Next, indicate on the diagram where you sit. Then write the names of all of your classmates on the remaining seats. The chances are good that you know the names of the people who sit closest to you.

Segal (1974) carried out a study on people who were training to work for the police. These recruits were assigned to seats in a classroom on the basis of their surnames, which were put in alphabetical order. After several weeks of training, the researcher asked the recruits to name their closest friends. He found that the student's surname was a good indicator of who formed friendships. In fact, it was more important than being the same age or sharing the same religious beliefs.

There are several reasons why physical proximity can lead to attraction:

- It is easier to get to know someone who is close by
- You are more likely to discover whether you have mutual interests
- It can lead to attraction because of the **exposure effect.**

THINK ABOUT IT

What effect do you think computer technology such as e-mail might have on the development of relationships?

Exposure effect

Have you heard the old saying, 'familiarity breeds contempt'? According to popular wisdom, seeing too much of someone may cause you to dislike them. Psychological research suggests the opposite: that repeated exposure to someone actually tends to increase our liking for them.

This could be due to the fact that repeated exposure to another person increases our familiarity. The more familiar something is, the more we tend to like it. For example, in the brief amount of time it takes to participate in an experiment, familarity can influence liking. Saegert et al (1973) told female undergraduates that they would be taking part in an experiment on the sense of taste. Pairs of participants had to enter a booth and taste various liquids. The participants interacted either once, twice, five, ten times, or not at all. Each participant then had to rate how much she liked the other participant. The results are shown below.

The results show that the more interactions they had with the other participant, the more they liked them.

Graph showing patterns of familiarity and attraction among female graduates

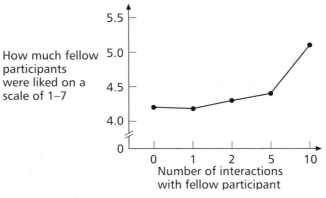

How much fellow participants were liked on a scale of 1–7

Number of interactions with fellow participant

Similarity

Do birds of a feather flock together? Research has shown that we tend to like people who are similar to us in interests, beliefs, attitudes and attractiveness. More specifically, similarity in attitude appears to be an important factor in forming friendships and relationships. In one study (Byrne, 1971) participants were asked to fill in a questionnaire which measured a number of their attitudes. Several weeks later, the same participants were given a copy of a completed questionnaire that was supposed to be filled in by another person. However, the researcher had manipulated the answers given so that half of the participants received questionnaires which expressed attitudes similar to their own; the other half had questionnaires which expressed attitudes different from their own. All of the participants were then asked to rate how much they liked the person who had filled in the questionnaire. Byrne found a strong positive correlation between similarity of attitude and liking.

? QUESTION

Why shouldn't the researcher conclude that similarity of attitude *causes* liking?

One criticism of the Byrne study is that the participants did not actually have contact with a real person. In a more realistic study, Griffitt and Veitch (1974) paid male volunteers to spend a week in a simulated fall-out shelter while the researchers measured their attitudes on a range of topics. At the end of the study, the men were asked to name three people they wanted to remain in the shelter and three people they would choose to get rid of. The results showed that the male volunteers wanted people who were similar to them in attitudes to remain in the shelter.

Physical attractiveness

Although people often do not like to admit it, the physical attractiveness of another person *is* a key factor in attraction. There could be at least two reasons for this. First, we tend to assume that physically attractive people have other socially desirable characteristics. This is called the **physical attractiveness stereotype**.

For example, Dion et al. (1972) showed male participants photographs of 'unattractive', 'attractive' or 'average-looking' women. The participants were then asked to rate the person on a number of traits not related to physical attractiveness. The results showed that the attractive women were rated as more intelligent and socially desirable than the unattractive women.

In a more recent study, Feingold (1992) used meta-analysis (a statistical technique) to review the evidence for the physical attractiveness stereotype. The experimental research showed that physically attractive people are perceived to be more intelligent, sociable and psychologically healthy than unattractive people. However, the correlational research revealed only a modest relationship between physical attractiveness and measures of personality and mental ability.

THINK ABOUT IT

Can you think of a reason why different investigative methods such as experiment and correlation should produce such different findings on the effects of physical attractiveness?

According to the physical attractiveness stereotype, when we choose a partner who is physically attractive, we may be assuming that person also possesses other socially desirable characteristics.

However, there may also be an evolutionary reason why physical attractiveness is important in choosing a partner. In general, men seem to place more emphasis on attractiveness than women. Before we look at the research, try the activity on page 298.

TRY THIS

Read through the 'lonely hearts' advertisements on the right, then make up a grid like the one shown below.

For each advert, fill in the appropriate information in the grid. Then answer the questions at the foot of the page.

♥ **Beautiful, wild, creative, 31-year-old female** seeks wild romance with a professional gentleman who aims for the top and has ambition and integrity.

♥ **36-year-old businessman**, tall, sense of humour, looking for female aged 25–35 who is attractive, intelligent and passionate.

♥ **Free-spirited, attractive, warm, desirable female** seeks a stable, interesting and contented male for a romantic relationship.

♥ **Is your star sign Libra or Gemini?** 32-year-old male, slim, fit and intelligent seeks blond, passionate female aged 20+ for love relationship.

♥ **Athletic, distinguished, 40 year old male** seeks slim, attractive female aged 30+.

♥ **Dogs, cats, rabbits better than men any day!** Prove me wrong. Attractive female, early 40s, seeks intelligent, professional man for friendship.

♥ **Stray tom cat** sees sophisticated feline for passionate romance and catnaps!

♥ **Sophisticated, attractive, young Asian woman** sought by a professional man for a romantic relationship.

♥ **Attractive yoga therapist** with a great body, seeks a tall, educated, successful man.

Gender of person writing advert	How they describe themselves	Qualities looked for in potential partner	Type of relationship sought

On the basis of your grid:

1 a) Are there any differences between the way males and females describe themselves?
   b) What are these differences?
2 a) Are there any differences between the qualities that males and females look for in potential partners?
   b) What are these differences?

Although you have only analysed a few adverts, you may already be able to see a trend or pattern in the type of qualities that men and women look for in their partners. Kendrick and Keefe (1992) looked at over 1,000 'lonely hearts' adverts from three different countries including the USA, India and Holland. They found that men tend to look for younger women, while women tend to prefer older men. Waynforth and Dunbar (1991) found other gender differences. They found that men and women tend to describe themselves in very different ways in the adverts. For example, 50% of female lonely hearts described their physical appearance (using such words as 'attractive' and 'curvaceous') compared to 34% of the males (who used words such as 'athletic' or 'handsome'). Also, when describing the qualities they were looking for in a mate, females were four times more likely than males to use words such as 'professional' or 'educated'. Male lonely hearts tended to use these terms when describing themselves.

Buss (1989) found that these gender differences also occur in different cultures. He presented participants from 37 different countries with a questionnaire about choosing a marriage partner. He found that women in all the cultures studied tended to be more selective and evaluated their partners on a number of criteria. Women were also more likely to emphasise the money-earning potential and status of the male. Males however, ranked physical attractiveness and youth as more important.

Why do these gender differences exist? **Socio-evolutionary theory** explains it in terms of different reproductive strategies. Males who want to increase their reproductive potential need to fertilise as many eggs as possible. As a result, they prefer traits of youth and beauty because these can be reliable indicators of health and fertility. Females are more likely to ensure their offspring survive if they choose mates who will help look after the offspring. Therefore, for females, status and dominance may be the selling points of a potential mate.

Despite gender differences, it appears that both men and women are realistic about their *own* levels of attractiveness. Some research has provided support for the **matching hypothesis**, which suggests that although we may prefer attractive people, we tend to choose partners who are similar to ourselves (are a 'good match') in terms of attractiveness.

Complementarity of needs

We saw earlier that similarity in attitudes and beliefs can bring people together. But what about the old saying that 'opposites attract'?

Research suggests that the answer depends on the stage the relationship happens to be in. In the early stages of a relationship, factors such as physical proximity and similarity tend to be important. Later in more long-term relationships, having needs that complement each other is important.

Kerchoff and Davis (1962) investigated the importance of complementarity. The participants in their study were couples who were 'seriously' attached. They were given personality and attitude tests and asked to indicate how satisfied they were in their current relationship. Six months later, the same participants were asked how their relationship had developed. The researchers found that for couples who had known each other for a short period of time, the best predictor of success in the relationship was similarity of attitude. However, for couples who had been together for more than 18 months, complementarity of needs was more important.

Biological basis

A more recent approach suggests that love may just be a matter of the right chemistry. Fisher (1997) suggests that there are three different stages in relationship-formation:

- lust
- attraction
- attachment

According to Fisher, these stages are biologically based, in that they are influenced by both **hormones** and **neurotransmitters**:

- **Hormones** are substances produced by endocrine glands which regulate bodily processes
- **Neurotransmitters** are chemicals that are released by nerve cells. Hormones are similar to neurotransmitters except that hormones travel over longer distances.

Fisher identified people who were attracted to a specific person. She used **Magnetic Resonance Imaging (MRI)** to identify which areas of their brain were active. The results suggested that:

- **lust** is controlled by the sex hormones testosterone and oestrogen
- **attraction** is caused by neurotransmitters such as dopamine and serotonin
- **attachment** is influenced by other hormones such as oxytocin.

Fisher believes that if the hormones and neurotransmitters can be identified it should be possible to design drug treatments which can calm the body down if emotions are out of control!

Research update

Recently, researchers (Duck 1995, Goodwin 1995 , Kitzinger and Coyle 1995) have pointed out that work on attraction still has a long way to go before it can help us understand how we choose our friends and partners. They have made a number of criticisms of previous research on the subject:

- Most studies were conducted in a laboratory setting and did not involve actual personal contact. Instead, participants were given photographs of 'attractive' or 'unattractive' people or 'attitude profiles' which were either similar or dissimilar to their own, and asked to rate that person according to a number of characteristics.

- Early research focused on the characteristics that drew people together rather than on the more intimate aspects of attraction.

● Most of the studies drew their participants from university undergraduates who were not representative of the population as a whole.

● Few longitudinal studies have been carried out to see how relationships develop over time.

● Few studies have considered how culture affects relationship development. For example, the importance given to 'romantic love' and the degree of choice in choosing relationships may vary from culture to culture.

● The great majority of research has focused on young, heterosexual relationships. There is less research on the nature of relationships among older people or among lesbians and gays.

Duck (1995) has argued that relationship development is much more complex than early research suggested. Recent research is attempting to address this limitation by focusing on the 'dynamics of relationships and the continously unfolding nature of relationship experience in real life and real time'. Psychologists today are keen to discover how early experience affects later relationship development; how relationships are managed over time, and how relationships are affected by social and cultural variations.

Summary

● Interpersonal attraction refers to the tendency to seek out the company of specific people.
● Rubin (1973) distinguished between liking and loving. Liking refers to a feeling of intimacy and regard for another person while loving refers to a deep sense of attachment.
● A number of factors influence whether we are attracted to another person. These include physical proximity, similarity and physical attractiveness. Complementarity of needs is important in long-term relationships.
● More recent research (Fisher 1997) suggests that attraction is biologically based and is influenced by our hormones and neurotransmitters.

20 Impression Formation

It's amazing. We've only just met, and yet already I've conceived an intense dislike for you!

Extraordinary I feel it too!

First impressions can be crucial

Imagine that you are being introduced to someone for the very first time. You will probably make a judgement about them very quickly – in most cases, without even being aware of it. But how do you form an impression of that person? What information do you look for and how do you interpret it?

Social perception

Social psychologists use the term **social perception** to describe how we observe and process information about other people. An important aspect of this process is **impression formation** or how we form impressions of others. As recent research has shown, the knowledge and ideas that are stored in our long-term memory will influence how we make judgements about others. As a result, social psychologists use the term **social cognition** to describe the cognitive (or mental) processes involved in forming impressions.

The importance of first impressions

Solomon Asch (1946) was one of the first psychologists to investigate how we form impressions of other people. According to Asch, the first information that we receive about a person tends to carry more weight than later information. This phenomenon has been called the **primacy effect**.

TRY THIS

In one experiment, Asch presented his participants with a list of traits about a hypothetical person.
As you read through these traits, put a plus sign (+) beside each desirable or positive trait and a minus sign (–) by each undesirable or negative trait. What is different about the order of traits in each list? How might this influence the impression formed of the hypothetical person?

Group A list	+ or –	Group B list	+ or –
intelligent		envious	
industrious		stubborn	
impulsive		critical	
critical		impulsive	
stubborn		industrious	
envious		intelligent	

You may have noticed that the list for Group A starts with positive traits and ends with negative traits. Group B was given the same list of traits but the order was reversed. Asch found that the order of the traits *did* make a significant difference. The descriptions given of the person were more favourable when the positive traits were presented first. He also found that some of the less desirable traits (such as 'critical' and 'impulsive') were interpreted in a positive way by the participants in Group A. In Group B, the same characteristics were interpreted in a negative way.

Look at some of the responses given by Asch's participants.

Group A participant:

'The person is intelligent and fortunately he puts his intelligence to work. That he is stubborn and impulsive may be due to the fact that he knows what he is saying and what he means and will not therefore give in easily to someone else's ideas which he disagrees with.'

Group B participant:

'This person's good qualities such as industry and intelligence are bound to be restricted by jealousy and stubbornness. The person is emotional. He is unsuccessful because he is weak and allows his bad points to cover up his good ones.'[22]

These two responses are clearly very different, and yet all the participants were given the same traits. It was simply that the traits were presented in a different order.

Luchins (1957) provided additional support for the primacy effect. He presented his participants with a story about Jim. The story consisted of two paragraphs. One of the paragraphs described Jim as a sociable, extraverted person who walked to school with his friends and talked to friends in the shop. The other paragraph described Jim as a more reserved, somewhat introverted person who walked home alone and did not speak to anyone in the shop. The paragraphs were then combined so that one group had the 'sociable' description of Jim followed by the 'unsociable' paragraph. The other group of participants had the paragraphs presented in the opposite order. (See if you can spot which paragraph shows Jim to be sociable and which shows him to be unsociable.)

Jim left the house to get some stationery. He walked out into the sun-filled street with two of his friends, basking in the sun as he walked. Jim entered the stationery store which was full of people. Jim talked with an acquaintance while he waited for the clerk to catch his eye. On his way out, he stopped to chat with a school friend who was just coming into the store. On his way out, he met the girl to whom he had been introduced the night before. They talked for a short while and then Jim left for school.

After school Jim left the classroom alone. Leaving the school, he started on his long walk home. The street was brilliantly filled with sunshine. Jim walked down the street on the shady side. Coming down the street towards him, he saw the pretty girl whom he had met on the previous evening. Jim crossed the street and entered a candy store. The store was crowded with students and he noticed a few familiar faces. Jim waited quietly until the counterman caught his eye and then gave his order. Taking his drink, he sat down at a side table. When he had finished his drink he went home.

All the participants were then asked to rate Jim on a number of characteristics. The results showed that 78% of the participants who read the 'sociable' paragraph first rated Jim as being friendly, compared to only 18% of the other group. (In the text above, the first paragraph shows Jim to be sociable, the second unsociable.)

However, Luchins also found that if there was a delay between the reading of the two paragraphs, or if the participants were distracted in some way, then the **recency effect** meant that the most recent information had the most effect.

Putting information together

Asch provided two different models to explain how we form an overall impression of a person. The first, called the **algebraic** model, suggested that each individual trait is equally important in forming impressions. The idea is that each trait (whether positive or negative) is added together to form an overall or global picture of the person. According to Asch:

> 'The total impression of the person is the sum of the several independent impressions. If a person possesses traits a, b, c, d, e, then the impression of him may be expressed as:

> *Impression* = a + b + c + d + e [23]

The second model Asch suggested is known as the **configural** model. According to this, certain pieces of information are more important than others. In other words, certain traits may set up a 'direction' and will influence how other traits are perceived. According to Asch:[24]

> 'The second view asserts that we form an impression of the entire person. We see a person as consisting not of these and those independent traits (nor the sum of ... traits) but we try to get at the root of personality. This would involve that the traits are perceived in relation to each other, in their proper place within the given personality. We may express the final impression as:

Impression =

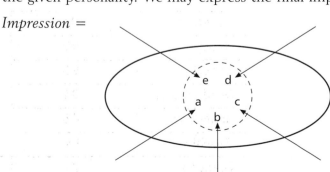

According to Asch, impression formation is a holistic process in which certain traits serve as anchor points around which all other information about a person is perceived. This model is consistent with the results of Asch's initial experiment described earlier, in which we saw that when positive traits were presented at the beginning of a list, they influenced how some of the less desirable traits were interpreted.

In the experiment described below, Asch further tested the idea that not all traits have the same weight in influencing impression formation.

KEY STUDY The experimenter read out a list of traits to two groups of participants. Each list described a hypothetical person. The lists are shown below:

Group A	Group B
intelligent	intelligent
skilful	skilful
industrious	industrious
warm	cold
determined	determined
practical	practical
cautious	cautious

The participants were all university students, and many were taking an introductory course in psychology. However, none of the participants was aware of the aim of the study.

The participants were told to try and imagine what the person described in the list would be like. They were given a checklist to record their impression, consisting of opposed pairs of traits such as generous/ungenerous, happy/unhappy. The participants were asked to choose the characteristics which would fit the impression they had formed of the person. The results are shown below:

Percentage of participants choosing the trait		
Traits	*Group A (warm)*	*Group B (cold)*
Generous	91	8
Happy	90	34
Honest	98	94
Good-natured	94	17
Important	88	99
Reliable	94	99
Humorous	77	13

As you can see, the impressions formed of the 'warm' person were more positive than the impressions made of the 'cold' person. Asch concluded that 'warm/cold' could be considered as **central traits** because they influenced how the other traits in the list were interpreted. Asch repeated the experiment and replaced the traits warm/cold with polite/blunt. The results are shown below:

Percentage of participants choosing the trait		
Traits	Group A (polite)	Group B (blunt)
Generous	56	58
Happy	75	65
Good-natured	87	56
Humorous	71	48
Important	94	96
Honest	87	100
Reliable	95	100

As you can see, the traits polite/blunt had much less influence on impression formation. As a result, Asch called these traits **peripheral traits.**

Questions

1. a) Identify one limitation with the sample used in the study.
    b) What effect could this have on the results of the study?
2. What is meant by the term 'single-blind' technique?
3. According to the warm/cold table:
    a) What percentage of participants in Group B thought the person was generous?
    b) Identify one trait which both groups of participants used to describe the hypothetical person.
4. a) What could Asch conclude from these results?
    b) Do these results support the algebraic or configural model of impression formation?

Source: Asch, S., 'Forming Impressions of Personality', in *Journal of Abnormal and Social Psychology*, 41 (1946), pp.258–90

Evaluation of Asch's experiments

Asch's work has been criticised by other researchers. One charge relates to the fact that the research was carried out in a laboratory setting and therefore did not involve any exposure to a real person. It could be argued that Asch's study lacked *ecological validity*. Kelley (1950) repeated Asch's experiment using a more realistic set-up. In his study, university students were told that their usual lecturer was unable to attend and instead they were to have a guest lecturer. Before the lecturer arrived, the students were given a short biographical sketch of him. The sketches were identical, except in one important respect: half the participants read that he was a 'warm' person, while the other half were told that he was a 'cold' person. The students were told that it was university policy to evaluate the performance of guest lecturers and that they would be asked to fill in a questionnaire at the end of the session.

Kelley found that the 'warm' lecturer was rated more favourably than the 'cold' lecturer. Furthermore, 56% of the students who were told the lecturer was 'warm' participated in class discussion, compared to 32% for the 'cold' lecturer.

Adapted from Kelley, H.H., 'The Warm–Cold Variation in First Impressions of People, *Journal of Personality*, 18 (1950), pp.431–5.

	Ratings given to the guest lecturer*	
Traits	**Warm description**	**Cold description**
Self-centred	6.3	9.6
Unsociable	5.6	10.4
Unpopular	4.0	7.4
Irritable	9.4	12.0
Humourless	8.3	11.7

* The higher the number, the more the person was thought to have the characteristic

Other psychologists have criticised the concept of central traits. For example, Wishner (1960) argued that whether a trait is considered to be central depends on its relationship to the other traits in the list. Wishner suggested that 'warm/cold' influenced the impression because they were the *only* social traits in the list and therefore were distinctive.

Rosenberg et al. (1968) expanded this idea and suggested that there are two basic dimensions which we use in forming impressions of others:

● social
● intellectual

Each of these dimensions has a 'good/bad' end. For example, 'good' social traits would include being sociable, helpful, warm and popular, while 'bad' social traits include being cold, humourless and unsociable. 'Good' intellectual traits include being skilful, scientific and persistent, while 'bad' ones include being frivolous, foolish and wasteful.

Rosenberg et al. identified two basic dimensions which we use in forming impressions of other people: social and intellectual

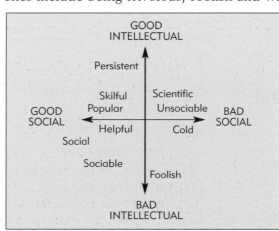

When meeting people for the first time we tend to rate them according to a personal 'checklist' of traits

According to Rosenberg's dimensions, 'warm' and 'cold' are social traits while the other traits that Asch used in the list are intellectual traits.

Despite the limitations described above, Asch's work made it clear that not all traits have the same weight in impression formation. Furthermore, an implication of Asch's work on impression formation is that people seem to have some idea about which traits are related to each other or belong together. Participants in Asch's experiments who knew that a person was 'warm' made an assumption that this person had other desirable characteristics, such as being generous, good-natured and happy.

What this seems to suggest is that people have their own **implicit theories of personality** ('implicit' means that it is not stated overtly). It is a bit like having your own internal checklist of traits which you use to rate other people. We tend to judge people according to the traits *we* think are important. We also make assumptions that if a person has one particular trait (like being attractive) he/she will have other related traits.

The concept of **implicit personality theory** may help to explain several aspects of impression formation:

● why different people do not form the same impressions of others
● how we go beyond the information that we have about a person to form a global or holistic impression of that person.

So how does this internal checklist or implicit personality theory develop? One explanation is provided by Kelly's notion of **personal constructs** (1955), which is described in detail on pages 171–74. However, it is worth describing here how personal constructs relate to impression formation.

Kelly suggests that we use personal constructs to help us make sense of the world around us. These personal constructs can be compared to spectacles or lenses through which we view the world. These constructs develop as a result of our experiences. For example, if you were brought up to believe that honesty is a really important trait, then you might tend to judge people according to how honest or dishonest they are.

Schemas and impression formation

As we saw earlier, the term **social perception** is used to refer to cognitive processes involved in impression formation. Recent developments in social cognition have identified some of the key processes involved. For example, the concept of **schemata** has replaced Asch's earlier notion of central traits.

According to Hamilton et al. (1980), impression formation is more than just deciding whether or not we like someone. It involves a number of cognitive processes, such as to how we pay attention to certain aspects of the person and not others, and how we organise and store information in our memory. Hamilton et al. define an impression as 'the perceiver's cognitive representation of another person.'

Perceiving a person is therefore more than just adding up all the bits of information we have about them. It also involves relating that information to the knowledge that we have stored in our **schemas**. Schemas are mental categories which consist of organised knowledge. Schemas will influence *what* we perceive, *how* we perceive it and what we remember. According to Taylor, Crocker (1987), there are four types of schemas:

- **person schemas** are mental categories which describe specific or typical individuals; for example, you may have a schema for specific people like the Queen or Michael Jackson.
- **self-schemas** are schemas which represent information about ourselves; you may see yourself as being a sporty, athletic person.
- **role schemas** contain knowledge which describes certain social groups and the roles that people occupy; for example, you may hold information about Americans as being materialistic and ambitious while Italians are impulsive and romantic. Role schemas are very similar to stereotypes.
- **event schemas** contain information about certain events like going to a wedding or going to a football match; they are also called *scripts* because they help us to anticipate what is expected in certain social situations.

TRY THIS

To get a feel for the different types of schemas:

a) Describe your event schema for 'going to a gig or concert.'
b) What information do you have stored in your 'role schema' about doctors?

How do schemas affect impression formation?
Research indicates that schemas are most likely to be used when:

- we have very little time to think about the information or have very little 'real' information to go on
- the 'facts' of the situation are consistent with our schemas (this is because we tend to think more about facts which do *not* fit our schemas)
- we are forming general impressions of a person rather than making a judgement about them on the basis of specific dimensions or traits.

People are also likely to use schemas that are triggered by visible characteristics such as physical appearance, dress or skin colour. Studies have shown that dress can influence our perceptions of others. Bickman (1971) demonstrated that people who are well-dressed are perceived as being more honest. In one study, money was left in a public telephone booth. If a person entered the booth and took the money, they were approached by a confederate. The confederate asked whether the person had found the money that had been left 'by accident' in the booth. The way in which the confederate was dressed varied. For half of the participants, the confederate was dressed in a smart suit. For the other half, the confederate wore scruffy work clothes. The confederate who was dressed in a suit retrieved their money twice as often as when they were dressed in scruffy clothes.

Physical attractiveness may also trigger the use of schemas. Dion et al. (1972) showed how physical attractiveness can influence the impressions we form of a person. The participants were asked to rate photographs of different people on a number of characteristics which had nothing to do with their physical attractiveness. The results showed that the people in the photographs who were more physically attractive were rated more favourably. For example, the attractive people were rated as more sociable, sensitive, kind and were thought to have better job prospects. This study also supports the concept of implicit personality theory, in that participants assumed that physical attractiveness would be correlated with other positive traits.

A study by Dovidio et al. (1986) showed how role schemas or stereotypes about race can also affect impression formation. White participants were shown lists of positive and negative characteristics such as ambitious, clean, lazy and stupid. Each characteristic was paired with either the word 'blacks' or the word 'whites'. Participants were told to press a button if they thought the words were associated with each other. The results showed that although participants' overt responses did not reveal stereotyping, they were quicker in pressing the button when associating a positive trait with whites than they were when associating a positive traits with blacks. The researchers concluded that the different reaction times revealed that the schemas of black people were less favourable than their schemas of white people.

Role schemas also exist in relation to gender. Broverman et al. (1972) asked a number of mental health professionals to describe the following people:

● a mature, healthy female
● a mature, healthy male
● a mature, healthy adult (sex unspecified)

The characteristics chosen for the healthy female were negative and included traits such as being emotional, submissive and easily influenced. The characteristics used to describe the healthy male and the healthy adult (sex unspecified) were basically the same and included more positive characteristics, such as being logical, self-confident and independent. The masculine traits were also associated with being well-adjusted.

Why do we use schemas?
Part of the reason we use schemas is that our information processing abilities are limited. As a result, we have to find ways of filtering or

categorising the amount of information which we receive. Schemas help us to make sense of information very quickly. As mentioned previously, we are most likely to make use of schemas when we have very little time to process information.

However, as the studies above show, using schemas has its disadvantages. We may use our schemas to make assumptions about an individual that are not true. Also, schemas are quite hard to change. This could be due to the fact that:

- people perceive things in a way that is consistent with their schemas
- people tend to ignore or disregard information which does not fit in with their schemas.

Summary

- Impression formation is the process by which we combine information about other people to form an overall evaluation or judgment.
- Asch showed that first impressions are important. This is referred to as the **primacy effec**t.
- Asch also showed that some traits (called **central traits**) exert a strong influence on how other traits are perceived.
- Schemas are mental categories which consist of organised knowledge. Schemas influence how we perceive, organise and remember information. They help us to expect certain types of information.
- Rosenberg et al. suggested that our impressions of others are based on two dimensions: social and intellectual.
- The impressions we form of other people are influenced by our schemas and personal constructs.

21 Social Influence

The term **social influence** refers to the ways in which our behaviour is affected by those around us. Although we may not always be aware of it, the behaviour of other people – sometimes their mere presence – can have an extremely strong influence on our own actions and behaviour. This chapter examines some of the research on social influence by considering issues such as social facilitation, conformity and obedience.

The pressure to conform is strong in all of us

Social facilitation

Some of the earliest research in social psychology was conducted by Triplett (1897). Triplett was interested to note that cyclists would often race faster if there were other cyclists present. He also noticed that if he asked children to turn a fishing reel as fast as they could for a set period of time, they would turn the reel faster if there were other children present doing the same thing. Triplett believed that this was because the children were competing with each other.

Similarly, Allport (1920) found that students would solve more multiplication problems if other students around them were also solving problems – even if they were specifically told *not* to compete.

This influence of co-actors on performance is known as the **coaction effect**. Zajonc et al. (1969) found it even applied to cockroaches, who would run away from a light source more quickly in pairs than alone!

Other research has found that the simple *presence* of other people, even if they are not doing the same thing, can affect performance. This is called the **audience effect**.

But research has found that the presence of others doesn't always *improve* performance. When performance *is* improved it is called **social facilitation**. When performance is made worse it is called **social inhibition**. A number of studies have shown that people perform better on *simple* tasks in the presence of an audience or co-actors, but do worse on *complicated* tasks.

Zajonc (1965) argued that the presence of others increases arousal. This is an innate reaction. We need to be prepared to respond to what others might do. Increased arousal makes **dominant responses** more likely. Dominant responses are responses that are most likely to be given in a particular situation. In simple or well learned tasks the dominant

Most of us feel nervous
in front of an audience ▶

response is likely to be correct, and so these tasks show social
facilitation. In complex or newly learned behaviour the dominant
response is likely to be incorrect, and so these tasks show social
inhibition.

Cottrell et al. (1968) found that if an audience was blindfolded so that
they could not observe the participants' behaviour, audience effects
disappeared. Cottrell argued that increased arousal is a *learned* response
rather than innate. Arousal is the result of **evaluation apprehension**.
That is, arousal increases because we have learned that others may judge
us or evaluate our performance. Bond (1982) proposed a **self-
presentation theory** of audience effects. People want to present a
favourable image to others. This means they need to concentrate on the
task, as well as worry about what the audience think of their
performance. On a difficult task there is more concern about how well
we appear to other people, and this extra worry diverts more attention
from the task in hand resulting in more errors.

THINK ABOUT IT

Suppose that you are learning to play snooker or pool. While you are practising, a crowd
of onlookers gather and laugh at you when you miss a shot. Would this make your
performance get better or worse? Would this be the same if you were a highly skilled
player?

However, audience and coaction effects have been observed in animals,
including ants and cockroaches. It is less easy to believe that
cockroaches are worried about 'looking good', although there is good
evidence that humans do. An alternative theory comes from Baron
(1986). He proposed **distraction-conflict theory**. Accordingly, an
audience or coactors will grab some of our attention. The competing
demands for our attention, from both the task and the other people,
increases levels of arousal. The increased arousal makes dominant
responses more likely, resulting in social facilitation or social inhibition.
Animals too can suffer attentional conflicts which can increase arousal.

The theory can also explain social facilitation effects without reference to arousal. The need to attend to a task *and* the presence of others (an audience or coactors), may result in *information-overload*. As a result, performers focus their attention on those cues most central to the task in hand. On a simple task with few things that we need to focus on, performance is increased. On a difficult task which requires attention to be divided on a variety of different things, performance is worse.

It seems possible that each of these theories can help us to understand social facilitation effects. The presence of others, then, can sometimes make us work *harder* (if not necessarily more accurately) on a task. For example, Dashiell (1930) found people would solve more multiplication problems but make more errors in the presence of others. But sometimes the presence of others can have the opposite effect in what is called **social loafing**.

Social loafing

Sometimes individuals will work less hard in a group than they will on their own. Each group member 'loafs', leaving it to the others in the group to make the extra effort. In one study, Latane et al. (1979) asked students to make as much noise as they could, alone or in groups, and found that the amount of noise that each person made went *down* the more people that were in the group. This was true even when participants wore headsets and blindfolds so that they were unable to monitor the performance of other members of the group. Research suggests that social loafing is most likely to occur when it has few consequences for the person involved. When a person knows that their individual effort will be monitored, or success on the task is important to them, they are likely to work as hard as ever.

It follows from this that, in order to maximise performance in places like factories or telesales offices, managers need to let workers know that their individual performance is being monitored and to offer rewards for productivity. Managers also need to be aware that, where workers are aware of each others' performance, they can develop their own norms for behaviour. For example, they may put pressure on group members to stop them from working too hard and making the rest of the group look lazy. As we shall see in the next section, group norms can exert powerful pressure on people to behave in particular ways.

Social norms

We all modify our behaviour depending on where we are and who else is present at the time. The way we respond to friends is different from the way we respond to parents, policemen and authority figures, etc. This is partly due to social rules which govern how we should behave. These can be formal, written rules like 'no parking', or informal, unspoken rules, like 'form a queue at a bus stop', 'use a knife and fork in a restaurant', etc. The informal rules sometimes tell us how to interpret the formal ones. For example, many people drive slightly above the 30 mph speed limit in built-up areas, because they do not want to be judged 'slow' by other drivers.

In a social situation such as eating in a restaurant, our behaviour is normally governed by well-defined social norms ▲

These formal and informal rules are called **social norms**, and they have a powerful influence on the way we behave. Different groups have different norms. Manual workers on a building site behave differently from office staff in a bank. Members of a rugby club act differently from members of the local women's institute. But wherever groups of people come together, it is common for a norm to emerge, to which members of the group are expected to conform.

What do we mean by conformity?

Conformity occurs when people behave in a certain way because of the pressure exerted by the presence of other group members. This pressure can be **formal** (e.g. they may not speak to you if they disapprove of your behaviour), or **informal** (e.g. you simply feel uncomfortable if you appear to 'stand out from the herd').

THINK ABOUT IT

Consider the different groups that you are associated with. Do you ever change your behaviour depending on who you are with? If so, why?

The formation of group norms

Sherif (1935) tested conformity using the **autokinetic effect**. This is a visual illusion in which a stationary spot of light seen in a darkened room appears to move around. People were asked individually to estimate how far the light moved. Different people gave different estimates, ranging from 2 to 8 inches. People were then grouped in pairs or threes and asked to state their estimates aloud. They were not told that they had to agree with each other; nevertheless, over a number of trials, there was a convergence in peoples' answers, so that members of a group all came to give a fairly similar response.

What this showed was the emergence of a group norm – in this case, the answers people were willing to give publicly. The study also revealed the informal pressure on people to conform to the group norms, and not be different from the rest.

Reasons for conformity

People may be influenced by others for various reasons:

● **Informational social influence:** the desire to be right. In many social situations we may feel uncertain about the right thing to do (e.g. which fork to use, what clothes to wear, etc.). We therefore take our cue from the behaviour of others.

● **Normative social influence:** the desire to be liked. We recognise that there are dangers in being different (deviant). People may not like us, or may make fun of us.

TRY THIS

Read the following situations:

a) You go to buy some meat in a supermarket that is different from the one where you normally shop. You see a group of people standing at the meat counter, but no obvious queue. You notice that some people take tickets from a nearby machine and you hear the shop assistant call out a number. Because of this, you take a ticket from the machine and stand at the counter, waiting for your number to be called.

b) You have just bought a new pair of trainers. They are a good fit, but rub at the heel slightly if the laces are not tied. However, all your friends wear trainers with laces untied, so you do the same.

Which situation shows **informational conformity**, and which shows **normative conformity**?

In Sherif's study, there were no 'right answers' to the question posed by the researchers. The findings may therefore reflect informational influence. At the time, few people thought that a situation in which there was an obvious right answer would produce such high levels of conformity.

Asch's research

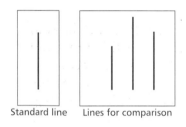

Standard line   Lines for comparison

In order to study the effects of conformity, Asch (1956) placed participants in groups of about six other people. Unknown to the participants, all the other members of their group were confederates of the experimenter. He then showed the groups pairs of cards like those shown here, and asked which of the lines on the right was the same length as the line on the left.

On each trial, the confederates answered first and the real participant was the last to answer. The groups were shown a series of different cards, and each time the correct answer was obvious. On the third trial, and several other, later trials, all the confederates deliberately gave the *same* wrong answer.

Asch found that nearly a quarter of the participants often conformed to the group answers; that about three-quarters conformed at least once; and that about a quarter of the participants never conformed. The overall average conformity for all the trials was 37%.

When interviewed afterwards, some participants said they had conformed because they thought they had misunderstood or the others maybe had better eyesight or were better informed. Their conformity arose from using others as a source of information, thus showing the impact of **informational social influence**. But most participants said they conformed because they did not want to look silly in front of the others. This showed the impact of **normative social influence**.

There have been a number of studies since Asch's original research, and they have tended to confirm his findings. For example, in a similar experiment, Crutchfield (1954) tested over 600 participants, five at a time. Participants were seated in individual cubicles and the answers of other (non-existent) participants were indicated by lights on a panel. The 'answers' were in fact provided by the experimenter. Findings were broadly similar to those of Asch.

Asch and others have since modified their research to investigate what factors might influence levels of conformity. The factors they have identified are:

● **Size of the group:** Asch found a ratio of about 3:1, (three confederates to one participant) was about the optimum for conformity. Below 3, conformity levels drop off; above 3, and conformity levels do not increase by much. Figures differ between researchers, but overall, groups of more than 5 or 6 have little additional impact in this type of study (Argyle, 1998). Gerard et al. (1968) argued that, since it is rare for large numbers of people to agree about something, when it does happen, people suspect collusion – i.e. they suspect that others are deliberately acting together to influence them

● **Status of the group:** people conform more if group members are perceived as having high status

● **Unanimity of the group:** if one confederate disagrees with the rest, even if they still disagree with the participant, conformity levels drop. This is probably because it lessens the fear associated with being the only dissenter

● **Task difficulty:** the harder the task (for example, if the lines in Asch's experiment are made more similar in length), the more people are likely to conform (informational social influence)

● **Personality factors:** research has investigated the nature of the conforming personality, but overall evidence for it is not strong, and situational factors are thought to be more important. Work done by Crutchfield and others suggests that perhaps a cluster of traits such as lower intelligence, lower self-esteem, and higher need for social approval may increase the likelihood of someone conforming.

● **Cultural factors:** More recent research reveals that conformity levels are lower in the USA and Europe than 40 years ago, and it is to be expected that as cultures and cultural norms develop and change, conformity levels will change with them. The research does suggest that in **collectivist** cultures which value group agreement and cooperation more highly (e.g. many Asian cultures), conformity levels tend to be higher than in cultures where individualism is more prized, e.g. America and Europe (Argyle, 1998).

Conformity isn't all bad

We need a certain amount of conformity for society to function. We all conform in many ways – in the clothes we wear, and how we behave in different situations – and to some extent this is desirable. For example, in a classroom it is not helpful if students are all talking and sitting facing away from the teacher. Individualistic Western cultures tend to stress the disadvantages of conformity such as loss of personal initiative or creativity. More collectivist cultures stress the advantages that conformity brings, in terms of increased social harmony and cohesion.

Evaluation of Asch's research

Strengths

+ Asch's work allows conformity to be studied in a controlled and systematic way.
+ His studies have stimulated a lot of further research.

Weaknesses

– Asch's research is highly artificial. In real life it is rare for us to be surrounded by strangers who deny the evidence of our eyes and not to be able to ask them what is going on.
– Demand characteristics mean that in experiments people often wish to please the experimenter. They may believe that something is occurring that they do not understand and conform because they do not wish to spoil the research. Indeed, some participants said just this when interviewed.
– Participants were subjected to stress in that they were made to appear different or else forced to lie.
– There were more non-conforming responses than conforming ones. A quarter of participants never conformed despite the pressures exerted by the experiment. Some researchers believe Asch's study reveals more about non-conformity than conformity.

Teenagers experience a strong pressure to 'belong' ▲

Types of conformity

An interesting distinction in types of conformity was made by Kelman (1961). He distinguished between:

● **Compliance**: conforming by doing something you privately *disagree* with in the face of social pressure
● **Internalisation**: conforming by doing something that you privately *agree* with so there is no internal conflict over your behaviour
● **Identification**: conforming to the behaviour of a person or group because you admire them, and perhaps wish to be like them, and be liked by them.

For example, if you feel guilty about verbally abusing a person or group, knowing it to be wrong, but do it anyway because your friends or peers do, this is compliance. If you join in abusing others but believe they deserve to be abused, this is internalisation. If you dress in the style of your favourite pop group and adopt some of their mannerisms or styles of speech, this is identification.

QUESTIONS

At a Weightwatchers' class, all members of the group promise not to eat cream cakes for the next month. One person then goes home and throws all his cream cakes in the bin. Another man goes to the nearby store and buys and eats a cream cake. In the class, both group members conformed to the group and made the same promise.

Which person has demonstrated **compliance** and which person has demonstrated **internalisation**?

Obedience

Obedience refers to 'doing as you are told' by someone – usually a person in authority. We are raised to obey authority figures, like parents, teachers and police officers.

A notorious case of obedience involving the American military occurred during the war in Vietnam in the 1960s. In a village called Mi Lai, a platoon of American soldiers rounded up several old men, women and children. Lt. William Calley, who was in command, gave the order to push the villagers into a ditch and shoot them. According to one of the soldiers involved, about 370 villagers were pushed into a ravine, many of them begging desperately to be spared. The soldiers 'kept right on firing' and all were shot. The massacre caused outrage in America. Calley was charged and tried. He pleaded that he was 'just following orders'.

Calley was found guilty but given a light sentence because it was never established whether or not there had been a clear order from higher ranks to kill civilians. In a follow-up to the incident it emerged that about 50% of the American public felt some sympathy for Calley and his men, on the grounds that being a soldier involves obeying without question.

Milgram's experiments in social conformity

Some of the most famous research in social psychology was conducted by Stanley Milgram (1963). Milgram set out to investigate the extent to which people would obey. He was interested to understand why it was that the police and military in Nazi Germany had obeyed orders to carry out the atrocities that were inflicted against Jewish people.

KEY STUDY

Milgram recruited 40 male volunteers through newspaper adverts offering $4.50 to people to go to Yale, a prestigious university in the USA, and take part in an experiment in learning. Each participant was introduced to another participant (in fact, a confederate of the experimenter). The two then drew lots to see who would be the 'teacher' and who the 'learner'. Again, unknown to the participants, the 'lots' had been fixed so that the real participant always took the role of teacher.

The learner was strapped to a chair in another room and his arm wired with electrodes. The learner's task was to learn a series of word pairs (e.g. 'blue'–'sky'). Every time the learner made a mistake, the teacher had to give an electric shock. This was done using a machine in another room that had a row of switches. There were 30 switches and each was labelled, starting with the first switch '15 volts slight shock', and going up 15 volts at a time to '450 volts danger: severe shock'. The machine was in fact a fake and no real shocks were administered. An actor, playing the role of the experimenter, was in the room with the teacher.

As the experiment progressed, the learner made mistakes and was given increasingly severe shocks by the teacher. The learner began to call out that it was painful and that he had had enough. The precise objections he raised, including at one point that his heart was bothering him, were prearranged by the experimenter. The teachers became increasingly worried and sought advice from the experimenter. The experimenter used a series of responses, also prearranged, from 'please continue', to 'you have no choice, you must go on'. As the shocks increased, the learner began to scream, and eventually shouted out that he refused to go on answering. After 315 volts he became silent. The teacher was told that no response should be treated as a wrong response and to continue with the experiment.

Milgram wanted to see how far people would go in obeying the experimenter. He predicted that few people would administer the highest levels, and psychiatrists he asked predicted that less than 3% of people would go all the way up to 450 volts. In fact, no one stopped before intense levels were administered (around the point at which the learner fell silent) and 65% of the participants went all the way up to 450 volts. It should be noted that the participants were not simply cruel or callous. Milgram noted the signs of distress that they showed, including sweating, trembling and frequently questioning the experimenter.

Questions

1. Why did the experimenter have prearranged responses to the participants' questions?
2. Give two criticisms of the sample Milgram used in this experiment.
3. What is meant by random sampling?
4. To what extent do you think Milgram's research had ecological validity?

Source: Milgram, S., 'Behavioural Study of Obedience', *Journal of Abnormal and Social Psychology*, 67 (1963), pp.391–8

Factors affecting obedience

How are we to explain such findings? Milgram conducted further studies to identify factors which influence obedience. These were:

- **Closeness of the learner:** with the learner in the same room only 40% of people administered 450 volts. When they had to hold the learner's hand to a 'shock plate', obedience fell to 30%. (These are still surprisingly high figures).

- **Closeness of the authority figure:** obedience fell to 21% if orders were given over the phone. Teachers often cheated and gave lower shocks than they were told to.
- **Status of the authority figure:** this derived from his position in a prestigious university. If he left the room and the experiment was taken over by a clerical assistant, obedience dropped markedly. When the study was carried out in a run-down-looking office, obedience also dropped.
- **Support from peers:** if paired with two other 'teachers' (confederates) who refused to go on, only 10% of participants went to 450 volts.

A fascinating aspect of social psychology is that it often provides insights that can radically alter the way in which we think about ourselves. We do not always behave as we think we would. Milgram's study is an example of this. It shows that situational factors can be a much more powerful influence on our behaviour than we generally realise. A soldier who disobeys an order in wartime risks being executed. There were no such dangers in Milgram's study.

One explanation for Milgram's findings is what he calls **agentic shift**. This refers to the extent to which we can shift responsibility for our actions onto someone else. Clearly, it is more difficult to shift responsibility if the experimenter is not even in the same room. At the same time, we must have trust in the experimenter: to some extent we must believe that they know what they are doing and accept their right to make demands on us. It is less likely we would obey a five-year-old in the same situation. Milgram points out that we are brought up to obey authority figures all our lives and, since these are seen as trustworthy, then we will obey other authority figures too, provided that their authority is also seen as *legitimate*. So the status of the authority figure is an important factor in agentic shift.

THINK ABOUT IT

What sorts of people would *you* be unlikely to obey? What does this tell us about the nature of obedience?

It is worth noting that a **uniform** often implies status and authority. Bushman (1988) found that strangers were more likely to give change for a parking meter when asked to do so by a woman wearing a uniform than by the same person dressed in a business suit or dressed scruffily.

Another issue in this research is **entrapment**. In Milgram's experiment, the shocks administered were small to begin with and escalated gradually. Participants did not know at what point to quit: if they stopped, they would have to admit they were wrong to have started.

Haritos-Fatouros (1988) reported that a similar technique is used to train torturers. First they are required to stand guard outside the torture cell; then inside; then they are asked to hold a piece of equipment. As a result they are gradually 'sucked in' to the process, each step representing just a small advance on the one before.

Evaluation of Milgram's experiment

Strengths

+ Milgram is criticised on ethical grounds (see below). But in his defence, Milgram carried out extensive debriefing of his participants. Afterwards, 'teachers' were reunited with 'learners' to show that no harm had been done and there were no hard feelings. In response to a questionnaire he sent out later, less than 2% of the participants were sorry for taking part, and many were glad to have done so, believing it gave insights that were important and feeling that more such research should be conducted.

+ Also in his defence, Milgram did not expect these findings. He did consult on the likely outcome, and no one else expected it either.

+ One positive outcome was that, in response to this and other similar research, the American Psychological Association decided to publish official guidelines to cover future research. We should note that studies like Milgram's breach those guidelines, and those of the British Psychological Society, and would not be permitted today.

+ Milgram's research shows not only the power of situational factors on our behaviour, but also the impact of social roles. The roles we play – parent, daughter, friend, teacher, student – also carry with them norms that govern how the role is to be played and what others expect from the person performing it. In Milgram's research, the participants played the role of 'participant in an experiment' – which is why the study may lack ecological validity.

Weaknesses

− Milgram was heavily criticised for his work by the public and professionals alike, in part probably because some of them did not like, and found it hard to accept, the implications of his work.

− One criticism is that his was an artificial laboratory-based experiment, and that its findings could not be applied to the real world. In particular, it was argued, participants knew they were in an experiment, which raised expectations of how they ought to behave, (i.e. obey the experimenter who is responsible for the research).

− Much criticism also focused on the ethical issues raised by the research. These include:

  ● **Deceit**: Milgram lied to his participants about the nature of the research, and about the fact that people were receiving electric shocks. In his defence it would be difficult to tell people about the true nature of the study in advance without spoiling the research.

  ● **The right to withdraw**: a rule of experimental research is that participants should be told at the start that they can withdraw at any time. Here, they often seemed not to realise that they were free to leave. In fact, the experimenters' prods ('You have no choice – you must continue') indicated the opposite. In his own defence, Milgram argued that people could have walked out whenever they wished. Again, if he had specifically told people that they did not have to obey, the point of the research would have been lost.

- **Stress**: participants were often greatly distressed by the research and did not find it easy to administer shocks. Some argue Milgram should have stopped the experiment once signs of distress were apparent.

Zimbardo's prison simulation study

One researcher who was particularly interested in the impact of social roles was Zimbardo. Zimbardo's prison simulation study examined the behaviour of people who demand obedience from others. Zimbardo et al. (1973) built a mock-prison in the basement of Stanford University, USA, and selected people to play the roles of prisoners and guards. Participants were screened to be mentally healthy and were assigned their role by the toss of a coin. On the day the study began, the 'prisoners' were arrested by the local police, stripped, deloused, given a prison uniform and put in the 'prison', where they were to remain 24 hours a day. They were told to refer to themselves and each other only by number. The guards wore uniforms, truncheons, handcuffs and reflecting sunglasses, and worked a shift system.

The study was meant to run for two weeks, but Zimbardo was forced to abandon it after just six days. The guards became increasingly nasty, inventing pointless rules and tasks for the prisoners like cleaning the lavatories with their bare hands, and depriving them of sleep. Not all the guards behaved badly, but the others did little to stop the ones who did. The prisoners became increasingly distressed. One went on hunger strike and another had to be sent home after Day 3 because he had become so upset.

These findings partly reflect the fact that participants were acting out **roles**. They were not criminals, but presumably they understood and acted in accordance with roles seen on television and in the media. Such processes may be at work in real prisons – indeed, institutions everywhere. Afterwards, some guards admitted to being seduced by the feeling of power their position gave them.

Deindividuation

Another contributory factor here is **deindividuation**. Deindividuation refers to the loss of personal identity and responsibility that can occur in a group. Often a crowd such as a lynch mob can seem to develop a 'mind of its own', and participants at lynchings feel shocked and ashamed of their own behaviour afterwards. Giving people uniforms and numbers can strip away their feelings of personal identity so that they behave in ways that they otherwise might not.

Evaluation

Strengths

+ Zimbardo examined the impact of social roles on behaviour under controlled conditions.
+ All participants were screened at the start to make sure that they were psychologically healthy and well adjusted.
+ The study showed that conformity and obedience are closely related.

People *conform* to norms associated with situational factors or social roles, and this can lead them to *obey* a person who tells them to do something.

Weaknesses

- Since Zimbardo's experiment was laboratory–based it could be seen as artificial. People were aware of being in a study. They may have conformed to their expectations of what the experimenter wanted, or felt that responsiblity for what happened did not lie with them.
- The study caused a lot of stress to participants. In fairness to Zimbardo, he did call a halt after six days, but by then many participants were very upset.

Obedience in the real world

The studies we have looked at so far can all be criticised as rather artificial. One study which has good ecological validity is that of Hofling et al. (1966). In the course of the experiment, 22 nurses at different hospitals in the USA were phoned by an unknown 'Dr Smith' and told to administer 20 mg of a drug 'Astroten' to a particular patient from a bottle in their medical cabinet. The bottle was labelled with the name 'Astroten'. The label also stated that the maximum daily dose was 10 mg. In fact, it contained a harmless substance.

By obeying 'Dr Smith', the nurses would be breaking four rules:

- not to accept instruction by telephone
- not to accept instructions from a doctor they do not know
- not to exceed the maximum dose
- not to administer a drug not on the list of permitted drugs

In the event, 21 out of 22 nurses obeyed the order!

When other nurses were asked what they would do, they said they would refuse to give the drug. This highlights Milgram's findings that people often do things that they believe they would not do if asked. (We should note that hospital practices have changed now, and that it is unlikely that any nurse would administer a drug in this way today.)

Some conclusions

What conclusions can we draw about obedience in the real world? Milgram's research suggests that people may reluctantly do unpleasant things to each other while acting under orders from superiors (such as soldiers in wartime). However, this ignores the motivational set or beliefs of those who do the obeying.

Sometimes people act out of a strong belief in the rightness or justice of their cause. They may experience no conflict with an inner conscience when told to inflict pain or suffering on others. Religious or political fanatics may be examples of this – so might soldiers fighting a 'just war'. Members of religious cults have been known to commit mass suicide on the orders of their leader.

However, although we often obey teachers and doctors, we do not do so all the time. For example, patients often ignore their doctors' advice

Come on, lads – let's kick some Anglo-Saxon ass!

Admirable spirit. Totally bonkers of course.

Fortunately, we do not always blindly follow where others lead us

about drinking and smoking. It is fair to say that social norms greatly influence our behaviour, but this does not mean that we simply follow blindly wherever others wish to take us. Sometimes we may actively resist them.

Minority influence

Sometimes, a person or small group of people can influence a majority. This is called **minority influence**. When Freud first put forward his theory of childhood sexuality, he immediately became the target of scorn, verbal abuse, and professional rejection. Vienna was outraged. But Freud persisted and developed his general theory, which has had a widespread impact on much psychological thinking. Many other great historical figures – for example, Martin Luther, Copernicus and Darwin – have eventually won through against resistance from a powerful majority. Moscovici et al. (1969) have identified some of the factors that can help minorities to change the opinions of the majority:

- **Consistency**: people who waver in their views will not convince other people. But if they are consistent in what they say, this can be effective. Moscovici et al. found that if a confederate minority *consistently* judged blue slides as 'green', they could persuade some of the majority to agree, but the minority could not do this if they wavered between blue and green.

- **Self-confidence**: stating opinions forcefully and firmly is more effective than seeming hesitant or unsure. Politicians would all like to convince us that they know what's best for the rest of us.

- **Defection**: if you can persuade just one or two people to your side, this punctures the sense of unanimity of the majority, and more may follow.

QUESTIONS

1 While performing a hard task, is the presence of a large audience more likely to result in **social facilitation** or **social inhibition**?

2 Distinguish between **informational social influence** and **normative social influence**.

3 Distinguish between **compliance**, **internalisation** and **identification**. Which is likely to produce the longest-lasting change in behaviour?

4 Identify *one* factor affecting levels of conformity for each of the following:

   a) a group
   b) a situation
   c) an individual

5 List *three* factors that influence the likelihood of obedience in Milgram's study.

6 What *two* traits should a person display if he wishes to change the views of the majority?

Summary

- Coaction effects and audience effects show how the presence of others can influence our behaviour. Performance of a simple task is often facilitated by an audience, and performance of a hard task is inhibited. The presence of others can also result in social loafing.
- Conformity is not mysterious: it is often simply the result of a desire to be right (informational social influence) or a desire to be liked (normative social influence).
- Levels of conformity may be influenced by situational, group, individual and cultural factors.
- Much of the laboratory research on conformity and obedience has low ecological validity and may be ethically suspect.
- Milgram's results may depend on agentic shift and entrapment. Zimbardo has revealed the power of social roles. Hofling has shown that high levels of obedience can be elicited in the real world for tasks that are potentially very damaging to other people.
- Moscovici has stressed that power and numbers are not everything, and that sometimes a minority group can change the opinions of the majority.

22 Prosocial Behaviour and Altruism

Ungrateful swine! He said I was only helping him so I could feel better about myself

Is there such a thing as altruism? ▲

Prosocial behaviour is behaviour that is intended to have a beneficial social effect. **Altruistic behaviour** is designed to benefit others when there can be no benefit to the person carrying it out. Nurses show prosocial behaviour in helping others, but they are not altruistic by this definition, because they expect to get paid for their work. **Cooperative behaviour**, where people work together for mutual benefit is not altruistic either.

Some critics have questioned whether there is such a thing as truly altruistic behaviour, since there are often rewards for helping others – even if it just means feeling better about yourself.

The evolutionary perspective

Animals often give warning signals at the approach of a predator. Birds give warning cries and rabbits thump their feet. On the face of it, this seems to contradict Darwin's theory of evolution, which predicts that the 'fittest' survive. Warning cries draw attention to the animal giving them and make them more likely to get killed by predators. Accordingly, we might expect altruistic animals to be killed off, leaving only selfish ones.

However, since Darwin, we have discovered a lot more about **genes**. Genes are inherited from our parents and determine what sex we will be, our eye colour and how tall we are likely to grow. Each child inherits half of its genes from the mother and half from the father.

Sociobiologists such as Wilson (1975) argued that altruism is built into the genetic code of animals and humans. He proposed a theory of **kin-selection**. The theory is that the gene pool is more likely to be maintained and increased if family members (kin) act to help each other. By helping those similar to us, we preserve similar genes to our own. As a result, those without altruistic genes are more likely to die out.

It follows from this that it can make sense to help others, even we sacrifice our own life in the process. A mother cat who dies to save three kittens will still ensure that more of her genes survive than if she had lived and the kittens had died, since each of the kittens will have half her genes.

In the wild, many animals will put themselves at risk in order to defend their young ▲

Kin-selection explains why we might behave altruistically to family members. However, in everyday life we also behave altruistically to friends and even strangers, who are not closely related genetically. An explanation for this is **reciprocal altruism**. This means that helping others is also beneficial to us because we can expect them to help us back at some point.

We do not have to be aware of genes in order to be affected and influenced by them. Trivers (1985) suggested that failure to repay a kindness may make us feel guilty and that helping others may make us feel good. In this way genes influence our behaviour, and those with altruistic genes are more likely to survive. However, others have argued that the simple fact that humans do something does not require us to invent genes to explain why they do it. We may have *learned* that it is right to help others, or be able to understand cognitively what the benefits are from helping others, and do so for these reasons rather than because of genes.

THINK ABOUT IT

If someone does you a favour, are you more or less likely to help them in the future? If you know they are selfish, does this influence your willingness to help?

Altruism and learning theory

If a baby cries when distressed, an association is formed between between distress and crying. **Classical conditioning** predicts that this association is learned, so that when a child hears others cry, or sees them show other symptoms of distress, he or she will also come to feel distressed. People are motivated to reduce the symptoms of distress they feel when others are unhappy by helping others.

Operant conditioning predicts that if you are rewarded for helping – for example, if parents praise you when you are good – then you are likely to repeat the behaviour in the future. In the same way, if your selfish behaviour is punished – for example, if you are scolded for it, or if you find that others are less likely to help you because of it – then you will be less likely to behave selfishly in the future. In this way children gradually learn to be helpful and not simply to satisfy their own selfish desires.

Social learning theory predicts that the people we observe around us provide **models** for us to imitate. If they behave in helpful ways, and especially if we see them rewarded for their helpfulness, we are likely to imitate this behaviour too. If they tell us selfish behaviour is bad, or if we see them punished for being selfish, we will be less likely to behave selfishly.

If models are inconsistent in their behaviour (sometimes helpful, sometimes not), children will grow up to be inconsistent in their behaviour too. Of course, models often *are* inconsistent, and it is rare for people to be always good or helpful or always bad and unhelpful. As a consequence, Mischel (1968) has proposed the idea of **situational specificity**. That is, the behaviours that we show, including prosocial ones, are a consequence of the specific situation in which they occur. People can learn that it is good to be helpful sometimes, but not always (see also Chapter 10, *Moral Development*, page 108).

Hartshorne and May (1928) conducted research on over 10,000 8- to 16-year-olds in a study lasting five years. Children were exposed to a variety of opportunities to behave in pro or anti-social ways. For example, they could steal a coin left in a puzzle box, or cheat when adding up their scores in a test. The researchers found that children would behave badly sometimes but not others – as Mischel would predict.

Bryan and Test (1967) found male motorists were more likely to offer to change a woman's flat tyre if they had recently passed another male role model doing the same thing. Macauley (1970) found people were more likely to put money in Salvation Army collection tins if they had seen other people doing the same. This shows how exposure to prosocial models can increase the likelihood of prosocial behaviour in others.

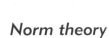

Research has shown that men are more likely to offer help if they have recently seen someone else do the same ▲

Norm theory

As we saw in Chapter 21, social norms are shared, agreed ways of behaving in society. Behaviours which are approved of are encouraged, and those that are disapproved of are discouraged. In this way, we learn and **internalise** the norms, so that we feel good about acting in accordance with them (because we feel it is right) and bad if we go against them (because we feel it is wrong). Berkowitz and Daniels (1963) suggested that a norm common to most societies is the norm of **social responsibility**. That is, we should look out for other people and help those in need.

However, in reality this is tempered by other norms. The norm of **equity** means that people should not take advantage, and that there should be a balance between what we put in and what we get out. For example, equity dictates that it is desirable to give temporary support to people who are out of work. But if such people are seen as 'scroungers', then society should not have to support them.

Similarly, the norm of **reciprocity** means that those who have been given help should be willing to offer help in turn if necessary at some later point and should not be ungrateful. The norm of **social justice** means that we should help those who are suffering through no fault of their own, but that if they bring suffering on themselves, they are to blame and are less deserving of our support.

Empathy

To **empathise** with another person is to be able to put yourself in their place and feel what they feel. It is not quite the same as sympathy, which implies taking the person's side as well. You may empathise with your enemies, but you are unlikely to sympathise with them.

Piaget argued that young children are **egocentric**: they are unable to see other people's points of view and so to empathise with them. Young children will respond to other peoples' emotions – for example, show fear if others do – but they may not know why the emotion is expressed or understand what to do about it it. For example, they may offer a toy to an upset child because the toy makes *them* feel happy. Children have to develop a **theory of mind**. This means they must be able to project themselves into the mind of others, in order to understand properly the distress of another person and to know what to do about it.

THINK ABOUT IT

If a three-year-old is shown a box of sweets and asked what they think is in it, they will probably say 'Sweets'. If you then open the box to show it contains marbles, they will be surprised. If you say that you are going to ask another child what is in the box, and ask, 'What do you think *they* will think is in it?' the child may now reply 'Marbles'.

However, a five-year-old will probably realise the other child does not know what she knows, and reply 'Sweets' again.

What does this reveal about young children's thinking?

It is worth noting that researchers such as Zahn-Waxler et al. (1992) have found that children often *will* offer appropriate comfort to someone in distress from quite a young age:

● A one-year-old infant may cry in response to another child crying, but offer little help.

● By 14 months a child will offer general comfort, though it may not be directed at the source of the distress (e.g. they may offer their favourite teddy to a child with a cut finger).

● By just 18 months a child will sometimes offer specific help, e.g. try to mend a broken toy, or offer a plaster for a cut finger.

By two years of age children engage in a wide range of prosocial behaviours, sharing things, offering protection to prevent injury or attack, and giving advice such as 'be careful'. This implies that even two-year-olds are not completely egocentric. We should also remember that the extent to which children appear egocentric often varies according to the testing situation (see Chapter 9, *Cognitive Development*, page 92).

According to Batson et al. (1981), empathy is what leads to altruism. According to the so-called **empathy–altruism theory**, we recognise the distress that others feel and wish to reduce it. Some people may be less

Young children are quite capable of altruistic behaviour ▲

likely or able to empathise than others. To help criminals empathise with other people, for example, schemes have been developed which reunite them with their victims so that they can talk to them and understand the distress they have caused. The hope is that this will make them less likely to re-offend in future.

Research suggests that, if we believe others are responsible for their own troubles, this may create feelings of disgust which may make helping less likely. If victims are not perceived to be to blame for their troubles, this will foster empathy and increase the chances of helping. Since some people hold to what is called the **just world hypothesis** – the belief that, fundamentally, people get what they deserve – this can lead to a tendency to *blame victims* for the trouble that they find themselves in. According to this view, a woman who gets raped must have been 'asking for it'; single mothers 'only have themselves to blame'; the starving should 'stop having children if they can't feed them' – and so on.

In contrast to Batson, Cialdini et al. (1981) proposed the **negative-state relief** model. According to this, seeing others suffer makes us feel bad, and so we help them to remove our bad feelings and make ourselves feel better.

Again, in contrast, Smith et al. (1989) proposed the **empathic joy** model, which suggested we help others because of the good feelings we experience for doing so.

Both these two theories suggest that helping others is a result of selfish motives rather than selfless ones. It is fair to say that the debate within psychology is unresolved, and that maybe each approach has something to offer.

QUESTIONS

1 Distinguish between **prosocial behaviour** and **altruistic behaviour**.
2 How might helping non-family members help to preserve your own genes?

Bystander behaviour

Imagine that a man is lying on the pavement in a city centre shopping precinct. He looks dazed and is calling out for help from passing shoppers. Would you be more or less inclined to help if:

● it was a child who had fallen over?

● it was all happening in a foreign hypermarket and you recognised that the victim was the same nationality as you?

● you had just heard that you had won £100,000 in the lottery?

What if there were other people in the area? Would their presence make any difference to how you felt and behaved?

The study of **bystander behaviour** looks at people's willingness to help a 'victim' who is observed to be suffering in the vicinity. In this situation we normally have two choices:

● We can decide to help in some way – **bystander intervention**

● We can decide *not* to get involved – **bystander apathy**

The case of Kitty Genovese

The case of Kitty Genovese, in which a young woman was attacked and murdered in New York City in 1964, prompted much concern and subsequent research.

The murder took place at about three o'clock in the morning. Over a period of 35 minutes, the murderer, Winston Moseley, a married man with two children, left the scene twice before returning to finish off his victim. She crawled to her apartment door, screaming repeatedly that she was being murdered and pleading for help.

Two weeks later the *New York Times*, acting on a tip-off from the police, published details of how 38 neighbours had witnessed the event from their windows and none had offered help. No one even phoned the police until it was too late.

The story is a shocking one, but the bystander apathy it describes is not as unusual as it seems. So why did none of Kitty Genovese's neighbours intervene to help her? What determines whether or not we go to the aid of someone in distress? How are we to reconcile the fact that ordinary people sometimes commit great acts of self-sacrifice and heroism to help others, yet at other times do nothing?

One attempt by psychologists to unravel the factors that can influence bystander behaviour is described below.

KEY STUDY   Piliavin et al. (1969) arranged for a male 'victim' to collapse on a subway train as it pulled out of a station in New York. In one condition, the victim smelled of alcohol and carried a bottle in a brown bag. In another condition he appeared sober and carried a cane. The race of the victim was varied, sometimes white, sometimes black.

During the experiment, observers noted the race and sex of all passengers in the carriage and those who helped. They timed how long it took for assistance to be offered, and if none was offered, a confederate offered assistance after 70 seconds. The researchers found that help was immediately offered in 95% of the trials in the sober condition. The drunk was helped in 50% of the trials. According to the norm of social justice (see above) this difference is what we would expect. Piliavin found more helping between members of the same race.

THINK ABOUT IT

Would you feel more or less guilty if you had to execute someone on your own or as a member of a firing squad?

What does this tell you about how the presence of others can affect our feelings of personal responsibility?

streams of shoppers pass by and scarcely give them a glance. Are these people drunk, sleeping or ill? Few bother to check.

In part, this may be because each of them is carrying out the kind of cost/benefit analysis referred to earlier. But it also reflects the fact that, since nobody else seems concerned, then we believe there is nothing to be concerned *about*. Many situations are ambiguous: we are not immediately sure what to make of them. In such cases we look to other people for guidance about how to interpret the situation.

Latané and Darley (1968) arranged for people to fill out a questionnaire in a room either on their own or with two other participants present in the room with them. While they were filling in the questionnaire, white smoke from a vent began to fill the room. Of the people on their own, 75% reported the emergency within four minutes. With others present, this dropped to just 12% – even though by the end of four minutes it was difficult to see clearly across the room.

This may in part reflect diffusion of responsibility. But in this study, unlike the one above, most participants were quite calm and unconcerned. This may indicate that in ambiguous situations we look to each other for cues and guidance. Since we do not like to look unnecessarily panicked or upset, we remain outwardly calm. The calm we see reflected around us can therefore lead us to conclude that what might otherwise be considered an emergency is not an emergency after all.

THINK ABOUT IT

A visit to the dentist is an unpleasant prospect for many of us, and possibly a painful one. But if you look at the faces of most of the people in the waiting room, most look calm.

If we rely on the appearance or behaviour of the people around us in an everyday situation like this, how are we likely to react in a more ambiguous situation?

When questioned afterwards, people in this study explained away the smoke as caused by 'a leak in the air conditioning', or 'steam pipes'. Because they had decided it was not an emergency, they were not unduly concerned.

Cognitive factors

Latané and Darley (1970) provided a five-step model to show the process we go through when deciding whether to offer help to someone in an emergency:

1 Notice the event
2 Interpret the event as an emergency
3 Assume responsibility, i.e. recognise it is up to you to do something
4 Decide what assistance to offer
5 Give help

TRY THIS

Which four steps in the model above are being referred to below?

● 'I really didn't know what to do for the best.'
● 'Accident, what accident?'
● 'It's got nothing to do with me.'
● 'It really didn't seem that serious.'

This model applies not only to bystanders who may witness an emergency in the street. For example, it also describes the process we go through in deciding whether to help victims of a disaster in a distant part of the world. If we fail to do any of the five things listed, then help is unlikely to be given.

QUESTIONS

1 Describe *four* social norms that influence prosocial behaviour.
2 Distinguish between the following *three* models for helping behaviour:

● **empathy–altruism model**
● **the negative state relief model**
● **the empathic joy model**

3 What is meant by the following terms:

● **diffusion of responsibility**
● **audience inhibition**
● **pluralistic ignorance**

Summary

- Prosocial behaviour is intended to have a positive social impact. Altruistic behaviour involves helping others for no personal gain.
- Evolutionary theory suggests that altruistic behaviour is coded into our genes. Altruistic behaviour helps preserve the gene pool by helping family members. Helping non-family members is also useful if others display reciprocal altruism.
- Learning theory suggests that prosocial behaviour is learned by direct association, reinforcement and by observing and imitating models.
- Norm theory suggests we internalise social standards of behaviour, including the norm of social responsibility. Other norms, such as those of equity, reciprocity and social justice, have an impact on prosocial behaviour too.
- The empathy–altruism model suggests we empathise with and wish to reduce the distress that others feel. Very young children are egocentric and may not be able to properly empathise. The just world hypothesis means people may have a tendency to blame victims for their plight, thereby reducing empathy and the willingness to help. The negative state relief model, and the empathic joy model suggest we may help others for somewhat selfish, egotistical reasons.
- Research suggests that the characteristics of the victim and the characteristics of the observers can influence bystander behaviour.
- Piliavin and others suggested that people may weigh up the costs and benefits in deciding whether to offer assistance.
- Latané and Darley suggested that factors like pluralistic ignorance and diffusion of responsibility can contribute to our understanding of bystander apathy. Sometimes, the more people there are around, the less chance a victim has of receiving help. They argued that the reason bystanders sometimes fail to offer help is not because they are truly apathetic or uncaring, but because the presence of others may lead us to believe an emergency is *not* an emergency, or that the responsibility for doing something is not ours.
- Latané and Darley have developed a cognitive model outlining five steps that people typically go through in deciding whether or not to offer assistance to a victim.

23 Aggression

War: the ultimate expression of man's innate aggression? ▶

Human history is littered with wars and acts of aggression. There is little doubt about our ability and willingness to inflict violence on each other (and on animals too). This chapter looks at why we are aggressive and what we can do to reduce aggressive behaviour.

What is aggression?

Aggression is behaviour that is intended to hurt or damage another person or property. Causing harm by accident, or in pursuit of some beneficial end – for example, when a surgeon cuts somebody open – is *not* aggression. Aggression may be verbal or physical. Psychologists also distinguish between **hostile** aggression, which is done simply to cause hurt, and **instrumental** aggression, in which hurt is caused in the pursuit of some other end (e.g. in self-defence).

Since aggressive behaviour often has unpleasant consequences, many people would wish to reduce it or, even better, get rid of it entirely. But the important question is *why* are we aggressive? Is it in our genes? Is it an instinct that we just can't control? This biological explanation seems a bit pessimistic. An alternative view is that aggression is learned behaviour, and that we learn from our environment when, and how, to be aggressive.

Once again, we are confronted with a nature/nurture debate. These are the two views we will consider in this chapter.

THINK ABOUT IT

Is it true that some people are more aggressive than others? Why do you think this is?

Biological approaches

If we can selectively breed animals to make them either more or less aggressive, and if (as seems to be true) some people just seem to be more aggressive than others, then it is tempting to believe that aggression stems from the physical make-up of individuals. Two things that might be important here are brain functioning and the influence of hormones.

The brain

A section of the brain known as the **hypothalamus** seems to have something to do with aggression. Stimulating this structure with an electrode can make animals behave either more or less aggressively depending on the area stimulated. For example, in one rather daring experiment, Delgado (1969) stopped a bull charging at him by electronically stimulating this part of its brain. It is also recognised that particularly aggressive people sometimes suffer from disorders of this region of their brain.

In a daring experiment Delgado stopped a charging bull in its tracks by electronically stimulating an electrode attached to the animal's hypothalamus ▶

However, in humans and primates the different regions of the brain are greatly interconnected. Delgado (1970) also found that stimulating the hypothalamus of a male monkey could make it more aggressive towards subordinate monkeys – but that it would not be more aggressive towards females, and would be submissive and show fear reactions to more dominant monkeys. This shows that – in monkeys, at least –

THINK ABOUT IT

If one part of the brain is usually responsible for aggressive behaviour, what options might this suggest for controlling the behaviour of someone who is particularly aggressive?

higher-order cognitive factors can have an influence on aggression and that aggressive behaviour is not automatic but depends on how situations are interpreted. It seems likely that cognitive factors also have a strong influence in much human aggression too.

Gender differences in aggression

A number of species such as primates establish **dominance hierarchies**. These are ladders of relative status. Aggressive encounters are most likely to occur between males who are close to each other in the hierarchy. There are advantages to being at the top of the ladder, including first access to food and females.

We know from research that on average boys tend to engage in more rough-and-tumble play than girls, and a number of studies have found that males are more physically aggressive than females. However it must be emphasised that that this is a general finding, and that some females may be more aggressive than some males. Boulton (1994) found that boys more often engaged in play fighting than girls and that the belief that it was important to be a good fighter was stronger in boys than girls. Daly and Wilson (1988) looked cross-culturally at the amount of assault and murder that occurred among people of the same sex (excluding members of the same family). They found that such aggression is far more common among males than females. This was true for all cultures at all points in their history that they studied. They also found that this aggression peaks in late adolescence and early adulthood.

An important part here may be played by the hormone **testosterone**. Hormones are chemicals produced by organs in the body which trigger and control activity in organs elsewhere in the body. Testosterone is a hormone usually found in much greater quantities in males than females. Studies have shown that, when the hormone is injected into male or female animals, they tend to become more aggressive. There is a dramatic increase in the amount of testosterone produced by males in adolescence. Daly and Wilson suggested this may be a time when males become preoccupied with issues of status, which can help win females and subdue other males.

The extent of the difference between males and females in aggression is, however, not clear: measures of aggression vary and figures are disputed. Dr George of London University (1994) interviewed 1,800 men and women in heterosexual relationships. Around 5% of the men reported one or more acts of violence against them by their spouse, compared to 1% of women. The **British Crime Survey** (1996) reported that nearly one third of victims of domestic violence were men, and nearly one half of these were attacked by women.

Given that men generally may feel more embarrassed to admit to being assaulted by women than vice versa and are therefore less likely to report attacks, the actual figures for violence suffered by men may be much greater – though we should not forget that levels of violence against women are probably also much greater than the figures suggest.

We should also recognise that female aggression may be influenced by hormones. For example, some women may sometimes become more aggressive pre-menstrually, or when they are pregnant.

Evaluation of biological theory of aggression

Strengths

+ It is not really surprising that our brains or hormones influence how we feel and how we behave, and there is much evidence that they do.

Weaknesses

- Most psychologists are keen to stress that we are not prisoners of our biology. We make choices about how to behave and are responsible for our actions.
- Research also suggests that differences in verbal aggression between the sexes are small. The fact that males tend to be stronger than females, and differences in the ways in which males and females are brought up, can account for differences in their aggressive behaviour. In modern industrialised societies, high-status males are often not the ones who are physically strongest or most physically aggressive.

Aggression as an instinct

Instinctive behaviour is behaviour that is automatic and unlearned. Instincts, whether animal or human, are inherited from our parents as part of our biological make-up. It is behaviour that is 'wired in'. Aggressive behaviour seems instinctive in some animals, and this raises the possibility that aggressive behaviour may also be instinctive in humans. We will now consider two instinct theories, those of Lorenz and Freud.

? THINK ABOUT IT

If aggression is an automatic, instinctive response, what does this imply about the way we should treat someone on trial for murder?

The ethological approach

Ethology involves studying animals in their natural environment. As a result of his studies of different animals, the ethologist Konrad Lorenz took the view that aggression in animals and humans is a form of instinctive behaviour. Lorenz defines aggression as: 'the fighting instinct in beast and man which is directed against members of the same species.' So we have a view of humans as natural warriors.

Lorenz argues that aggressive responses are **adaptive**, i.e. useful for survival. Animals often have to fight for food, mates and territory. The strongest animals win, and so are more likely to survive and reproduce. This ensures that the fitness of the species is increased.

However, if all the weaker animals are killed in the struggle, this is bad news for the species as a whole. There are less of them – and it is best for a species if as many members survive as possible. Animals can always die through accident or disease, and the fewer of them that there are, the greater the risk of the species becoming extinct.

Lorenz believed that, to help prevent members of a species from killing each other, animal aggression takes particular forms. When fighting another member of the same species, the fighting is done in a particular way according to a **ritualised** pattern. So if two stags decide to fight, they may eye each other up for a bit and then clash horns. This does have its dangers, of course, but it is a quite different form of behaviour from one stag waiting until its opponent is half asleep, and then sneaking up to spear him through the belly with an antler! Fighting rituals help minimise the damage done.

Lorenz argued that to avoid members of the same species killing one another, animal aggression takes 'ritualised' forms

In ritualised fighting, when one animal has had enough, it can often surrender before getting badly hurt or killed. This can be done through an **appeasement ritual** in which the defeated animal signals 'surrender' by making itself vulnerable to the victor. So a wolf might surrender by lying on its back. This submissive posture exposes its soft throat and underbelly. But this is not (usually) an act of suicide, since the wolf to whom it surrenders will usually stop attacking it at this point. Having won the fight, and whatever it was fighting for, the victor has little to gain from continuing the conflict and risking further injury.

Lorenz and human aggression

Lorenz argues that humans have the same instinct for fighting as animals. We naturally compete with each other for scarce resources. But we have less need for ritual in fighting since we do not have big teeth or sharp claws with which to hurt each other. The problem with human aggression is that because of our technology, and the development of weapons, the fighting instinct in humans is no longer adaptive. The development of weapons technology means that humans now can and do kill each other very easily. We do not have the rituals that effectively prevent us from doing this. Furthermore, even if things like crying and pleading can sometimes succeed in stopping aggression, these behaviours have no chance to work if the attack is immediately fatal or occurs at a distance – for example, if you are using a high-velocity rifle or dropping bombs on someone. So where our aggressive instinct may have served us well in the past, now, with the advance of human technology, the human instinct for aggression is really out of hand and threatens the survival of the whole species.

Evaluation of the ethological approach

Strengths

+ Human wars are often fought over resources such as territory. Lorenz reminds us that we may not be so very different from other animals in this respect.

Weaknesses

- Animal aggression is very different from what humans do. The forms that human aggression can take, and the reasons for it, seem much more varied.
- The more intelligent an animal is, the less need there is for automatic, instinctive behaviour. The point about intelligence is that it makes an animal more flexible in its behaviour.
- 'Instinct' seems a poor explanation for modern human warfare, which involves killing at a distance. A bomber pilot, after all, is killing people he cannot even see, so his behaviour cannot be an instinctive response to anything.

THINK ABOUT IT

In what way is human aggression different from aggression in animals? Consider the possible causes of aggression, the different forms that aggression can take, and the impact of higher-order cognitive processes (reason).

The psychoanalytic approach

Freud argued that we are born with two basic instincts. One is the life instinct, **eros**, which involves life-enhancing things such as love, creation, reproduction, etc. Initially, Freud suggested this was the only instinct we have. But later, in response to the horrors of World War I, he came to the view that we also have a darker side, an aggressive and self-destructive instinct: **thanatos**, the death instinct. These two instincts operate in the unconscious mind and make up the **id**. Essentially they conflict with each other, though they can interact in strange ways, leading to masochistic or sadomasochistic behaviour.

For Freud, therefore, our aggressiveness is closely linked to the strength of the impulses that come from the id, and the ability of our ego and superego to deal with and control them (see Chapter 6, *Freud and Psychoanalytic Theory*, page 42). Someone who is very aggressive probably has a strong aggressive instinct.

Freud argued that instinctual energy builds up over time. If our instinctual desires are not met or expressed, tension develops, and the need to express them becomes stronger. The eventual expression of such a need reduces tension, so that we feel more comfortable again – at least for a while. This process of 'getting things out of our system' Freud called **catharsis**. In the case of aggression, the longer we go without finding some way of releasing our aggressive energy, the more it builds, and the more uncomfortable we feel.

Fortunately, Freud believed, there are a number of ways we can meet this need without actually hurting other people or ourselves:

- we can channel it into aggressive fantasies and imaginings

- we can achieve catharsis by watching aggressive acts by others – for example, either in ritualised sports such as boxing or perhaps by watching violent films

- We can also **sublimate** our aggressive instincts – in other words, find a socially acceptable way of expressing them. People with high levels of aggression may find an outlet in the jobs they do (e.g. butcher or soldier) or in sport (e.g. rugby).

Evaluation of the psychoanalytic approach

Strengths
+ Freud's views are thought-provoking and have led to much debate and further research.

Weaknesses
- Freud's theory has been criticised as unscientific (see Chapter 6).
- The idea that viewing aggression can be cathartic has been challenged. Some feel that exposing people to violent films encourages them to be more violent rather than less. We will return to this topic later.
- Human warfare often seems to be fuelled as much by cultural influences and learning (e.g. love of one's country, loyalty to comrades), as by underlying instinct.
- The argument for the existence of an aggressive instinct seems to be circular. People are thought to be aggressive because they have an aggressive instinct, and are believed to have an aggressive instinct because they are aggressive. We may as well say someone who is funny must have an instinct for humour, or someone who does well at school has the studying instinct.

The frustration–aggression hypothesis
This explanation of human aggression was originally put forward by Dollard et al. (1939) and is based on **drive theory**, which is in many ways similar to instinct theory. Drive theory states that behaviour is determined by the particular **drive state** we happen to be in. Hunger is a drive state that means you will act to reduce hunger by finding food. In the same way, aggression is a drive state that means you will behave

aggressively. An aggressive drive state, according to the frustration–aggression hypothesis, is caused by frustration.

All frustration leads to aggression, and all aggression is caused by frustration. Frustration arises when we are prevented from getting something we want. So the blocking of a desired goal causes frustration, which leads to aggression.

THINK ABOUT IT

You badly want to watch a TV programme but your sister is watching the other channel and she has the remote. Might this produce any aggressive feelings in you? How would the frustration–aggression hypothesis explain this?

Evaluation of the frustration–aggression hypothesis

Strengths
+ It seems to be true that people are sometimes aggressive because of feelings of frustration.
+ This theory has been linked to **scapegoating** (see Chapter 24, *Prejudice and Discrimination*) and has been used to explain why some groups may become targets for aggression when people are frustrated; e.g. frustrations caused by times of economic difficulty may result in an increase in racist violence.

Weaknesses
– The theory is circular, like instinct theory. That is, it suggests people are in an aggressive drive state because they are behaving aggressively, and they are behaving aggressively because they are in an aggressive drive state.
– Not all aggression is caused by frustration. For example, football hooligans who engage in mindless violence even though their team has just won, do not seem to be obviously frustrated.
– Frustration does not necessarily lead to aggressive behaviour. There are a number of other possible ways of coping with frustration, from laughing it off to bursting into tears.

In fact, the original frustration–aggression hypothesis has undergone a number of revisions. Berkowitz (1989) suggested that frustration may cause anger, but whether or not this leads to aggression often depends on higher-order cognitive factors. For example, before lashing out physically, we may pause to think *why* we are upset and whether there may be other ways to cope with our feelings. Sudden feelings of intense anger, though, may result in an aggressive response before higher-order cognitions have a chance to operate – for example , when we strike out in a 'blind rage' without thinking.

TRY THIS

Link the **terms** on the right to the **definitions** on the left.

Catharsis	the intent to hurt someone for the sake of it
instrumental aggression	behaviour aimed at stopping an attack
thanatos	male hormone implicated in aggression
ethology	expressing an impulse and thereby reducing tension
testosterone	hurting someone in pursuit of some other end
hostile aggression	the death instinct in Freudian theory
appeasement rituals	unlearned behaviour
instinct	the study of animals in their natural habitat

Summary

- Biological approaches to aggression look at the ways in which physical structures in the body, or innate mechanisms like instincts, influence aggressive behaviour.

- A region of the brain called the hypothalamus seems to play a role in aggressive behaviour, as do hormones. Higher levels of the male hormone testosterone may make aggression more likely, and may contribute to observed sex differences in aggression. Female hormones may also sometimes influence aggressive behaviours in women. Humans are not, usually, however, simply prisoners of their biology, and cognitive factors probably play a major role in much aggressive behaviour.

- The view that aggressive behaviour is instinctive was proposed by Lorenz and also by Freud. Lorenz believes aggression is adaptive in animals, and has used evidence of the fighting rituals of some species to support his ideas. He believes aggression is no longer adaptive in humans because of the development of weapons technology.

- Freud believed we inherit an aggressive instinct, as part of the id.

- Both of these theorists have been challenged by others. Animals may not provide a reliable guide to human behaviour. Freud's work is unscientific. Instinct theory presents a circular argument.

- The frustration–aggression hypothesis was built around drive theory. But although frustration may explain some aggression, the original theory was too simple and has since been modified.

- Like instinct theory, drive theory is circular.

What kind of example is this father setting his child?

Learning approaches

According to learning theory, aggressive behaviour is learned, just like all other behaviours, through the processes of classical conditioning, operant conditioning, and observation and imitation.

In classical conditioning, if a stimulus producing a response is paired with a second stimulus, then in time, the second stimulus will also trigger the same response. (Remember Pavlov's dogs? Food was paired with the sound of a bell, and eventually dogs would salivate just at the sound of the bell.) Accordingly, Berkowitz (1967) argued that we learn to associate certain **cues** (like guns) with aggression. He suggested that anger may sometimes result in aggression, but that the likelihood of an aggressive response is influenced by cues. He found that participants who were made angry showed a higher level of aggression, (measured by their willingness to give electric shocks to a confederate of the experimenter), if there was an aggressive cue around, such as a gun, than if there was a non-aggressive cue such as a badminton racket. This has become known as the **weapons effect**.

Evaluation of classical conditioning approach

Strengths

+ Berkowitz alerts us to the fact that objects or cues in the environment may affect levels of aggression. This implies a strategy for reducing aggression: minimise the number of aggressive cues, e.g. by banning guns and violent videos.

Weaknesses

- The weapons effect has been confirmed by some, but not all, researchers who have looked for it.
- We should also note that such measures of aggression are rather artificial. Participants know they are in an experiment. Further, the opportunity to shock someone with no fear of retaliation is not something that usually occurs in real life.

Operant conditioning

The principle behind operant conditioning is that responses that are reinforced tend to get repeated. If you behave aggressively and benefit from it, it is likely that you will behave aggressively again. So, if a school bully can gain sweets, money, or some form of fearful respect from his classmates (i.e. is rewarded for bullying), he is likely to continue bullying.

Research has found that children who respond to aggression with **counter-aggression** (i.e. who hit back), and are successful in doing so, are much more likely to use counter-aggression in future. A possible problem is that having learned that aggression can be rewarding, they may then go on to attack another child. Those who are not successful with their counter-aggressive behaviour are less likely to be counter-aggressive in future.

Evaluation of operant conditioning approach

Strengths

+ The theory seems intuitively reasonable and is supported by research. It can explain some instances of bullying, and why some people may become victims. Obviously, there is little point in being aggressive if you just keep getting beaten up as a consequence. A problem, however, is that if other children see you as someone who just 'gives in', you may be more likely to become a target for future attacks.

+ As men are, on average, bigger and stronger than women, their physical aggression is likely to be more successful (and therefore rewarding) than female aggression. This may help provide an explanation for the general finding that males are more aggressive than females.

Weaknesses

– The principles of classical and operant conditioning are derived from research on animals and are unlikely to give an adequate explanation for all human behaviour. In particular they say little about how cognitive factors and moral reasoning may influence aggressive behaviour.

Observational learning

According to observational learning, we learn different kinds of aggressive responses and the situations in which they are appropriate, by observing what others say and do. A classic demonstration of this approach is the research by Bandura and others.

KEY STUDY   Bandura (1965) showed children a film of an adult behaving aggressively towards a Bobo doll (a large, weighted rubber doll that would bounce back upright when pushed). Depending on which group they were in, the children saw either:

1   the adult rewarded with praise or sweets for being aggressive

2   no consequences to the adult for aggressive behaviour

3   the adult punished for their aggression

When the children were allowed to play with the doll themselves the first two groups were aggressive towards it, but the third group, who had seen the adult punished for aggressive behaviour, were much less so. Interestingly, Bandura found that when children who had seen an adult punished were offered rewards for behaving aggressively, they were quickly able to show that they could imitate the aggressive behaviour of the adult. This shows that we can learn aggressive responses from watching others, and that we may imitate this behaviour, though we are less likely to do so if we think the consequences of doing so may be punishing for us.

Bandura's research showed that children were quick to copy aggressive behaviour by adults

Source:
Bandura, A., Ross, D. & Ross, A., 'Transmission of Aggression Through Imitation of Aggressive Models', in *Journal of Abnormal and Social Psychology*, 63 (1961), pp.575–82

What this means is that, if we are exposed to people behaving aggressively, we may copy them – a process called **modelling**.

Questions
1. Are there any problems in using 'hitting a Bobo doll' as a measure of aggression?
2. Can you think of any ethical problems raised by this study?
3. How far do you think this study applies to aggression in the world outside the laboratory?

The research also indicates that models who are seen as similar to us, warm, or powerful are particularly likely to be imitated. This highlights the importance of the role that parents and peer groups have in shaping our behaviour. Cognitive factors have an important role. If we are thinking of behaving aggressively, we will often consider the likely consequences. Since every person's learning history is different, it is not surprising that we all have different views of the world and that we differ in our aggressive responses, just as we do in other forms of behaviour.

THINK ABOUT IT

What sorts of people do you think *you* would be especially likely or unlikely to imitate?

Given the importance of models – and especially parental models – let us now consider how parents can influence aggressive behaviour in their children and examine the role of the media.

Child-rearing styles
Research by Sears et al. (1957) suggested that parents who are firm but fair; who set clear standards; who punish fairly and consistently and who explain clearly to their children why their behaviour is wrong, are more likely to have children who show good self-control and are less aggressive.

They labelled parents like this as **authoritative** parents. Such parents act as models, showing fairness and reason as a way of resolving disputes. By contrast, parents who are inconsistent in their punishment, and who either use very little discipline (**permissive** parents) or who are very strict and use harsh discipline (**authoritarian** parents), are likely to produce more aggressive children. Parents who give in to childrens' aggressive demands teach children that aggressive responses are likely to be rewarded. Parents who use frequent physical punishment may foster anger and hostility in their children. At the same time they provide models of aggressive behaviour that their children can imitate to help deal with these emotions, perhaps by being aggressive towards other children.

The media and aggression

The role of the **media** (the press, radio and perhaps especially television and video) in promoting aggressive behaviour has been widely discussed. Certainly, constant exposure to violent models can teach people new forms of aggression and runs the risk of violent behaviour being imitated. Thomas and Drabman (1974) found that violent programmes can **desensitise** people – i.e. make them progressively more tolerant of aggressive behaviour. For example, eight-year-olds who watched a violent programme were less likely to tell an adult about a fight going on between two children than those who had seen a non-violent programme. In the same way people who are used to seeing violence on television may become more accepting of violence in real life.

We all know *how* to do many things that we normally *don't* do, because we have learned that certain forms of behaviour are socially unacceptable. But if everybody else was doing these things and they seemed normal things to do, then we might be more likely to do the same. In the same way, if we observe people behaving aggressively, we may feel it is acceptable for us to behave agressively too. In other words, observing others behaving aggressively may *reduce our inhibitions* against behaving aggressively ourselves.

In contemporary culture, aggression is often seen as heroic

THINK ABOUT IT

Jot down some of the things that you know how to do but are inhibited from doing. It may make an impressive list!

How many films can you think of in which males are presented as heroes partly because they are good at hurting the 'bad guys'? How might this influence the way in which men come to think about behaving aggressively?

This point about reducing inhibitions becomes even stronger if the violence we see appears to be **morally justified** (i.e. is good and right). Consider the plot of the average Hollywood action-adventure blockbuster. Usually it takes the form of a man ('good guy'), who encounters a problem ('bad guys'), which he solves through violence (usually by killing the bad guys). As a result of this he is hailed as a hero. Successfully inflicting violence on others is therefore seen as the sort of thing good guys and heroes do. Suffering violence, or being defeated, is the lot of the bad and the weak. Maybe this helps explain the pride some people may take in 'being hard'. To them, hurting others is associated with heroism.

Aggression and gender stereotypes

It is worth noting that it is usually *men* who are cast in such roles. This may reflect a wider cultural distinction in which women are seen as more passive and men as more aggressive and active.

Smith and Lloyd (1978) found that a baby dressed in pink was encouraged by women to be passive. They gave it cuddly toys to play with and spoke soothingly to it. When the baby was dressed in blue, the women encouraged it to be more active and bang toy hammers around. Research suggests that parents are sometimes less tolerant of aggressive behaviour in their daughters than in their sons. It is possible, therefore, that sex differences in aggression may reflect differences in the way males and females are brought up, beginning when they are very young. This may be a reflection of cultural values, and offers support for social learning theory.

Overall, the extent to which aggressive behaviour is influenced or inspired by the media is not clear. A field experiment by Parke et al. (1977) studied male juvenile delinquents living in small groups in low-security institutions. The researchers began by measuring the boys' normal levels of aggressive behaviour, and dividing them into two groups. Over a one-week period one group was shown violent films and others non-violent films. The boys exposed to violent films did show increases in levels of aggression, though the biggest effect was on boys who were already fairly aggressive. This supports the idea that TV *does* make a difference. However, there are problems with such studies, the main objection being that institutionalised delinquent boys are not representative of the general population.

QUESTIONS

1 What is the 'weapons effect'?
2 Suggest two reasons why someone might become a bully in school.
3 What does it mean to say a sample is not 'representative of the general population'?

Correlational studies

There have been a number of correlational studies which show a link between watching violence on TV and aggressive behaviour. But, being correlational, they tell us nothing about cause and effect. It could be that people enjoy violent films because they are already aggressive. On the other hand it could be that watching violent films makes people

Does violence on TV encourage aggression in real life? ▲

aggressive. What we can say is that TV and the media generally represent just one socialising influence among many. If they have an effect (and they might), they are certainly not the only factor involved – so we cannot really blame all aggression on TV.

Evaluation of the social learning approach

Strengths

+ Social learning theory is supported by a number of studies which use humans, rather than animals, as participants.

+ The theory has intuitive appeal. To say we can learn aggressive behaviour is not to say anything that is surprising. The focus of research must be, (and largely is), to achieve a better understanding of how aggression is learned, and the conditions under which aggressive behaviour becomes more likely. Social learning theory is contributing to this debate, and it alerts us to the wide variety of models in our environment from which we can learn.

+ It helps us to understand the concerns that some people have about violence in the media. The theory would predict that observing violent models may increase the likelihood of violent behaviour among the observers (and not decrease it because of catharsis, as Freud might argue).

Weaknesses

– It has little to say about the influence of innate or biological factors on aggressive behaviour.

Cultural and group influences

Group norms

Group norms also have an impact on aggressive behaviour. **Norms** are shared ways of behaving. In the UK, unlike in many other countries, people form queues at bus stops because there is a norm for queueing. Similarly, there are norms for aggression. Soldiers, rugby players or boxers may all be expected to display more physical aggression than, say, hippies, or chess players or supporters of CND. Religious groups like Quakers may stress non-violence, whereas criminal groups like the Mafia see violence as a legitimate way of achieving what they want. So people may become more or less aggressive because of pressures to act in ways that are appropriate for the particular groups to which they belong.

Another possibility is that aggressive people may choose to join particular groups, (e.g. a boxing or rugby club) because they provide a potential outlet for their aggressive impulses. Interestingly, a study by Marsh et al. (1978) found that football fans often enact rituals such as chanting, 'skirmishing' at half-time, chasing away visiting fans after the match, etc., without much real violence occurring. Football hooliganism, then, could be said to involve a culturally transmitted understanding of what is involved in carrying it out.

Cultural influences

Wade and Tavris (1996) point out that Eskimos regard even mild protest as a serious threat, and that in Eskimo society the display of anger is viewed as intolerable, appropriate only for babies, sick people, the insane – and white people. This reflects the fact that Eskimo society is close-knit and that people have to cooperate to survive. The way in which a society socialises its members, therefore, can influence both the amount of aggression and the forms of aggression that the society may experience. Wade and Tavris suggest that societies that value competition and power are more likely to foster aggression, both within that society and towards outsiders.

Scott (1992) has found big variations in the incidence of murder around the world. For example, the rate is about seven times higher in the USA than in the UK. This may be due to factors such as the availability of weapons and the acceptability of aggressive behaviour. Also, where violence has come to be seen as a legitimate feature of conflicts between groups, it becomes an accepted part of the culture and as such, more probable. In countries like Northern Ireland, where opposing groups have, for many years, used violence against each other, violence may come to be seen as the normal way of dealing with problems, and so future violence is more likely.

Reducing aggression

Can aggression be effectively reduced, or at least controlled? To the extent that aggression is a result of brain function or hormones, either surgery or some kind of hormone therapy or drugs might appear to offer some form of solution. Freud believed that providing people with opportunities to express aggressive impulses in acceptable ways, for example through sport, could reduce their aggressive impulses. He also argued that watching aggressive actions could reduce aggressive feelings in people. There is little support for this view today. Indeed, social learning theory predicts that exposure to aggressive models may increase, rather than decrease, levels of aggression.

To the extent that aggressive responses are learned then there are a number of possible strategies for reducing them. *Reducing the number of aggressive cues in the environment* – for example by banning the sale or carrying of weapons – may be useful. The principles of operant conditioning suggest that aggressive responses should not be reinforced, and clearly parents and teachers have a responsibility here. Adults should not 'give up' in the face of persistent aggressive behaviour by children, since this negatively reinforces children for their bad behaviour. At the same time it makes sense to *reinforce cooperative and helpful behaviour*.

The principles of observational learning suggest that it may be wise to *limit the number of aggressive models* that people are exposed to, and to make sure that where such models are seen, their aggressive actions are not seen to be rewarding. Again, *exposure to cooperative or helpful*

Does exposure to violent films and videos make children more aggressive?

models would be useful. This has implications for the ways in which parents and others conduct themselves, and also for the sorts of films and videos that children (and perhaps adults) should view.

While punishing aggressive responses may be useful, we should be aware that this may also provide models of aggressive behaviour that can be imitated. Some countries employ capital punishment to deter people from committing terrible crimes like murder, but just how successful capital punishment is as a deterrent has long been debated. Generally speaking it seems likely to be more successful in deterring calculated violence, where people have time to consider the possible consequences of their actions, than in preventing unpremeditated violence that results from a sudden 'blind rage'.

Cognitive strategies may also be helpful. Research suggests that some aggressive people are more likely to interpret the behaviour of other people as hostile. *Helping aggressive people to re-evaluate the behaviour of others* may therefore be useful.

For example, it may be that the reason our nextdoor neighbour did not respond to our cheery 'good morning' was *not* because he was being deliberately rude or provocative, but simply because he had other things on his mind. Toch (1985) believes *training in social skills* that help people to communicate more effectively and also to deal more skilfully with provocation may help people to avoid difficulties. After all, there are different ways of talking to people, and some are less likely to give offence than others. A chance to develop good communication skills may make it less likely that others will interpret your behaviour towards them as hostile, and therefore less likely that they will feel hostile towards you. Also, if we can encourage angry people to see the funny side of things, or to feel empathy, then aggressive responses are less likely. Ohbuchi et al. (1989) found that people reacted less aggressively to bad behaviour if they received an apology for it. In part this is because apologising to someone indicates that you respect them and did not mean to cause them harm.

QUESTIONS

1　What style of child-rearing is least likely to produce aggressive children?
2　Give two reasons why males tend to be more physically aggressive than females.
3　Give three ways in which the media may contribute to increased aggression in society.
4　Suggest two ways of reducing the levels of aggression in society.

Summary

● The debate concerning the causes of aggression is another variation on the nature/nurture debate. The nature side focuses on biology, the brain, hormones and instincts, while the nurture side focuses on learning, classical and operant conditioning and social learning theory. As with most such debates, our understanding is improved by considering the influence and interaction of both sides of the argument.

● The fact that social and cultural factors can affect levels of aggression and also influence the forms that aggressive behaviours take is evidence in support of the impact of learning.

● There are a wide variety of sources from which aggressive responses can be learned. A better understanding of this learning is important for attempts to reduce the levels of aggression in society.

● Cognitive factors also play an important part in human aggression. Helping people develop communication skills, to see that the behaviour of others is often not hostile, and to find non-aggressive ways for coping with their own anger, may all be useful in reducing the likelihood of aggressive responses.

24 Prejudice and Discrimination

Prejudices are common, but they can be dangerous. The ethnic cleansing in Kosovo which resulted in NATO countries bombing Yugoslavia in the summer of 1999 is a recent example of the destructive power of prejudice. This chapter will discuss the causes of prejudice and ways to reduce and overcome it.

What is prejudice?

The key to this term lies in the word itself. To be **prejudiced** is to *pre-judge*. This means to hold opinions about something or someone which are not based on examination of the facts. Often, we make judgements about other people simply on the basis of the groups they belong to. Many of our views about old people, or women, or particular ethnic groups, are formed in this way. In some cases we can be prejudiced in favour of a group, as when we think our team is best and want them to win. More often, however, we are prejudiced *against* people and things – and it is this negative aspect of prejudice that psychologists are particularly interested in exploring. Of course, the positive and negative sides of prejudice are often linked. If you want your team to win, you must want the other team to lose. Common prejudices include ageism, sexism and racism.

Secord and Backman (1964) claim that all attitudes (including prejudiced attitudes) have three main components, which they refer to as an **ABC**:

A **An affective component**. This is the feelings you have, i.e. your emotional response, to particular things (e.g. 'Wossnames' fill you with feelings of disgust and anger).

B **A behavioural component**. This refers to what you do as a result of your attitude (e.g. you may just ignore all Wossnames, or, in an extreme case, you may try to kill them).

C **A cognitive component**. This consists of the thoughts or beliefs that you hold about something or someone (e.g. all Wossnames are dirty and stupid).

Clearly, these three things are related. How you think about someone may affect how you feel about them, which in turn may affect what you do. Of course, you may not do anything as a result of your attitude, and it is relatively rare to go to the extreme of trying to kill people. But a particular form of response, and one that is widespread in society, is to

Groups such as the infamous Ku-Klux-Klan express their prejudice through extreme racist behaviour and language.

discriminate against members of particular groups. To discriminate *between* people is just to point out ways in which they are different, e.g. these are males and these are females. There is nothing wrong in this. To discriminate *against* people, however, is to treat them unfairly, and so is morally wrong.

For example, to give jobs to members of one particular group (say, men), rather than to people in another group who are equally capable (say women), is an example of discrimination against a group. In this case the prejudice is called **sexism**.

We can think of prejudice as an attitude, usually negative, that one holds towards other people because of their group membership. It is also possible to be prejudiced against objects, animals and events – for example, some people may have a prejudice against snakes.

THINK ABOUT IT

Think of a prejudice that you may have. Try to identify the **three** components mentioned above in your prejudice.

A final important point is that prejudiced views are often *very difficult to change*. People who dislike Wossnames may have met very few, if any, of them. When you point this out to them, they will declare they don't *want* to meet them; they often have a fund of stories (often anecdotal) to support their views. They will usually make sweeping generalisations from a few Wossnames to all Wossnames (something they would never tolerate if directed against themselves or members of their own group). For example, someone may say 'all students are lazy'. If you are a student, you will probably dispute this, realising that it is wrong and that some students may be lazy, but many are hardworking.

'Them and us'
Central to the problem of prejudice is a *'them and us'* attitude. Typically, the groups to which we think we belong (the **in-groups**), are the ones we value most. We see these groups as better than other groups (**out-groups**), and also treat in-groups more favourably. Tajfel (1971) calls this **in-group overevaluation**, and **out-group rejection**. Of course, your in-group is someone else's out-group. Here we have a recipe for conflict which is reflected in the long and bloody history of human warfare and oppression. The tendency to value your own cultural or ethnic group over others is called **ethnocentrism**.

Prejudice exists in nearly all cultures in some form or another. But how can we explain this? What gives rise to prejudiced attitudes? Some people seem to be more prejudiced than others, and so some psychologists have sought to explain prejudice in terms of the functioning of the *individual*, seeking to explain what it is about a person that makes them this way. Others emphasise that prejudiced attitudes often reflect the ways in which whole *groups* of people feel about other groups, and have focused on group-level explanations for prejudice. Let us turn our minds, then, to explanations for the causes of prejudice.

Prejudice: individual-level theories

These explanations for prejudice focus on particular aspects of the person that make them likely to hold prejudiced attitudes. We will consider theories to do with the authoritarian personality, the dogmatic person, the role of frustration, and the impact of learning.

The authoritarian personality

One of the most appalling and extreme examples of racial prejudice in human history was Hitler's attempted mass-extermination of the Jews during World War II. Shortly after the war, Adorno and others seeking to explain this atrocity questioned about 2,000 people about their views on immigrants, the law, politics and their general values. They also asked them about their childhood and the ways in which their parents treated them. They concluded that some people may be more prone to racist attitudes than others, and that this was often a reflection of the way they were treated by their parents as children.

The researchers designed a questionnaire to measure the extent to which people were prejudiced against Jews. They went on to find that people who were prejudiced in this way were often also prejudiced against other foreigners, homosexuals, blacks, and indeed out-groups generally. Adorno believed that such people had a particular kind of personality that he called an **authoritarian personality**.

The Nazi extermination of the Jews in World War II was driven by extreme racial prejudice

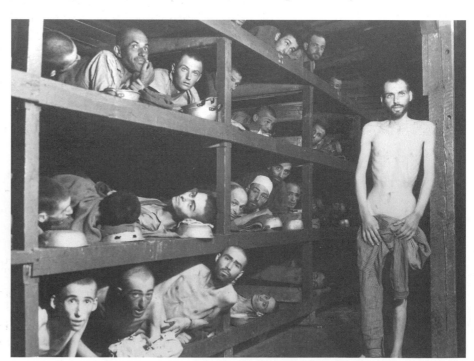

Strictly brought-up children may display an exaggerated respect for authority in later life ▲

Adorno et al. (1950) found that authoritarians often held rather rigid attitudes toward authority. They argued that such people probably had very strict parents who tolerated very little argument and punished them heavily when they were children. In later life, such people showed a great respect for authority and conventional values, favoured the harsh punishment of offenders and were intolerant of out-groups. The strictness of their upbringing also produced a lot of anger and hostility which could not be directed at their parents, because their parents were seen as powerful and because they had been brought up to respect them. Drawing on Freudian ideas, Adorno et al. argued that, as a result, much of their hostility was repressed and redirected (or **displaced**) onto other, weaker and, by their standards, unconventional, people such as minority groups.

Adorno designed the **F-scale**, a questionnaire to measure authoritarianism and the extent to which people were prone to the sort of Fascist attitudes that give rise to extreme racism. The questionnaire did not ask directly about attitudes to racist groups. Instead it contained statements with which people were required to agree or disagree. Some examples are given below.

Adorno, T.W., Frenkey-Brunswick, E., Levinson, D.J. & Sanford, R.N., *The Authoritarian Personality*, (Harper & Row, New York, 1950) ▶

Examples of questions in Adorno's F-scale Questionnaire

	Agree	Disagree
• Homosexuals are hardly better than criminals and ought to be severely punished	☐	☐
• Obedience and respect for authority are the most important virtues children should learn	☐	☐
• People can be divided into two distinct classes: the weak and the strong	☐	☐

QUESTIONS

What difficulties are there in trying to measure peoples' attitudes using a questionnaire?

Evaluation of Adorno's research

Strengths

+ Adorno alerts us to the fact that some people may form prejudices more readily than others.
+ Research has supported a link between high scores on the F-scale and prejudiced attitudes.
+ Many psychologists accept that the ways in which parents raise their children can affect the attitudes their children form.

Weaknesses

- Adorno obtained information by asking people for reports of how they were raised as children, and memory can be unreliable.
- The data is only correlational, and so cannot tell us about cause and effect. Differences in education or class background might equally well explain the results.
- People may simply have learned prejudice from prejudiced parents, rather than be displacing any pent-up hostility.
- We cannot explain the horrors of Nazi Germany as being simply the result of a sudden, mass outbreak of strict parenting suffered by German children. We need also to consider factors like the economic depression and cultural attitudes of the time.

The dogmatic individual

Adorno's questionnaire was only really designed to measure attitudes reflected by the far right in politics. (Fascists are described as far right, conservatives less so. Communists are far left, socialists less so). However, Rokeach (1960) pointed out that prejudice is not confined to people like fascists. For example, those on the left in politics can have their prejudices too. Rokeach argued that what really characterises prejudiced individuals is that they have a **closed mind**. In other words, such people tend to see things in a rather rigid fashion and are not open to new ways of looking at things. Rokeach called such people **dogmatic**, and produced a questionnaire of his own, known as the **dogmatism scale**, to measure this feature.

Rokeach suggested that people who are prejudiced against ethnic groups do not reject them simply because they have different-coloured skin or look different in some way. They reject them because they have different values and lifestyles. And since they have closed minds, they are unable to understand that there may be different, but equally valid, ways of doing things. They believe that their way is the *right* way. If other people are different, then they are less worthy or wrong, and therefore may threaten the right way of doing things.

Evaluation of Rokeach

Strength

+ Both Adorno and Rokeach argue that there may be a prejudiced personality type. Some people are just more likely to be prejudiced than others. This seems to fit with our everyday experience.

Weakness

- It remains unclear why this should be the case. Does a tendency towards prejudice reflect an innate predisposition, a learned tendency or a mixture of the two? We shall consider learning theory shortly.

The frustration–aggression hypothesis

Another individual-level approach to prejudiced behaviour is the **frustration–aggression hypothesis** (see Chapter 23, *Aggression*, page 338). This sees aggression as an innate response to frustration, and has been used to support the view that frustrated individuals may vent their aggression on minority groups, and perhaps even physically attack them. It has also been suggested that at certain times, perhaps during an economic recession, people are liable to feel frustrated by the lack of jobs or money, and this may cause levels of prejudice and aggression to rise. Indeed, Hovland and Sears (1940) made a study of official records of lynchings that occurred between 1882 and 1930 in the American South, and found that, as the price of cotton fell, reflecting a worsening economic situation, the number of attacks on blacks increased.

QUESTION

Data showing a link between variables is called a **correlation**. What sort of correlation was found in the study above?

Scapegoating

The tendency to take out our frustrations on particular individuals or groups is known as **scapegoating**. Scapegoats are people we blame for our own problems – and whom we may attack. Typically, they are individuals or groups perceived as weaker than ourselves (since there is no point attacking the strong), and minority groups are often targets. In the Depression of the 1930s, it seems that blacks were seen as scapegoats in the American South.

Scapegoating is not uncommon. For example, it is not unusual for racists in times of economic difficulty to claim that 'they' (whoever 'they' are) are coming over here and taking all of 'our' jobs (a statement that is rarely supported by statistics, since in times of economic difficulty, it is usually the minority groups who suffer most). At one time, in Germany and elsewhere, it was common to blame Jews for social problems. In Germany more recently, new economic difficulties have led to immigrant Turks becoming targets for racist attacks. In the UK, people of Afro-Caribbean and Asian origins in particular have been (and are) frequent targets for racism.

Evaluation of frustration–aggression hypothesis

Strengths

+ The frustration–aggression hypothesis helps us understand links between social conditions or times of economic difficulty and increases in racism.

Weaknesses

– The recession in Britain in the 1980s did not lead to any great increase in racist attacks.
– The theory is really only directly applicable to individuals. It does not explain why one group (say, whites), is prejudiced against another group (say, blacks). We need to consider wider, cultural attitudes here. We will not, for example, understand the extremes of racial prejudice found in places like Kosovo, Rwanda or South Africa, if we ignore past and present cultural attitudes in those regions.

 – The theory does not explain how target groups can change, e.g. why immigrant Turks are targets in modern Germany rather than Jews. Again, wider, cultural attitudes need considering.

Learning theory and prejudice

One possible explanation of how some prejudices are acquired is offered by **classical conditioning**. The Nazis in Hitler's Germany may have spoken about Jewish people in ways that conveyed feelings of disgust or loathing. The repeated association of these negative feelings with the word 'Jew' might have resulted, in time, in Jewish people evoking these feelings in many Germans. Alternatively, classical conditioning explains that if a member of one particular group was aggressive or unpleasant to somebody else, the negative feelings that person experienced could be generalised towards all members of that group.

Operant conditioning could also be relevant here. If a person is reinforced for prejudiced behaviour, perhaps by praise from prejudiced parents or peers, then that prejudiced behaviour is more likely to be repeated in future. In terms of **social learning theory**, prejudiced behaviour and emotional responses can be learned from observing models in the environment. Once again, therefore, if parents, peers, or the wider culture express prejudiced attitudes, these can be learned and internalised by children until eventually their attitudes come to be seen as right and proper. This is often the purpose of propaganda in times of war. People are encouraged to believe that the citizens of their country (the in-group) are brave lads fighting for what is good and right, whereas the enemy, the out-group, are cruel, wicked foreigners.

THINK ABOUT IT

Can you think how learning theory might be used to explain how someone could acquire a prejudice against the supporters of a particular football team?

People do not always ▲
conform to type

Stereotyping

The ease with which people seem to learn prejudices is startling. But *why* is this? Given that we know that people are all individuals in their own right, why is it that we so often find ourselves making statements like 'all Wossnames are…'? The answer seems to have something to do with the ways in which we process and deal with information.

The world is a complicated place. Every person and object within it is unique, but to make sense of it, we have arranged them into categories – so these are 'tables', these are 'chairs', these are 'fruit' and these are 'vegetables', etc. This simplifies life and makes the world easier to understand. In the same way we categorise groups of people according to age, sex, race, occupation, etc.

A **stereotype** is a set of ideas about a group of people, what they are like and how they behave. Stereotypes are useful up to a point. The problem is that they represent a simplified view. One consequence of this is that people in a particular group may seem to us to be much more similar to each other than they really are.

For example, we know from personal experience that the people in the groups to which we belong are all very different from each other. But because we lack knowledge about out-groups there is a tendency *to see the members of a particular group as being all the same*. In this way, young people often think that old people are much more similar to one another than they really are. In the same way, the elderly are aware that older people are all different, but tend to view young people as being all the same. This is what lies behind statements like 'all women are passive', 'all men are rapists' and 'all policemen are wonderful'.

THINK ABOUT IT

How might older people stereotype young people, and vice versa?
See if you can give stereotypes for:

a) teachers
b) people with glasses
c) motorcyclists

Furthermore, the simple act of putting people into categories highlights the way in which they are different from each other. This is, after all, the basis on which the categorising is done. Stereotyping, therefore, serves to emphasise differences and can lead us *into thinking that groups are much more different from each other than they actually are.*

In stereotyping, we put people in categories of one sort or another, usually on the basis of their physical appearance. For example, if we see someone in a pin-striped suit and bowler hat, carrying a copy of *The Financial Times* and a rolled umbrella, we are likely to categorise them in a certain way. We will make assumptions about their sex, job, class, the type of car they drive, the way they vote, their hobbies – and so on. Of course, they could be a Hell's Angel on the way to a fancy dress party. But it is precisely because we cannot expect to think of all the possibilities that we do use stereotypes – and often find them useful.

We know from studies of perception and memory, that the way we think about the world affects the way we perceive and remember it. Perception and memory are **interpretative**. That is, we tend to interpret events in the light of what we already know (or *think* we know). As a consequence, we are more likely to notice something that confirms our stereotypes or prejudices, than something that might undermine them. Buckhout (1974) showed a group of white participants a drawing in which a casually dressed white man holding a razor threatened a smartly dressed black man on a train. Half of the participants wrongly remembered the black man as holding a razor.

What is more, our understanding, or lack of it, affects the way we interact with the world – often in complex ways. For example, Word et al. (1974) found that white students were likely to give black people shorter, less friendly interviews than white people. They were not really aware of doing this, but not surprisingly the black interviewees tended to do less well as a result. In this way, not only was discrimination against blacks maintained, but the white students' stereotypes and prejudice were justified – since the blacks' poor performance simply served to reinforce the whites' prejudiced opinion of them.

THINK ABOUT IT

How might stereotyping contribute to sexism?

Evaluation of stereotyping theory

Strengths
+ An understanding of stereotyping does add to our understanding of how prejudices are formed and maintained.

Weaknesses
– It is not clear where particular stereotypes come from, nor why some are more negative than others.

TRY THIS

Match the **terms** on the left to the **definitions** on the right.

the authoritarian personality	has a closed mind
in-group overevaluation	blaming others for our troubles
scapegoating	a questionnaire to measure authoritarianism
ethnocentrism	rating groups 'we' belong to very highly
the dogmatic personality	displaces anger onto minority groups
discrimination	disliking other ethnic groups
F-scale	treating a person or group unfairly

Prejudice: group-level theories

Group-level explanations for prejudice look beyond the individual to consider the impact of wider, social forces, such as cultural attitudes or the attitudes of groups to which the individual belongs.

Realistic group conflict theory

It is by no means clear that prejudice *must* result from perceived differences between groups, since different groups often seem to cooperate and get along nicely. Sherif argues that prejudice will often arise between groups that are *competing* with each other for resources.

KEY STUDY

Sherif et al. (1961) conducted a series of field experiments on boys aged about eleven at summer camp in the USA. The first stage of the experiment involved the boys being split into two groups at camp which were placed in different cabins located away from each other. Each group lived and played together separately from the other group for a week. The boys in each group became friends, found nicknames for each other, found a name for their group (e.g. the 'Eagles' and the 'Rattlers'), and even made up their own flags. By the end of the first stage, each group had developed a strong sense of a group identity.

After a week, when each group had developed a strong group spirit, the second stage of the experiment began. The two groups were brought into competition with each other in games such as football and tug-of-war. The winners were given prizes, the losers received nothing, so that in effect both groups were competing for scarce resources (prizes).

Not surprisingly, the competition was intense, but it quickly developed in ways that were unpleasant. Initially, this just took the form of name-calling and teasing, but soon things got worse. The Eagles burned the Rattlers' flag. The Rattlers attacked the Eagles' cabin, damaging and stealing property. The two groups became extremely hostile to each other, calling each other names like 'sissies,' 'big-heads,' 'cheats' and 'cowards', at the same time praising their own group members at every opportunity. After just two weeks of competition, the groups developed and displayed strong prejudices towards one another.

Sherif suggests that these same forces are at work in the world generally. Where different groups or countries compete with each other for land, jobs, food, minerals or other scarce resources, this competition is likely to foster prejudiced attitudes. (Note that the experiment did have a third stage, in which Sherif attempted to reduce the tensions between the boys. We will look at this later on.)

Source:
Sherif, M., Harvey, O.J., White, B.J., Hood, W.R. & Sherif, C.W., *Intergroup Conflict and Cooperation: The Robber's Cave Experiment* (University of Oklahoma, Norman, Oklahoma,1961)

Questions

1. What was the purpose of the first stage of the experiment?
2. Describe in your own words what is meant by 'realistic group conflict theory'.
3. What **ethical problems** are raised by Sherif's study?

Minimal groups

Tajfel (1971) believed that competition is not always needed for prejudice. Sometimes, just knowing that you are in a group that is different from another one is sufficient in itself. In one study, he and his colleagues assigned 14- and 15-year-old boys to different groups by asking them to estimate the number of dots flashed on a screen for a fraction of a second. The boys were given false feedback and in reality were assigned to the groups on a random basis (i.e. entirely by chance). Each boy then had to sit alone and assess the performance of the others on a task. They consistently rated the performance of their group members above that of members of the other group. Billig and Tajfel (1973) even found similar results when people were told they had been assigned randomly.

A **minimal group** is one that is defined on the basis of almost no (minimal) information. This means that people are put into groups on an arbitrary basis, and there is no real basis for distinguishing between them. Even between such groups, it seems, prejudice can be easily established. One possible explanation for this, outlined below, is to do with the impact of **social norms**.

Norms of competitiveness

As we have seen, **social norms** are shared ways of thinking and behaving (see page 314). People may learn norms that suggest that different groups are in competition with them, even when they may not be. In a competitive society, we are encouraged to see ourselves as in competition with others. At school we compete against each other in team games; schools compete against other schools; and in adult life we compete against everyone else for jobs and status. If we are used to seeing each other, and other groups especially, as competitors, then this in itself may foster prejudice between groups, *even when no competition actually exists.*

We are taught to compete with other groups from an early age ▶

Conformity to norms

Norm theory suggests that we learn what kind of behaviour is expected in different situations. Similarly, members of a group learn not only which out-groups are suitable targets for prejudice, but also the form that such prejudice should take – from ignoring them to killing them (e.g. the Ku-Klux-Klan).

THINK ABOUT IT

Try and suggest norms for behaving in the following situations:

● a rock concert
● a church service
● a pub

In different ways we all conform to social norms ▲

Minard (1952) found that black and white miners in Virginia worked well and cooperated together underground. Above ground, however, they did not mix and expressed prejudiced attitudes to each other. What we have here is a **situational norm**. Prejudice did exist, but it was only expressed in certain situations.

Often, the wider culture will provide cultural norms which influence the form prejudice will take and the target group against which it is directed. Pettigrew (1959) found that whites in the southern states of the USA were prejudiced against blacks, but not against other minority groups, and they did not score highly on Adorno's F-scale. Cultural norms, therefore, dictated that it was *blacks* who should be the targets of prejudice: personality factors did not seem to be a major influence.

Once norms of behaviour are established, we can feel great pressures to conform to them (see Chapter 21, *Social Influence*, page 312). This can serve to maintain and spread prejudices once they exist. Pettigrew (1971) suggests that conformity to norms is a major factor in prejudice and that it can be very difficult to resist pressure to conform to a prevailing prejudiced view.

For example, imagine that your colleagues and boss at work are from your ethnic group, and though pleasant enough otherwise, consistently express racist attitudes, use racist terms, and tell racist jokes. How easy would you find it to criticise them or tell them that they were being offensive? You could end up by losing their friendship, cooperation, your chances of promotion – perhaps even your job. So instead you say nothing – perhaps even make the odd racist comment or joke yourself. In this way you end up supporting and adopting racial prejudice.

Social identity theory

Another possible explanation for much of the hostility that groups feel towards each other is that part of our identity lies in our group membership. Tajfel argued that a person's self-image contains both a **personal identity** and a **social identity**. When groups interact, they often do so on the basis of the norms and roles specified for their particular group. So group membership can influence the clothes we wear, the places we go, the things we do, the music we listen to and many other things that contribute to our sense of who we are.

We all like to feel that we are 'OK' people. If we are OK, then the groups we are in must be 'OK' too. It may be that we may increase the value of in-groups, and decrease the value of out-groups, simply out of a sense of insecurity or a need to think well of ourselves. In other words, in-group overevaluation can boost our self-esteem.

At the same time, if we downgrade our opinion of out-groups, we can also feel good about ourselves by **social comparison** ('we' are better than 'them'). This can lead to out-group rejection. This also helps to explain why prejudices can be so hard to change. It is because our own sense of self-worth is bound up with our prejudices. Something which threatens our prejudice may also threaten our self-esteem. This may be why we cling to our prejudices so tightly, and resist, and get angered by, attempts to change them.

Reducing prejudice

As we have seen, prejudices can be socially divisive and destructive. But can anything be done to reduce or overcome them?

A good starting point is to ensure that different groups enjoy *equality before the law*. If the legal system and social institutions are actively prejudiced, there is little hope for improvement. The Race Discrimination Act, the Sex Discrimination Act and the Disability Discrimination Act attempt to give all members of society equal status in the eyes of the law. We should remember that true legal equality is often won only through prolonged struggle. Even now, racial equality is only just beginning to be achieved in South Africa after years of struggle and bloodshed.

Legal equality is an important first step, but it does not guarantee social equality. We should not expect prejudiced attitudes to disappear overnight. Race and sex discrimination are still common in the UK, although people are aware that they have to take care how they practise it. To do away with prejudice requires us to do something very difficult: to change the way that people think and feel about other people. And for all the reasons we have already mentioned – cognitive processing, self-esteem, pressures to conformity – this is not something that can be achieved easily or quickly.

Increasing contact

One way to reduce prejudice may be to encourage **increased contact** between groups. The more that we get to know about different groups, the more likely that our stereotypes will be undermined. It will help us realise that members of other groups are all different from one another, just as members of our own in-group are. Contact with different groups will also help us to realise that people in particular groups are not so very different from people elsewhere. Deutsch and Collins (1951) found that housewives in a mixed housing estate in New York reported decreases in their racial prejudice, whereas housewives in a segregated estate (i.e. where blacks and whites lived apart) in New Jersey reported that their racial prejudice was unchanged, and in some instances, went up.

But increased contact, in itself, is not enough. Remember the case of the miners who showed prejudiced attitudes above ground, despite having regular contact below ground? In a review of the literature, Secord and Backman (1964) concluded that, although prejudice may be reduced in a particular situation by increased contact because stereotypes are disconfirmed, there is often little generalisation to other situations.

Encouraging non-competitive contact

Brown (1988) argued that, for increased contact to be helpful, it should be non-competitive. If groups meet only to compete with each other, prejudice is likely to result – as Sherif's study of the boys at summer camp showed. Members from different groups also need to meet each other under conditions where they share **equal status**. In other words, if you have a low opinion of a particular group, but you only ever encounter them doing low-paid, menial work, this may simply serve to reinforce your prejudice against them. Clearly, the ways in which people are portrayed in the media can have an impact here too.

Positive role models

This also highlights the need for **role models** in society. If a particular group has members who are seen to occupy high-status positions in society, it encourages other members to aim high as well. On the other hand, if for example there are no working-class, black or women judges, members of these groups may feel that being a judge is simply not an occupation they can reasonably aspire to – thereby reinforcing the white, male, middle-class view that these other groups simply haven't got 'what it takes' to hold responsible positions in the community. As a result, prejudice remains firmly entrenched (and judges may reflect a rather narrow body of opinion).

Exposure to high-status role models can raise expectations and aspirations

Promoting cooperation

Earlier in this chapter, we described how prejudices had flared between two rival groups at a boys' summer camp in the USA during an experiment conducted by Sherif et al. But this was not the end of the story.

In the final stage of the experiment, Sherif and his team tried to counter the prejudice they had produced. The first method they used was simply to encourage the two groups of boys to play together without competition. But simply allowing opportunities for non-competitive contact in this way was not effective. The method they eventually found that *did* work to a great extent was to get the boys to cooperate together to achieve something that both groups wanted. This is sometimes referred to as the **pursuit of superordinate goals**. Putting the boys in situations where they had to cooperate with each other – for example, to fix a broken water supply, or to tow their truck up a hill to get it restarted – was found to be quite successful in breaking down 'them-and-us' thinking. As a result, much of the hostility was reduced and many of the boys in the two different groups became friends.

Cooperating to achieve a joint goal can help reduce prejudice ▶

This sort of technique has been tried in schools. Aronson et al. (1978) have described the use of the **jigsaw technique**, where children are put into small learning groups, each containing a mix of children from different ethnic backgrounds. Each group is given a problem to solve. Each child in the group is given a piece of information (part of the jigsaw) that will help solve the problem. The problem can only be solved if all the children in the group pool their resources and work together. In solving problems in this way, children learn to cooperate, not compete, and they develop more positive attitudes towards each other, and to school. But again, researchers have found that, while such techniques can do a lot for attitudes in the classroom, they only have a limited impact in the wider world outside.

Overcoming prejudice through education

Education may help combat prejudice in a number of ways. Ignorance is an important element in prejudice. Educational programmes for reducing prejudice should therefore focus on providing information about out-groups. If people gain an understanding of different cultures and lifestyles and come to appreciate cultural differences as simply providing different ways of being human, they are less likely to fall victim to crude stereotypes and prejudices.

Another method is to let children experience at first hand what it feels like to be on the receiving end of prejudice. In a famous study, schoolteacher Jane Elliot told a class of white schoolchildren that those with brown eyes were inferior to those with blue eyes. Brown-eyed children had to wear collars so that all could see their inferior status. They were ridiculed by the teacher, denied privileges and told not to mix with the blue-eyed children.

The blue-eyed children were delighted at their new superior status, and quickly joined in with ridiculing those with brown eyes. But the following day, the teacher said that she had made a mistake, and that it was the blue-eyed children who were inferior. Now blue-eyed children had to wear collars and face ridicule and denial of privileges.

Not surprisingly, when children were in the group labelled as inferior, they felt greatly upset and their school performance suffered. But interestingly, when the experiment ended, and the children were reunited as one, big, friendly and happy group, the school performance of *all* the children went up.

Interviewed years later as adults, the participants revealed that this experiment had a lasting effect on them. They were not prejudiced against racial groups and they argued that there should be more such experiments in schools.

Elliot's study is one of the few that seems to have produced long-lasting effects that generalise quite widely. Experiencing prejudice at first-hand gave these children an intuitive understanding of just how horrible it can be.

QUESTIONS

1   What ethical criticisms could you make of Jane Elliot's experiment?
2   Give two practical problems associated with research involving children.

We have seen that many attempts to reduce prejudice have a limited impact. This is because these attempts cannot in themselves alter the fact that prejudices are embedded in the wider culture. Outside the schoolroom or workplace, groups are not all treated equally and prejudices are still widespread. Models of prejudiced behaviour still exist for others to learn from and imitate, and norms of prejudice and discrimination still demand conformity. The legal system, the media, and schools all have an important part to play in combatting prejudice – but even so, changing social attitudes is likely to be a very slow process.

TRY THIS

Fill in the gaps in the sentences using the words and phrases listed below:

increased contact   **social identity theory**   **the jigsaw technique**
realistic group conflict theory   **pursuing superordinate goals**   **resources**
norms of competitiveness   **in-group overevaluation**

Sherif's theory, called ...., suggests that prejudice may arise between groups when they are competing for ....

Because of .... groups may believe they are in competition even when they are not.

According to .... the groups that we belong to say something about who we are, and this may result in ....

Deutsch and Collins conclude from their research on housing projects that .... can help reduce prejudice.

Sherif found that .... helped in reducing prejudice, and this has been used in the classroom in what is known as ....

Summary

- Prejudice is an example of an attitude, usually negative. Prejudice involves a combination of thoughts, feelings and behaviours that are hard to change.
- Both the notion of an authoritarian personality, and the notion of the dogmatic person see prejudice as a personality problem.
- Prejudices can be learned through classical and operant conditioning and through observing models. Stereotyping helps explain why prejudices are learned so easily.
- Realistic group conflict theory suggests prejudice is likely to occur between groups when they are competing for resources.
- Social norms and social identity theory also help to explain why prejudices arise and how they are expressed and maintained.
- Reducing prejudice is hard, but increased contact between groups, the pursuit of superordinate goals, and education may all help.

Environmental and Comparative Psychology

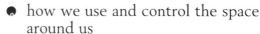

Environmental psychology explores how the physical and social environment affects behaviour. Environmental psychologists are interested in:

- how we use and control the space around us
- how animals and humans mark out and defend territory
- how crowding affects behaviour
- how being part of a crowd affects human behaviour.

The aim of **comparative psychology** is to compare animal and human behaviour in order to further our understanding of human behaviour. Comparative psychologists are interested in:

- how animals learn in their natural environment
- the social behaviour of animals, including territoriality.

Both environmental and comparative psychology use animal research to further our understanding of human behaviour.

25 Personal Space, Privacy and Territory

An Englishman's home is ▲
his castle

Imagine that you are visiting another country for the first time. The people there speak the same language as you, but their behaviour is very different. Instead of queueing for a bus, everyone stands in a crowded circle touching and chatting to each other. How would you cope in such a place? You might feel uncomfortable if you are used to living in a culture in which people generally maintain a greater space or distance between themselves and others.

The concept of personal space

The idea of **personal space** was first introduced by Katz (1937) and has its roots in biology and anthropology (the study of human beings). However, psychological interest in personal space has increased over the last 25 years.

You will know from experience that you adjust your position and distance from others depending on who the 'others' are, what you are doing and where you happen to be.

THINK ABOUT IT

- How do you sit when you are talking with a friend in a café?
- How do you feel when a stranger stands too close to you?
- Do you have a favourite seat in class or at the pub?

What does this tell you about the nature of personal space?

The term **personal space** refers to our *sense of distance between ourselves and others, and how we choose to position ourselves in relation to them.* According to Sommer (1969), personal space is an area with invisible boundaries surrounding your body, into which you do not let other people intrude. It is like an invisible bubble which helps you keep a comfortable distance between yourself and others.

The idea of personal space as an invisible bubble which you carry around with you may seem a bit strange. Your personal space may shrink for friends and family and lovers, and expand for strangers and people in authority. Your sense of personal space is unique to you and has been influenced by the culture in which you have grown up.

TRY THIS

To find out what your own sense of personal space is like, try the following activity:

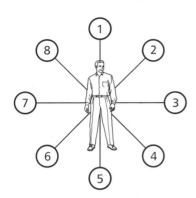

Imagine that you are in the middle of the figure below. Each of the eight numbers represents a door through which someone is about to enter. You are in the centre, facing Door 1, with Door 5 at your back. Make a mark on each of the lines to show how close you would allow a person to come before you felt uncomfortable. Finally, connect up the 8 points you have marked.

You now have the shape of your personal space. How does it compare with the shape of other people's personal space?

Why do we need to have personal space?
Psychologists believe that having a sense of personal space helps in a number of ways:

● **preventing stimulus overload:** personal space helps us to maintain distance from others and to avoid being exposed to too many sights and sounds

● **behavioural freedom:** personal space helps to ensure that our behaviour is not controlled by others

● **communication:** personal space can be used as a form of non-verbal communication.

Based on American research, Hall (1966) suggested that there are four types of personal space **zones** that we use in our interaction with others. The zones are described in the table below:

Hall, E.T. , *The Hidden Dimension* (Doubleday, New York, 1966)

Zone	Description	Distance	Activities
Intimate Distance	appropriate for close or intimate friends	0–50 cm	comforting, making love, wrestling
Personal Distance	used with friends and acquaintances	50 cm – 1.2m	conversations, eating out
Social Distance	used in conducting business interactions	1.2m – 5.1m	discussions with employer or clients; job interview
Public Distance	used for public meetings, interactions with public figures	5.1m –	rock concert, public lecture

TRY THIS

Check that you understand what you have read by filling in the gaps in the sentences, using the words listed below.

- **communicate**
- **four**
- **intimate**
- **the environment and human behaviour**
- **invisible bubble**
- **information overload**

Environmental psychologists are interested in studying the relationship between
....

Personal space can be thought of as an .... Our personal space helps us to prevent .... and to help us .... with others.

There are .... different zones which we use in interacting with others.

.... distance is the distance we use for interacting with our loved ones.

Factors affecting personal space

There are a number of factors which influence your sense of personal space. These factors include:

- culture
- gender
- age
- personality.

Cultural differences

Research suggests that culture may affect the distance we maintain in our interactions with others. Hall (1966) carried out several cross-cultural studies on personal space. He found that people from contact cultures such as the Mediterranean, Arabic and Hispanic cultures, interact at closer distances than North Europeans and North Americans. Arabs, for example, tend to have conversations at a distance of only 30 cm, while Americans tend to talk to each other at 1–3.5 metres.

KEY STUDY Little (1968) investigated the interaction distances of university students in five different countries: Scotland, Sweden, Italy, Greece and the USA. Participants were asked to arrange several pairs of small plastic dolls so that they looked 'natural' and were facing each other and making eye-contact. The psychologists then recorded the average distance between the dolls for each of the students. The results showed that the Mediterranean students placed the dolls much closer together than the North Europeans. The results are shown below:

Country	Interaction distance (cm)
Sweden	30
Italy	27
Greece	23
USA	30
Scotland	35

Source:
Little, K.B., Cultural
Variations in Social
Schemata' in *Journal of
Personality and Social
Psychology*, 10 (1968),
pp.1–7

Questions

1. What is the dependent variable in this study?
2. This study was carried out in a laboratory setting. Give one advantage of studying personal space in a lab setting.
3. Suggest two problems that psychologists might face in carrying out cross-cultural research on personal space.

Gender differences

Research suggests that gender also influences our sense of personal space, and that females tend to interact with other females at closer distances than males do with other males. However, when the pairing is male and female, females tend to prefer larger distances than males.

There is also research to suggest that the personal space of men and women has different 'shapes'. For example, Fisher and Bryne (1975) conducted an experiment in which a confederate sat down close to a student who was studying in a library. They found that regardless of the gender of the confederate, male participants felt more threatened when the confederate sat opposite. Female participants felt more threatened when the 'confederate' sat down next to them.

THINK ABOUT IT

Can you think of any reasons why male participants felt more threatened when the confederate sat opposite?

Age differences

Psychologists have found that younger children interact at closer distances than older children or adults. According to a study by Aeillo and Aeillo (1974), after the age of six the rule seems to be that the older the child, the larger the social distance. The results of the study are shown below:

Aiello, J.R., & Aiello, T., 'The Development of Personal Space: proximic behaviour of children 6 through 16', *Human Ecology*, 2 (1974), pp.177–189.

After the age of six , children prefer to put greater social distance between themselves and other people ▶

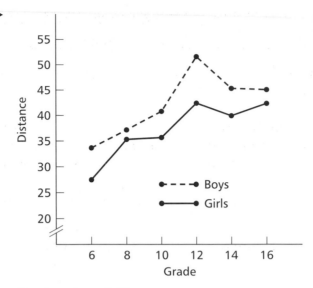

Personality differences

One other factor which may influence the amount of personal space maintained in social interactions is personality. The research seems to suggest that certain types of people prefer rather larger personal distances when interacting with others. The aspects of personality which affect personal space are:

Aspect of personality	Description
Extraversion–introversion	● introverts prefer larger distances
Levels of anxiety	● anxious people prefer larger distances
Self-esteem	● people with low self-esteem prefer larger distances
Locus of control *(the degree to which people believe that internal or external factors control the things that happen to them)*	● people with an external locus of control (who believe that the things that happen to them are due to luck or fate) prefer larger distances

Space invasion

How do you deal with a situation when someone invades your personal space and gets too close for comfort? One strategy is to try to escape from the situation. Konecni et al. (1975) arranged for a same-sex confederate to stand on the same side of a street either 1, 2, 5 or 10 feet from a person waiting to cross. The researcher found that the closer the confederate stood, the quicker the other person crossed the street. Participants in the study dealt with having their space invaded by leaving the scene as quickly as possible.

TRY THIS

Check your understanding by filling the gaps in the following brief summary. Choose from the following terms:

- anxiety
- females
- males
- contact cultures
- external locus of control
- self-esteem
- younger
- internal locus of control
- extraversion–introversion

Cultures which permit or encourage physical closeness between people are known as ....

Research suggests that in general .... interact at closer distances than ....

In terms of age, the .... the child, the smaller the social distancing.

There are a number of personality factors at play in personal distancing, including .... and ....

Feeling control over what happens to us is known as .... and encourages closer distancing.

Having your space invaded can also increase your level of arousal. Middlemist et al. (1976) carrried out a field experiment in a men's urinal (you may like to reflect on the ethics of this particular piece of research!). For half of the participants, the confederates used a urinal which was next to the one the participants were using. For the other half, the confederates used a urinal further away. What emerged was that the closer the confederate, the longer it took the participant to begin to urinate and the faster to finish. Both of these behaviours are signs of stress.

However, not all 'space invasions' are negative experiences. Sometimes the situation dictates whether interacting with someone at close range is a good or a bad experience. If a 'friendly' stranger invades your personal space, the evidence seems to show that you are less likely to feel threatened. This is described on page 380.

THINK ABOUT IT

In a crowded lift a stranger is standing too close to you for comfort. What are some of the ways you might try to deal with this?

Most people say that they would turn away, avoid eye contact, count the rivets in the roof or show signs of physical withdrawal like folding their arms.

In a study by Storms and Thomas (1977) male confederates sat either 6 inches or 30 inches away from a male university student. The confederate treated half of the students in a friendly way, the other half in an unfriendly way. The researchers measured how much the students reported liking the confederate. They found that the friendly confederate was liked the best, even though he had potentially invaded their sense of personal space by only sitting 6 inches away. The unfriendly confederate was liked less when he sat close rather than when he sat farther away.

Applications of personal space

Earlier in this chapter we outlined Hall's work on the four personal distance zones.

- Which zone do you think would lead to the best results in a learning situation?
- Which zone would be most effective for a doctor/patient or therapist/client situation?

Questions like these have stimulated psychologists to study the practical implications of personal space.

In a well-known study, Sommer (1979) found that there was a relationship between *where* students sat in a classroom and the marks they received. He carried out a correlation study which showed that students who sat in the middle or front section of the classroom received more attention from the teacher, were more likely to participate in the classroom activities and also received better marks. The figures below show how seating position affected student participation. As you can see, the participation rates were higher for students sitting in the front row and in the middle row.

In summary

- Personal space is like an invisible 'bubble' of distance between ourselves and others

- Each of us has a unique or individual sense of personal space

- Our sense of personal space is affected by a number of factors including personality, culture, gender, and age

- The sense of personal space is relevant to activities such as teaching and doctor–patient relationships.

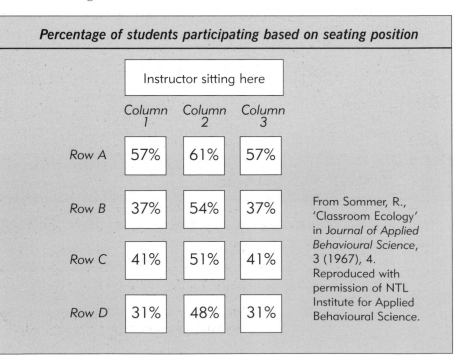

Percentage of students participating based on seating position

Instructor sitting here

	Column 1	Column 2	Column 3
Row A	57%	61%	57%
Row B	37%	54%	37%
Row C	41%	51%	41%
Row D	31%	48%	31%

From Sommer, R., 'Classroom Ecology' in *Journal of Applied Behavioural Science*, 3 (1967), 4. Reproduced with permission of NTL Institute for Applied Behavioural Science.

Sommer suggested that this happens because students at the side of the classroom may have more difficulty in seeing and hearing the teacher. Students at the side of the room may have less eye-contact and less communication with the teacher. They may also be less motivated than students who sit near the front.

More recent research has confirmed that the most effective zone for teacher–student interaction is at either 'personal' or 'intimate' distance. It seems that when it comes to learning and study, proximity is a bonus!

Psychologists have also studied the most effective distances for doctor–patient and therapist–client interactions. The research shows that the most productive distance is an intermediate one. Stone and Mordenn (1976) asked university participants to talk about personal issues with therapists at various distances: 2 feet, 5 feet and 9 feet. They found that students were more comfortable and more willing to give the most information at 5 feet.

THINK ABOUT IT

- If you hadn't prepared your work for a lesson and wanted to avoid being asked a question by the teacher, where in the class would you be most likely to sit?

- Have you noticed that people on a bus tend to put their belongings on the seat next to them so that no one else can sit down? Why do you think they do this?

Mind if I join you?

Territory

According to environmental psychologists, we spread out our belongings in order to protect our territory. In the previous section, personal space was compared to a 'bubble' – an area that surrounds your body. In this sense it is quite different from the concept of **territory**. Personal space is invisible and also portable, in that you carry it around with you. A territory tends to have clear boundaries and is usually a physical space which individuals or groups feel they own. Territories also tend to be larger than personal space. So a territory can be defined as *a physical area which is owned or controlled by a person or group*.

You probably feel that you already have an idea of what a territory is, and can probably think of a number of examples of how we defend territory:

- always sitting in the same seat in a classroom or pub
- having hedges or fences which mark the boundaries of your property
- personalising the physical space that you use by pinning up photographs and pictures
- marking off your territory on a crowded beach with a wind-breaker, deckchairs and strategically-placed towels.

A teenager's bedroom is an example of primary territory ▲

A school classroom is an example of secondary territory ▲

A crowded tube train is an example of public territory ▲

Territory, therefore, is any space which you 'own' to some degree – either permanently or temporarily. **Territoriality** is the tendency to defend or protect your space against intruders.

Types of territory

According to Altman (1975) there are three main types of territories which we use:

1 **Primary territory:** this type of territory is owned on a relatively permanent basis and is seen as being central to the day- to-day lives of the occupants. **Examples**: your home, your bedroom

2 **Secondary territory:** this is a territory which is shared with others but which is regarded to a degree as being 'yours'. **Examples**: classroom, seat in pub

3 **Public territory:** a space or area which belongs to everyone and is occupied on a 'first-come, first-served' basis. **Examples**: train carriage, doctor's waiting room

The research on territories has revealed a number of interesting things about our behaviour:

1. The habit of personalising territories

Practically everyone personalises their primary territories in some way or other. But people also tend to personalise some of their secondary territories. For example:

● locals sometimes keep a personalised mug in their pub

● churchgoers have been known to 'reserve' their pew by leaving a personal prayerbook or Bible there.

Personalising a territory is simply asserting your control over it. Hansen and Altman (1976), for example, found that students who dropped out of university had previously displayed fewer personal items in dormitory rooms or in their flats. The study suggests that these students did not feel a sense of ownership over their physical space.

2. Home ground advantage

Territorial dominance refers to the fact that an individual or team of people dominates interactions with others because the interaction is all taking place on their own territory. For example, Coleman (1968) reported that his patients appeared submissive when consulting him in his doctor's surgery, but when he made house calls, they were more confident and assertive.

In competitive sports, territorial dominance is better known as **home ground advantage**. It is widely recognised among sportspersons that teams competing on home ground tend to have an advantage and that this leads to a higher number of 'home wins'.

This could be because the home-team players usually have more support in the crowd and are more familiar with the physical playing

In competitive sports like baseball, 'home teams' usually score a greater number of wins, due to confidence and familiarity of being on home ground

area. Schwartz and Barsky (1977) analysed the results of 1,880 baseball games, 182 professional football games and 542 professional hockey games. Their analysis showed that there was a home advantage for all sports, in that teams won more home games than they lost.

3. *Defensible space*

According to Oscar Newman (1972) we can be affected by the architecture and style of the buildings we live in. The key to his theory was the idea of **defensible space**. A defensible space is *any space which is arranged in such a way that crime is deterred and residents can keep a watch on it*. Newman had noticed that certain types of buildings were particularly prone to vandalism and crime – especially high-rise flats in inner-city areas, where there were many public areas which could not be supervised, such as stairwells and lifts. In many of these areas, special groups had been formed to defend their shared property against theft and vandalism by non-residents.

High-rise flats in inner-city areas are particularly vulnerable to crime and vandalism

Newman's work was based largely on the Pruitt–Igoe housing project in America. The project consisted of 277,764 apartments for low-income families. Each building contained over 80 dwellings. Within three years of opening, the project had a vacancy rate of up to 70% and was crime-ridden. Because of the number of people living in the project, it was impossible to tell residents from non-residents. The buildings were built on open ground with no territorial boundaries between them. Each building had several entrances and surveillance of who came and went was minimal.

One building, however, was an exception. The residents in this building made use of a chain link fence which had been left by the builders to protect the area around their building. In Newman's terms, the fence provided the residents with defensible space. As a result, the level of vandalism in that building decreased significantly and the vacancy rate was only 5%.

Newman's research showed that if a housing development was to be safe and secure, it needed to be thought of as a **zone of territorial influence**; that is, it should look as if it belonged to the residents, and there should be ways in which areas such as entrances could be kept under watch.

383

One effect of marking out our territory is that it may help to protect us from crime. In 1979, Brown compared the external appearance of homes that had been burgled with homes that had not been broken into. She found that symbolic barriers had played a part in protection and that houses which had not been broken into typically had name and address signs, hedges and rock borders. It seemed therefore that territorial markers could operate as boundaries and keep away intruders.

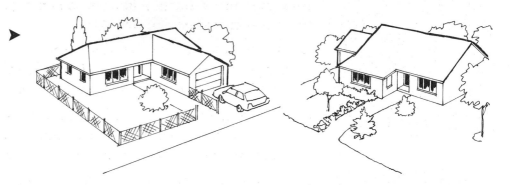

Symbolic barriers such as the fence around the left-hand house make it less likely to be burgled than the house on the right.

Summary

- A territory is defined as a physical area which is owned or controlled by a person or group.
- The difference between personal space and territory is that personal space is an invisible bubble which moves around with the person, while territory refers to a fixed space.
- There are three different types of territories: primary, secondary and public.
- Defensible space is a space which can be protected or defended by others.

26 Crowds and Crowding

Top: a high-density urban environment

Below: a sparsely populated low-density environment

An important distinction in environmental psychology is between the terms **crowding** and **density**:

- **Density** is an *objective* measure of the amount of physical space per person. For example, density could refer to the number of people per room or the number of people within a dwelling.

- **Crowding** refers to the *subjective* or personal feeling of there being too many people within a given space. Crowding depends on the person's subjective appraisal of the situation.

For example, imagine you are sunbathing on a secluded part of a beach (low density) and someone decides to set up camp right next to you. In this situation, you may experience a sense of crowding. However, if you attend a rock concert where you are packed elbow-to-elbow with hundreds of other people (high density), you may not be aware of being crowded in this situation.

The effects of high density

One way of investigating the effects of high density has been through animal research, usually in a laboratory setting. The results suggest that – for animals at least – high density has negative effects. The following key study is a good example of the type of animal research that has been carried out.

KEY STUDY Calhoun (1962) built an enclosed area which could house 48 rats. The enclosure consisted of a 10ft x 14ft platform which was divided into four cells as shown in the diagram on page 386.

In the enclosure, there were ramps which connected all the pens except Pens 1 and 4. This resulted in the animals crowding into the other two pens. Calhoun called these two pens 'behavioural sinks'. Adequate food and water was presented and the number of rats soon increased to 80. Calhoun found that the rats engaged in a number of unusual behaviours. For example, the male rats showed a significant increase in sexual activity. The female rats were not very successful in rearing their young and many of the pups died. Some of the adult rats resorted to cannabalism. Calhoun concluded that the changes in the rats' social behaviour was due to high density.

'Calhoun's pens' – an
experimental environment
developed by Calhoun to
explore the effect on rodents
of high-density living
conditions

Reproduced with
permission of Ikliyo Tagawa
Garber

Questions

1. What was one effect of high density on these animals?
2. Give one problem with generalising results from animal studies to humans.
3. How appropriate is it to generalise from Calhoun's research to humans?

Source:
Calhoun, J.B., 'Population
Density and Social
Pathology', in *Scientific
American*, 206 (1962),
pp.139–48

Another study by Calhoun (1973) also demonstrated the negative effects of crowding in animals. In this study, mice were placed in a large enclosure. They were provided with enough food and water for 4,000 mice. However, Calhoun found that the population did not increase beyond 2,200. Once the population reached 2,200, the pups began to die and the adults were not able to reproduce successfully. As a result, the colony became extinct. As Calhoun points out, the extinction of the colony could only have been due to overcrowding since there were no predators and adequate food and water were provided.

Crowding and stress

So, if overcrowding in rats produces negative effects, what about other species? Christian et al. (1960) studied how density affected the population of deer in a natural setting. Again, there was plenty of food available, and the number of deer increased to 300. However, two years later, half of the population died and the size of the population declined to 80. Autopsies carried out on the animals showed that their adrenal glands were enlarged, suggesting the animals had experienced prolonged stress.

QUESTIONS

1 What is one problem with studying the effects of crowding in a **laboratory** environment?
2 What is one problem with studying the effects of crowding in a **natural** environment?

Crowding experiments on humans

The animal research led researchers to predict that high density would also have negative effects in humans. One of the first crowding experiments with human participants was carried out by Freedman et al. (1971). The researchers divided groups of all-male or all-female students into groups of 5 or 9 and placed them in rooms of 35, 80 or 160 square feet. The participants were given a number of tasks to perform, such as proof-reading and counting rapid clicks. Much to their surprise, the researchers found that the difference in density did not affect the participants' performance on the tasks.

However, other research suggests that high density *can* affect human behaviour. Density may lead to the experience of crowding when density:

● interferes with our goals
● leads to information overload
● prevents us from controlling outcomes or predicting future events.

One laboratory experiment showed that, in common with other environmental stressors, crowding can have **after-effects**. Sherrod (1974) asked female participants to work in groups of eight on various tasks, in either a large or small room. In one condition, the participants were provided with a sense of control by being told that they could leave the room if they wanted to. The initial results showed that neither density nor a sense of control affected task performance. However, when the same participants were asked to work on another task in a large room, the results showed that participants who had previously experienced crowding (being in the small room) and were not told they could leave the room, showed poorer performance of their task. The study suggested that although being exposed to crowding may not have immediate effects, it can affect *later* performance.

Rodin et al. (1979) found that a sense of control also affected participants' experience of being in a crowded lift. Participants who were standing near the control panels in the lift reported feeling less crowded and perceived the lift as being larger than participants who were not close to the control panel.

Corridors or suites?

A number of studies on crowding have been carried out on university students living in halls of residence. Some halls of residence consisted of long corridors with 30–40 students on each corridor. The students' rooms opened straight onto the corridor:

In a study of the effects of crowding, it was found that people standing closest to the control panel of a lift felt 'less crowded' than those further away

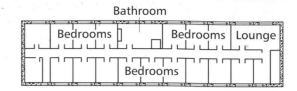

Other halls of residence were built in 'suites', with six residents sharing a lounge area and a bathroom, as shown below:

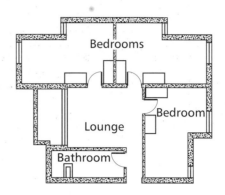

In summary

- **Density** *refers to the amount of physical space per person, while* **crowding** *refers to the subjective feeling that there are too many people within a space.*

- *Animal studies have revealed a number of negative effects of high density, including difficulties in reproduction, infant mortality and, in extreme cases, extinction.*

- *Early research on the effects of high density in human participants suggested that density did not affect behaviour. More recent research indicates that high density can increase physiological arousal, decrease willingness to help others and give rise to after-effects in task performance.*

Baum and Valins (1977) investigated the environmental effects of corridors versus suites. Both living arrangements were identical in terms of the amount of space per person and the number of residents on each floor. In both designs, students had to share a bedroom with one other student. However, Baum and Valins found a number of differences in how students responded.

For example, students living on corridors:

- felt more crowded
- felt they experienced more unwanted interactions with others
- were more likely to report a desire to avoid other people
- performed worse on laboratory tasks that required co-operation.

Research has also been carried out on university students who, because of accommodation shortages, have been required to 'triple up' (i.e. live as a group of three in rooms originally designed for two). Karlin et al. (1978) found that students who were 'tripling up' experienced more stress and felt they had less control over the environment. Furthermore, these effects disappeared when the students returned to sharing with just one other person.

Of course, university students living in cramped conditions are not the only people who complain of feeling crowded. Research suggests that simply *expecting* a crowd (even if one does not actually materialise) is enough to cause stress. Baum and Koman (1976) observed the behaviour of participants who were expecting either a small or large group of people to appear. Participants who were anticipating the larger group reported feeling less comfortable and more crowded, and tended to sit in corners away from people.

Crowding: behavioural and emotional aspects

So far we have focused on the situational factors associated with crowding. However, research by Montano and Adamopoulous (1984) provides an overview of the **behavioural** and **emotional** (affective) consequences of crowding.

According to their research, there are four situations which make people feel crowded, three associated emotional responses and five associated behavioural responses. These are summarised below:

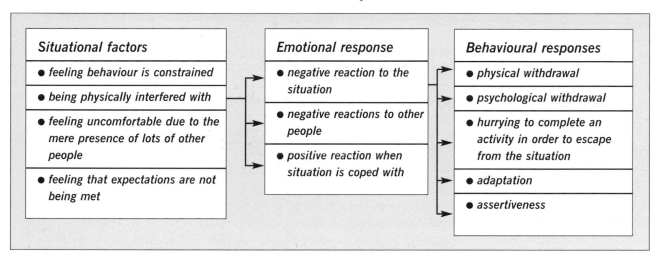

Situational factors	Emotional response	Behavioural responses
• feeling behaviour is constrained	• negative reaction to the situation	• physical withdrawal
• being physically interfered with	• negative reactions to other people	• psychological withdrawal
• feeling uncomfortable due to the mere presence of lots of other people	• positive reaction when situation is coped with	• hurrying to complete an activity in order to escape from the situation
• feeling that expectations are not being met		• adaptation
		• assertiveness

The table clearly shows that crowding produces a number of negative reactions, both to other people and to the crowding situation itself. There is some evidence to support this. Bickman et al. (1973) found that high density affected people's willingness to help others. The researchers 'dropped' envelopes which were stamped and addressed in a number of halls of residence which varied in terms of density. Some of the students were living in halls with high density, while others lived in halls with medium or low density. Helping behaviour was measured by the number of envelopes which were picked up and posted. The results are shown below:

	Density		
	High	*Medium*	*Low*
Percentage of people who posted envelopes	58%	79%	88%

THINK ABOUT IT

Do you think that retrieving an envelope is a good measure of helping behaviour? Explain your answer.

TRY THIS

Match up the **situational factors** which create the experience of crowding with the appropriate everyday **examples:**

Situational factor	*Example*
feeling behaviour is constrained	not being able to appreciate watching a sports event because there are too many spectators
expectations not being fulfilled	being bumped into by other people on a crowded tube train
feeling physically interfered with	feeling distressed in a crowded lift
feeling uncomfortable due to physical presence of other people	being unable to move from a seat on a crowded train

Finally, research suggests that high density can result in an increase in physiological arousal. For example, Evans (1979) asked participants to volunteer for a study which would last over three hours. The participants were grouped in either a small or large room. The researchers recorded the participants' blood pressure and heart rate before and after the experiment. The results revealed higher levels of arousal in the high-density condition.

Most of the research described above identifies the negative effects of high density on humans. However, not everyone is affected in the same way by high density. Individual differences such as personality, age and gender may also influence a person's response to density.

Crowd behaviour

THINK ABOUT IT

What is your idea of a crowd? When does a **group** of people become a **crowd**? How does your behaviour change when you are part of a crowd?

Psychologists use the term **crowd** to refer to a *substantial number of people (often strangers) who are in the same place at the same time* and who often engage in 'unusual' behaviour. You will know from personal experience that crowds can behave in irrational ways!

One of the first researchers to study how being part of a crowd can affect behaviour was Le Bon (1895). He believed that when a person becomes part of a crowd, their behaviour is influenced by more primitive instincts. According to Le Bon, when a person joins a crowd he:

'descends several rungs in the ladder of civilisation. Isolated, he may be a cultivated individual; in a crowd, he is a barbarian – that is a creature acting by instinct.'[25]

Le Bon identified three characteristics of crowds which affect human behaviour:

- **anonymity**: loss of individual identity; there is a decline in the person's sense of responsibility for their actions since they are unlikely to be identified

- **contagion**: this occurs when an idea or behaviour spreads very quickly throughout a crowd (e.g. like a 'Mexican wave')

- **suggestibility**: this occurs when the unconscious or instinctual parts of the personality influence the person's behaviour.

Le Bon's concept of anonymity was later replaced by the term **deindividuation** (Festinger, 1952). Deindividuation occurs when a person loses their sense of individual identity because they are part of a group. Festinger et al. (1952) investigated the nature of deindividuation in a laboratory experiment. University students were invited to take part in a group discussion under one of two conditions. In the deindividuation condition, participants were asked to wear a large grey coat, and the discussion took place in a room with very dim lighting. In the other condition, participants were in a well-lit room and were not asked to wear a grey coat. During the discussion, the participants were encouraged to make hostile remarks about their parents. The researchers found that participants in the deindividuation condition were more willing to make hostile remarks than the other participants.

Zimbardo (1969) also investigated the effects of deindividuation by asking female participants to give electric shocks to a confederate (in reality, no shocks were given). In one condition, the participants were placed in a dimly lit room and wore white coats and hoods which covered their faces. In another condition, the participants were placed

In Zimbardo's study of deindividuation, participants wore white hoods to mask their identity. Robbed of their individuality, they were found to be more willing to inflict pain than participants who could be identified

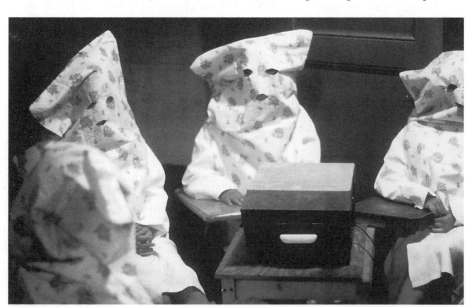

in a well-lit room, dressed in their own clothes, and given a large name-tag to wear. Zimbardo found that the deindividuated participants were more willing to administer electric shocks to the confederate and pressed the shock button for twice as long as the participants who could be easily identified.

THINK ABOUT IT

Why was it important that all the participants were the same gender?

Crowd baiting

There is evidence that deindividuation also occurs outside of the laboratory environment. In the USA, Mann (1981) carried out an analysis of newspaper reports of 'crowd baiting'. He found that when someone was threatening to jump from a building, a crowd would often gather to egg them on. In many cases, the crowd would begin chanting, 'Jump! Jump!' to the person who was deciding whether or not to end their life. The analysis revealed that there were several factors which influenced this behaviour:

- **size of the crowd:** crowd baiting was more likely to happen when the crowd size approached 300
- **time of day:** the behaviour was most likely to occur in fading light
- **distance from the victim:** crowd baiting was most likely to occur if the victim was between the 8th and 12th floor of the building
- **size of city**: crowd baiting was more likely to occur in large cities.

THINK ABOUT IT

Using your knowledge of crowd behaviour, why do you think most crowd baiting occurs in large cities?

Hysterical contagion

Le Bon's concept of contagion, whereby ideas and behaviours spread quickly through a crowd, has been supported by a number of studies. There are several recorded cases of mysterious illnesses sweeping through a school or a factory. When medical investigators have been called in to find the physical cause of the epidemic, they have often been unable to find anything. Psychologists use the term **hysterical contagion** to explain why group members experience physical symptoms such as nausea and dizziness which have no physical cause. Psychologists suggest these symptoms are the result of social influence.

For example, in the USA in June, 1962, a number of female employees in a factory (62 out of a workforce of 200) reported being bitten by an insect and experienced nausea, a rash and numbness. When health officials searched the factory for the offending creature, they found five ordinary insects, none of which could have caused the women's symptoms. When the women were asked to describe the insect which bit them, some of them described it as a small black bug while others described it as a white insect. The epidemic occurred during a period of great stress within the factory. A new supervisor had just been appointed and most of the women were working overtime to meet production deadlines. The first women who reported being bitten were 'social isolates' who did not have many friends at work and were not very popular. Then the 'bug' seemed to spread to other women. The researchers (Kerchoff and Beck, 1962) concluded that this was an example of hysterical contagion, and that the mysterious illness caused by the 'bug' unconsciously allowed the women to express their stress and anxiety.

In conclusion, research supports the notion that being part of a crowd encourages people to engage in behaviour that they would never engage in if they were alone. Le Bon's description of a civilised, cultivated person being transformed into a creature acting by instinct does seem appropriate.

Summary

- The term 'crowd' is used to refer to a group of people (usually strangers) who engage in particular forms of behaviour.
- Le Bon (1895) was the first person to study crowd behaviour and identified three features of a crowd which affect behaviour: anonymity, contagion and suggestibility.
- Festinger (1952) introduced the concept of deindividuation and showed how people change their behaviour when they are anonymous.
- Zimbardo's research showed that deindividuation may encourage people to lose their sense of individual responsibility and self-restraint.

27 Comparative Psychology: Other Research Using Animals

A chimpanzee uses a
stick as tool to capture
ants in an anthill ▲

Comparative psychology developed from the work of the behaviourists and the ethologists. In this chapter the findings from ethological research are explained and applied to how animals learn in their natural environment. The chapter focuses on why psychologists study animals and how this research can help us to understand human behaviour.

Why do psychologists study animal behaviour?

Imagine you are watching a wildlife programme on TV. The camera is following a chimpanzee who is looking for food. The chimpanzee finds a large nut which is too hard to open with his mouth or teeth. The nut is also too hard to be cracked open with a bit of wood. The chimpanzee walks for about 80 metres to another tree and retrieves a large piece of granite that he had used earlier to open a nut. He then lodges the nut between two rocks and cracks it open using the granite. Why are we surprised at this animal's ability to locate and access food?

Psychologists are interested in studying animal behaviour for a number of reasons. First, studying animal behaviour can help us to understand human behaviour because we can make comparisons between what animals do and what humans do. Secondly, animal behaviour is fascinating in its own right both to researchers and to ordinary people. Millions of television viewers tune in each week to programmes like *Wildlife on One* and *The Natural World*.

Another reason why psychologists are interested in animal behaviour is a practical one: in many instances, it is easier to study animals than humans. For example, most of the research on learning has been carried out an animals. It is no wonder, then, that psychologists are interested in understanding how animals acquire certain behaviours and how they adapt to their environment.

What is comparative psychology?

Comparative psychology involves studying the behaviour patterns of different species in order to develop general principles to explain their actions. The main aim of comparative psychology is to compare animals and humans in order to reach a better understanding of human behaviour.

Comparative psychology developed from two other disciplines:

● **behaviourism** (see Chapter 7, *The Behavioural Approach*, page 54)
● **ethology** – the study of animals in their natural habitat.

Given that ethology played an important role in the development of comparative psychology, it is worth describing in some detail the aims and methods of ethological research.

Ethology

Ethology can be defined as the scientific study of animals in their natural environment. As a discipline, it developed largely in Europe and many of the researchers were trained biologists. These researchers observed a variety of animals in nature. When they did conduct experiments, they attempted to simulate the animal's natural setting.

Famous ethologists include:

● Konrad Lorenz (1903–89)

● Karl von Frisch (1886–1982)

● Niko Tinbergen (1907–88)

Both ethologists and comparative psychologists are interested in explaining *how* animals behave as well as *why* they behave in certain ways. According to Tinbergen (1963), there are four different ways of answering 'why' animals behave in certain ways. These four questions involve asking about:

● the **function** of a behaviour: how the behaviour helps the animal to adapt or survive
● the **mechanism** of a behaviour: what causes or triggers a behaviour
● how a particular behaviour has **developed** within the individual
● how the behaviour has **evolved** from the animal's ancestors.

In general, ethologists focused on **species–specific** behaviour (behaviour patterns which are consistent within the same species). Early ethologists recognised that there were regularities in the behaviour patterns of animals. They observed that an animal will perform the same behaviour pattern over and over again. They also recognised that different members of the same species behave in a very similar way.

The early ethologists believed that a lot of animal behaviour was **instinctive** (innate) and not influenced to any great degree by learning. Lorenz observed similar behaviour patterns in different species. For example, the courtship behaviour of different species of ducks was very similar, even though their habitat was different.

Lorenz suggested that the behaviour patterns of animals could be divided into two types:

- instinctive
- learned.

Instinctive patterns were inherited and did not depend on experience. Learned behaviour patterns were acquired and were dependent on experience.

The concept of instinct persisted until the 1950s and 1960s. However, a limitation of the concept is that it is not possible to categorise behaviour patterns into inherited ones or learned ones. Most behaviour is influenced by both factors.

Despite the limitations of the concept of instinct, it is possible to identify a number of important generalisations from the ethological research:

- some behaviour patterns are expressed in exactly the same way by all members of the same species under similar conditions
- a behavioural response can be triggered by a very simple stimulus.

THINK ABOUT IT

Lorenz and Tinbergen (1938) studied the 'egg-retrieval' response of the greylag goose. The greylag goose lays its nest on the ground. The nest is made of grass and shaped like a bowl. On occasions, if an egg rolls out of the nest, the egg-retrieval response is triggered. Lorenz and Tinbergen observed that the goose retrieves the egg in an orderly or stereotyped way. For example, the goose will:

- turn to face the egg
- extend its neck outward so that its head is just above the egg
- place the underside of its bill against the egg
- roll the egg backwards.

Lorenz and Tinbergen found that even if the goose loses contact with the egg, it will continue to move backwards towards the nest. Furthermore, if the egg was removed by the researchers, the goose continued to perform the entire egg-retrieval response. In other words, once the response had been initiated it had to be completed – even if the egg had disappeared!

What stimulates the egg retrieval response?

The egg-retrieval response is not unique to the greylag goose. In fact, a similar response can be observed in all ground-nesting birds.

Observations such as the egg-retrieval response led Lorenz and others to put forward the notion of a **fixed pattern action (FAP)**. This is an innate behaviour pattern which is spontaneous and consistent among all members of a species. Lorenz suggested that fixed action patterns have a number of characteristics:

- the behaviour usually appears in the same form or pattern
- every member of a species generally behaves in the same way (the behaviour is **species–specific**)
- the behaviour will occur in animals even if they have been isolated or prevented from practising the behaviour
- the behaviour is usually triggered off by a specific stimulus
- once triggered, it is inflexible and will not change even if the situation changes
- it serves only one purpose; it will not be used in other contexts even if the behaviour would be appropriate

In fact, not all behaviour patterns are as rigid as Lorenz suggested, even though they follow essentially the same script. Dawkins and Dawkins (1974), for example, showed that while the drinking behaviour of chicks follows an identical pattern, there is some variation in the time intervals between drinks (rather like a group of drinking companions in a pub, where one or two always drink faster than the rest). Barlow (1977) suggested that because of these differences we should talk of **modal action patterns (MAPs)** – meaning that, although the sequence of behaviour is ultimately the same, it is not as fixed and identical as Lorenz originally suggested. The concept of a modal action pattern is a more flexible concept and allows for differences in terms of how individual members of a species adapt to their environment.

We can see from this that ethologists are interested in studying the consistency of behavioural patterns among individuals of the same species. They are also interested in comparing species to see if there are similar patterns of behaviour.

Ethologists also recognised that a behavioural response can be triggered by a very simple stimulus. For example, the female tick can survive in a trance-like state for 18 years without a meal. This trance-like state can be broken by the odour of a particular acid which is given off by the skin glands of mammals (von Uexkull, 1934). Once the female tick locates the smell of the acid, she is instantly ready to find her meal. She will locate her host and use temperature and tactile cues to help her find an appropriate place to burrow in. To appreciate the way that simple stimuli can trigger complex behaviour, read the following Key Study.

KEY STUDY

Male stickleback (left) in the 'threat' position ▲

Pelkwijk and Tinbergen (1937) studied the fighting responses of male sticklebacks, a species of small fish. When a male stickleback enters the territory of another male, the following response was observed:

'Not only do they dart towards the opponent with raised dorsal spines and opened mouth, ready to bite, but, when the opponent does not flee at once but resists, the owner of the territory does not actually bite, but points its head down and standing vertically in the water, makes some jerky movements as if it were going to bore its snout into the water. Often it erects one or both ventral spines.'

So if one male assumed the threat position, the other male would attack him. Under experimental conditions, male sticklebacks were placed in glass tubes and exposed to other males in a number of postures. The only posture which triggered an attack was the vertical posture.

Pelkwijk and Tinbergen also presented male sticklebacks with a number of models like the ones shown below. They were interested to identify which features of the model (colour, shape or size) triggered an attack.

In experimental conditions, sticklebacks in the vertical posture would be attacked ▶

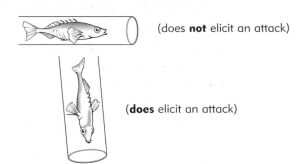

(does **not** elicit an attack)

(**does** elicit an attack)

They found that the important feature was the presence of a red belly. The shape or size of the model did not matter. Even unrealistic-looking models would be attacked if the red belly colour was present. Pelkwijk and Tinbergen concluded that the male stickleback's fighting behaviour was caused by two stimuli: posture and the colour of the belly.

Source:
Pelkwijk, J., Ter, J. & Tinbergen, N., 'Einer Eizbiologische Analyse Einiger Verhaltensweisen von Gasterosteus Aculeatus', *L. Zeitschrift für Tierpsychologie*, 1, pp.193–204

Even unrealistic models would be attacked if the red belly colour was present ▶

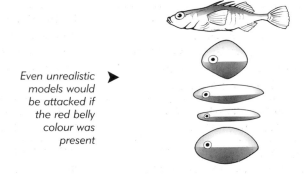

Questions
1. Which stimuli cause fighting behaviour in the male stickleback?
2. Give one advantage of studying animals in the laboratory.

Sign stimuli
The stickleback's threat posture is another example of a fixed action pattern. This vertical posture is performed by all males of the species, and the response is stereotyped.

The characteristics of stimuli which trigger a response (in this case, posture and belly colour) are called **sign stimuli**. Ethologists believed that the recognition of the stimulus *and* the response to it were both inborn.

Comparative psychology and ethology

Although comparative psychology developed in close assocation with ethology, there are some important differences between them.

- Ethologists are happy to study animals in their own right. Comparative psychologists are interested in *comparing* animal and human behaviour in order to understand human behaviour better. Comparative psychology developed mainly in America and was heavily influenced by the behaviourist approach. Most research by comparative psychologists takes place in a laboratory setting.

- While ethologists focused on instinctual behaviour, comparative psychologists are more interested in the role of learning and experience. Since comparative psychologists do most of their research in the laboratory, they are restricted to studying certain species such as rats, pigeons, cats and dogs.

The main differences between ethology and comparative psychology are outlined below:

	Ethology	*Comparative psychology*
Focus of research	Study of animal behaviour in the animal's natural environment	Comparison of animal and human behaviour
Methods	Observation of animals in their natural habitat, limited use of experiments in semi-natural conditions	Research usually conducted in laboratory or experimental conditions
Main interest	The study of how/why animals behave in a certain way; emphasis is on the consistency of behaviour within species and instinctual behaviour	Comparison of animal and human behaviour in order to better understand human behaviour; emphasis is on the role of learning
Species studied	A variety of species, including birds, fish and insects	A few species such as rats, dogs and pigeons
Disadvantages	Carrying out research in the natural setting means there is little control over the environment; researcher may lack knowledge of the animal's past history; not all behaviour patterns are easy to observe; more difficult to draw conclusions about cause and effect	Behavioural patterns of the animal can be affected by the artificial conditions of the laboratory; cannot study the animal in its complete context

In the next section on how animals learn, we will see the influence of both the ethological and comparative approaches.

SECTION 7 | *Psychology For You*

How animals learn

Consider the following examples:

- **Adult black-headed gulls** eat each others' offspring. Therefore the adults must learn to distinguish their own chicks from other chicks so they know which ones to care for and which ones to eat.

- **The nutcracker bird** lives on pine nuts and has to store food for the winter. The food may be scattered over 1,000 km and the bird has to remember landmarks in order to locate the food even when it is covered by snow.

- **Imo**, a Japanese macaque monkey, tried washing sweet potatoes in the sea to remove the sand before she ate them. The other monkeys imitated her behaviour and soon most of the troop became potato-washers.

These examples illustrate the importance of learning in animal behaviour. Think again about the examples. None of this behaviour fits into our earlier definition of an instinct. An animal that returns to a nesting place or relocates food which has been stored is showing evidence of learning.

Learning is another term which psychologists do not find easy to define. However, learning can be said to have taken place when experience with an external event results in a relatively permanent change in behaviour.

An implication of this definition is that it is now assumed that an animal's learning is the product of its particular nature and needs and circumstances. However, there are some general principles or ways of learning that most animals seem to have in common.

According to Grier and Burk (1992), there are at least ten different types of learning, but they can all be classified into one of three categories:

1. **associative** learning
2. **non-associative** learning
3. **complex** learning

1. Associative learning

Associative learning occurs when there is a change in an animal's behaviour as a result of one event being paired or associated with another. Associative learning includes **classical conditioning, operant conditioning** and **taste aversion.** Since conditioning is described in detail in Chapter 7, *The Behavioural Approach* (pages 54–70), only taste aversion will be discussed here.

Taste aversion occurs when an animal has eaten or swallowed an object or substance which produces illness. As a result, the animal will avoid any further consumption of that substance. Garcia et al. (1974) presented rats with a food (or fluid) which had a distinctive taste, and then exposed them to radiation. Even very small amounts of radiation cause nausea. The researchers found that the rats would avoid the food which had been paired with the radiation. Furthermore, it took only one trial for the rat to avoid the food. Taste aversion also occurred even when there was a long delay (up to seven hours) between eating the food and being exposed to radiation and nausea.

THINK ABOUT IT

How could taste aversion help an animal survive?

2. Non-associative learning
Non-associative learning includes:

● habituation
● sensitisation.

In simple terms, frequent exposure to something leads to getting used to it and eventually we stop responding to it. **Habituation** involves the gradual fading of a response to a stimulus. For example, a visitor to your home may comment on the extremely loud noise that your refrigerator makes. You are probably unaware of it because you have habituated to it.

In the same way, animals can recognise stimuli but learn not to respond to them each time. For example, Tinbergen (1948) showed that chicks could habituate to the presence of a shadow flying overhead. Models which varied in shape and in size were flown over the chicks. When a particular model was flown in one direction it resembled a hawk (which is a predator), and when it was flown in the other direction it resembled a goose. The 'hawk' model always resulted in an escape response but the chicks did not try to escape from the 'goose' model.

In Tinbergen's experiment, the chicks would recognise the shape of a hawk, but would not attempt to escape from the 'goose' model (far right) ▶

(Plus signs (+) indicate models that elicited an escape response from the chicks)

THINK ABOUT IT

Why would habituation be an advantage to an animal?

Sensitisation occurs when an animal shows an increased response to a stimulus. For example, if birds see one of their flock being captured by a predator, the birds will show a stronger escape response to the appearance of that predator.

3. Complex learning

There are a number of different types of complex learning. They include:

- latent learning
- observational learning
- imprinting
- insight learning
- spatial learning.

Latent learning

In **latent learning**, the fact that the animal has learned a response may not be immediately obvious. Information which the animal has previously learned is stored until it becomes useful. Latent learning can occur without reinforcement.

Buxton (1940) allowed rats to explore a large maze over a period of time. There was never any food in the maze and the rats were removed from the maze at different places each time. The rats were deprived of food for 48 hours and then fed in the 'goal box' of the maze. After being fed, they were placed back in the start box. Buxton found that the majority of the rats ran straight to the goal box without making a single mistake. The rats had previously learned the layout of the maze, and put this knowledge to good use when they wanted to reach the food.

Observational learning

An example of learning by **observation** and **imitation** occurs in chaffinches. Chaffinches learn their songs from older birds by imitation. It has been shown that if each individual chaffinch does not hear the song of other adults, the chaffinch song will be less complex.

Another example of observational learning is the potato–washing behaviour of the Japanese macaque monkey mentioned earlier. Ethologists who were studying the animals left potatoes for them at the edge of the forest. The following year, they observed that the monkeys were taking the potatoes to the sea to wash them. Imo had been the first monkey to try washing the potatoes, and the behaviour was imitated by the other monkeys. Interestingly, the first monkeys to copy Imo were monkeys of her own age.

Imprinting

Imprinting is another kind of learning in animals and one that reveals the 'pre-programmed' or genetic nature of a behaviour. In this sense, it is something of a curiosity for psychologists, because it combines an instinctive element and learning. Imprinting involves the young animal forming an association, or identifying with, another animal or object.

The best-known example of imprinting was demonstrated by Lorenz when he showed that baby ducks and goslings, which normally follow their mothers away from the nest after hatching, could be made to follow a substitute figure. For example, when he reared the goslings himself, the goslings would follow him as soon as they were old enough to leave the hatching box, and would ignore their real mother. Lorenz in fact had to introduce them to water and give them their first lessons in swimming!

Lorenz concluded that there was an inherited mechanism that was primed to switch on at a critical period after hatching and led to imprinting on the largest moving object around at the time. And it lasted! Months later, when the goslings had turned into mature birds, if offered a choice between Lorenz and the mother, they waddled over to Lorenz. It seems that the young birds had learned the identity of their first care-giver and never forgot it.

Imprinting occurs in other species as well. Young shrews become imprinted on the odour of the individual nursing them between 5 and 14 days after birth. If that 'nurse' is a substitute mother of another species they will follow a cloth impregnated with her odour even when returned to the natural mother after 15 days. They have learned the identity of the female that nursed them when they were younger, and they show that they remember her odour.

THINK ABOUT IT

How would imprinting help a black-headed gull chick avoid being eaten?

Ethologists were interested in exploring the *timing* of imprinting. Did it have to occur at a precise time after hatching and in the animal's lifespan? Originally, Lorenz claimed that there was a **critical period** for imprinting: anything up to 25 hours after hatching. 'Critical' here means that imprinting had to take place within 25 hours, or the chance to imprint would be permanently lost. However, other researchers including Guiton (1959) have shown that imprinting can take place five days or even later after hatching. In view of this flexibility, it is now more acceptable to think of the interval of time available for imprinting as a **sensitive period** depending in part on the environmental circumstances. The term **sensitive period** refers to a period of time in which learning is most likely to occur.

Insight learning

Insight learning is a more advanced form of learning. Insight learning involves the individual solving a problem by thinking about it and mentally 'trying it out' before putting it into action. Previous specific experience is not required. A good example of insight learning was demonstrated by Kohler (1925), using Sultan, a chimpanzee.

Kohler hung a banana from the ceiling in a room. On the floor, a box had been placed off to one side. The banana was too high for Sultan to grab by reaching or jumping. When he first entered the room, Sultan paced around in an agitated way for about five minutes, then took hold of the box, placed it under the banana, climbed on to the box and grabbed the banana. Kohler changed the procedure, for example, by raising the height of the banana and increasing the number of boxes. However, the same behaviour was successful for Sultan. It seemed that Sultan had suddenly hit on a solution.

Kohler did not explain *how* this process of problem-solving happened, he simply described it. But it does seem that the chimp was using knowledge picked up in one situation and applying it to another.

Spatial learning

This is a very common form of learning and involves the animal learning its surroundings and familar places. It means that an animal must learn to orient its way in space.

A good example is the female digger wasp. When a digger wasp has dug her burrow in the ground, she flies off to collect food for her offspring. In the process of leaving the burrow on the first hunting trip, she circles the area for a few seconds, then flies off. In her absence the researcher (Tinbergen, 1929) moved the pine cones from around the nest into a circle at the side. When the wasp returned, she tried to find the entrance to her nest in the newly arranged circle of pine cones. Her behaviour suggested that she had previously learned something about the objects and landmarks and their location in relation to the nest entrance.

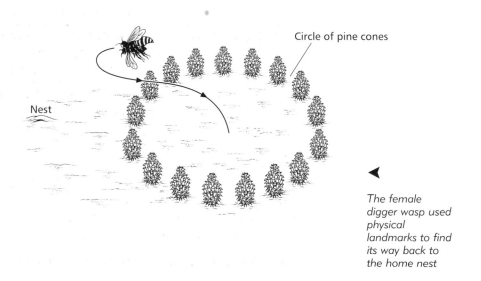

Circle of pine cones

Nest

The female digger wasp used physical landmarks to find its way back to the home nest

Other examples of learning among animals are **adaptive**, in that they help a species to survive in their environment. Some of the more spectacular of these examples are to do with migration. Many animals travel thousands of miles each year. Some of this behaviour is clearly instinctive and unlearned: for example, young cuckoos fly from Britain to Africa in the autumn without their parents flying with them to show them the way. Other birds, however, seem to rely on learning. Adult starlings driven away from their home territory before the migration season will fly in the correct direction to reach the place where they had spent the winter before. In this case, learning clearly influences their behaviour.

In summary

- *Comparative psychology is the study of patterns of behaviour in different species in order to develop general principles to explain their actions. The main aim of comparative psychology is to compare animal and human psychology in order to better understand humans.*

- *Ethology was an important influence on the development of comparative psychology. Ethologists prefer to study animals in their own right, rather than make comparisions between humans and animals.*

- *Ethological research emphasised instinctive behaviour such as fixed action patterns and recognition of sign stimuli.*

- *Research within comparative psychology has focused on the role of learning. There are three main categories of learning: associative learning, non-associative learning and complex learning.*

The social behaviour of animals

In Chapter 21, *Social Influence* (page 312), we described in some detail how human behaviour changes when other people are present, as a result of social facilitation, conformity and crowding behaviour. But what of the social behaviour of animals?

Social organisation refers to how members of a species interact with each other. In some cases, social organisation is fairly rigid, as in the case of social insects such as ants. In other examples, social organisation is more flexible. Sometimes animals take out 'temporary membership' of the social organisation. For example, tigers usually live and hunt alone, but make contact for breeding purposes.

Comparative psychologists have identified four different types of social organisation among animals:

Social organisation	Description
1. Societies	A group of animals living together for a substantial period of time; animals usually organise themselves into a hierarchy
2. Flocks/schools	A less complex type of organisation sometimes involving hundreds or thousands of individuals, but still with a degree of social interaction
3. Aggregations	Species which are not attracted to each other but which 'bump into each other' during a shared activity such as eating or drinking
4. Colonies	A large number of animals such as insects interacting continuously

Sociality in animals

Animals vary in the degree to which they socialise with each other (known as **sociality**). At one end of the scale, there is the heron, who is usually alone, and at the other end of the scale there is the organised society of worker and soldier ants who service their queen.

In order to study the degree of **sociality** in animals, psychologists:

● create artificial animal groups

● isolate individual animals

● study natural variations within a species, such as when one member of the species holds itself aloof from the others.

The research seems to suggest that socialising with others is a mixed blessing for animals. It is worth considering both the advantages and disadvantages of sociality.

Advantages of sociality

- **Physical benefits:** living in a social group can offer a physical advantage to animals. For example, emperor penguins huddle together closely as they incubate their eggs during the winter. As a result, heat is conserved. Penguins on the outside of the huddle swap places more than birds in the middle and the end result is that all the birds receive appropriate shelter.

- **Protection against predators:** Groups of animals are more likely to spot danger and to see off the predator than a solitary member of the species. Groups have some obvious advantages when it comes to avoiding ending up as someone else's lunch. For example, red-billed weaver birds are more likely to spot a hawk (a potential predator) when there are two or more birds present.

- **Finding food:** a group of animals foraging for food together are likely to outperform a solitary hunter. They can signal to each other where food is to be found – as honey bees do. They may also be able to tackle larger prey and use tactics such as taking it in turns to chase prey until the quarry is exhausted.

- **Defending a territory:** not all animals are territorial in the sense of defending an area within which they find food and rear their young. With the exception of gibbons, this is actually rare among primates. However, it is fairly common among birds and fish. For example, wagtails defend their territory vigorously against other birds and behave aggressively towards intruders. Robins also fiercely defend their territory by flying straight at the intruder and making a high-pitched call. As a result, intruders are more likely to be 'seen off' by groups of birds than by individuals.

Disadvantages of sociality

- **Food sharing:** in simple terms of meals per day, living in a group is not necessarily an advantage for the individual hunter. The spoils of hunting have to be shared. In a lion pride, for example, the lionesses are the best stalkers and hunters, but it is the lions who take the biggest portion of the prey (literally the 'lion's share'). Consequently, social living can create extra competition for food.

- **Interference:** another problem with living in a group is interference from other members of the species. For example, lions are not very tolerant of the young. When a male lion (or group of males) take over a pride, they kill the cubs who are present. As we saw earlier, black-headed gulls will eat the offspring of neighbouring gulls.

- **Health hazards:** another problem facing social animals is the spread of infections. A good example is the swallow bug, a bloodsucking parasite which attacks cliff swallows (Brown and Brown, 1986). Cliff swallows nest in large colonies (up to 3,000 pairs of birds), and the swallow bug lives in the nests and attacks the chicks. The result is that affected chicks do not grow properly.

On balance, group living does provide animals with some clear advantages; but there are also serious disadvantages. Living in groups or colonies increases competition for food, increases the risk of disease and may make the animals more likely to be seen by predators.

Territories

In Chapter 25, *Personal Space, Privacy and Territory* (page 374), we introduced the idea of human territoriality. Clearly, non-human animals are also territorial creatures.

In general terms, a **territory** is a defended area. Hinde (1956) was interested in identifying the purpose of territories for animals. According to Hinde, territories can be used for:

● mating
● raising young
● feeding
● a combination of these purposes.

What are the benefits and costs to animals of having a territory? According to Huntingford and Turner (1987) the costs include:

● acquiring a territory may involve getting rid of the previous occupant
● maintaining a territory takes up energy
● defending a territory increases the risk of being injured.

There are, however, advantages of having a territory:

● less risk of infection or disease spreading since animals are spaced out
● food supplies may last longer if fewer animals are using them
● decreased danger from predators, since scattered individual animals are harder to locate.

Hayes (1994) distinguishes between the different types of territories used by animals, and identifies five different types as described below:

Type of territory	Description
Range	the actual space through which a species moves, mates and finds food (but there is no active sense of ownership)
Home range	the area where the animal spends most time
Seasonal territory	the area that an animal takes over during a specific part of the year
Nested territory	one animal will behave in a territorial way but other members of the species are allowed to occupy areas within the main territory
Colonial territory	animals nest together in large groups but each group is allocated a smaller individual area within the territory

One factor which affects territoriality in animals is the abundance of food. When there is very little food available, animals may leave their territory to find other resources. They may, however, return to their territory at various intervals just to stake their claim. When food is very abundant, the owner of the territory will not bother to frighten off intruders – presumably because there is less reason to defend the territory.

Summary

- Living together for animals has certain benefits, including better protection against predators, more efficient hunting and more effective territory defence.
- Social living can also be a disadvantage in relation to sharing food, the risk of communal disease and interference.
- Some species have an active sense of territoriality, while other species live a largely solitary existence.
- There are a number of different types of territory, including seasonal, colonial and nested territories.
- Animals may weigh up the costs and benefits associated with defending a territory and may be less likely to defend when food is plentiful.

The Biological Approach

The link between mind and body is perhaps one of the great unresolved mysteries. Understanding something of how our bodies work – for example, how our brains are structured for the job of thinking, how our hormones may affect how we feel, and how our thoughts and feelings may in turn affect our body – is an important part of understanding ourselves. This section introduces you to the human brain and looks at issues concerning emotion and stress.

28 Structure and Function of the Nervous System

Although the human brain only weighs about 3½ pounds, it is a very complicated piece of machinery and contains over 10 billion nerve cells. The brain regulates all of the body's functions and controls our behaviour. The brain also monitors activity in every cell in our body. In order to do this, it has to *receive* information from the body's sense receptors. The brain also needs to *transmit* information to the body's muscles and glands.

Structure of the nervous system

The structure of the nervous system is shown in the diagram below. As you can see, it has two major divisions: the **central nervous system (CNS)** and the **peripheral nervous system (PNS)**. The peripheral nervous system is also subdivided into other systems. We will describe briefly the nature of each part of the nervous sytem.

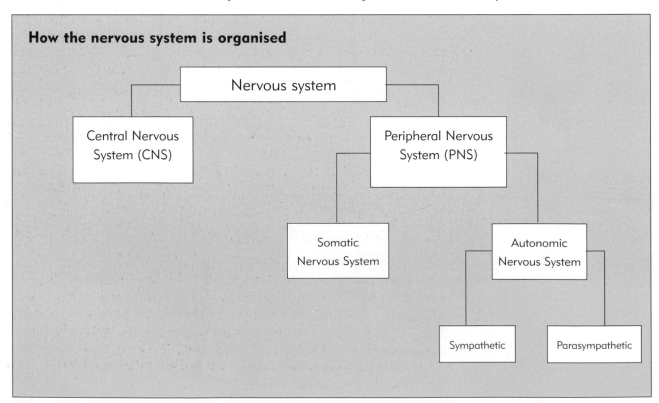

How the nervous system is organised

The central nervous system

The central nervous system consists of the **neurons** (nerve cells) in the brain and spinal cord. The **spinal cord** extends from the bottom of the brain to the base of the spine. The spinal cord does two important jobs. It delivers sensory information from the rest of the body to the brain. The spinal cord also transmits the brain's commands to the body. (For a more detailed discussion of the structure of the brain, see page 412). Therefore the spinal cord acts like a bridge between the brain and the rest of the body.

The peripheral nervous system (PNS)

The **peripheral nervous system** consists of all the neurons which lie outside the central nervous system. The PNS connects muscles, glands and sense organs to the central nervous system. The role of the PNS is to provide the central nervous system with information from sensory receptors and to pass on commands from the brain to organs and muscles. The PNS can be further divided into two parts:

1 the **somatic** nervous system
2 the **autonomic** nervous system

1. The somatic nervous system

The **somatic nervous system** regulates the voluntary movements of the body's skeletal muscles. For example, when you are playing football, the somatic nervous system controls the voluntary movement of your muscles.

2. The autonomic nervous system (ANS)

The other part of the peripheral nervous system is called the **autonomic nervous system (ANS)**. The autonomic nervous system controls the muscles, internal organs and glands over which we have no voluntary control. For example, bodily processes such as digestion and respiration are regulated by the autonomic nervous system. The ANS has two jobs:

Function	Carried out by:
trouble-shooting: prepares the body for situations which require higher levels of arousal or energy	sympathetic division
house-keeping: helps body to conserve energy	parasympathetic division

Because it has these two different jobs to carry out, the ANS is further divided into two parts: **sympathetic** and **parasympathetic**.

● The **sympathetic division** has the role of being a 'trouble-shooter'. In a stressful situation, the sympathetic nervous system alerts the brain for a 'fight or flight' response. This involves increasing the body's heart-rate, blood-sugar level, adrenaline and blood flow to the muscles and slowing down digestion. Once the emergency is over, the parasympathetic nervous system (the 'housekeeper') reverses all those processes.

● The **parasympathetic division** also plays a role in maintaining the body, conserving energy and regulating the elimination of waste products from the body.

TRY THIS

Match the **parts of the nervous system** on the left with their **functions** on the right

Parts of the nervous system	*Function*
somatic nervous system	prepares body for 'fight or flight'
central nervous system	conserves the body's energy
parasympathetic	consists of neurons in the brain and spinal cord
autonomic nervous system	controls voluntary movements of skeletal muscles
peripheral nervous system	controls muscles and organs over which we lack voluntary control
sympathetic nervous system	connects muscles, glands and sense organs to the central nervous system

Brain structure and function

One way of dividing up the structures of the brain, is to think of the brain as having three main layers:

1   The **central core** includes structures deep within the brain which are involved with processes such as breathing, digestion and heart rate
2   The **limbic system** is located within the central core and plays an important role in emotional and sexual behaviour
3   The **cerebral cortex** is the brain's 'outer layer'

1. The central core

The **central core** is the part of the brain which regulates internal bodily processes. It consists of five structures, each of which has its own role in controlling the internal state of the body:

● medulla
● pons
● reticular activating system
● thalamus
● cerebellum

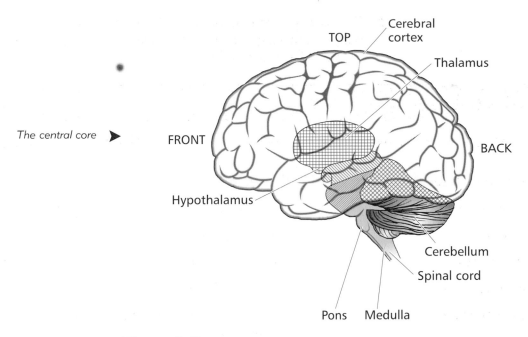

The central core ▶

Labels: TOP, Cerebral cortex, Thalamus, FRONT, BACK, Hypothalamus, Cerebellum, Spinal cord, Pons, Medulla

The medulla

The **medulla** is located just above the spinal cord and is responsible for many of our vital functions, such as reflexes, heart-rate and respiration. Because of this, damage to the medulla can be life-threatening.

The medulla is also important because it is the cross-over point at which nerve fibres extending down from the brain and nerve fibres coming up from the body cross or intersect. This crossing-over explains why the left side of the brain controls the right side of the body.

The pons

Directly above the medulla is a large bulge called the **pons**. In Latin, the word *pons* means 'bridge', and the pons acts like a bridge in the sense that some of its nerve fibres connect to the cerebellum. The medulla and the pons both contain the **reticular activating system (RAS)**, a network of neurons which is involved in arousal and attention. The reticular activating system is also involved in regulating sleep.

Cerebellum

Behind the medulla and the pons is a large structure called the **cerebellum** ('little brain'). Damage to the cerebellum affects motor responses, balance and the ability to co-ordinate movement.

Thalamus

The **thalamus** is located deep within the brain and is generally described as the 'relay station' of the brain. This is because it receives sensory information from other parts of the nervous system and is responsible for transmitting that information to other parts of the brain. Therefore all sensory information (with the exception of smell) passes through the thalamus before being sent to the cortex.

In summary

- *The brain has three main layers: the central core; limbic system and cerebral cortex.*

- *The central core consists of five different structures:*

  - *the **medulla** controls vital functions like heart-rate;*

  - *the **pons***

  - *the **reticular activating system (RAS)** is involved in arousal and sleep*

  - *the **cerebellum** affects balance and movement*

  - *the **thalamus** transmits sensory information to the cortex*

2. The limbic system

The **limbic system** consists of a number of structures including the:

● amygdala
● hippocampus
● hypothalamus

Rather like a thermostat, the limbic system enables our bodies to maintain a constant environmental climate – a process called **homeostasis**. The limbic system regulates blood-sugar level, body temperature and blood-pressure. According to Ornstein and Thompson:

> 'The limbic system is also strongly involved in the emotional reactions that have to do with survival, such as sexual desire or self-protection through fighting or escaping. One way to remember limbic functions is that they are the "Four F's" of survival: feeding, fighting, fleeing and sexual reproduction'[26]

The limbic system ▶

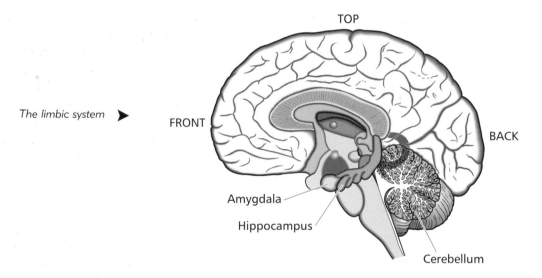

Amygdala

One important structure of the limbic system is the almond-shaped **amygdala** (from the Latin word for 'almond'). The amygdala is located deep within the temporal lobe and appears to have several functions, one important one being the control of rage. Animal research has shown that electrical stimulation of certain parts of the amygdala can result in the animal violently attacking an object or other animal. If certain parts of the amygdala are destroyed, the animal usually becomes very placid and tame.

The amygdala also governs how animals interpret the emotional importance of certain stimuli. For example, Kluver and Bucy (1937) found that lesions in the amygdala of monkeys meant that they were unable to recognise appropriate food, dangerous stimuli or appropriate sexual partners.

Other research with monkeys suggests that lesions in the amygdala cause the animal to misinterpret the facial expressions or gestures of other monkeys and to react in an inappropriate manner. Finally, the amygdala also receives sensory information such as smell, sight and sound.

Hippocampus

The **hippocampus** is the largest structure in the limbic system and gets its name from the Greek word for 'sea horse', because of its shape. The hippocampus has an important role to play in memory, particularly the formation of long-term memory. Our knowledge of the hippocampus is based on clinical evidence of patients suffering from amnesia. One of the most famous of these is 'H.M.', who suffered from epilepsy and underwent surgery to remove the hippocampus in order to reduce the severity of his seizures. After the surgery, H.M was able to store a certain amount of information in short-term memory, but was unable to transfer it into his long-term memory store. Long after the operation, when he was asked how old he was, and what year it was, he replied, 'Twenty-seven' and '1953' – his age and the year when he underwent surgery.

Similar memory loss has been found in other patients who had their hippocampus removed. Creating **lesions** (damaging or destroying a part of the brain) in the hippocampus of animals does not result in the same degree of memory impairment. Instead, animals have difficulty in learning certain responses. For example, Olton et al. (1978) observed the behaviour of rats in a maze. The maze had a number of different alleys and food was located at the end of each one. Normally rats would tend to try each of the alleys. However, rats with lesions of the hippocampus would enter the same alley over and over again without trying any of the other ones.

Hypothalamus

The **hypothalamus** is located just below the thalamus (*hypo-* means 'beneath' or 'less than'). Although it is only the size of a pea, the hypothalamus is the most important part of the limbic system. It is the hypothalamus which helps the body to maintain a stable state by regulating the body's temperature and heart-rate.

For example, if the body's temperature drops, the hypothalamus causes the blood vessels to constrict. The hypothalamus also regulates feeding and drinking. Research has shown that damage to the hypothalamus can result in abnormal feeding and drinking behaviour in animals.

The hypothalamus also regulates the body's hormonal system by controlling the pituitary gland which is attached to the base of the hypothalamus. **Hormones** are chemical substances which are secreted by certain glands in the body and affect bodily processes. The pituitary gland has been called the **master gland** because it controls the activity of other glands. Because the hypothalamus controls the pituitary gland, it in effect controls the entire hormonal system.

3. The cerebral cortex

The term **cortex** means 'outer layer' or 'covering'. The **cerebral cortex** is the region of our brain which enables us to plan, reason and make

In summary

- The **limbic system** consists of the amygdala, hippocampus and hypothalamus.

- The **amygdala** controls emotional reactions such as rage.

- The **hippocampus** is involved in memory.

- The **hypothalamus** helps to regulate body temperature and heart rate. It also regulates the body's hormonal system.

decisions. Although the cerebral cortex is only one-eighth of an inch thick, it contains billions of neurones. The cerebral cortex consists of two halves or hemispheres. Each hemisphere is responsible for the opposite side of the body – so, for example, the right side of the brain controls movements on the left side of the body. Although the hemispheres look the same, they are responsible for different functions as shown below:

Right hemisphere	**Face recognition**
	Spatial tasks
	Recognition of objects
	Non-verbal material
	Analysing information in an integrated way
	Negative emotions
Left hemisphere	**Language**
	Verbal material
	Memory for words/numbers
	Positive emotions

The fact that the hemispheres are involved in different types of functions is often referred to as **lateralisation of function** or **hemispheric specialisation**.

The notion that the cerebral hemispheres were specialised for different functions was supported by Paul Broca, a French surgeon of the 1860s. Broca discovered that patients with speech impairments all had damage to a region in their left hemisphere (now known as **Broca's area**). He also found that patients who had damage to the same area in the right hemisphere had no problems with language.

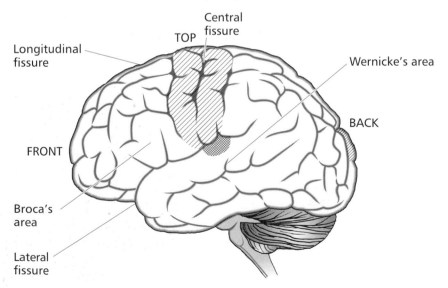

Another surgeon, Carl Wernicke, discovered that damage to a different part of the left hemisphere produced a different kind of impairment.

This area, now known as **Wernicke's area**, was located in the temporal lobe. Damage to this region resulted in patients losing their ability to understand the language they heard correctly – even though they could still speak fluently. This confirmed the notion that the left hemisphere plays an important part in language.

The hemispheres are connected by a band of nerve fibres called the **corpus callosum**. The corpus callosum is responsible for the transfer of information between the hemispheres.

The surface of the cerebral hemispheres is made up of ridges and grooves. There are three grooves (or **fissures**) which serve as landmarks and help divide the cerebral cortex into four distinct regions called lobes. Once you have worked out where the fissures are located, the geography of the brain is easier to understand.

- The **longitudinal fissure** separates the left hemisphere from the right
- The **central fissure** runs across the top of the brain and separates each hemisphere into a 'front' and 'back'
- The **lateral fissure** runs along the side of the brain and divides each hemisphere into a 'top' and 'bottom'

The lobes of the cortex

The fissures described above divide each hemisphere into four lobes as follows:

1 The **frontal lobe** is located at the front of the brain directly in front of the central fissure
2 The **parietal lobe** is located behind the central fissure and above the lateral fissure at the top of the brain
3 The **temporal lobe** is located along the side of each hemisphere just below the lateral fissure
4 The **occipital lobe** is located at the back of the brain

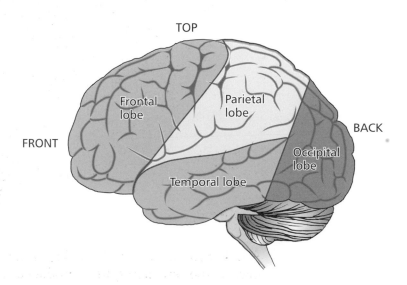

The four lobes of the cerebral cortex ▶

It is worth remembring not only *where* the lobes are located but also the functions of each one.

1. The frontal lobe

The **frontal lobe** is often considered to be the 'executive' part of the brain. Like a director of a corporation, it is responsible for planning and decision-making. The frontal lobe is also involved in evaluating whether an event or object is threatening. The frontal lobe contains the **primary motor cortex**, a long, narrow strip just in front of the central fissure. The motor cortex directly controls body movements by transmitting information to the muscles.

Damage to the frontal lobe can have several serious effects. The person:

- may not be able to organise their behaviour in order to reach a certain goal

- may repeat a particular behaviour over and over again and be unable to change a strategy.

- may find it difficult to make an appropriate emotional response in a given situation

2. The parietal lobe

The parietal lobe contains the **primary somatosensory cortex**, a thin strip located just behind the central fissure which receives information about touch, temperature, pressure and pain from internal organs and muscles. Areas of the body which have many tactile receptors (like the hands) will have large sections of the somatosensory cortex devoted to them. The somatosensory cortex also receives information about the position of our body parts and their movements (called **proprioceptions**).

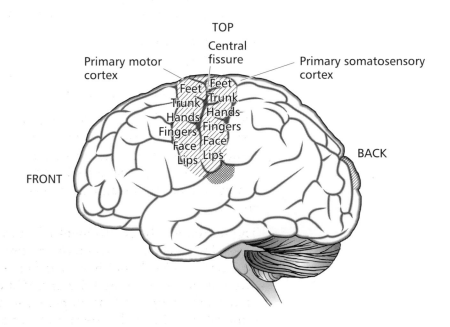

It therefore has an important role to play in how information from the various senses are integrated. The parietal lobe also integrates information from the senses with information stored in memory.

Once again, damage to the parietal lobe can have serious consequences. For example, a person with parietal lobe damage may have difficulty in locating the position of their body parts in space. Damage to the *left* parietal lobe may mean the person is unable to write or unable to read. Finally, damage to the parietal lobe may result in **hemi-neglect** in which the individual ignores information from one side of space, usually the left. Individuals with hemi-neglect:

> 'may not eat food on the left side of the plate, draw the left side of objects, read the left side of words, use the left side of the body and in severe cases, they may even deny that the left side of the body belongs to them'[27]

Initially, all information on the neglected side will be ignored. Over time, some items can come to be processed, but the neglect will never totally disappear.

Finally, parietal damage can also result in:

● visual agnosia
● tactile agnosia

Agnosia is an impairment in recognising objects using a particular sense like touch, hearing or vision. In **tactile agnosia** the sufferer is unable to identify an object through touch alone. In **visual agnosia**, the sufferer cannot recognise objects by looking at them. They may be able to report the shape, colour or size of the object, but are unable to integrate this information so as to be able to identify the object.

3. *The temporal lobe*
The **temporal lobe** has four main functions:

1 auditory processing
2 memory
3 emotion
4 visual recognition of items

The temporal lobe contains the **primary auditory cortex** which is concerned with hearing. Damage to the primary auditory cortex can result in hearing loss. An important type of auditory processing which occurs in the temporal lobe is speech perception. Damage to the left temporal lobe can mean that a person loses their ability to *understand* speech.

The temporal lobe is also involved in memory. The case of 'H.M.' (see page 415) showed that when the hippocampus in the temporal lobe was destroyed, H.M. found it very difficult to learn any new information. More recent research by Frisk and Milner (1990) suggests that removal of the left temporal lobe impairs memory for verbal material, while removal of the right temporal lobe affects memory for spatial information.

Since some parts of the limbic system are located in the temporal lobe, this lobe is also involved in motivation and emotion.

Finally, the temporal lobe is responsible for the processing of visual information, particularly the perception of complex patterns. While the parietal lobe helps us to identify the *location* of objects in space, the temporal lobe helps us to identify *what* the item is.

Damage to the temporal lobe can result in **auditory agnosia**. In this case, the sufferer can hear a sound, but cannot identify or recognise it.

4. Occipital lobe

The **occipital lobe** is located at the back of each hemisphere. It contains a sensory area called the **primary visual cortex**. Damage to the entire primary visual cortex can cause total blindness. However, a small lesion to the visual cortex can create a 'hole' in part of the field of vision. Although the occipital lobe is the key player in vision, as we have already discovered, the temporal and parietal lobes also play a part in visual processing.

TRY THIS

Can you label the diagram correctly, using the terms listed below? *Hint*: Start by identifying the **fissures**, indicated by the darker lines on the diagram.

- **pons**
- **lateral fissure**
- **parietal lobe**
- **medulla**
- **occipital lobe**
- **longitudinal fissure**
- **spinal cord**
- **cerebellum**
- **frontal lobe**
- **central fissure**
- **temporal lobe**

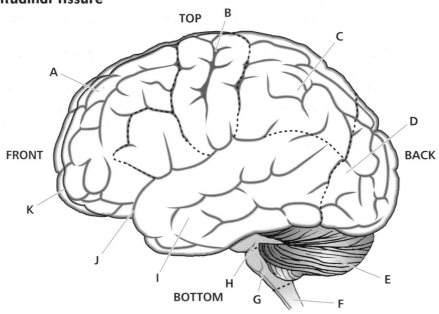

Summary

- The central nervous system consists of the brain and spinal cord
- The peripheral nervous system consists of all the neurons which lie outside the central nervous system.
- The peripheral nervous system consists of the somatic nervous system (which controls the voluntary movements of the body's skeletal system) and the autonomic nervous system (which controls the muscles, organs and glands over which we have no voluntary control).
- The autonomic nervous system is made up of the sympathetic division (which prepares the body for 'fight or flight') and the parasympathetic division (which helps the body to conserve energy).
- The brain has three major layers: the cental core, the limbic system and the cerebral cortex.
- The central core regulates the body's internal processes. It contains a number of elements, each of which has its own role in controlling the internal state of the body. These include the medulla, pons, reticular activating system, thalamus and cerebellum.
- The limbic system helps to maintain a constant climate within the body and consists of the amygdala, the hippocampus and the hypothalamus.
- The cerebral cortex is the outer layer of the brain and is divided into two halves or hemispheres. The hemispheres are specialised for particular functions. For example, the left hemisphere is specialised for language.
- There are three important landmarks on the surface of the cerebral hemispheres which divide the cortex into four lobes. The landmarks include the longitudinal fissure, the central fissure and the lateral fissure. These divide each hemihere into four lobes: the frontal, parietal, temporal and occipital.
- The frontal lobe is responsible for planning and decision-making and contains the primary motor cortex.
- The parietal lobe contains the primary somatosensory cortex and receives sensory information.
- The temporal lobe is involved in hearing and visual recognition. It also has a role to play in memory and emotion.
- The occipital lobe is concerned with vision and contains the primary visual cortex.

29 Ways of Investigating the Brain

In recent years, advances in science and technology have resulted in more sophisticated ways of studying how the brain works. Some of these methods allow researchers to investigate specific areas of functioning; others provide only a general overview. The participants used in the research also vary, and include:

● non-human animals

● humans with brain damage

● humans who have 'normal' brain functioning

It is important to include people who have normal brain functioning because otherwise the research could provide a biased view. These participants provide a comparison and help researchers understand better how people with brain damage are affected.

1. The lesion method

The word **lesion** literally means 'wound' or 'injury'. A lesion involves damaging or destroying a part of the brain. This method is based on the assumption that if damage to a particular part of the brain results in certain functions or behaviours being disrupted, then that part of the brain must be involved in that function. Lesions can be deliberately produced or can occur naturally.

With non-human animals, researchers can deliberately cause damage to a specific region of the brain. There are several ways of producing lesions. One way involves inserting a fine wire (called an **electrode**) into a particular region. An electrical current is then passed through the electrode that destroys the surrounding tissue. The researcher then carefully observes how the lesion affects the animal's behaviour.

For example, Aronson and Cooper (1979) found that male cats with lesions in the amygdala became less selective in their choice of partner. After lesions were created, the male cats would attempt to mate with other male cats and would even try to mount members of other species.

Ethical issues

Some researchers feel that such research on animals is unethical and tells us very little about how the human brain functions. Researchers who carry out such studies must follow the ethical guidelines concerning animals (see Chapter 4, *Ethical Issues in Research*, page 27).

With humans, researchers have to rely on cases of brain damage that have occurred naturally, either due to an accident or disease. An early example is the case of Phineas Gage, a railway worker who suffered a steel rod through his skull. He survived the accident but it had serious effects on his personality. Recently researchers reconstructed the extent of Phineas's brain damage by using his preserved skull. They concluded that his damage was similar to having a frontal lobotomy which resulted in problems in decision-making and emotion.

Limitations of the lesion method

- There are ethical problems, in that once an area of the brain is destroyed or damaged it can never be restored.
- It is not always possible to determine whether damage to a particular part of the brain affects performance because that part is crucial to the ability to perform the task, or because it connects with other areas of the brain which are also crucial (Banich, 1997).
- In animal experiments, the researcher has control over the size and location of the lesion being created. However, in humans who have suffered accidental damage, there is often damage to other areas. This makes it more difficult to identify specifically which part of the brain is responsible for which function. It is also difficult to assess the extent of the damage since the researcher would not know what the participant's behaviour was like *before* the accident occurred.
- Generalisation from animal research to humans is difficult because human brains are organised differently from animals', and animals have limited behavioural responses compared to humans.

2. Electrical stimulation of the brain

This technique involves delivering mild electric currents to specific areas of the brain. The aim is not to damage the area but simply to stimulate it.

Researchers use electrical stimulation for two purposes:

1 It helps to identify which structures of the brain are connected to each other. For example, if electrical stimulation in one part of the brain results in increased activity in another part of the brain, then they must be connected to each other in some way.

2 It helps researchers to understand the relationship between specific areas of the brain and behaviour. For example, Penfield (1955) stimulated certain parts of patients' brains while they were waiting for surgery. He found that stimulating a particular part of the brain (primary motor cortex) caused the patients to move, while stimulation of another part of the brain (primary auditory cortex) caused patients to hear buzzing noises.

Limitations of electrical stimulation

- Artificial electrical stimulation of the brain cannot duplicate the natural electrical activity within the brain.

3. Chemical stimulation of the brain

This technique involves introducing small amounts of chemicals directly into the brain of an animal in order to *stimulate* or *inhibit* specific groups of neurons. The chemicals used can include drugs, hormones or neurotransmitters. Researchers then observe how these chemicals affect the animal's behaviour.

When a part of the brain is more active than usual, it uses more glucose (its main energy source) and produces more protein. If researchers could measure either the glucose used or protein produced, they would therefore be able to determine which parts of the brain were active. In practice, this is impossible, but researchers can inject a radioactive chemical which is similar to the glucose. If certain areas of the brain are very active, traces of the radioactive chemical can be found in these areas. Unfortunately, however, the only way to identify areas with large amounts of the radioactive chemical is to kill the animal and take cross-sections of its brain.

Limitations of chemical stimulation

- If a concentrated chemical is used it can damage the animal's brain tissue.
- Different animals respond differently even when the same substance is injected in the same place within the brain (Fisher, 1964).

4. Recording the brain's electrical activity

Since nerve cells (neurons) work by producing electrical impulses, another way of understanding how the brain works is by recording the **electrical activity** within the brain. This technique can be used with both non-human animals and humans.

In non-human animals, it is possible to place electrodes directly into certain cells and identify what type of stimuli causes a particular cell to fire. In humans it is more difficult to record the activity of individual cells or group of cells, so researchers record the general level of activity within the brain.

An **EEG (electro-encephalogram)** is a way of recording the patterns of electrical activity within the brain by placing electrodes on a person's scalp. The electrodes pick up the electrical signals occurring within the brain, which are usually quite small, and amplify them. These signals are then transmitted to a recording machine which produces a visual display of the electrical activity. EEGs are able to provide a millisecond-by-millisecond account of the brain's activity.

EEGs have helped researchers to study the processes involved in sleep and dreaming. They are also useful in diagnosing epilepsy and other disorders such as brain tumours.

Limitations of the EEG method

- EEGs only provide an overview of what is happening in the brain. They cannot be used to identify the specific region of the brain producing the activity (Banich, 1997).

5. Single-cell recording

In animals, it is possible to record the electrical activity (or **firing rate**) of a single brain cell. This technique involves inserting a micro-electrode inside or near a particular nerve cell. Once the researcher has established what the cell's base-line firing rate is, it is possible to observe if the cell increases or decreases its rate of firing in response to certain types of stimuli. For example, Hubel and Wiesel (1968) used this technique to record the activity of individual cells in the visual parts of the brain of cats and monkeys.

Limitations of single-cell recording

- The technique is not appropriate for humans so it is difficult to generalise the results based on animals.
- It can destroy brain tissue.
- The technique provides information about individual cells or groups of cells, but does not provide information about the brain's *overall* level of functioning. Trying to build up a map or overview of the brain using this technique could take forever.

6. Brain-imaging techniques

Brain-imaging techniques are both safe and non-invasive and can produce images of different regions. Three brain-imaging devices are used:

- Computerised Axial Tomography (CAT scan)
- Magnetic Resonance Imaging (MRI)
- Positron Emission Tomography (PET scan)

CAT scan

CAT scans have an important function in diagnosing brain abnormalities such as blood clots, tumours or areas of damaged tissue.

The patient undergoing the scan lies on a table with his or her head in the middle of a machine which takes a number of X-rays at different angles. This information is fed into a computer which produces a three-dimensional picture of the brain.

Limitations of CAT scans

- As with X-rays, CAT scans involve exposing patients to potentially harmful radiation.
- CAT scans cannot show the actual functions of the brain.
- The instruments involved are not very sensitive, so the image produced is not very clear.

Magnetic Resonance Imaging (MRI)

Magnetic Resonance Imaging involves the use of magnetic fields and radioactive waves (as opposed to X-rays) to create an image of the brain.

The patient is placed in a machine which creates a strong magnetic field. As a result, certain atoms and other particles which are sensitive to the magnetic field align themselves in the same direction (rather like magnetised iron-filings). This magnetic field is interrupted by radio

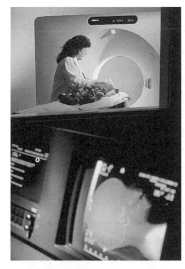

CAT scans convert X-ray data into a three-dimensional picture of the patient's brain. The picture can be seen on the video monitor in the foreground

waves from a radio antenna placed around the patient which excites the atoms and other particles. The time taken for the atoms to return to their original position is recorded by the computer and converted into a visual display. MRIs are more sensitive than CAT scans and produce a very clear and precise image.

Limitations of Magnetic Resonance Imaging
– Like the CAT scan, MRI is unable to tell us about how the brain functions – only about brain anatomy.
– MRI cannot be used on patients who have metal in their body that is not connected to hard tissue (for example, a metal clip on an artery), because the magnetic field could cause the metal to dislodge.

PET scans
Unlike the imaging techniques described so far, **PET scans** *are* able to provide information about brain function.

PET uses a radioactive substance which allows researchers to identify which areas of the brain are active at any point in time. The person undergoing the scan is injected with a radioactive form of glucose which is similar to the glucose which supplies the brain with energy. The more active a brain cell, the more of this radioactive glucose it is likely to absorb. The radioactive substance gives off a particle which has a positive charge. When this particle collides with an electron that has a negative charge, energy is given off in the form of light.

In PET scanning, the patient's head is surrounded by a ring of special cells that detect the light produced by this activity in the patient's brain. Active areas of the brain produce a lot of light. This information is fed into a computer which converts the information into a visual display which shows which parts of the brain are most active.

PET scans are useful because they help researchers to identify which areas of the brain are active when we are carrying out a specific task.

Limitations of PET scanning
– Involves the introduction of a foreign substance into the body.
– Since it involves radiation, a person should not have more than 4–5 scans per year.
– The scans from a single individual do not always provide enough information to build up an accurate image of the brain. Therefore researchers often use a number of participants and average the results. This means the PET scan is not always accurate at determining localisation of function for a given individual.

Summary

- Researchers are interested in investigating both the anatomy of the brain and how the brain functions. Techniques include the lesion method, electrical and chemical stimulation of the brain, recording the brain's electrical activity and brain-imaging.
- The lesion method involves damaging or destroying a part of the brain.

- Electrical stimulation involves delivering a mild electric current to specific areas of the brain.
- Chemical stimulation involves introducing chemicals directly into the brain and observing the effect on behaviour.
- Another way of studying the brain is to record the brain's electrical activity. This can be done by EEGs and by single-cell recording.
- Brain-imaging techniques involve producing maps of different parts of the brain. CAT scans, MRI and PET scans are all examples of brain-imaging techniques.

TRY THIS

Fill in the gaps in the sentences below using the following terms:

- **CAT**
- **MRI**
- **EEG**
- **stimulation**
- **lesion method**

One problem with the .... is that once a part of the brain is damaged or destroyed, it can't be restored.

An .... involves placing electrodes on a person's scalp.

.... is more sensitive than CAT scans and produces a very clear image.

Electrical .... involves delivering mild electrical currents to specific areas of the brain.

.... scans are useful in diagnosing brain abnormalities such as blood clots.

30 Emotion

Just a touch of hayfever, Captain

Can you imagine what life would be like without emotions?

Can you imagine what life would be like without emotions? In some ways it might have its attractions. You would be spared the experience of being frightened, angry or embarrassed. But you would also miss out on the great human experiences of being in love and feeling excitement, joy and happiness.

Although psychologists have not been able to agree on a precise definition of an emotion, most psychologists agree that an emotion is *a relatively brief display of a feeling which is a response to environmental stimuli*. But emotions consist of more than just feelings.

The components of emotion

Most psychologists agree that emotion has four different components:

- **physical arousal**: this includes bodily changes such as increased heart-rate or blood pressure
- **cognitive processes**: i.e. how we interpret or make sense of the situation
- **subjective feeling**: the emotion we experience, such as anger or fear
- **behavioural reaction**: how we act in response (such as running away)

Expressing and recognising emotions

Many species of animal communicate their emotions by their facial expressions and by their posture. This applies to humans as well. We know from our everyday experience that a person's facial expression is a good guide to how that person is feeling.

Darwin was among the first to study the similarity in facial expression between primates and humans

TRY THIS

The situation described below could cause a number of reactions. For each reaction, identify whether it is a:

- **behavioural reaction**
- **cognitive process**
- **physical reaction**
- **subjective feeling**

Situation	Reactions	Aspect of emotion
While you are driving a cat runs out in front of you	realise that this is an emergency	
	slam on brakes	
	feel frightened	
	heart pounds	

When you have finished, you will have a good example of the different components of an emotion.

Are emotional expressions learned or innate?

Charles Darwin (1859) believed that the ways in which humans express emotions have evolved from the way animals express emotion. He believed that emotional expressions are innate responses. If emotional expressions are innate, then it is reasonable to expect that people from different cultures will show their emotions through the same facial expressions.

Research suggests that there are six basic emotions which can be expressed by the human face. According to Ekman (1973) and Izard (1990) these six emotions are:

Fear   Anger   Happiness   Sadness   Surprise   Disgust

TRY THIS

Try to display each of the **six** emotions to a friend in a facial expression.
Can your friend tell which emotion you are displaying?

Cross-cultural studies

Several psychologists have carried out cross-cultural research on how emotion is expressed. If there are similarities across cultures – especially isolated cultures – then this would support the notion that emotional expressions are innate.

Ekman and Friesen (1980) studied the South Fore people in a remote area of New Guinea. None of the people had been exposed to Western culture. The researchers wanted to see whether South Fore people were able to identify the facial expressions of Western people. The researchers presented stories to the participants like the one below:

> 'She is sitting in her house all alone and there is no one else in the village; and there is no knife, or bow and arrow in the house. A wild pig is standing in the door of the house, and she is afraid the pig will bite her.'

The people were then given three different photographs of Westerners and asked to choose the one which best showed the emotion the person in the story would be feeling. The South Fore people had no difficulty choosing the correct photograph.

In a second study, the researchers wanted to investigate whether the facial expressions of the South Fore people were the same as those of Westerners. The researchers asked the South Fore participants to make the facial expression that they would have if they were happy to see their friends or if they were angry. The facial expressions were recorded. These were shown to American undergraduates who were asked to identify the emotion being experienced. Although the students had some problems in distinguishing between fear and surprise, in general they were able to identify accurately the emotions being expressed by the South Fore participants.

These results seem to indicate that people do show similar facial expressions when experiencing emotions, and also, that people are able to interpret accurately the facial expressions of people from different cultures. So what role does culture play in the expression of emotions?

According to Ekma and Friesen (1975) each culture has its own rules about what emotion is appropriate in a particular situation. This can lead to a person hiding their true feelings, or expressing an emotion that they do not actually feel. Ekman and Friesen argue that the expression of emotion follows **display rules**. These determine whether or not it is appropriate to express a particular emotion. For example, Samurai women in Japan smile to express their grief when their husband dies. In other cultures, this would be seen as inappropriate.

In one experiment, Japanese and American undergraduates were shown a distressing film, first on their own and then in the presence of an experimenter. The researchers recorded the people's facial expressions. While they were watching the film alone, the American/Japanese students displayed the same facial expressions. However, when they watched the film in the presence of another person, the Japanese students were less likely to express negative emotions. This is due to the fact that Japanese culture discourages the public display of emotion. It seemed that the participants were subject to different display rules.

The physiology of emotion

As we saw in Chapter 28, *Structure and Function of the Nervous System*, the autonomic nervous system has two parts: the sympathetic and parasympathetic. The part of the nervous system which deals with emotion is the **autonomic nervous system (ANS)**.

The **sympathetic division** prepares the body to expend energy, increasing the level of adrenaline and raising heart-rate. The **parasympathetic division** is responsible for activating functions which occur when we are in a relaxed state. This includes most of the body's general maintenance needs, such as digestion and elimination of waste products. Once the emergency has passed, the parasympathetic division helps to slow down heart-rate, resume normal breathing and 'maintenance' activities such as digestion.

TRY THIS

In an emergency you experience the following physical reactions. For each one, identify whether it involves the sympathetic or parasympathetic system by placing a tick in the appropriate column.

Physical reaction	Sympathetic	Parasympathetic
dilation of pupils		
breathing slows		
salivation is stimulated		
digestion is inhibited		
bladder contracts		

Emotion and the brain

As we saw earlier, there are a number of brain structures which seem to play an important role in emotions:

- the hypothalamus
- the amygdala
- the limbic system
- the cerebral cortex

Although the **hypothalamus** is very small (it weighs about 4 grams) it influences a wide range of behaviours. For example, animal research has shown that if certain parts of the hypothalamus in cats are electrically stimulated, the animals displayed aggressive behaviour such as hissing, growling and baring their teeth (Delgado, 1969).

According to research, the **cerebral cortex** may be responsible for *inhibiting* emotions such as aggression while other structures like the hypothalamus are responsible for the production of emotions. For example, Bard (1934) removed the entire cerebral cortex of cats and found that they responded with 'sham rage' (i.e. rage which occurs without any external stimulus). However, if the cat's hypothalamus was also removed, the aggressive attacks disappeared. Bard concluded that the hypothalamus has an important role to play in the production of emotion.

However, other areas of the brain such as the limbic system are also important.

Research has shown that damage to a part of the limbic system known as the **amygdala** significantly reduces animals' level of aggression. Rosvold et al. (1954) investigated the effects of amygdala lesions on a group of monkeys. A lesion was made in the most dominant monkey's amygdala which resulted in the monkey losing his status in the dominance hierarchy. When a lesion was made in the next-most dominant monkey, he too lost his status. However, when a lesion was made in the monkey who was third in the hierarchy, his aggressive behaviour did not decrease nor did he lose his status. This could have been due to the fact that he returned to a much less competitive environment since the two most dominant monkeys had already lost their place in the hierarchy. It may be that the lesions affected how the animals interpreted information and the environment around them.

Humans who suffer from a condition known as **intermittent explosive disorder** also show less aggression when a part of their amygdala is destroyed. For example, Mark and Ervin (1970) treated a 34-year-old man who had suffered brain damage resulting in dramatic changes in his behaviour including aggressive outbursts. He would suddenly attack strangers or members of his own family. When other treatments failed to reduce his violent behaviour, he agreed to have a *lesion* in the amygdala which eliminated his violent behaviour.

Electrical stimulation of parts of the amygdala can lead to rage and violent attacks. There are a few cases of *electrical stimulation* of the amygdala in humans. For example, one woman suffering from a brain disorder received electrical stimulation of the amygdala as part of her therapy. She reported strong feelings of aggression.

Research has shown that animals continue to respond emotionally even when their internal organs do not provide feedback to the brain

Interviewer: 'How do you feel now?'

Patient: 'I feel like I want to get up from this chair. Please don't let me do it. Don't do this to me. I don't want to be mean.'

Interviewer: 'Feel like you want to hurt me?'

Patient: 'Yeah. I just want to hit something. I want to get something and just tear it up. Take it so I won't. *(Hands her scarf to the interviewer. Interviewer hands her a stack of paper which she tears to shreds).* I don't like to feel like this.'[28]

Role of the cerebral hemispheres in emotion

Recent research has focused on the cerebral hemispheres of the brain and the role they play in emotion. It appears that the two hemispheres are specialised for emotion. The left hemisphere seems to be involved with positive emotions and the right hemisphere with negative ones. For example, Gur et al. (1994) found that the right hemisphere tends to be more active when a person is experiencing a negative emotion (being asked to think about a negative event) and the left hemisphere is more active when a person is experiencing a positive emotion (when a person is asked to think about a positive event).

Researchers have also studied patients with brain damage to the right and left hemisphere. Patients with damage in right hemisphere have difficulty in producing facial expressions associated with emotion.

Measurement of emotional arousal

When a person is aroused their sweat glands are activated and they will perspire, particularly on the palms of their hands

When a person is in a relaxed state, their breathing rate is low, their heart-rate is slow and their muscles are relaxed. When a person is in an aroused state, the opposite of these responses occurs. Although there are some differences in arousal for different emotional states, there is quite a lot of overlap. Therefore it is useful to measure a person's *overall* level of arousal without necessarily trying to distinguish one emotion from another.

There are several ways to measure physiological arousal, including **EEGs** and **EKGs** (which measure electrical activity in the heart). Another way is to measure **galvanic skin response (GSR)**. When a person is aroused, their sweat glands are activated and they will perspire, particularly on the palms of their hands. The perspiration lowers the electrical resistance of the skin, which can be measured by GSR.

Lie-detectors

Another instrument which is able to measure heart-rate, breathing rate, blood pressure and GSR all at the same time is the **polygraph test**, or **lie-detector**. The lie-detector is based on the assumption that when a person is lying there will be changes in their physiological arousal. There are, however, problems with the use of the standard polygraph test. Some people who are used to lying may produce very little arousal to both the control and critical questions.

More recently, Lykken (1988) developed another way of asking questions called the **guilty knowledge test**. This appears to be a more reliable technique. It involves presenting multiple choice questions which contain information that only the guilty person would know. For example, the person could be asked:

> *'The burglar dropped something when he ran away from the scene of the crime. Was it a hat/ knife/ a watch/ car keys/ a glove? If you are the person who committed the crime, you will know what it was.'*

Using this method, 90% of guilty people have been shown to be correctly identified.

However, according to Eysenck (1996), there are a number of problems with using physiological measures of arousal:

- It is usually very difficult to identify *which* emotion a person is experiencing on the basis of physiological measures of arousal.

- Although the various physiological measures are all supposed to measure arousal, measurements from different methods (e.g. EEGs, EKGs and GSR) do not correlate well with each other.

The self-report

As we have already discussed, we use other people's facial expressions as a guide to what emotion they are feeling. However, we all know of situations where we have tried to control our facial expressions in order to hide our true emotions (e.g. not letting someone see you cry or see your anger). One way to find out how people are feeling is to ask them using a **self-report measure**. This might involve giving an individual a list of words like 'angry', 'happy', 'anxious' and 'frightened', and asking them to indicate which words express how they are feeling at that particular time. However, a disadvantage of using self-report measures is that the person may not answer honestly, particularly if they are experiencing negative emotions.

Theories of emotion

There are four important theories which try to explain what causes emotion and how the various components of emotions relate to each other, each named after the researchers who developed them. The theories are:

- the James–Lange theory
- the Cannon–Bard theory
- Schachter's cognitive labelling theory
- Lazarus's theory of cognitive appraisal

James–Lange theory (1884)

Although William James (an American psychologist) and Carl Lange (a Danish physiologist) worked independently in different countries, they suggested very similar explanations of emotion at about the same time. Commonsense tells us that if we unexpectedly encounter a wild animal we will feel frightened and run away. In this situation, experiencing the emotion of fear comes first and *causes* the behavioural response of running away.

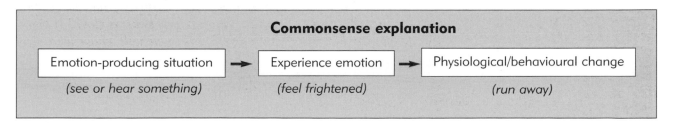

According to the James–Lange theory, this sequence of events is in fact incorrect. Their theory suggests that emotion-producing situations elicit a number of physiological responses (such as increase in heart-rate or sweating) and behavioural reactions (such as running away). The brain receives information about these reactions before we experience emotion. The theory is suggesting that emotional experiences are the *result* of changes within our body rather than the *cause*.

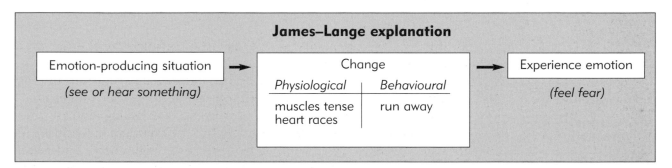

According to this theory, then, the emotions that we experience are a result of the sensory feedback from our muscles and internal organs and our behaviour. According to James:

> '[*the truth is that*] we feel sorry because we cry, angry because we strike, afraid because we tremble and not that we cry, strike or tremble because we are sorry, angry or fearful'.[29]

Evaluation of James–Lange theory

Strengths

+ This was the first modern theory of emotion and influenced research for over a century.
+ If the James–Lange theory is correct, each emotion should have its own distinctive pattern of bodily changes. Without this the brain would not be able to decide which emotion should be experienced. There is research to support the idea that different emotions are associated with distinct physiological responses.

    For example, Ax (1953) set out to identify the physiological responses associated with anger and fear. The participants were told that the research was investigating high blood-pressure and would involve measuring some of their physiological responses. There were two conditions in the study. In the 'angry' condition, participants were exposed to a 'technician' who made rude and unpleasant remarks. In the 'fear' condition participants were given electric shocks. The researcher recorded a number of physiological responses including blood-pressure, muscle tension, GSR, hand/face tension, and found that there were important differences for the two emotions. For example, the responses of the participants in the 'fear' condition were similar to those associated with an increase in adrenaline (increased heart-rate and increased breathing). The responses from participants in the 'angry' condition were similar to those caused by an increase in adrenaline and noradrenaline which also increased arousal.

+ According to the James–Lange theory if sensory feedback from the body is important, then people who have suffered damage to the spinal cord should experience less intense emotions. If the injury is higher up on the spinal cord, the area of sensory loss is large. This means the person receives little or no sensory feedback from those areas. If the injury is lower down, the brain may still receive feedback from other undamaged areas.

Hohmann (1966) asked a number of people who had spinal cord damage about the intensity of their emotional feelings. He found that the location of the damage was indeed related to their ability to experience emotion. People who had damage to the higher parts of the spinal cord reported experiencing less intense emotions than people who had damage to lower portions of the spinal cord. However, although the lack of sensory feedback affected their feelings, it did not alter their behaviour. For example, one of the patients described dropping a cigarette while he was in bed and alone at home. Although he was aware that he was in a potentially life-threatening situation, he did not experience the emotion of fear. However, he was eventually able to reach the cigarette and put it out. It would appear that people can respond to events, despite lacking the ability to feel emotions.

Weaknesses

– Animal research has shown that animals continue to respond emotionally even when their internal organs do not provide feedback to the brain. Sherrington (1906) carried out surgical procedures on dogs which involved severing the spinal cord and vagus nerves. The vagus nerves are responsible for taste and other sensations from the abdomen. Despite the fact there could be no sensory feedback to the brain, the dogs showed normal emotional reactions.

– Other critics have pointed out that there are not enough physiological responses to correspond to every different emotion. Furthermore, physiological responses are very similar across different situations. For example, heart-rate will increase when we are exercising, when we are fleeing from danger and when we are physically attracted to another person. Finally there are a number of different emotions which cannot be distinguished simply by their physiological reactions.

Cannon–Bard theory (1927)

This theory is based on the work of two physiologists, Walter Cannon (1927) and Philip Bard (1929). It suggests that the physiological changes and the experience of emotion occur *independently* of each other. According to the **Cannon–Bard theory**, a part of the brain called the **thalamus** is activated when a person is in an emotion-producing situation. The thalamus sends information to the cortex which results in the subjective experience of emotion. At the same time, the thalamus sends information to the hypothalamus which results in physiological changes. So the emotion that we experience and physiological reactions are seen as separate and independent processes. This is in contrast to the James–Lange theory which suggests that the physiological changes cause the emotion.

The Cannon–Bard theory ▼

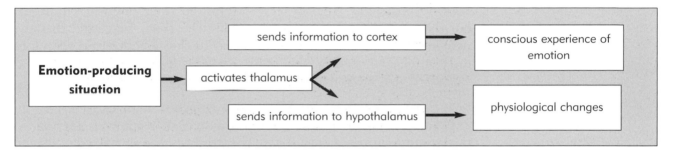

Evaluation of Cannon–Bard theory

Strengths

+ Commonsense tells us that sometimes we can experience an emotion before any physiological changes have occured. For example, we may feel frightened and only later experience wobbly legs! The Cannon–Bard theory can account for this, since the experience of emotion and physiological reactions are separate.
+ The theory focuses on the physiological basis of emotion (e.g. the thalamus sends information to the cortex and hypothalamus).

Weaknesses

– The Cannon–Bard theory assigns a central role to the thalamus. However, more recent research has shown that it is the *hypothalamus* and the *limbic system* which are important in emotion.
– The theory assumes that the thalamus is activated by any emotion-producing situation. But the theory does not explain how we distinguish between situations which are emotional and ones which aren't.

Schachter's cognitive labelling theory

Both the James–Lange theory and the Cannon–Bard theory focus on the automatic physiological processes in experiencing emotion. Stanley Schachter (1962) changed all that. Schachter suggested that *cognitive factors* have an important role to play in emotion. According to Schachter, in order to experience emotion *two* factors must be present:

● physiological arousal
● cognitive assessment (appraisal) of the situation

As a result, Schacter's theory is often referred to as the **two-factor theory** or **cognitive labelling theory**.

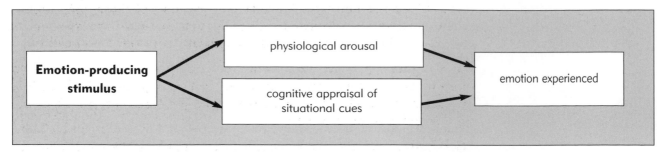

Schachter's cognitive labelling theory ▲

An earlier study by Maranon (1924) supported this idea. In this study, 210 people were injected with adrenaline and then asked to describe their feelings. The majority (71%) reported their physical symptoms but did not report feeling any emotion. The study suggested that the people attributed their physical arousal to the injection and therefore did not feel the need to label their arousal as 'emotion'. The study also suggested that arousal alone was not enough to create an emotion.

Schachter expanded on Maranon's research and carried out an experiment to investigate the influence of cognitive factors in interpreting an emotional state. The study is somewhat complicated because of the number of different conditions and is described below.

KEY STUDY The participants used in the laboratory experiment were male undergraduates, studying an Introductory Psychology course. The participants were told that the aim of the study was to see how vitamin supplements affected their vision. Participants were asked if they were willing to accept an injection of 'Suproxin', a vitamin supplement. Surprisingly enough, 184 out of the 195 participants agreed to have the injection. In reality, the injection did not contain a vitamin supplement. Half of the participants received an injection of adrenaline to increase their level of arousal and the other half received a 'placebo' injection of a saline solution which would not affect their level of arousal or have any side effects.

The participants who were given the adrenaline were then allocated to one of three conditions:

1   **Informed condition:** participants in this condition were informed about the side effects of the injection of adrenaline. They were told they might experience increased heart rate and mild trembling. Therefore these participants had an appropriate explanation for their physical symptoms.

2   **Uninformed condition:** participants were not told anything about possible side effects of the injection of adrenaline. These participants would not have an appropriate explanation for their arousal.

3   **Misinformed condition**: participants were misinformed about the possible side effects. They were told that they might experience itching and a numb feeling in their feet. None of these symptoms is related to adrenaline. Therefore these participants were provided with an inappropriate explanation for their arousal.

So far, then, we have one group of participants who were given a placebo and another group who were given an injection of adrenaline. Those given the adrenaline were then split into three groups: informed, uniformed and misinformed.

The final part of the experiment involved exposing the participants to different situations designed to make them feel angry or happy. In the angry condition, the participants interacted with a confederate who complained about the way he had been treated during the experiment. The other participants in the happy condition interacted with a confederate who acted happy by throwing paper aeroplanes around the room and being silly. The researchers measured the emotional state of the participants by observing their behaviour through a one-way mirror and by giving them a questionnaire to complete about their emotional state. The researchers predicted that:

● participants in the informed condition who knew what side effects to expect would attribute their arousal to the injection and therefore would not experience a change in emotion
● participants who were uninformed or misinformed would experience the most emotion since they did not have an appropriate explanation for their arousal
● When participants were not provided with an explanation for their arousal, the situation that they were in ('angry' or 'happy') would affect how they interpreted their emotional state.

The results for the participants exposed to 'happy' confederate are shown below:

Results for participants exposed to a happy confederate	
Condition	Score on questionnaire*
Informed	0.98
Uninformed	1.78
Misinformed	1.90
Placebo (saline injection)	1.61

The higher the score on the questionnaire, the greater the happiness reported

The researchers found that the participants were not willing to express their anger on the questionnaire. They were however, more willing to express their anger when they thought they were alone with the confederate. The table on page 440 shows the participants' responses to the confederate. (The researchers did not provide results for participants in the misinformed condition.)

Results for participants exposed to angry confederate	
Condition	**Anger units***
Informed	-0.18
Uninformed	+2.29
Placebo	+0.79

* The higher the number, the more anger reported by participants

Although the results of Schacter and Singer's study were not as clear-cut as they had predicted, the results did show that physiological arousal on its own is not enough to cause a change in emotion. We tend to look to the situation for an appropriate interpretation of the emotion we are feeling.

Questions

1. Give one problem with the sample used in this experiment.
2. Identify two ethical problems with this experiment.
3. Why did one group of participants receive a placebo injection of saline solution?
4. According to the results:
   a) Which of the participants were least influenced by the presence of the happy confederate?
   b) Which participants showed the most angry responses?
5. Give one reason why the participants may not have been willing to express anger on the questionnaire.

Source:
Schachter, S. & Singer, J.,
'Cognitive, Social and
Physiological
Determinants of
Emotional State',
Psychological Review, 69
(1962), pp.379–99

Evaluation of Schachter and Singer

Strengths

+ The theory was one of the first to focus on cognitive factors in emotion (Eysenck, 1996). Schacter and Singer's study showed that the emotion the participants experienced depended on the situation they were exposed to and their interpretation of it.

Weaknesses

− The study took place in the artificial environment of a laboratory. It is difficult to know how well these results would apply to real life.
− The sample used in the study was not representative since all the participants were male undergraduates. Also, because they were studying psychology, it could be argued that they were not 'innocent'.
− The participants' mood before the experiment began was not measured so it is difficult to determine how much the experimental procedure affected their emotional state.
− According to Schacter and Singer, five of the people who received an injection of adrenaline did not show the expected physiological responses. As a result, they excluded these people from the rest of the study. Also, Schacter and Singer failed to provide results in the anger condition for misinformed people.

Lazarus's theory of cognitive appraisal

A more recent theory which emphasises the importance of cognitive processes in experiencing emotion is Richard Lazarus's theory of **cognitive appraisal** (1982). According to Lazurus, before we respond emotionally to a stimulus, we weigh up the situation and make a cognitive appraisal of it. Lazarus suggested that this appraisal takes place in three stages:

● primary appraisal
● secondary appraisal
● re-appraisal

According to Smith and Lazarus (1990):

> 'How a given individual reacts emotionally to an encounter depends on an evaluation of what the encounter implies for personal well-being... If we know how a person evaluates the relationship with the environment, we can predict that person's emotional reaction.'[30]

Primary appraisal

In primary appraisal, we assess the impact of the situation on our well-being. For example, we may decide that the situation is a positive one, a stressful one or is irrelevant to our well-being. Lazarus believed that there were two components or parts of primary appraisal:

● **Motivational relevance** refers to the extent to which the situation is important or relevant to us. In other words, it refers to how much we have at stake in the situation.
● **Motivational congruence–incongruence** refers to whether the situation would help or inhibit the achievement of our personal goals.

So, in primary appraisal, we assess how relevant the situation is to us and the effect it could have on our personal goals.

Secondary appraisal

Secondary appraisal involves assessing our capacity for coping with the situation. Lazarus identified four aspects of secondary appraisal:

1 accountability
2 problem-focused coping
3 emotion-focused coping
4 future expectancy

Accountability involves considering who will take the blame if the situation turns out to be negative and who will take the credit if the situation proves to be a positive one.

The other three aspects of secondary appraisal are concerned with evaluating the person's potential for dealing with the situation. In **problem-focused coping**, the individual considers their ability to act directly on the situation in order to meet the demands presented. An example of problem-focused coping is deciding to give up a stressful job.

Emotion-focused coping involves the person adjusting psychologically to the situation. This could include seeking emotional support from friends or relatives or taking up a hobby. Finally, **future expectancy** refers to the possibility that there could be changes within the situation which would make it less threatening.

Re-appraisal

The third stage of cognitive appraisal is **re-appraisal** and involves monitoring the situation and how well we are coping with it

One study which supported Lazarus's theory was carried out by Speisman et al. (1964). In it, participants watched a gruesome film showing aboriginal boys taking part in an initiation ceremony which involved cutting their penises with a flint knife. By varying the soundtrack, participants were divided into four conditions:

- In **Condition A**, the pain suffered by the boys was emphasised

- In **Condition B**, the boys' expectations of becoming adults were emphasised

- In **Condition C**, the importance of the initiation rite was emphasised

- In **Condition D**, no commentary was provided

While participants were watching the film their physiological arousal was measured. Despite the fact that they all saw the same film, the participants in Condition A had the highest level of arousal. When the importance of the initiation rite and the boys' expectations were emphasised in the accompanying commentary, the participants experienced lower levels of arousal. The study supports the notion that how we appraise a situation influences the experience of emotion.

Evaluation of Lazarus's theory

Strengths
+ The theory recognises that an emotional response depends upon how we interpret or appraise the situation.
+ The theory identifies different coping strategies that people use.

Weaknesses
− Cognitive appraisal theory under-emphasises the physiological aspects of emotion.

Summary

- An emotion can be defined as a relatively brief display of a feeling in response to environmental stimuli.
- Emotions have four different components; physiological, cognitive, behavioural and subjective feeling.
- People from different cultures do show similar facial expressions when experiencing emotion. However, each culture varies in terms of which emotion is appropriate in a given situation.

- The autonomic nervous system plays an important role in emotion. The sympathetic nervous system prepares the body for an emergency situation and the parasympathetic helps restore the body's normal functioning.
- There are a number of brain structures concerned with emotion including the hypothalamus, the amygdala, limbic system and cerebral cortex.
- The left hemisphere of the brain seems to be involved in positive emotions and the right hemisphere with negative ones.
- There are a number of ways to measure emotional arousal, including EEGs, GSR and polygraphs. Questionnaires have also been used which involve the person indicating their current emotions.
- According to the James–Lange theory, emotional experiences are the result of changes within the body.
- The Cannon–Bard theory suggests that physiological change and the experience of emotion occur independently of each other.
- Schachter's cognitive labelling theory suggests that physiological arousal on its own is not enough to cause a change in emotion. An appropriate interpretation is also needed.
- Lazarus emphasises the importance of cognitive appraisal in experiencing emotion.

31 Stress

Although the word stress is a familiar word in our daily vocabulary, providing a precise definition of stress has proved to be extremely difficult. According to Selye, everybody has it, everybody talks about it, yet few people have taken the trouble to find out what stress really is.

Defining stress

Part of the problem with defining stress is that there are different aspects to it. For example, if you try and identify three things which cause you stress, you may come up with a list of situations or events (such as moving house, starting a new job or studying for exams). These events or situations are called **stressors**. Therefore one way of approaching stress is to focus on the things which *cause* stress.

Argument and confrontation can be acutely stressful for some people ▲

Now try to think about how being stressed *affects* you. You may experience physical changes such as increased heart-rate; emotional effects such as feeling tense; and cognitive effects such as not being able to concentrate. Stress may also affect your behaviour so that you may not be able to perform tasks as well as you usually do. This approach to stress focuses on how we *respond* to stress.

Finally we know from our own experience that what is stressful for one person may not be stressful for another. As a result, Lazarus suggests that:

> 'stress resides neither in the situation nor in the person; it depends on a transaction between the two. It arises from how the person appraises an event and adapts to it.'[31]

According to this perspective, stress depends on the interaction between the person and his or her environment. It occurs when an individual perceives a stressful situation and feels they are unable to meet the demands of that situation.

So are we any closer in coming up with an appropriate definition of stress? Most psychologists would agree that stress is a pattern of physiological, emotional, cognitive and behavioural responses to circumstances which are perceived to threaten our well-being. The following diagram summarises the various perspectives on stress:

Stress as a stimulus	*Stress as a response*	*Stress as a process*
focus is on events and situations which cause stress	focus is on how people respond to stressors	focus is on the interaction between the person and the environment

It may be useful to approach the study of stress by using the diagram above and to focus on:

- events and situations which cause us stress (stress as a stimulus)
- the effects of stress (stress as a response)
- cognitive appraisal (stress as a process)

Stress as a stimulus

Bearing in mind that people differ in terms of how they respond to stressful events and situations, it is possible to identify four main causes of stress. These include:

- stressful life events
- minor hassles of daily life
- work-related stress
- environmental sources of stress.

Stressful life events

We all know that sudden changes in life can be stressful. Even happy events like getting a new job or winning the lottery may mean that we have to undergo great change or adjustment.

Holmes and Rahe (1967) set out to investigate how major life events affect health. They developed the **Social Readjustment Rating Scale (SRRS)** to measure the amount of stress associated with particular life events.

The scale was developed by presenting adults with a list of 43 life events such as divorce, pregnancy and retirement. They were asked to compare each life event to marriage, which was assumed to be a happy event but one which also requires a considerable amount of adjustment. Using marriage as a standard comparison (assigned 50 points), they were asked to rate the amount of readjustment needed to cope with each life change on a scale from 1 to 100. The greater the number of points assigned to each change, the more stressful it was for the person experiencing it.

The points assigned to each life event are called **life change units (LCU)** and are shown in the table on page 446.

The Holmes And Rahe Social Readjustment Rating Scale (1967)

Life event	Life Change Units (LCU)	Life event	Life Change Units (LCU)
1 Death of spouse	100	22 Change in responsibilites at work	29
2 Divorce	73	23 Son or daughter leaving home	29
3 Marital separation	65	24 Trouble with in-laws	29
4 Jail term	63	25 Outstanding personal achievement	28
5 Death of a close family member	63	26 Wife begins or stops work	26
6 Personal injury or illness	53	27 Begin or end school	26
7 Marriage	50	28 Change in living conditions	25
8 Fired at work	47	29 Revision of personal habits	24
9 Marital reconciliation	45	30 Trouble with boss	23
10 Retirement	45	31 Change in work hours or conditions	20
11 Change in health of family member	44	32 Change in residence	20
12 Pregnancy	40	33 Change in schools	20
13 Sex difficulties	39	34 Change in recreation	19
14 Gain of new family member	39	35 Change in church activities	19
15 Business readjustment	39	36 Change in social activities	18
16 Change in financial state	38	37 Mortgage or loan less than $10,000	17
17 Death of a close friend	37	38 Change in sleeping habits	16
18 Change to different line of work	36	39 Change in number of family get-togethers	15
19 Change in number of arguments with spouse	35	40 Change in eating habits	15
20 Mortgage over $10,000	31	41 Vacation	13
21 Foreclosure of mortgage or loan	30	42 Christmas	12
		43 Minor violations of the law	11

Holmes, T.H., & Rahe, R.H., 'The Social Readjustment Scale', *Journal of Psychosomatic Research*, 11 (1967), pp.213–18

Once the scale was developed, Holmes and Rahe gave it to a number of patients who had experienced major life changes before they became ill.

When the scale was given, the life change units were not shown. Instead the patients were asked to tick the changes which had occurred during a certain period of time (for example, in the last six or twelve months). The individual's life change units were added up to give a total life change score. Research has shown that people whose life change units totalled 300 points were more susceptible to physical and psychological illness than people who scored 200 points or less (Holmes, Masuda, 1974).

THINK ABOUT IT

Do you think that a person who has an increase in their financial state will experience the same stress as someone who has a decrease in their financial state?

Evaluation of the Social Readjustment Rating Scale

Strengths

+ The scale provides a way of measuring the amount of adjustment needed for a number of specific life events.
+ The scale includes a wide variety of events which most people experience in their adult life and which they would find stressful.
+ It acknowledges that life changes, even positive ones, can cause stress.
+ It has significantly influenced the research in stress and health.

Weaknesses

− The scale does not measure the *degree* of stress experienced by the individual; some life changes will be very stressful for some people but not others.
− Most of the recent research suggests that there is only a weak association between major life events and disease (Brett et al., 1990).
− Coolican (1996) points out that some of the life events on the scale are related, so that if a person has experienced one of them, they are likely to experience another; for example, marital separation may result in a change in financial state and a change in living conditions.
− Some items on the scale are not specific enough (e.g. business readjustment, revision of personal habits).

Daily hassles

Although major life events such as the death of a loved one are stressful, luckily they do not happen very often. What other factors affect the amount of stress that we experience? According to Kanner et al. (1981), daily life is full of minor hassles such as losing doorkeys, being stuck in a traffic jam or having a flat tyre. The researchers therefore developed a scale to measure the stress involved in these everyday hassles.

The **Hassles Scale** consists of 117 events and respondents are asked to indicate the extent to which they have been frustrated by them during the past month. Lazarus et al. (1985) have found positive correlations between scores on the Hassles Scale and reports of psychological symptoms. Research also indicates that daily hassles may be linked to physical health as well.

Weinberger et al. (1987) studied a group of older patients who suffered from arthritis. The patients were asked to complete:

● a questionnaire about the severity of their arthritis and their overall general health
● a modified version of the Daily Hassles scale
● a modified version of the Social Readjustment Scale.

The researchers found that the scores on the Daily Hassles scale were a better predictor of health than the number of major life events experienced. In fact, the more hassles they experienced, the poorer their general health and more severe their symptoms of arthritis.

It could be that, since daily hassles occur frequently, they may have more effect on the individual's stress levels. Lazarus et al. (1985) identified a number of factors which cause daily hassles. These were:

Factors	*Examples*
time pressure hassles	too many things to do
health hassles	physical illness
worries about future security	financial or job-related worries
work hassles	not getting on with colleagues
household hassles	DIY, house repairs

Work-related stress

THINK ABOUT IT

Can you write down three jobs or occupations that you think are stressful? What is it about them that makes them stressful?

You may have included jobs such as fire-fighters, air-traffic controllers and nurses. But any job can be stressful if certain factors occur within the working conditions, as illustrated in the diagram below.

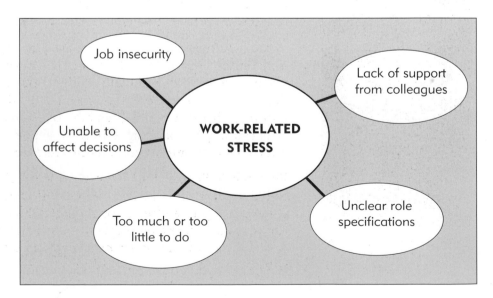

There are a number of occupations in which employees have limited opportunities to discuss work-related issues with their colleagues. As a result, they are unable to talk through problems and may end up feeling very isolated.

Another factor which creates stress at work is **insecurity**. This may be because there are frequent changes in the working conditions (such as changes in procedure or policy) or changes in the workforce (e.g. a new boss who suddenly wants to change everything).

People also find it difficult at work if they do not have clearly defined **roles and responsibilities**. If you are unclear about where your responsibilities begin and end, it is very difficult to know whether you are doing a good job.

Work overload is often given as a cause of stress at work. Work overload occurs when the demands of the job exceed the person's capability to meet them. Strangely enough, **work underload** can also be stressful. Underload occurs when a person's skills and abilities are not being utilised. This can have negative effects on the person's psychological well-being.

Finally, research indicates that employees who work within organisations that encourage **participation in decision-making** are more satisfied with their jobs and have lower levels of stress (Ivancevich, Donnelly, 1975). This may be because having influence in decision-making increases a person's sense of autonomy and control.

Environmental sources of stress

Research within environmental psychology has identified a number of stressors within the environment. They include:

- noise
- heat
- pollution

Of all environmental stressors, the one that has been most thoroughly researched is **noise**. Within the environment there are a number of sources of noise such as traffic, sirens, neighbours and aircraft.

What exactly is noise? When you are playing *your* stereo very loud, this is definitely not noise. However, when your next door neighbour is playing *her* stereo loudly late at night, this is noise. The most common definition is that noise is 'unwanted sound'. The sound may be unwanted because it is unpleasant (the sound of a car alarm); because it is harmful (the piercing sound of a pneumatic drill); or because it interferes with important activities like sleep.

Research indicates that if the noise level rises above 90 decibels (the sound made by a large lorry when it is about 50 feet away from you), there are negative effects for the individual. The research also suggests that it is not just the physical characteristics of noise that are important. It is also the amount of *perceived control* that the individual has over the situation.

Noise is a major source of stress in the environment

to decrease. The researchers suggest that there might be an inverted 'U'-shaped relationship between temperature and aggression. Up to a certain point, increases in temperature result in an increase in aggression. Beyond this point, an increase in temperature leads to a decrease in aggression because it becomes too hot to bother.

According to Rotton and Frey (1980), temperature also has an effect on the daily number of psychiatric emergencies. The evidence showed that on hot days there were more emergencies.

Air pollution

Most of us are probably aware that the air we breathe is filled with toxic substances. **Pollution** has created environmental problems such as toxic rain and the depletion of the ozone layer. The type of toxic substances that we are exposed to include industrial waste, car exhaust fumes and aerosol-spray emissions. A recent study has suggested that around 10,000 people per year in England and Wales die early as a result of air pollution (Brown, 1994). Evidence also suggests that high levels of pollution affect our health and our behaviour. In one study, Evans et al. (1987) investigated the effects of ozone in California. The study found that people who lived in polluted areas tended to respond more negatively to major life events than people who were not exposed to pollution. However, this data was correlational.

Specific pollutants such as carbon monoxide have also been investigated. Beard and Wertheim (1967) exposed participants to various concentrations of carbon monoxide. The level of carbon monoxide on busy roads during rush hour varies from 25 to 125 parts per million (**ppm**). In the study, the participants were exposed to concentrations of carbon monoxide from 50 to 250 ppm. After exposure, participants were asked to estimate how much time elapsed during specific time-intervals. Prolonged exposure to carbon monoxide significantly decreased their ability to make accurate judgements of time.

Much of the air we breathe is polluted ▲

Stress as a response

Physiological responses to stress

As we saw in Chapter 30, *Emotion*, any type of threat can trigger the fight-or-flight response, in which the sympathetic nervous system prepares the body for an emergency.

One of the first researchers to study the effects of prolonged stress was Hans Selye (1936). Selye worked with laboratory animals and exposed them to a variety of stressors such as heat, cold, mild shock and pain. Selye believed that all stressors elicit the same biological response. In other words, he believed that the stress response was **non-specific**, in that it did not vary as a result of the stressor. He described the organism's response to the stressor as the **general adaptation syndrome**. This consisted of three stages:

1 **Alarm reaction:** the organism becomes aware of the existence of a threat, and the fight-or-flight response is generated. The general level of resistance to the stressor is reduced. However, at the end of this stage, the body is prepared to deal with the stressor.

2 **Resistance stage:** if the stress continues, the organism may progress to the second stage. Here, the body is trying to adapt to the stressor and the level of general resistance is above the normal level. Although the organism may not show any obvious signs of stress, the ability to resist new stressors is decreased.

3 **Exhaustion stage:** if the stress cannot be overcome, the body's resources will be used up and the ability to resist will be very limited. If the stress continues, the organism is susceptible to disease or death.

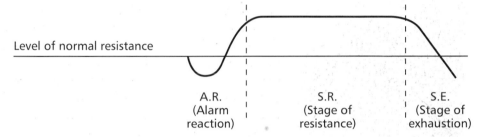

Level of normal resistance

A.R. (Alarm reaction)   S.R. (Stage of resistance)   S.E. (Stage of exhaustion)

According to Selye, not all stress is harmful. He believed that moderate levels of stress (called **eustress**) were adaptive, but that high levels of stress could cause disease and death:

Strengths

+ Selye's model is a good starting point for understanding how human beings cope with stress.
+ Selye's research showed that although arousal is initially an adaptive response, if it continues it can lead to disease.

Weaknesses

− Selye's model does not account for individual differences in how people respond to stress.
− His model was based on research with animals, so may not generalise to humans.

Although our physiological response to stress is automatic, our *psychological* responses are based on how we perceive the stressor and on our ability to cope with it. Psychological effects of stress can occur at an emotional, cognitive or behavioural level.

Emotional effects	depression anxiety anger fear
Cognitive effects	poor concentration impaired memory
Behavioural effects	fatigue problems with sleeping

Stress as a process

According to this perspective, stress is not just a stimulus or a response. It is a 'process' in which the individual makes a **cognitive appraisal** of the situation. According to Lazarus and Folkman (1984), there are two stages in our cognitive appraisal:

1 **primary appraisal** involves deciding whether a demand threatens your well-being
2 **secondary appraisal** involves deciding whether you have the resources to meet the demand.

1. Primary appraisal

As described in Chapter 30, *Emotion*, primary appraisal involves weighing up an event and deciding whether it is:

● irrelevant to you
● relevant but not threatening
● stressful.

For example, if the weather forecast warns of severe flooding in the South of England, this situation could be:

● **irrelevant** to you, because you live in Scotland
● **relevant** but not threatening, because you live on high ground
● **stressful** because you live in a ground-floor flat near a river in southern England.

Lazarus sugggests that if we decide that the event is threatening, then we will consider the event further in terms of three features:

● **harm/loss:** relates to the amount of damage that has already happened
● **threat:** refers to future harm
● **challenge:** refers to any positive outcome or benefit.

2. Secondary appraisal

In secondary appraisal, we decide whether or not we have the necessary resources to deal with the threat. The amount of stress we experience depends on the match between the demands of the situation and our ability to cope. If the demands of the situation significantly outweigh our resources, we will experience stress.

Since people vary in the way they evaluate a stressor and their ability to cope with it, they are likely to experience different levels of stress even when faced with the same stressor.

More recent research also supports the notion of individual differences in responding to stress. Kobasa (1979) introduced the concept of **hardiness** to explain why some people cope better with stress than others. Kobasa studied business executives who had experienced long-term stress. She found that some of the executives became ill while others remained healthy. According to Kobasa, the 'hardier' executives tended to have certain personality characteristics such as:

- **a sense of commitment:** some executives had a clear sense of purpose and involvement; they were willing to turn to other people for help

- **control:** some executives believed that they had control over events in their lives while others believed that events just happened to them

- **a sense of challenge:** some executives tended to view change as a challenge rather than as a threat.

Coping strategies

Some stress is an inevitable part of everyday life. We are able to reduce the negative effects of stress by using **coping strategies**. Lazarus and Folkman (1984) suggested that there are two different types of coping strategies:

1. **Emotion-focused coping** involves trying to control and reduce the negative emotions associated with stress. This type of coping is most likely to be used when the individual believes that it is not possible to change the stressful situation. Example of emotion-focused coping include:

   - seeking support from other people
   - distracting attention from the problem by engaging in other activities
   - releasing pent-up emotions.

2. **Problem-focused coping** is aimed at directly changing the situation or increasing our ability to deal with it. Examples of problem-focused coping include:

   - clarifying the nature of the problem
   - considering alternative courses of action
   - deciding on the most appropriate course of action and implementing it.

D'Zurilla & Sheedy (1991) assessed people's problem-solving ability (i.e. their ability to define problems and suggest a variety of ways to cope with them). At a later date they measured their stress symptoms. They found that people who were better at solving problems had lower levels of stress.

There are a variety of means of coping with the negative effects of stress. Anti-anxiety **drugs** (e.g. Valium) can reduce the physical symptoms of stress, but these are often addictive and have unpleasant side-effects. They tend to address the symptoms rather than the underlying causes of stress. Other methods like **meditation** and **relaxation techniques** (e.g. systematically relaxing the muscles of the body) can reduce arousal and lower blood pressure. Also, regular **exercise** can help cope with stress by lowering adrenaline levels. **Biofeedback** involves connecting people to machinery that provides information (visual or auditory) about internal states like blood pressure and heart rate. People can learn to deliberately regulate these internal processes, and can reduce high blood pressure or the frequency of tension headaches.

Teaching people to identify the symptoms of stress, to evaluate the ways in which they deal with stressful situations and providing better strategies for coping with stress can all be useful. It is important that people feel they have some control and that they are able to change things for the better. **Cognitive strategies** involve eliminating negative thoughts ('there's nothing I can do') and emphasising positive ones ('it will help if I do this'). **Stress management programmes** address problem behaviour. They encourage people to take a realistic view of what they should demand of themselves, and teach things like time management so that people do not become overwhelmed by work at the last minute. **Assertiveness training** helps people to confront social situation that they may find stressful.

Summary

- Psychologists have studied the factors that cause stress, how people respond to it, and how we appraise stressful situations.
- Stress can result from major life changes but also from daily hassles. Some stress is work-related, other stress comes from the environment (noise, heat, pollution).
- Reactions to stress include Seyle's general adaptation syndrome. Stress can have emotional, cognitive and behavioural effects.
- The same stressors can produce different responses in people. This may be linked to how individuals make a cognitive appraisal of the situation.
- Lazarus argued that there are two stages of cognitive appraisal. Primary appraisal involves deciding whether a situation threatens our well-being. Secondary appraisal involves deciding whether we can cope with the situation.
- Kobasa (1979) found that 'hardy' individuals cope better with stress than other people. Such people see change as a challenge, have a sense of commitment and believe they have control over events that happen to them.
- There are several strategies that can help people to deal with stress.

Exam Questions

Section 2: Research Methods

1. Zimbardo assumed that a large city would produce more anonymity and less sense of responsibility than a smaller city. He conducted an identical experiment in New York (population 8 million) and in Palo Alto (population 100,000). He placed an apparently abandoned car, with the number plate removed and the bonnet left open, on a street in the two cities, and observed people's reactions. In New York, within 10 minutes a man, woman and child about 9 years old came by and began to remove parts of the car. Within 24 hours the car was completely stripped. In Palo Alto after 72 hours the car remained untouched, except for one person who politely put the bonnet down when it began to rain.

   (a) The study described above is a **field experiment**.

   (i) Explain one practical problem with a field experiment.

   (2 marks)

   (ii) Explain one advantage in conducting a field experiment.

   (1 mark)

   (b) Zimbardo used an **opportunity sample**. What do you understand by the word 'opportunity' in psychological research?

   (1 mark)

   (c) A **dependent variable** is what is observed or measured by an experimenter. What was the dependent variable in the study described above?

   (3 marks)

   (d) Identify and explain one ethical problem with the study described above.

   (3 marks)
   OCR (MEG) 1998

2. As part of your GCSE coursework you have been asked to plan an experiment using an independent groups design. The aim is to find out if it is easier to recall a list of 30 words which is **organised** (List One) or the same list of 30 words which is **not organised** (List Two). The order of the words in List One is randomised to make List Two.

   (a) Write a suitable hypothesis for your experiment.

   (2 marks)

   (b) In your experiment state:

   (i) the independent variable

   (1 mark)

   (ii) the dependent variable

   (1 mark)

   (c) You used the **same** words in List One (organised) and List Two (not organised).

   (i) Explain why you should use the same words in each list.

   (2 marks)

   (ii) Describe how you could *randomise* the words in List One to make List Two.

   (2 marks)

   (d) You have been asked to use an independent groups design.

   (i) Explain what is meant by the term *independent groups design*.

   (1 mark)

   (ii) State and explain **one** advantage of an independent groups design.

   (2 marks)

   (e) (i) Explain what is meant by the term *extraneous variable*.

   (2 marks)

   (ii) Name **one** extraneous variable which should be controlled in this experiment and explain why it is necessary to control it.

   (2 marks)

   (f) You have decided to test your participants' memory for the 30 words using a *recognition task*. Describe how you would do this.

(3 marks)

(g) Write a debriefing which is suitable for the participants in your experiment.

(2 marks)
NEAB 1998

3. A psychologist wanted to know if people formed impressions of others by making judgements about their accents. She asked for volunteers from her local college and these participants were randomly divided into two groups. There were 24 female volunteers and 13 male volunteers. One group listened to a tape recording of a Liverpool woman with a Scouse accent, while the other listened to a London man with a Cockney accent. Both speakers read the same extract from a newspaper. The participants rated each person for Intelligence, Honesty, Sense of Humour and Laziness using a scale from 1 to 10, with 1 being low and 10 being high. The results showed that the Scouse (Liverpool) accent was scored higher for Intelligence, Honesty and Sense of Humour, and that the Cockney (London) accent was scored higher for Laziness. The psychologist concluded that the participants formed a better impression of the female speaker because of her Scouse accent.

(a) Write a hypothesis for the study.

(1 mark)

(b) What are the dependent and independent variables in the study?

(2 marks)

(c) Do you think the psychologist's conclusion was correct? Explain your answer.

(4 marks)

(d) You have been asked to design a better study to investigate how people respond to the accents of others.

(i) Describe the type of research method you would use and give reasons for your choice.

(5 marks)

(ii) Identify **and** briefly describe the way you would choose your sample of participants.

(3 marks)

(iii) Outline the procedure you would follow, giving reasons for your choice.

(4 marks)

(iv) Describe how you would debrief the participants who took part in your study

and explain why this is important.

(6 marks)
SEG 1997

4. Outline **one** ethical and **one** practical problem with using animals in research.

(4 marks)
OCR (MEG) 1998

5. Describe **two** findings from research into animal behaviour and say how these findings might be applied to human behaviour.

(9 marks)
OCR (MEG) 1997

Section 3: Two Major Approaches to Development

1. Describe Freud's explanation of how gender identity is formed in either boys or girls.

(4 marks)

2. Explain one criticism of the work of Freud.

(2 marks)
NEAB 1997

3. Compare and contrast the psychodynamic with the social learning explanation of personality.

(15 marks)
SEG 1991

4. A study was carried out to see if children who had developed a superego would be more likely to feel guilt than children who had a weak superego. Each child was asked to take care of an expensive vase that was being heat treated in an oven. The child was told that when the vase had been in the oven for the right amount of time, a red light would come on, and when this happened they should switch off the oven at once. The children watched the vase for a while but eventually they would play with other toys in the room. The psychologist, who was looking through a one-way mirror, would then turn on the light and replace the glass with fragments of a broken one through a concealed hatch in the oven. When the psychologist returned to the room they made a note of how guilty the child appeared about the broken vase.

(a) What was the aim of the study?

(1 mark)

(b) What is the superego?

(2 marks)

(c) According to Freud, how does the superego develop in a child?

(3 marks)
OCR (MEG) 1991

5. Read the story below and answer the questions which follow.

Fluffy's a star!

Fluffy the cat turns on his favourite TV programme all by himself. Fluffy's owner, a psychologist, said, "I shaped Fluffy's behaviour over a period of a month, and now I only have to give him a chocolate drop every now and then when he turns on the television. This keeps Fluffy producing the behaviour."

(a) The story above illustrates:

    (i)   classical conditioning
    (ii) operant conditioning
    (iii) latent learning

(Tick your choice)

(1 mark)

(b) Earning 'chocolate drops' for turning on the TV is an example of:

    (i)   primary reinforcement
    (ii) negative reinforcement
    (ii) secondary reinforcement

(Tick your choice)

(1 mark)

(c) Explain how Fluffy's owner might have shaped the cat's behaviour.

(4 marks)
NEAB 1996

6. *Schedules of reinforcement*

In operant conditioning, there are five main types of reinforcement schedule. These are described below:

Schedule of reinforcement	Description
Continuous	Reinforcement is reinforcement given every time the correct behaviour is performed
Fixed ratio	Reinforcement is given after a regular number of correct behaviours (for example, every 5th time)
Variable ratio	Reinforcement is given after a variable number of correct behaviours (for example, on average, every 5th time)
Fixed interval	Reinforcement is given, only after a fixed time since the previous reinforcement (for example, every 30 seconds)
Variable interval	Reinforcement is given, only after a variable time since the reinforcement (for example, on average, every 30 seconds)

Which schedule of reinforcement best describes the following behaviour:

(a) gambling at a fruit machine (one-armed bandit)

(1 mark)

(b) receiving your weekly wage

(1 mark)

(c) pressing the call button of a lift several times because the lift doesn't always come first time

(1 mark)

(d) doing some fruit-picking for money and being paid for every 10 boxes that you fill?

(1 mark)
OCR (MEG) 1993

7. How would a psychologist define reinforcement?

(2 marks)
OCR (MEG) 1993

Section 4: Developmental Psychology

1. (a) What is temperament?

(5 marks)

(b) Describe a psychological study of temperament and outline its main findings.

(10 marks)

(c) Describe any **two** explanations of personality development. Then identify and explain two differences between them.

(15 marks)
SEG 1997

2. (a) According to Rogers, what is unconditional positive regard?

(2 marks)

(b) Explain **one** difference between Rogers' theory of personality and Cattell's theory of personality.

(2 marks)
OCR (MEG) 1997

3. Describe and evaluate **one** study in which the effects of maternal deprivation were investigated.

(6 marks)
NEAB 1998

4. Discuss the contribution of **either** Ainsworth **or** Rutter to our understanding of attachment between children and their parents.

(6 marks)
NEAB 1996

5. Describe and evaluate Bowlby's theory of maternal deprivation.

(9 marks)
OCR (MEG) 1998

6. *(a)* Explain the difference between accommodation and assimilation.

(6 marks)

(b) Describe **two** characteristics of pre-operational children according to Piaget.

(6 marks)

(c) Describe **one** study that suggests that Piaget's ideas may be wrong.

(8 marks)

(d) Explain how Piaget's ideas have influenced children's education.

(10 marks)
SEG 1996

7. Identify and explain **one** major difference between the theories of Piaget and Bruner.

(3 marks)
OCR (MEG) 1998

8. *(a)* Outline **two** psychological explanations of moral development.

(14 marks)

(b) Describe **one** way in which peers might influence an individual's moral behaviour.

(10 marks)

(c) Describe how pro-social reasoning develops in most children.

(6 marks)
SEG 1998

9. Kohlberg used stories that had a moral dilemma. From your knowledge of psychology describe **one** other way of measuring moral development.

(2 marks)
OCR (MEG) 1996

10. Describe and evaluate **two** psychological explanations of sex role development.

(9 marks)
OCR (MEG) 1997

11. *(a)* Explain what psychologists mean by gender concept.

(6 marks)

(b) Describe **two** psychological theories of the development of gender and explain **one** difference between them.

(16 marks)

(c) Describe **one** way in which others, for example teachers, promote and reinforce gender differences.

(8 marks)
SEG 1998

Section 5: Cognitive Psychology

1. *(a)* What is perception?

(4 marks)

(b) Describe **one** study that suggests that perception is influenced by nature.

(8 marks)

(c) Describe **one** study that suggests that perception is influenced by nurture.

(8 marks)

(d) Explain why psychologists cannot agree whether perception is learned or innate.

(10 marks)
SEG 1996

2. *(a)* Explain what is meant by *reconstructive memory*.

(4 marks)

(b) Use psychological evidence to name and explain one way in which the accuracy of eyewitness testimony might be improved.

(4 marks)
NEAB 1998

3. Outline at least **three** problem-solving techniques suggested by psychologists. Give an example for each one of how it can be used in an everyday situation and indicate how useful the technique is.

(9 marks)
OCR (MEG) 1996

4. Describe and evaluate **two** theories that

psychologists have proposed to explain how children acquire language.

(9 marks)
OCR (MEG) 1998

5. From your knowledge of psychology, identify and describe **one** ethical and **one** practical problem of attempting to teach animals language.

(4 marks)
OCR (MEG) 1997

6. *(a)* What is IQ and how is it calculated?

(4 marks)

(b) Describe one use of an IQ test.

(6 marks)

(c) Describe and explain one limitation of IQ tests.

(10 marks)

(d) Outline the view which suggests that intelligence is influenced mainly by heredity.

(10 marks)
SEG 1998

Section 6: Social Psychology

1. *(a)* How do friendship patterns change as children grow older?

(6 marks)

(b) Describe and explain **two** reasons why one person may be attracted to another.

(14 marks)

(c) Describe **two** studies that show how the presence of other people might affect an individual's behaviour.

(10 marks)
SEG 1997

2. Why is affiliation important for humans?

(4 marks)
SEG 1997

3. Describe **one** study in which the *primacy effect* in impression formation was investigated.

NEAB 1998

4. *(a)* When forming impressions of others, what is the primacy effect?

(5 marks)

(b) Explain how an implicit personality theory might create an impression of someone when we meet them for the first time.

(10 marks)

(c) Give **one** example of how the media act as filters of information.

(5 marks)
SEG 1998

5. Describe and evaluate **one** study in which conformity was investigated.

(6 marks)
NEAB 1998

6. Name **two** factors which might affect conformity to group pressure. Use evidence from psychological studies to support your answer.

(6 marks)
NEAB 1996

7. *(a)* What is altruism?

(5 marks)

(b) Describe **one** psychological study of altruism.

(10 marks)
SEG 1998

8. Using psychological evidence, describe **three factors** which might affect helping behaviour.

(9 marks)
OCR (MEG) 1997

9. *(a)* Describe **one** way in which child rearing styles might affect a child's aggression.

(4 marks)

(b) Compare and contrast **two** different theories of the origins of aggression.

(16 marks)

(c) According to psychologists, how can aggression be reduced?

(10 marks)
SEG 1996

10. Using psychological research, describe **two** ways of reducing prejudice.

(8 marks)
OCR (MEG) 1998

11. *(a)* What is prejudice?

(3 marks)

(b) How does discrimination differ from prejudice?

(3 marks)
SEG 1998

12. Read the following description of a famous study conducted in 1966.

While on duty a hospital nurse received a telephone call from Doctor Smith about a patient on the ward.

Doctor Smith asked the nurse to give the patient a drug called Astroten. The bottle containing the drug was clearly labelled:

ASTROTEN
MAXIMUM DOSAGE: 10MG.
(MUST NOT BE EXCEEDED)

Doctor Smith told the nurse to give the patient 20mg. of Astroten. Taking instructions over the telephone and giving more than the maximum dosage were strictly against hospital rules. When the nurse started to take the medicine to the patient, a researcher stopped her and explained the purpose of the study.

(a) Which of the following terms best describes the nurse's behaviour:

(i) inhibition
(ii) obedience
(iii) compliance

(1 mark)

(b) Explain one factor which may have influenced the nurse's behaviour.

(2 marks)

(c) Name one ethical issue which is involved in studies like the one described above.

(1 mark)
NEAB 1996

Section 7: Environmental and Comparative Psychology

1. What do psychologists mean by environment?

(4 marks)
NEAB 1998

2. Using psychological evidence, explain how crowding or being part of a group may affect behaviour. (You may like to consider animal/human studies as well as bystander apathy and social contagion in your answer)

(9 marks)
OCR (MEG) 1996

3. What is meant by 'defensible space'?

(1 mark)
OCR (MEG) 1997

4. Outline **two** emotional and/or behavioural responses we may experience when people invade our personal space.

(4 marks)
OCR (MEG) 1998

5. Psychologists have identified **three** types of territory: primary, secondary, and public territory. Give **one** example of each.

(3 marks)
OCR (MEG)1998

6. Give **one** example of an instinct and describe how it might affect a person's behaviour.

(3 marks)
SEG 1998

7. Explain **three** characteristics of innate behaviour in animals.

(9 marks)
OCR (MEG) 1998

8. (a) What is the method used by psychologists to study animals in their natural habitat?

(1 mark)

(b) Give **one** advantage of using this method of study.

(2 marks)

9. (a) What is meant by the term 'fixed action pattern'?

(2 marks)

(b) Describe an example of a fixed action pattern that you have studied.

(3 marks)
OCR (MEG) 1997

Section 8: The Biological Approach

1. (a) From the list below, tick the **three** phrases that correctly describe the effects on the body of stimulating the *parasympathetic nervous system*.

☐ Salivation increases   ☐ Salivation decreases
☐ Heart rate increases   ☐ Heart rate decreases
☐ Pupils dilate   ☐ Pupils constrict

(3 marks)

(b) Name **one** hormone which is associated with the flight or flight response.

(1 mark)

(c) Describe a study which supports the idea that *social situation* and *physiological changes* act together to determine the emotional response that people experience. Include details of how the study was carried out and give the results of the study.

(4 marks)
NEAB 1998

2. The term *localisation* suggests that different areas of the brain are specialised for different functions. Name **two** other special areas of the brain and describe their functions.

(4 marks)
OCR (MEG) 1997

3. Identify **three** problems that psychologists face when investigating the brain.

(6 marks)
OCR (MEG) 1997

4. Brain damage can be caused by operations, strokes, accidents, illnesses, etc. Describe **two** findings psychologists have made from the study of brain-damaged people.

(4 marks)
OCR (MEG) 1996

5. *(a)* Describe the James–Lange theory of emotion.

(3 marks)

(b) Describe evidence against the James–Lange theory of emotion.

(3 marks)
NEAB 1998

6. Use your knowledge of psychology to discuss the suggestion that a certain amount of arousal can be helpful to performance.

(4 marks)
NEAB 1997

7. Give **two** psychological effects of stress.

(2 marks)
NEAB 1996

8. Using psychological evidence, describe **two** environmental sources of stress.

(6 marks)
OCR (MEG) 1996

References

1. Freud, S., 'Some Psychical Consequences of the Anatomical Distinctions between the Sexes' in J. Strachey (ed. and trans.), *The Standard Edition of the Complete Psychological Works of Sigmund Freud*, 19, (Hogarth Press, London). Original work published 1925
2. Freud, S., ibid.
3. Watson, J., 'Experimental Studies on the Growth of Emotions' in Murchison, C. (ed.), *Psychologies of 1925* (Clark University Press, Worcester, Mass., 1926)
4. Hirschorn, P., in Medcof, J., & Roth, J., (eds.), *Approaches to Psychology* (Open University Press, Milton Keynes, 1979)
5. Kohlberg, L., 'The Development of Children's Orientations Towards a Moral Order: 1. Sequence in the development of moral thought', *Vita Humana*, 6 (1963), pp.11–33
6. Birns, B., The Emergence and Socialisation of Sex Differences in the Earliest Years', in *Merrill-Palmer Quarterly*, 22, 5 (1976), p.229
7. Adapted from Grant, L.: 'First Among Equals', *The Guardian*, 22 October 1994
8. Freud, S. (1933): 'Femininity' (Lecture 33), in *New Introductory Lectures on Psychoanalysis*, Penguin Freud Library (Penguin, Harmondsworth, Middx., 1973)
9. Kohlberg, L., 'A Cognitive-Developmental Analysis of Children's Sex Role Concepts and Attitudes' in Maccoby, E.E. (ed.): *The Development of Sex Differences* (Stanford University Press, Stanford, 1966)
10. Quoted in Allport, G.W. & Vernon, P.E.: 'The Field of Personality' in *Psychological Bulletin*, 27 (1930), pp.677–730
11. Tavris, C., *Psychology*. (HarperCollins, New York, 1933)
12. Cattell, R., 'Advances in Cattellian Personality Theory' in Pervin, L.A., *Handbook of Personality* (Guildford Publications, New York, 1990)
13. Eysenck, H.J. (ed.): *The Measurement of Personality* (MTP, Lancaster, England, 1976)
14. Eysenck, H.J., *The Biological Bases of Personality* (Charles C. Thomas, Springfield, Illinois, 1967)
15. Costa, P.T., and McCrae, R.R., 'Bullish on Personality Psychology', *The Psychologist*, 6 (7), 1993, pp.302–3
16. Kelly, G., *The Psychology of Personal Construct* (Norton, New York, 1955)
17. Cazden, G.B., *Child Language and Education* (Holt, Rhinehart & Winston, New York, 1972)
18. Gross, R., *Psychology: The Science of Mind and Behaviour*, 3rd edition (Hodder & Stoughton, London, 1996)
19. Lenneberg, E.., *Biological Foundations of Language*, (Wiley, New York, 1967)
20. Lenneberg, E.., ibid.
21. Savage-Rumbaugh, E.S., in Lewin, R., 'Look Who's Talking Now', *New Scientist*, April 1991
22. Asch, S., 'Forming Impressions of Personality', in *Journal of Abnormal and Social Psychology*, 41 (1946), pp.258–90
23. Asch, S., ibid.
24. Asch, S., ibid.
25. Le Bon, G., *Psychologie des Foules* ('The Crowd'), (Unwin, London, 1903)
26. Ornstein, R. & Thompson, R., *The Amazing Brain* (Houghton Mifflin, Boston, 1985)
27. Banich, M., *Neuropsychology: The Neural Bases of Mental Function* (Houghton Mifflin, Boston, 1997)
28. King, H.E., 'Psychological Effects of Excitation in the Limbic System' in D.E. Sheer (ed.), *Electrical Stimulation of the Brain* (University of Texas Press, Austin, Texas, 1961)
29. James, W., 'What is an emotion? *Mind*, 9 (1884), pp.188–205
30. Smith, C. and Lazarus, R., 'Emotion and Adaptation', in Pervin, L.A., *Handbook of Personality, Theory and Research* (The Guilford Press, New York, 1989)
31. Lazarus, R.S., & Folkman, S., *Stress, Appraisal and Coping*, (Springer, NY, 1984)

Index

Page references in *italics* indicate diagrams or illustrations.